T0303936

Also in the Variorum Collected Studies Series:

OM PRAKASH
Precious Metals and Commerce
The Dutch East India Company in the Indian Ocean Trade

GEORGE BRYAN SOUZA
Portuguese, Dutch and Chinese in Maritime Asia, c.1585–1800
Merchants, Commodities and Commerce

DENNIS O. FLYNN AND ARTURO GIRÁLDEZ
China and the Birth of Globalization in the 16th Century

A.R. DISNEY
The Portuguese in India and Other Studies, 1500–1700

M.N. PEARSON
The World of the Indian Ocean, 1500–1800
Studies in Economic, Social and Cultural History

RODERICH PTAK
China, the Portuguese, and the Nanyang
Oceans and Routes, Regions and Trade (c.1000–1600)

G.V. SCAMMELL
Seafaring, Sailors and Trade, 1450–1750
Studies in British and European Maritime and Imperial History

C.R. BOXER
Dutch Merchants and Mariners in Asia, 1602–1795

S. ARASARATNAM
Maritime Trade, Society and European Influence in Southern Asia, 1600–1800

ASHIN DAS GUPTA
Merchants of Maritime India, 1500–1800

C.R. BOXER
From Lisbon to Goa, 1500–1750
Studies in Portuguese Maritime Enterprise

C.R. BOXER
Portuguese Merchants and Missionaries in Feudal Japan, 1543–1640

VARIORUM COLLECTED STUDIES SERIES

On the Economic Encounter Between Asia and Europe, 1500–1800

Om Prakash

Om Prakash

On the Economic Encounter Between Asia and Europe, 1500–1800

LONDON AND NEW YORK

First published 2014 by Ashgate Publishing

2 Park Square, Milton Park, Abingdon, Oxfordshire OX14 4RN
711 Third Avenue, New York, NY 10017

Routledge is an imprint of the Taylor & Francis Group, an informa business

First issued in paperback 2018

ISBN 978-1-4094-1828-3 (hbk)
ISBN 978-1-138-37583-3 (pbk)

British Library Cataloguing in Publication Data
A catalogue record for this book is available from the British Library.

The Library of Congress has cataloged the printed edition as follows: 2014932466

VARIORUM COLLECTED STUDIES SERIES CS990

For Santosh
for her unstinting love and support

CONTENTS

This volume contains xvi + 346 pages

ACKNOWLEDGEMENTS

Grateful acknowledgement is made to the following persons, institutions, journals and publishers for their kind permission to reproduce the papers included in this volume: South-South Exchange Programme for Research in the History of Development (SEPHIS) and the University of Malaya (for article I); Manohar Books, New Delhi (II); University of Leiden Press (III); SAGE Publications Ltd (V); Fondazione Istituto Internazionale di Storia economica 'F. Datini', Prato (VI); the Aligarh Historians Society and Professor Irfan Habib (VII); Boydell and Brewer, Woodbridge (VIII); Walburg Pers Editions, The Hague (IX); Academia Press, Gent (X); Koninklijke Brill NV, Leiden (XI); Asian Studies Center, Michigan State University, East Lansing, MI (XII); Cambridge University Press (XIII); and Peter Lang Publishers (XIV).

Every effort has been made to trace all the copyright holders, but if any have been inadvertently overlooked the publishers will be pleased to make the necessary arrangement at the first opportunity.

PUBLISHER'S NOTE

The articles in this volume, as in all others in the Variorum Collected Studies Series, have not been given a new, continuous pagination. In order to avoid confusion, and to facilitate their use where these same studies have been referred to elsewhere, the original pagination has been maintained wherever possible. Article XI has necessarily been reset with a new pagination, and with the original page numbers given in square brackets within the text.

Each article has been given a Roman number in order of appearance, as listed in the Contents. This number is repeated on each page and is quoted in the index entries.

INTRODUCTION

The history of the economic contacts between Asia and Europe dates back to at least the early years of the Common Era. Asian luxury goods – Chinese silk, Indonesian spices, Indian textiles and so on – found their way to Europe via the Middle East and the Mediterranean involving a complex network of exchange. In the fifteenth century, goods of Chinese and southeast Asian origin were obtained in fair quantities by Indian and west Asian merchants at Malacca and transported to the port of Cambay on the west coast of India. A part of this cargo was re-exported to west Asia, both for consumption within the region and to be sent on to Europe via the Mediterranean. The two channels used for the purpose were the Red Sea and the Persian Gulf.

This pattern of exchange, which had been in operation for centuries, underwent a structural modification following the discovery by the Portuguese at the end of the fifteenth century of the all-water route to the East Indies via the Cape of Good Hope. Among the historic consequences of the discovery was the overcoming of the transport technology barrier to the growth of trade between the two continents. The volume of this trade was no longer subject to the capacity constraint imposed by the availability of pack animals and river boats in the Middle East. Both the old and the new routes were in use throughout the sixteenth century but by the early years of the seventeenth, when the northern European companies had successfully challenged the Portuguese monopoly of the all-water route, the latter had almost completely taken over the transportation of goods between the two continents. In addition to their transportation, the procurement of the Asian goods was also now organized by the Europeans themselves, who had for the first time arrived in the East in any number.

On their arrival in the East, the Portuguese and later the other European merchant groups, came face to face with a fairly extensive and sophisticated network of Indian Ocean trade. Given the long tradition of a significant volume of maritime trade being carried on from their respective ports, involving the generation of additional revenue in the form of customs and other duties paid by the visiting merchants, most Asian states of the period welcomed these merchants, making available to them the use of all facilities the ports might have to offer. The Europeans by and large were treated as no exception to this general policy. Indeed, the fact that countries such as India attached a high premium to the precious metals brought in by the Europeans to pay for the goods they procured, made them particularly welcome. This brings us to what was traditionally the most outstanding characteristic feature of Euro-Asian trade, namely the necessity for the Europeans to pay for the Asian goods overwhelmingly in precious metals. This essentially reflected the inability of Europe to supply western products at prices that would generate a large enough demand for them to provide the necessary revenue for the purchase of Asian goods. Europe at this time probably had an overall superiority over Asia in the field of scientific and technological knowledge but as yet did not have the cost advantage that came with the Industrial Revolution in the nineteenth century. This put the Asian, and particularly the Indian, producers with their considerably lower labour costs and a much longer history of sophisticated skills in handicrafts of various kinds, in a position of advantage over their European counterparts in the production of a variety of manufactured goods. The only major item that Europe was in a position to provide to Asia was precious metals. The growth of Euro-Asian trade, therefore, was critically dependent upon an increase in the availability of these metals. In this context, the working of the Spanish American silver mines and the import of large quantities of American silver into Europe during the sixteenth and early seventeenth centuries was a development of critical significance.

The Europeans operated in the Indian Ocean alongside the Indian and other Asian merchants with no special privileges being available to them. It was only in the second half of the eighteenth century when the English East India Company assumed political authority in Bengal that the situation changed somewhat to the advantage of the Company.

This collection of essays deals with some of the aforementioned issues in relation both to the Indian merchants as well as the European corporate enterprises – the Portuguese *Estado da India* and the Dutch and the English East India companies – and the private traders between the sixteenth and the eighteenth centuries.

The first essay in the collection not only introduces many of the issues discussed in the rest of the volume, but indeed also goes over some ground not covered subsequently. One such issue is the economy-wide implications of European trade with reference to questions of income, output, employment and prices.

A detailed discussion of the Indian merchants' participation in the Indian Ocean trade on the eve of the Europeans' arrival in the Ocean forms the subject matter of the second essay. The central role of India and her merchants in this trade is explained in part in terms of her mid-way location between west Asia on the one hand and south-east and east Asia on the other. The other circumstance relevant in this regard was the subcontinent's capacity to put on the market a wide range of tradable goods at highly competitive prices.

Essay numbers three and four deal with the Portuguese – both the *Estado da India* as well as private traders – involvement in the Euro-Asian and the Indian Ocean trade. An important issue analyzed in the third essay deals with the implications of the Portuguese trade for the Indian merchants engaged in the Indian Ocean trade. It is argued that the Portuguese cartaz system, in so far as it entailed only a small additional fiscal burden, was indeed no more than a minor irritant. The fourth essay briefly analyzes the pattern of functioning and the scale of operations of the major components of the Portuguese enterprise in Asia.

The relationship of the private Portuguese trading community with fellow Asian merchants as well as with the competing European private traders and corporate enterprises in the Indian Ocean/ South China Sea complex in the late eighteenth century, discussed in the fifth essay, was essentially one of acute rivalry often bordering on unconcealed antagonism. But at the same time, there were important and unexpected areas of cooperation between individual Portuguese private traders on the one hand and individual and non-Portuguese European traders and even European corporate enterprises on the other.

In the seventeenth and the eighteenth century, the Dutch East India Company was the largest of the European corporate enterprises engaged in a large and growing trade between Asia and Europe. What distinguished it most from its principal rival, the English East India Company, however, was its large scale participation in the trade of the Indian Ocean as an integral part of its overall trading strategy. This element constitutes one of the central issues discussed in the four essays from number six to nine.

The European private traders' operations in the Indian Ocean are analyzed in essay numbers ten and eleven, the former dealing with the trade originating in the Bay of Bengal and the latter with that in the western Indian Ocean. The attitudes of the corporate enterprises towards the private traders differed a great deal depending largely on the degree of involvement of the enterprise in the Indian Ocean trade. The Dutch East India Company, which was the only corporate enterprise engaged in substantive Indian Ocean trade, stood at one end of the spectrum and over the greater part of its existence was uncompromisingly hostile to employees illegally engaged in private trade. It is another matter that the employees nevertheless managed to do so. The brief involvement of the French East India Company in the Indian Ocean trade from the Bay of Bengal in the first half of the eighteenth century represents in some sense the other end of the spectrum involving a formal collaborative arrangement between the Company and its employees together with Indian merchants. English private merchants, who simultaneously worked for the Company, and accounted for a very large proportion of the total European private contingent, particularly during the eighteenth century, were in the happy position of enjoying the patronage of the Company for their Indian Ocean enterprises, while taking full advantage of the Company's growing political power in the subcontinent. In the 1720s and the 1730s, the important Surat-Mocha link from the western Indian Ocean was dominated by Sir Robert Cowan, the governor of Bombay and his collaborator Henry Lowther, chief of the English factory at Surat. Their activities covered a wide range from trading, freighting space on vessels owned by Cowan wholly or in part, freighting space for his cargo on other merchants' – both European and Indian – ships, loaning funds on respondentia, arranging insurance and money transfers, acting as attorney for fellow English private traders, recovering bad debts on their behalf and generally networking with them.

Essay numbers twelve and thirteen are concerned with the manufacturing and trade in Indian textiles during the seventeenth and the eighteenth century. The first of the two essays describes the varieties manufactured in Bengal, a region traditionally famous for its high quality cotton muslins and calicoes. Following the assumption of political authority by the English East India Company in the region in the second half of the eighteenth century, the market based system, it is argued in the following essay, was replaced by one embedded in coercion of the intermediary merchants and the manufacturing artisans. The sector, however, was resilient enough to adjust to the new pressures and manage to survive intact.

The last but one essay is the only one in the volume which goes both into the pre-colonial and the colonial period in India and indeed into the early years of independence. It argues that the relationship between long distance trade, coinage and wages underwent a change in crucial respects as between the pre-colonial and the colonial period.

The concluding essay in the collection argues that the eighteenth century, consisting of two sub-phases with the cut-off point lying somewhere around 1760, constituted a distinct category in the history of Bengal. The successor state established in the province in the early years of the century by Murshid Quli Khan turned out to be a perfectly stable political entity till it was itself overrun by the English East India Company in the 1750s, inaugurating the establishment of colonial rule in the subcontinent.

I might mention here that the principal repository of the Dutch East India Company archives in The Hague, familiar to generations of scholars as the Algemeen Rijksarchief (ARA) was rechristened Nationaal Archief (NA) in 2002. Many years earlier, the volumes containing the bulk of the Dutch East India Company documentation preserved at this archives had been redesignated from the earlier Koloniaal Archief or KA volumes to Verenigde Oostindische Compagnie or VOC volumes and assigned new numbers. The former change relates to essay numbers V, VI, VIII, X, XII and XV while the latter is applicable only to essay number XII. These changes have not been incorporated into the notes to the essays.

On rereading the essays included in this collection, I find that there is a certain amount of overlap across essays dealing with similar themes but in varying depth and emphasis. I ask for the reader's indulgence in this behalf.

I would like to convey my deep appreciation to Professor Samuel Jubé, the Director of the Institute for Advanced Study, Nantes, France where this volume was completed during my stay there as a Fellow, for all his help and cooperation.

OM PRAKASH

Institute for Advanced Study
Nantes, France
January 2014

I

Euro-Asian Encounter in the Early Modern Period

I

EURO-ASIAN ENCOUNTER IN THE EARLY MODERN PERIOD

The process of decolonization that the immediate post-World War II period witnessed brought to an end one of the most outstanding – if also the most shameful – characteristic features of the modern age. This was the domination of one people over another generally referred to as colonialism. In its economic dimension, colonialism assumed an extremely important role in determining the nature and the rate of economic growth both in the metropolitan as well as in the colonized world in the nineteenth and the first half of the twentieth century. This served to considerably widen the gap between the income levels and the standard of economic performance generally between the developed countries of the west on the one hand and the underdeveloped countries of the Third World viz. Asia, Africa and Latin America on the other. According to Angus Maddison, one hundred and fifty years ago, the gap in mean per capita share of gross domestic product between the richest and the poorest global regions, namely Western Europe and Africa, was probably three to one. Today this gap between a rich country such as Switzerland and a poor country such as Mozambique is a mind-boggling four hundred to one.[1] To what extent colonialism has or has not been directly or indirectly responsible for this state of affairs has been a subject of intense debate over the last half a century or so. This lecture is not about this debate although some of the issues raised by it will indeed be commented upon. What this lecture will seek to do is to analyse the relationship between Europe and Asia where many countries eventually became the victims of colonialism. The analysis will be confined to the early modern period viz. the period from the sixteenth to the eighteenth centuries. In the main, this period formed the backdrop to the phase of the formal colonial relationship between countries in the two continents, although as we shall see there were cases where monopsonistic and monopolistic privileges were sought and obtained by the Europeans in

1 David, S. Landes, *The Wealth and Poverty of Nations, Why Some Countries Are So Poor and Some So Rich*, New York, 1998, p. xx.

Asia and even formal territorial control established in parts of the continent during this early period. Though economic relationship was by no means the only vehicle of contact between the two continents, the lecture will be confined to this relationship.

ASIAN MARITIME TRADE IN THE PRE-EUROPEAN PERIOD

The history of economic contacts between Europe and Asia goes back into antiquity. Fairly regular commercial contacts are known to have flourished during the days of the Roman Empire. The precise strength and range of these contacts until about the early part of the second millennium A.D., however, remain somewhat obscure. But there can be very little doubt that the rise of long-distance Asian maritime trade stretching from Gombroon in the Persian Gulf to Nagasaki in Japan along what I have elsewhere described as the great arc of Asian trade had important implications for the value as well as the composition of the water-cum-land trade between west Asia and southern Europe via the Mediterranean. In Asian maritime trade, by far the longest distance was covered by the route that connected Aden to Canton. There is evidence to suggest that this route was in regular use at least from the seventh century. The principal group which had initiated trade on the route was the Persian merchants who had, however, been supplanted by and large by Arab merchants since about the ninth century. The principal stops on the way were either Cambay or Calicut on the Indian west coast and a port such as Palembang in Sumatra. It would seem that at some time during the twelfth century Chinese junks also began operating on this route in an important way. There is evidence that the Chinese merchants established commercial contacts with places such as Sri Lanka, Kollam on the Malabar coast and Hurmuz in the Persian Gulf. The Chinese participation in trade on this route would appear to have reached important levels by the early years of the fifteenth century. Between 1404 and 1433, a series of seven commercial-cum-naval expeditions was dispatched from China under the command of Admiral Cheng Ho. The first of these expeditions is believed to have consisted of as many as 62 ships and 28,000 men. The fourth voyage is reported to have reached Hurmuz and Aden, while those that followed claimed to have touched even the East African ports of Mogadishu and Malindi. But in 1433 the Chinese authorities abruptly withdrew from these ventures and, indeed, there is no record of these long-distance voyages having ever been resumed. In the meantime, the Arabs had also gradually pulled out of this long-distance route.

Whatever the reasons behind the Chinese and the Arab withdrawal from long-distance trade, it signalled a basic alteration in the organizational structure of Asian trade. The new structure was based on the segmentation of the great arc of Asian trade into three divisions – the Arabian Sea, the Bay of Bengal and the South China Sea. The ports of Cambay or Calicut and Malacca (founded at the beginning of the fifteenth century), which had until then served essentially as victualling and stopping points on the long route between west Asia and China, now became terminal ports. The role of these ports in providing a reasonably assured market in the goods brought in, as well as in making available those sought after by the visiting ships, besides offering facilities such as anchorage, ware-housing and banking, cannot be overemphasized. In the course of the fifteenth century, Malacca became a truly major centre of international exchange and a meeting point of traders from the East and the West. Increasingly, the participation of the Arab merchants became confined to the trade between west Asia and the west coast of India. This left the trade between the west and the east coasts of India on the one hand, and the eastern Indian Ocean region on the other, almost exclusively in the hands of Indians – the Gujaratis more than anyone else, but also the Chettis, the Chulias and other groups from the Coromandel coast, besides the Oriyas and the Bengalis. The participation of the Chinese merchants was now restricted by and large to controlling the trade between China and Malacca, while the Indonesian and the Malay merchants hardly seem to have ventured beyond the inter-island and the port-to-port trade in the Malay-Indonesian region. In sum, Indian merchants from different regions of the country constituted an important trading group operating in the Ocean.

It is true that the ships that left Cambay for Malacca each year included many owned and operated by Arab, Persian, Turkish and other merchants from west Asia, but all these groups together were overshadowed by the Gujaratis who controlled the bulk of the trade on the route. The goods that the Malacca-bound ships leaving Cambay carried were, in part, coloured woollen clothes and glassware from the Mediterranean, and items such as rose-water, opium, indigo and silver from west Asia. But a large part of the cargo would seem to have consisted of textiles manufactured in Gujarat – mainly of coarse cotton, though more expensive varieties including those manufactured from fine-quality cotton and silk also seem to have figured in the list. The cargo obtained in exchange at Malacca included Chinese goods such as silk and porcelain, Indonesian spices such as pepper, cloves, nutmeg and mace, besides woods and aromatics, and precious and non-precious metals such as Malayan tin. In addition to Malacca, the Gujarati ships from Cambay called at ports such as Aceh, Kedah, Tenasserim/Mergui and Pegu. The goods carried to these ports were broadly similar to those carried to Malacca: the goods brought back were largely of local origin, rather than cosmopolitan as in the case of Malacca. A part of the large conglomerate of goods brought to Cambay was obviously destined for consumption in Gujarat, as well as the large north Indian hinterland supplied by it. But a good proportion would seem to have been re-exported mainly to west Asia, the most important ports in the region at this time being Aden and Jeddah. The other important constituent of the cargo to west Asia was textiles manufactured in Gujarat. These were predominantly those manufactured from coarse cotton and intended for mass consumption, though superior varieties manufactured from fine cotton and silk also figured in the list. The route from Cambay to Aden would seem to have been dominated by the Arab, Persian and other west Asian merchants though the Gujarati merchants also operated on this route in an important way.

The Indonesian spices and other items imported from Cambay into Aden and other west Asian ports found their way in significant quantities, in addition to the markets of west Asia, to

Europe via the Mediterranean. The two routes used for the purpose were those via the Red Sea and the Persian Gulf. While the Red Sea route terminated at the Egyptian port of Alexandria on the southern coast of the Mediterranean and involved only a small stretch of overland transportation, the Persian Gulf route made use of the Tigris or the Euphrates rivers and a fair amount of caravan transportation across Iraq and the Syrian desert. Important among the Mediterranean destination ports on this route were Tripoli (of Syria) and Beirut. This traffic was handled exclusively by the west Asian merchants. At the Mediterranean ports, the goods were procured mainly by the merchants from Venice and Genoa. While both the Red Sea and the Persian Gulf routes had been in use since antiquity, the relative amount of traffic on either at any given point in time depended partly on political circumstances. While during the eighth and the ninth centuries the Persian Gulf route was the dominant one, the decline of the Abbasid caliphate and the rise of the Fatimids of Egypt tilted the balance from the eleventh century onward significantly in favour of the Red Sea route. This was also the period which witnessed a significant expansion in the volume of Euro-Asian trade. Evidence from the end of the fourteenth and the early years of the fifteenth century suggests that volume-wise the Alexandria trade was considerably larger than – nearly double on average – the one via Beirut. However, since the latter handled the expensive spices much more, the difference between the two ports was much smaller in terms of value.[2]

RISE OF AN EARLY MODERN WORLD ECONOMY

In a well-known passage in his *An Enquiry into the Nature and Causes of the Wealth of Nations*, Adam Smith, the father of modern economic science, argued that "the discovery of America and that of a passage to the East Indies by the Cape of Good Hope are the two greatest and most important events recorded in

2 C.H.H. Wake, "The changing pattern of Europe's pepper and spice imports, ca. 1400-1700", *The Journal of European Economic History*, vol. 8(2), 1979, pp. 364-9.

the history of mankind."[3] While there clearly is an element of exaggeration in this statement, it nevertheless underscores the critical role of the two events in the emergence of an early modern world economy. The three principal segments of this economy, namely Europe, the New World, and Asia effectively came together in an interactive fashion for the first time directly as a result of the great discoveries of the last decade of the fifteenth century. The New World was discovered for the first time. As for Asia, what the discovery of the all-water route via the Cape of Good Hope achieved was the overcoming of the transport-technology barrier to the growth of the Euro-Asian trade. The volume of this trade was no longer subject to the capacity constraint imposed by the availability of pack animals and river boats in the Middle East. It was indeed a critically important coincidence that the discovery of the Cape route and of the New World took place almost simultaneously. For without the enormous quantities of American silver reaching Europe through the sixteenth century, the enhanced trading opportunities between Europe and Asia opened up by the Cape route would essentially have been frustrated. Euro-Asian trade had traditionally been one involving the exchange of Asian luxury and other goods basically against European silver and, to a smaller extent, gold. The 'bullion for goods' pattern of trade was an outcome of the inability of Europe to supply goods that could be sold in Asia in reasonably large quantities at competitive terms. Europe at this time had an undoubted overall superiority over Asia in the field of scientific and technological knowledge, but not as yet the distinct cost advantage that came with the Industrial Revolution in the late eighteenth and nineteenth centuries. This put the Asian, and particularly the Indian producers, with their considerably lower labour costs and a much longer history of sophisticated skills in handicrafts of various kinds, in a position of advantage over their European counterparts in the production of a variety of manufactured goods. As a result, Europe really had no option but to pay for the Asian goods overwhelmingly in terms of precious metals.

[3] Adam Smith, *An Enquiry into the Nature and Causes of the Wealth of Nations*, 1776, reprinted from the sixth edition, London, 1905, vol. 2, p. 139.

Ever since the fourteenth entry or so, the output of precious metals in Europe had by and large been stagnant raising fears of deflationary tendencies cropping up. This, coupled with the bullionist inhibitions regarding the export of precious metals, would almost certainly have created a situation where the non-availability of significant additional quantities of precious metals for export to the East would by and large have rendered the opportunities opened up by the availability of the Cape route quite redundant. It is in this context that one must appreciate the critical significance of the two great discoveries – that of the New World and of the Cape route to the East Indies – having taken place almost simultaneously. It is from this time onward that one can legitimately speak of the emergence of an early modern world economy embracing in an organic and interactive manner all three of its principal components, namely the New World, Europe, and Asia.

THE PORTUGUESE ESTADO DA INDIA

The spice monopoly

Since the Cape route had been discovered by the Portuguese, they immediately monopolized it and even got the Pope to legitimize the arrangement. Was their trade on this route a net addition to the Euro-Asian trade in spices and other goods or did it represent largely a diversion of the trade along the long-established water-cum-land route via the Mediterranean? There is very little doubt that in the early years of the sixteenth century the Portuguese policies were indeed instrumental in spelling almost a total disaster for the trade along the old route. The attempt at monopolizing the spice trade was unambiguous. It called for a total exclusion of Asian shipping from the Persian Gulf and the Red Sea: the instructions to Pedro Alvares Cabral, in charge of the first major commercial voyage to India that left Lisbon in March 1500, included the initiation of steps designed at blockading the passage to the Red Sea. The rest of the Asian trade would be regulated to exclude trade in spices. The instrument used to implement this policy was the cartaz, a safe-conduct that all Asian ships were obliged to carry on pain of seizure in the event of non-compliance.

The document obliged the Asian ship to call at a Portuguese-controlled port and, following the establishment of the Portuguese customs houses there, to pay customs duties before it proceeded on its voyage. Enemies of the Portuguese and banned goods such as spices were not to be carried. There is some evidence that an equivalent of the cartaz existed in the Asian seas before the arrival of the Portuguese, but there can be little doubt that the scale on which this restrictive measure was used by the Portuguese was unprecedented. The measure indeed represented an institutional constraint on the freedom of navigation on the high seas.

The policy of exclusion of the merchants from Calicut, Cambay and other ports on the west coast of India from the Red Sea and the Persian Gulf was highly successful. Hurmuz at the entrance to the Persian Gulf was captured in 1515: the failure to capture Aden was made up for by the dispatch each season from Goa of a fleet to lie off the entrance to the Red Sea, usually cruising between Aden and Bab-el-Mandeb and returning to Hurmuz in April. Raids on departing fleets at Calicut were common and the result was practically a ruination of the spice trade with the Persian Gulf and the Red Sea. It was reported as early as 1504 that the Venetian galleys calling there found no spices at either Alexandria or Beirut. Two years prior to that, concerned at the loss of the substantial revenues that the spice trade used to bring him, the Mamluk of Egypt had sought the good offices of the Pope to try and dissuade the Portuguese from choking the flow of spices through the Red Sea!

The dislocation in the spice trade, however, proved only temporary. By the second decade of the sixteenth century cracks had already begun to appear in the Portuguese system. A series of circumstanes combined to produce this result. A key element in the situation was the financial priorities and compulsions of the Estado da India. Given the rather precarious state of the finances of this body, it was imperative that no opportunity of taxing Asian shipping by making it call and pay duties at Portuguese controlled ports such as Malacca, Goa and Diu be missed. Hurmuz, taken in 1515, was one such strategically located port. Pepper and other spices passing through the port and destined for consumption within west Asia posed no problem: the choice between tax revenue and the cost of the infringement of the European monopoly arose only in respect of that part of the cargo which would eventually reach Venice or Genoa via Aleppo. The choice was made in favour of the tax revenue and, as Niels Steensgaard has suggested, between 1524 and 1543 an average of 90,000 xerafins was earned as customs duties per annum at Hurmuz. Steensgaard's characterization of the Portuguese enterprise as 'redistributive' in character has in part at its base such parasitical siphoning off of a part of the profits of Asian trade. Another circumstance that prompted the Portuguese to allow pepper shipments to pass Hurmuz was the desire to earn the goodwill of Persia against an increasingly aggressive Ottoman empire. Whatever the motivation, the Portuguese decision involved a diversion of the spice trade from the Aden-Cairo-Alexandria axis to the Basra-Baghdad-Aleppo axis.

But that diversion was strictly temporary, and from the late 1530s onward the Red Sea spice trade began to revive. After an initial vigorous and successful phase, the Portuguese blockade of the Bab-el-Mandeb became increasingly ineffective for a variety of reasons. For one thing, considerations of strategy as well as of economics often obliged the Porguguese authorities to issue a limited number of cartazes for the Red Sea ports. Thus, as early as 1515 Albuquerque found it necessary to grant the Samudri raja a certain number of cartazes for the merchants based at his port, enabling them to resume trade with Aden and Jeddah. On other occasions, a similar concession was extended to other puppet rulers. Important business associates such as Khwaja Shams-ud-din Gilani as well as merchants providing credit to the Estado had to be similarly accommodated. In some cases, such as in that of Gilani, trade in pepper was explicitly permitted, while in most others the understanding was that pepper would continue to be treated as a prohibited article. But for all practical purposes, the distinction made little difference and nearly all ships going to the region carried pepper legitimately or clandestinely. And then, of course, there was the trade in pepper carried on by various categories of the Portuguese in contravention of the official policy.

The network of this trade included the Red Sea and there was very little the Portuguese official machinery was able to do about it.

It needs to be emphasized that the Estado simply lacked the resources in men and ships to sustain an effective blockade of the Red Sea year after year. The only area in which the Portuguese were reasonably successful was in preventing ships from Malabar from going to the Red Sea. But shipping from Kanara and the Bay of Bengal continued to carry Indian pepper to the Red Sea from the late 1530s and the early 1540s onward, mainly through the agency of the Gujarat merchants. It seems that considering the expense and the poor rate of success, the Portuguese abandoned the Red Sea expeditions around 1569, clearing the way for a full-fledged revival of the Red Sea traffic in pepper. C.R. Boxer, who has traced this revival, is of the opinion that the volume of Aceh pepper reaching Jeddah at the end of the sixteenth century was larger than what the Portuguese were taking to Lisbon by the Cape route.[4]

The procurement of pepper

In keeping with the traditional composition of the Asian imports into Europe, the principal item sought by the Portuguese Crown in Asia was spices – overwhelmingly pepper – though some other goods were also procured. Throughout the sixteenth century, an overwhelming proportion of the pepper imported into Lisbon was procured on the southwest coast of India where the first purchases were made at Calicut on the Malabar coast where Vasco da Gama had landed. But relations with the *pardesi* merchants of the town as well as the samudri raja deteriorated fast. The conflict with the merchants had its origin mainly in the Portuguese insistence on being provided with pepper before the Red Sea merchants had been served. The Portuguese attack on a *sambuk* was retaliated by their factory being looted which, in turn, led to an attack on the port and a bombardment of the town in 1501 that lasted for two days. The era of peaceful trading which, occasional instances of

---

[4] C.R. Boxer, 'A note on Portuguese reactions to the revival of the Red Sea spice trade and the rise of Atjeh, 1540-1600', *Journal of Southeast Asian History*, vol. 10(3), 1969, pp. 415-28.

violence notwithstanding, had been the norm in the Asian waters for centuries, had finally been shattered by the Portuguese. At any rate, it was found more expedient to shift the centre of pepper procurement to Cochin where the more cooperative Mappila and the Syrian Christian merchants were used as brokers and intermediaries. With the aid of the dependent raja of Cochin, the Portuguese tried to establish a monopoly in pepper there. But since the raja had no real control over the areas where pepper was grown or over the routes used for its transportation, the monopoly never really worked in any effective sense. At his own level, of course, thc raja provided all help by giving protection to the river boats bringing pepper to Cochin, by guaranteeing loans raised by the Portuguese from private sources, as well as by providing loans himself.[5] The friendly relationship between the Estado and the Mappila merchants at Cochin, however, did not last very long. By the end of the third decade of the century, the merchants had declared a holy war – *jihad* – against the Estado. This hostility continued in one form or another into the seventeenth century.

The procurement of pepper in India was organized by the Estado while the sales in Europe were through contract sales based until the middle of the century at Antwerp and thereafter in Lisbon. The liquidity problems of the Portuguese Crown forced a major reorganization of the trade with Asia in 1564 when the first of a series of contracts giving over trade on the Cape route to private parties was concluded. The remaining part of the century witnessed a variety of experiments being carried out in an attempt to identify the optimal strategy that would ensure to the Crown maximum monopoly revenue without obliging it to be directly involved in the conduct of the trade with Asia. In 1570, the trade in pepper and other spices was opened to free competition, although the Crown also continued to participate in the trade itself and retained its monopoly on the export of precious metals to Asia. The Asian contract system was introduced in 1575. The

[5] Jan Kieniewicz, 'The Portuguese factory and trade in pepper in Malabar during the sixteenth century', *The Indian Economic and Social History Review*, vol. 6(1), 1969, pp. 68-9.

first beneficiary of the new arrangement was the Augsburg merchant Konrad Rott and associates who included the Milanese merchant Giovanni Batista Rovalesca. Under this arrangement, Rott received intact the royal monopoly of the Cape route – the procurement of spices in Asia, their shipment to Europe, the provisioning of the carracks in Lisbon and Goa, and the distribution of pepper in Europe. Just before his death in 1580, dom Henrique renewed the Rott-Rovalesca contract for another five years. Each year, the contractors were supposed to purchase in India a total of 30,000 quintals of pepper – 15,000 on their own account and 15,000 on the Crown's account. The contractors were free to sell their half of the pepper as they chose; the Crown would also sell all of its 15,000 quintals (which cost it nothing) to the Rott-Rovalesca consortium at 32 cruzados per quintal. The consortium thus enjoyed exclusive European distribution of Portuguese pepper.[6] A sharp decline in the European price of pepper, however, forced Rott out of business. In February 1586, a new Asian contract was concluded for a period of six years with Rovalesca in association with Giraldo Paris. This group was required to supply to the Crown 30,000 quintals of pepper per annum at a price of 16 cruzados per quintal.[7] The Casa da India sold the pepper to the European contractors at prices negotiated each year in Lisbon. The contract system continued until 1598 when following the English and Dutch intervention in the seaborne spice trade, private enterprise was no longer willing to take up the pepper contracts. In any event, the experiment with the contract system had not been particularly satisfactory for either side. The syndicates were consistently unable to import the quantities specified in the contracts and never managed to make adequate profits. The bankruptcy of Rott has already been noted: his Milanese counterpart Rovalesca was also forced to follow suit.

---

6 James C. Boyajian, *Portuguese Trade in Asia under the Habsburgs 1580-1640*, Baltimore and London, 1993, p. 20.

7 Hermann Kellenbenz, "Autour de 1600: le commerce du poivre des Fugger et le marche international du poivre", *Annales Economies-Societes-Civilisations*, vol. 11(1), 1956, pp. 1-28.

Redistributive enterprise?

Given the manner in which the Portuguese Crown dealt with the matter of the procurement, the transportation, and particularly the disposal of the Asian pepper in the European market, the Danish historian, Niels Steensgaard, characterized the Portuguese Euro-Asian pepper trade as a redistributive enterprise. As he so succinctly put it, "the Portuguese pepper monopoly was not a business but a custom house."[8] He had then gone on to contrast this with the productivity enhancing nature of the northern European companies' – particularly the Dutch East India Company's – trading operations between the two continents from the beginning of the seventeenth century onward. The success of the companies was based not upon government monopolies or the use of violence but on their ability to compete in the market. For by adopting specific policies in relation to stocks, pricing and the mode of the disposal of their goods, the companies made impressive gains in the transparency and the predictability of the markets in which they operated. This is essence constituted what Steensgaard described as the Asian Trade Revolution of the early seventeenth century. While certain key elements in Steensgaard's formulation continue to be valid, the overall characterisation of a redistributive enterprise for the entire Portuguese trading operations both between Europe and Asia as well as those within Asia is probably in need of revision. This is partly because the companies were not quite as devoid of the use of monopoly and violence as Steensgaard's model in a pure form would seem to imply. More importantly, we now know that the Portuguese enterprise was indeed very much more than a simple Euro-Asian trade in pepper, the commodity mainly responsible for the characterisation of the trade as redistributive in nature.

It is, therefore, important to keep the matter in perspective and not overstate the redistributive dimensions of the Portuguese Asian enterprise in its entirety. Pepper was indeed the raison d'etre of the Portuguese Euro-Asian trade in the beginning

---

[8] Niels Steensgaard, *Carracks, Caravans, and Companies: The Structural Crisis in the European-Asian Trade in the Early 17th Century*, Copenhagen, 1973, p. 100.

accounting in the first two decades of the sixteenth century for as much as 95 percent of the total Asian cargo imported in physical terms and 85 percent in value terms.[9] However, the situation changed considerably from the 1580s onward with the physical share of pepper coming down to 68 percent during 1587-88, to 65 percent during 1600-03 with an increase to 69 percent during 1608-10.[10] More importantly, a recent study by James Boyajian suggests a dramatic decline in the proportion of pepper to total Portuguese imports over the period 1580-1640 to a mere 10 percent. According to him, by far the most important item of import during this period was cotton and silk textiles accounting for as much as 62 percent of the total value imported, followed by precious stones (14 percent) indigo (6 percent) and spices other than pepper (5 percent).[11] If pepper accounted for no more than 10 percent of the total imports from Asia, the redistributive dimension of the Portuguese Euro-Asian trade as viewed from the European end would assume a very different quantitative profile from that suggested by Niels Steensgaard. At the heart of Boyajian's analysis is his almost revolutionary revision of current orthodoxy in the matter of the relative role of the private Portuguese traders in the Euro-Asian *carreira* traded over the period. It has traditionally been conceded that the *carreira* ships did indeed carry on a regular basis a certain amount of private cargo under a variety of arrangements. The novelty of Boyajian's estimates consists in his view of the magnitude of the private cargoes carried abroad these ships overwhelmingly on the account of the New Christian merchants who were descendants of Iberian Jews forcibly converted to Christianity at the end of the fifteenth century. According to Boyajian, private cargoes accounted for an almost unbelievable

---

[9] The physical estimates are based on Genevieve Bouchon, "L'inventaire de la cargaison rapportee de l'Inde en 1505", *Mare Luso Indicum*, Vol. III, Paris 1976, and *Navires et Cargaisons retour de l'Inde en 1518*, Paris, 1977. The value estimates are calculated from Magalhaes Godinho, *Os D'escobrimentos e a Economia Mundial, Lisbon, 1963-71*, Vol. III, p. 11.

[10] Niels Steensgaard, "The return cargoes of the Carreira in the 16th and early 17th century" in Teotonio R. de Souza (ed.), *Indo-Portuguese History: Old Issues, New Questions*, New Delhi, 1985, p. 22.

[11] James C. Boyajian, *Portuguese Trade in Asia*, Table 3, p. 44.

93 percent of the total value imported over the period 1580-1640 from Asia. Certain methodological problems with the Boyajian estimates do indeed raise questions about the precise extent of the private Portuguese merchants' trade between Europe and Asia. But there can be little doubt that the significant upward revision of the overall role of these merchants in Euro-Asian trade is in the right direction. This would considerably erode the redistributive dimension of the pepper trade at the European end.

Portuguese intra-Asian trade

What about the Asian end of the Portuguese trading operations as an element in the redistributive potential of these operations? We have already seen that the Estado da India's attempt at monopolizing the Indian Ocean spice trade was short-lived. In respect of the bulk of the remainder of the trading activity carried on by the Portuguese either on an official or on a private basis, there was no component of a redistributive enterprise whatever. The Estado itself engaged in a certain amount of trade within Asia, mainly in the Bay of Bengal with Malacca as the principal point of origin and termination of voyages. In the decade of 1511-20, the *Fazenda Real* (or royal treasury) carried out a number of exploratory commercial voyages and a whole series of crown routes (*carreiras*) was created. This was done in close cooperation with the Keling merchant community of Malacca, whose doyen at the time was one Nina Chatu. The cooperation often took the form of ventures undertaken jointly by the Crown and Nina Chatu. One such venture was the voyage of the *Sao Joao* which left Malacca for Martaban in Burma in August 1512, returning in May 1513. The same ship was then sent to Pulicat, again in partnership with Nina Chatu.[12] However, for a variety of reasons, the period over which the involvement of the Portuguese Crown as an entrepreneur in intra-Asian trade lasted was comparatively brief.

The phase of the Crown involvement in intra-Asian trade was followed from the second half of the sixteenth century onward

[12] Sanjay Subrahmanyam, "The Coromandel-Malacca Trade in the 16th Century: A Study of its Evolving Structure", *Moyen Orient & Ocean Indian XVI-XIX*, vol. 3, 1986, pp. 55-80.

by a fairly intensive participation in this trade by private Portuguese traders, many of whom were at the same time employees of the Estado. Another major group of private traders participating in intra-Asian trade was that of the New Christian merchants, also using this channel to obtain a variety of Asian goods for transportation to Lisbon abroad the *carreira* ships as private cargo. A large number of the private traders operated on the basis of the so-called 'concession' system introduced in the 1550s. This system was essentially in the nature of a benefice conferred by the Crown mainly on the so-called *casado* merchants. A concession conferred on the grantee the right to make a voyage between two specified ports in the Indian Ocean and/or the China Sea. By the 1580s, the concession system had become a major component of the Portuguese trading network in Asia. Luis Thomaz has listed a total of 34 concession voyages in operation in the 1580s covering the China sea, the Indonesian archipelago, and the Bay of Bengal.[13] The New Christian merchants of Goa invested in both the *carreira da India* as well as in intra-Asian trade. Indeed, the profits from intra-Asian trade financed a good part of the cargo that the New Christian merchants put on the *carreira* ships at Goa for Lisbon on their private account. In the 1580, Goa's merchants, according to Boyajian, shipped about 250,000 cruzados in silver and other goods each year to Macao on the China-Japan carracks. In return, they extracted from Japan more than 500,000 cruzados of silver annually, much of which returned to Goa and Cochin as silk, musk and porcelain and gold coin, after yet another exchange in Macao.[14] A large part of this cargo eventually found its way to Lisbon. This particular trading strategy anticipated in an important manner what the Dutch East India Company did on a much more elaborate scale and with a much greater degree of intensity in the seventeenth century.

---

[13] Luis Filipe F.R. Thomaz, "The Portuguese in the seas of the Archipelago during the 16th Century", pp. 81-85. Originally published as "Les Portugais dans les mers de l', Archipel au XVI siecle", *Archipel, 18* (1979). Available in translation as *Trade and Shipping in the Southern Seas, Selected Readings from Archipel (18)*, 1979, Paris, 1984, pp. 75-91.

[14] James C. Boyajian, *Portuguese Trade in Asia*, p. 84.

A reference to the trading activities of the Dutch East India Company, which we shall analyse in some detail below, also serves to remind one that in so far as the Dutch monopoly of finer spices involved a gross under-payment to the producers in the Spice Islands, the label of redistributive enterprise would apply as much to this segment of the Dutch Company business as it would to the pepper trade of the Portuguese Crown. Indeed, Steensgaard himself recognizes this when he says, "the Dutch East India Company was not a 'pure' type: it contained features in its constitution, in its structure and its policy, more reminiscent of a redistributive enterprise than of a business."[15] Again, the absence of the "use of violence" by the companies is a construct that poses problems. In its trade within Asia, the Dutch East India Company took extensive steps to obtain exclusive right in particular products and markets and minimize competition by indigenous merchants, making a judicious use of violence in the process.[16] The Company also made an optimal use of the pass system to keep Asian competitors out of the trade in monopoly products such as spices and regulate their trade in several others, such as Malayan tin. If some violation of the prescribed policies and procedures, say by the Indian traders, was tolerated, it was only because the cost of unlimited conflict in the form of possible disruptions to its trade in the Indian subcontinent would have been unacceptably high for the Company.[17]

If one goes beyond Steensgaard and defines the notion of "ability to compete" to include both belief and confidence in

---

[15] Niels Steensgaard, *Carracks, Caravans and Companies*, p. 141. A few pages earlier, Steensgaard writes, "One may therefore raise the question as to whether the Dutch East India Company ought not to be considered a redistributive enterprise using organized violence with a view to the acquisition of income" (p. 133).

[16] As the Dutch historian, Hans van Santen, has put it, "Violence was a necessary part of the market strategy of the VOC", H.W. van Santen, "De Verenigde Oost-Indische Compagnie in Gujarat en Hindustan, 1620-1660," Ph.D. thesis, Leiden University, 1982, p. 208.

[17] Om Prakash, "Asian trade and European impact: A study of the trade from Bengal 1630-1720," in Blair B. Kling and M.N. Pearson (eds.), *The Age of Partnership, Europeans in Asia Before Dominion*, Honolulu, 1979, pp. 43-70.

competitive trade, the sustained opposition of the English and the Dutch companies to the entry of rival European companies into Euro-Asian trade creates problems. The Dutch Company, for example, was clearly hostile to the first Danish expeditions of the 1610s and the early 1620s to India.[18] The VOC's action in seizing two of the Genoese East India Company's vessels in the Sunda Straits in April 1649 was a clear example of the use of force to keep a potential competitor out, though ostensibly the step was taken because the vessels were carrying Dutch crews and merchants.[19] Also, in the 1720s, the Dutch and the English companies successfully formed a coalition both in Europe as well as in Bengal to keep the newly formed Ostend Company out of the lucrative Bengal trade. It was basically the pressure by the two companies that led to the suspension and later the abolition of the Ostend Company. There, of course, was nothing they could do about the same set of merchants regrouping themselves under different nomenclatures. It is, therefore, imperative that the question of the differences between the policies followed by the Portuguese on the one hand, and by the Dutch and the English on the other, which certainly were by no means inconsiderable, be kept in perspective.

THE DUTCH AND THE ENGLISH EAST INDIA COMPANIES

Even though the Asian Trade Revolution of the early seventeenth century consisted in the English and the Dutch East India companies being different from the Portuguese Estado only in a limited way, there nevertheless was another kind of Asian Trade Revolution under way at precisely the same time. This revolution consisted in an enormous expansion in the volume and value of seaborne Euro-Asian trade as well as a major diversification in the composition of the goods imported into Europe as well as the

---

[18] Om Prakash (ed.), *The Dutch Factories in India, 1617-1623*, New Delhi, 1984, pp. 31-33, 35; Holden Furber, *Rival Empires of Trade in the Orient, 1600-1800*, Minneapolis, 1976, pp. 201-202; Sanjay Subrahmanyam, *The Political Economy of Commerce: Southern India, 1500-1650*, Cambridge, 1990, p. 282.

[19] Sanjay Subrahmanyam, *The Political Economy of Commerce*, p. 293.

range of Asian sources where these goods were procured. A related development was the near-wiping out early in the seventeenth century of the water-cum-land route between the two continents that had been in use for centuries.

The Dutch East India was founded in 1602 by a charter granted by the States-General, the national administrative body of the Dutch Republic. The Euro-Asian trade carried on by the Portuguese was running into serious problems in the last quarter of the sixteenth century. This, coupled with the loss, in 1585, of Antwerp's position as the staple market for Asian goods in north-western Europe as a result of the blockade of the Scheldt, gave the merchants from the northern Netherlands a strong incentive to challenge the Portuguese monopoly of the Cape route and participate directly in the Euro-Asian spice trade. The first stage was the establishment in the 1590s of a number of so-called 'pre-companies', the most important of which was the one known as the 'Old Company'. It was on the account of this company that eight vessels were sent out to the East in 1598. The profit on the voyage was estimated at around 400 percent. Since the ships sent to the East on the individual account of different companies competed with each other fiercely, the inevitable result was an increase in the cost price of the pepper and other spices and a decline in their sale prices in the Netherlands. It was with a view to prevent such cutthroat competition that the various companies were merged together in March 1602 to form the United Dutch East India Company. The other major north-west European Company engaged in the Euro-Asian trade was the English East India Company. The great success attendant upon the venture of the Old Company of Amsterdam into the Euro-Asian trade had caused great consternation among the English merchants engaged in the spice trade from the Levant. The fear of the Dutch domination of the spice market in northwestern Europe thus served as the catalyst that led a group of London merchants to apply to the Crown for a monopoly charter for the East India trade. The request was granted and on 31 December 1600 was born the 'Company of Merchants of London trading into the East Indies'.

Initially, both the Dutch and the English concentrated on the procurement of pepper and other spices which, as in the sixteenth century, continued to account for an overwhelming proportion of the total Asian imports into Europe. But unlike, and indeed mainly because of, the Portuguese, the Dutch and the English procured their pepper in Indonesia rather than on the southwest coast of India. The result was a marked shift in the Asian loci of the Euro-Asian seaborne trade form India to the Indonesia archipelago. This was the Asian counterpart of the shift of the European loci of this trade from Lisbon to Amsterdam and London. It was nearly three quarters of a century before the Asian loci shifted back to India in response to the change in European fashions assigning an increasingly important role to textiles and raw silk in the Asian imports into Europe. In the case of the Dutch East India Company, for example, spices, including pepper, came down from an imposing 74 percent of the total imports in 1619-21 to 68 percent during 1648-50 and to a mere 23 percent during 1698-1700. On the other hand, textiles and raw silk went up from 16 percent in 1619-21 to an incredible 55 percent at the end of the seventeenth century. There was a decline thereafter, but in 1778-80 textiles and raw silk accounted for half of the total imports. Because of the smaller geographical range of the Asian operations of the English East India Company, goods procured in India accounted for an even greater proportion of the total Asian imports into England. At the end of the seventeenth century, this figure stood at as much as 95 percent and at 84 percent in 1738-40.[20]

The role of bullion

The central characteristic feature of Euro-Asian trade, namely the necessity for the Europeans to pay for the Asian goods overwhelmingly in precious metals, however, remained unchanged throughout the entire period between the sixteenth and the eighteenth centuries. This particular phenomenon has sometimes

[20] J.R. Bruijn, F.S. Gaastra, and I. Schoffer, *Dutch Asiatic Shipping in the 17th and 18th Centuries*, The Hague, 1987, Vol. 1, Table 41, p. 192. Calculated from K.N. Chaudhuri, *The Trading World of Asia and the English East India Company, 1660-1760*, Cambridge, 1978, pp. 508-10.

been ascribed to the rigidity of consumer tastes in the East, which rendered the Asian markets for European goods extremely small and static. Alternatively, it has been suggested that the absorption of precious metals by India or China reflected the hoarding habits in these societies.[21] But as pointed out earlier, a more convincing explanation of this phenomenon is the inability of Europe to supply western products with a potential market in Asia at prices that would generate a large enough demand for them to provide the necessary revenue for the purchase of the Asian goods. The only major item Europe was in a position to provide to Asia was precious metals. The growth of the Euro-Asian trade, therefore, was critically dependent upon an increase in the availability of these metals. In this context, the working of the South American silver mines and the enormous import of American silver into Europe during the sixteenth and the early seventeenth centuries was a development of critical significance. Although the American silver initially arrived into Spain, a large part of it eventually found its way to Amsterdam, mainly via Hamburg. In fact, from the early years of the seventeenth century the Dutch were the undoubted masters of the European bullion trade and Amsterdam the leading world centre of the trade in precious metals.[22] It is an indication of the international standing of this city as a market for precious metals that the English East India Company also obtained a large part of its requirements of these metals in Amsterdam. An analysis of the Dutch and the English East India companies' exports to the East Indies over the seventeenth and the eighteenth centuries testifies to an unambiguous pattern where precious metals dominated the total exports throughout the period. An important implication of this 'bullion for goods' model of Euro-Asian trade was that as far as the Europeans were concerned, the profit from the trade was derived almost entirely from the sale of Asian goods in Europe rather than also from the sale of European goods in Asia.

---

[21] Rudolph C. Blitz, 'Mercantalist policies and the pattern of world trade, 1500-1750', *Journal of Economic History*, vol. 17, 1967, pp. 39-55.

[22] J.G. van Dillen, 'Amsterdam als wereldmarkt der edele metalen in the 17de en 18de eeuw', *De Economist*, vol. 72, 1923, pp. 538-98, 717-30.

Dutch intra-Asian trade

If India was at the centre of the European trading companies' Euro-Asian trade, it was equally central to the extensive amount of trade the Europeans, both the corporate enterprises as well as private traders, carried on within Asia using the Indian Ocean-South China Sea trading network. The critical role played by India was as much a function of her capacity to provide cost-competitive manufactured goods – predominantly cotton and other textiles – in the case of the Europeans engaged in intra-Asian trade, as it had been traditionally in the case of the Indian and other Asian merchants similarly engaged in this trade. The principal European corporate enterprise engaged in intra-Asian trade in a substantial manner and as an integral part of its overall trading strategy, namely the Dutch East India Company, got involved to this trade in the first place in order to procure Indian coarse cotton textiles at source. These textiles were the principal medium of exchange throughout the Malay Indonesian archipelago and it was nearly impossible for the Company to obtain supplies of pepper and other spices except in exchange for these textiles. While these textiles could have been procured within the region at places such as Aceh, the acute business instinct of the Company took it, within a few years of its arrival in Asia, to their source, the Coromandel coast and Gujarat. The large and assured availability of highly cost-competitive textiles in India with a large demand both in Southeast Asia and West Asia was thus the starting point of the Dutch East India Company's involvement in intra-Asia trade, which eventually grew to a point where this branch of trade became of as much concern to the Company as its Euro-Asian trade. As early as 1612, Hendrik Brouwer, a future governor-general of the East Indies, had described the Coromandel coast as the "left arm of the Moluccas and the surrounding islands because without textiles that come from there, the trade in the Moluccas will be dead."[23]

The three principal elements in the Dutch strategy of participation in intra-Asian trade were Indian textiles and raw silk, Indonesian spices, and Japanese silver. The initial supply of

[23] J.E. Heeres (ed.), *Corpus-Diplomaticum Neerlando-Indicum*, The Hague, 1907, Vol. 1, p. 154.

investment funds brought in from Holland was invested first in Indian textiles, a large part of which was then sold against spices. While a part of the spices was sent home, the remainder constituted, together with the remaining Indian textiles, the basis of entry into a number of branches of trade within Asia. Among the most prized of these was the trade with Japan, where nearly half of the value of the goods sent consisted of Indian textiles and raw silk. As of 1639, when the 'closed country' era began in Japan, the Dutch East India Company was the only European entity permitted to operate in the country, giving the Company a significant differential advantage over its rivals. This advantage lay in the large amount of silver, a critical input for the Indian and several other trading areas, that the Japan trade provided. Given the large and persistent differential in the gold-silver bi-metallic ratio between the two countries, it was highly advantageous for the Company to convert a large part of the Japanese silver it procured into gold at Taiwan. The Chinese gold could then be invested profitably in the procurement of textiles on the Coromandel coast, where the basic currency unit in use was the gold pagoda. The point to emphasize is that, by about the middle of the 17th century, the Dutch East India Company had become a major participant in intra-Asian trade with trading links all along the great arc of Asian trade. Indian textiles, raw silk, and later opium, which turned out to be a highly profitable item, sold in large quantities all over the Indonesian archipelago, were among the key commodities in the Dutch Company's framework of intra-Asian trade. Given the importance the Company attached to this trade, its employees were not allowed to engage in it on their individual account. That, however, did not prevent them from doing so on a fairly large scale on a clandestine basis. Indeed, in a high-value, low-bulk item such as opium which was ideal for contraband trade, the volume of the clandestine trade was often as large as that on the Company's own account.[24]

Turning next to the English East India Company and the private English traders, one finds that while the involvement of the Company in intra-Asian trade was negligible and confined

[24] Om Prakash, *The Dutch East India Company and the Economy of Bengal, 1630-1720*, Princeton, 1985, pp. 15-23, 83-9.

essentially to the first half of the 17th century, private English traders based in India constituted by far the largest and the most enduring group of Europeans engaged in the trade of the Indian Ocean and the South China Sea. These traders operated from ports on both the east and the west coasts of India. Over the 17th and the early years of the 18th century, the Coromandel ports witnessed English trading activity on a much larger scale than did ports in Bengal. Masulipatnam was the principal port used on the Coromandel coast, but around the turn of the century more and more private English shipping moved on to Madras. In Bengal, the principal port was Hughli until it was replaced by Calcutta in the early years of the 18th century. In course of time, Calcutta emerged as the most important port of English private trade in India. On the west coast, English private trade began at Surat in the early years of the 17th century, but moved on to Bombay in the 18th century.

POLITICAL AND ECONOMIC ENVIRONMENT

What was the nature of the political and economic environment in which the European corporate groups and the private traders were obliged to function while carrying on their trading activities in Asia? In other words, if the range of alternative scenarios under which the Europeans functioned in different parts of Asia in the early modern period is conceptualized as a broad spectrum, where precisely would South Asia, for example, figure in that spectrum? One might begin by drawing attention to the fact that in the pre-European phase of the history of commercial exchange in the Indian Ocean-South China Sea complex, there was a well-established tradition of foreign merchants being welcome at the Asian ports, since they were perceived as providers of additional business to the local merchants and of additional income by way of customs duties etc. to the ruling authorities. The visiting as well as the resident foreign merchants were, by and large, left to manage their affairs themselves, including the arrangements they might make with their local counterparts, their business dealings in the market, and so on, without the administration unduly interfering in their decision-making processes. The Asian port at which such autonomy was allowed in the most unconstrained fashion was probably that of Malacca, which in the course of the 15th century had become a major centre of international exchange, and a meeting point of traders from the East and the West. Foreign merchants resident in, and operating from, the port could broadly be divided into four groups: (a) the Gujaratis, (b) other Indian merchant groups and merchants from Burma, (c) the merchants from Southeast Asia up to and including the Philippines, and (d) the merchants from East Asia, including the Chinese, the Japanese and the Okinawans. Each of these four groups was even allowed to have a *shahbandar* of its own, who managed the affairs of that particular community autonomously of the local authorities.

European naval superiority

To who extent was this scenario modified by the arrival of the Europeans in the Indian Ocean at the beginning of the 16th century? By far the most crucial element in the new situation was the armed superiority of European ships over their Asian counterparts. A glaring example of this disparity was provided in April 1612 when six English ships congregated off the Arabian coast and hijacked, in succession, fifteen passing Mughal ships from India, culminating in the capture of the great 1,000-ten vessel *Rahimi*, which belonged to the mother of the Mughal emperor. The prizes were taken to a nearby anchorage and plundered at will. It is true that the *Rahimi* was armed with some fifteen pieces of artillery and that the soldiers aboard her carried muskets, but these were merely anti-personnel weapons. Indian vessels, which often relied on rope and treenails to hold their planks in place, lacked the strength both to withstand heavy artillery bombardment from without, and to absorb the recoil of large ordinance firing from within.[25] The fact that the English could do this with impunity reflected not only the vulnerability of the Indian mercantile vessels but also the absence of a Mughal navy capable of retaliating

---

[25] Geoffrey Parker, *The Military Revolution, Military Innovation and the Rise of the West, 1500-1800*, Cambridge, 1988, pp. 107-8.

against such high-handed action. The flotilla at Dhaka and the fleet maintained by the Sidis at Janjira near Bombay were clearly inadequate to support an offensive against European ships. It was indeed not without reason that in 1662, on being approached on behalf of the king of the Maldive islands to use his good offices to persuade Emperor Aurangzeb to impose a ban on English and Dutch shipping to the islands, the *faujdar* of Balasore pointed out that even if the emperor could be persuaded to oblige the king, he was in no position to do so since he was 'master only of land and not of the sea.'[26]

Dutch spice monopoly

In the 17th century, the Dutch and the English also took over the cartaz system from the Portuguese, though in a modified format and under the nomenclature of the 'pass' or the 'passport' system. It was, however, only the Dutch East India Company which, given its high stakes in intra-Asian trade, took the system with a certain amount of seriousness. The Verenigde Oostindische Compagnie (VOC) also followed the Portuguese precedent in attempting to monopolize both the Euro-Asian and the intra-Asian trade in spices. By the early 1620s, on the basis of agreements wrested from the authorities in many of the islands in the Moluccas, the Dutch had acquired effective monopsony rights in nutmeg and mace. The case of cloves was somewhat more complex. There was large scale smuggling between the producing areas and Makassar, enabling the English, among others, to obtain large quantities of this spice. Though from 1643 onwards the VOC had managed to reduce such smuggling, it was only after the conquest of Makassar in 1669 that the Dutch fully controlled the trade in cloves. Finally, as far as pepper – which was a substantially more important item of investment in the Indies than all the other spices put together – was concerned, inspite of the conclusion of exclusive agreements with a number of states in the region, the Company never acquired effective monopsony rights in the spice.

[26] Nationaal Archief (N.A.), Letter from the Dutch Director at Hughli to Batavia dated 26 October 1662, Verenigde Oostindische Compagnie, (VOC) 1240, f.1380vo.

The totality of the control achieved by the VOC in the case of spices other than pepper in the Euro-Asian trade is exemplified by the almost incredible fact that for the entire period between 1677 and 1744, the Company managed to sell cloves in Amsterdam at the fixed price of 75 stivers per Dutch pound.[27] A similar stranglehold was enjoyed by the Company in the intra-Asian trade in these spices. The fact that the Moluccas enjoyed world monopoly in the production of these spices, grown in particular islands covering a limited geographical space, which could be effectively policed, was the key to the success of the VOC in controlling the production and the trade in these items. By the same token, pepper, which was grown on the island of Sumatra over extensive tracts, could never be brought under the monopoly net, the formal monopsony agreements with several regional powers notwithstanding. For precisely the same reason, the Portuguese had an essentially similar experience with this spice on the south-west coast of India in the sixteenth century.

What did the Dutch spice monopoly entail for the Company on the one hand, and for the producers and the Asian traders dealing in them on the other? I have argued elsewhere that by increasing the rate of gross profit on these spices to incredibly high levels, often running to a thousand or more percent, the spice monopoly became a major element in the unquestioned domination of Euro-Asian trade by the Dutch through the 17th century. A similar domination was achieved in the intra-Asian trade by using the spice monopoly as a major entry device into many branches of the network. The unusually high profit was, of course, at the expense of the producers of these spices, as well as the Indonesian and other Asian traders who used to carry on a large-scale intra-Asian trade in them. This can be seen as institutionalized coercion by one group over another that had not been a feature of Asian trade in the pre-European phase. In terms of the placement in the spectrum discussed earlier, the situation in the Indonesian archipelago would indeed represent one end of the spectrum with a clear-cut and substantive differential advantage available to the VOC.

---

27 Kristof Glamann, *Dutch-Asiatic Trade, 1620-1740*, Copenhagen/The Hague, 1958, p. 33.

Japan

Together with the spice monopoly, exclusive access to the bullion-providing Japan trade was the other principal circumstance behind the VOC's unprecedented success in penetrating the Indian Ocean-South China Sea trading network. But ironically, the conditions under which the Company was obliged to operate in Japan were diametrically opposite to those in the Indonesian archipelago, placing the Company, as it were, at the other end of the spectrum of conditions under which the European corporate enterprises functioned in Asia. In a coercion-based regime, if it was the VOC that resorted to coercion over the producing and the trading groups in the Indonesian archipelago, it was itself the victim of coercion at the hands of the political and the commercial establishment in Japan.

The beginnings of the rise of a non-market governed commercial regime in Japan can be traced to 1604 when, under a new arrangement termed the pancado, the Portuguese were obliged to sell their principal import into Japan, namely Chinese raw silk, at a price determined arbitrarily by a guild monopsony consisting of a group of merchants from the five imperial cities of Edo (Tokyo), Osaka, Kyoto, Sakai and Nagasaki. In 1631, when they protested against the arrangement, the Portuguese were told that they were free to leave the country. In 1633, they actually had to sell at prices lower than even the pancado price.[28] The same year the pancado arragement was extended to cover a part of the Chinese raw silk brought in by the Dutch East India Company as well. Following the promulgation, in June 1636, of the *sakoku* or the 'closed country' edict and the expulsion of the Portuguese in 1639 consequent on the suspected involvement of their Catholic missionaries in the Shimbara rebellion in 1637, the Dutch became the only European merchant group to be allowed to operate in Japan. In May 1641, they were ordered to move to the islet of Deshima, off the Nagasaki harbour, to which they were henceforth confined, besides being subjected to a range of commercial restrictions. These included a ban on the export of gold, the prescription of

---

[28] George Bryan Souza, *The Survival of Empire: Portuguese Trade and Society in China and the South China Sea, 1630-1754*, Cambridge, 1986, p. 60.

days on which the Company could offer its goods for sale, until which time they had to be kept in sealed warehouses, and the extension of the pancado system to the entire lot of Chinese raw silk the Company imported into Japan. The 1672 introduction of the system of *shih shobai* which the Dutch translated as *taxatie-handel* (appraised trade), effectively extended the pancado system to all imports. On the basis of the samples collected from the Dutch factors, the different commodities imported were evaluated unilaterally by selected members of the Nagasaki Chamber of Commerce. This arrangement had an immediate and substantial adverse effect on the profitability of the trade, and in 1675 the Batavia Council wrote to the governor of Nagasaki that although the Company traded with 'all corners of the globe', it had 'never yet found a single other place where the purchaser fixed the price.'[29] The appeal that the 'appraised trade' system be rescinded, however, fell on deaf ears and the Dutch chief at Nagasaki, Martinus Ceaser, could do little but express his frustration as follows, 'But it seems that the Japanese have finally laid aside all sense of honour and decency whilst we perforce must dance to their piping in everything.'[30] The fact that the Japan trade was nevertheless of enormous value for the Company through the 17th century only serves to underscore the critical role that bullion played in the early-modern Asian trade.

India

What was the situation in India like which, as we have seen, was at the centre of the Europeans' trading activities. We have already noted that in the 16th century, the Portuguese managed to obtain monopsonistic privileges in the procurement of pepper on the Malabar coast. On the strength of the assistance provided to the raja of Cochin in throwing the Portuguese out, the Dutch East India Company inherited, in 1663, similar monopsonistic privi-

---

29 Pieter van Dam, in F.W. Stapel *et al.* (ed.), *Beschryvinge van de Oost-Indische Compagnie*, The Hague, 1927-54, Book II, Part I, p. 454.

30 C.R. Boxer, 'Jan Compagnie in Japan 1672-74 or Anglo-Dutch Rivalry in Japan and Formosa', *Transactions of the Asian Society of Japan*, Second Series, 7 (1930), p. 170.

leges. But given identical problems of policing and enforcement, the situation was indeed comparable to that in Sumatra rather than that in the Molluccas.

Outside of the Malabar coast, however, the situation in India was very much in the mould of the Malacca model, characterized by the absence of coercion on either side. In terms of the spectrum of alternative scenarios, the placement of the Europeans operating in India would be right in the middle of the spectrum. In the subcontinent, the relationship between the ruling authorities and the different European groups was by and large an amicable one, based essentially on perceived mutual advantage. The authorities basically looked upon the European companies' trade in their area as a net addition with the attendant benefits that such growth of trade entailed for the economy. More immediately, the resultant increase in the customs revenue, which in the case of the Mughal empire accrued directly to the central treasury, and probably constituted a head of revenue in importance next only to land revenue, was an important consideration. An equally important consideration would seem to have been the 'bullion for goods' character of the Europeans' trade. The fact that the companies paid for the goods obtained in the subcontinent overwhelmingly in terms of precious metals made them probably the single-most important conduit for the import of these metals into the country. The domestic output of these metals being practically nil, their import, in reasonably large quantities, was critical, among other things, for the successful conduct of the subcontinent's monetary system. As a result, European requests for permission to trade and the establishment of factories were routinely granted by Mughal imperial authorities and by regional authorities in the Coromandel coast. The rate of customs duty that European companies were obliged to pay was ordinarily the same as that payable by the Indian and other Asian merchants operating from the region. Indeed, imperial administration often went a step further and exempted these companies from the payment of transit (rahdari) duties, giving them a differential advantage vis-à-vis their own nationals. It is another matter that local and the provincial authorities, whose income streams would have been adversely affected by such exemption, usually managed to ignore imperial orders and continued charging rahdari duties. Under this dispensation the companies operated in the market basically as yet another group of merchants availing no special privileges in their dealings with the Indian merchants or artisans. By the same token, they were at liberty to function in the system like any other merchant group, without restriction on the use of systematic infrastructures. Their factors and representatives were allowed to travel throughout the empire, buy and sell where they found it most profitable to do so, and deal with their Indian counterparts on terms strictly determined by the market.

Conflict resolution

The absence of coercion, however, did not preclude occasional conflict between Indian political authorities, on the one hand, and European trading companies, on the other. In such an event, both sides were concerned that the conflict did not escalate beyond a point. At work was, indeed, a rather finely tuned balance between unquestioned European maritime superiority as against their almost total vulnerability on land for a long time. Scholars such as Frederick C. Lane and, more recently, Niels Steensgaard have gone to the extent of arguing that 'the principal export of pre-industrial Europe to the rest of the world was violence'. While there is an element of truth in this formulation, it is imperative that it is not torn out of context. Violence on the sea was a weapon of the last resort to be used as sparingly as possible, for the simple reason that it was by no means a costless process. Ordinarily, both sides would first seek to resolve conflict and only in the event of a deadlock would either side resort to actual violence.

An example of a potential area of conflict between the authorities and the Dutch East India Company, given its large-scale participation in intra-Asian trade, was the violation of the Company's pass policy by the Indian merchants engaged in the Indian Ocean trade. The trouble the Company faced at Surat in 1648-9 is a case in point. Following the conquest of Malacca in 1641, and the subsequent conclusion of monopsony agreements with the principal tin producing regions in the Malay peninsula, the Company sought to restrict direct access for Indian vessels to the 'tin ports' north of Malacca, and get them to carry out all their trade at Malacca itself. This strategy, however, proved largely ineffective as long as these vessels had continuing free access to the Bay of Bengal port of Aceh on the northern tip of Sumatra. The extensive trade carried on by the Aceh merchants with Sumatran and Malayan ports made Aceh a large market for Indian textiles, as well as a major procurement point for items such as pepper and tin. Indeed, on the basis of the passes issued by the queen of Aceh, it was even possible for the Indian merchants to sail to the east Sumatran and west Malayan ports and carry on trade there. Particularly useful in this regard was the link to Perak, then a vassal state of Aceh and abundantly provided with tin. The implications of this for the VOC were quite severe. In 1646, no tin could be bought in the Malay peninsula and no pepper could be sold at Malacca. A full-scale response was evidently called for and on 3 July 1647, Batavia resolved that 'the Moors of Surat, Coromandel, Bengal Pegu, etc. be prohibited from the trade both in Achin [Aceh] and in the tin quarters [of peninsular Malaya] on pain of seizure [of their vessels] as legitimate prize if they come there in the future'. Patrolling of the approaches to Aceh, as well as to ports such as Kedah, Perak and Johor was intensified. The factors in India were instructed not to issue passes for Aceh or any of the other ports declared out of bounds.[31]

Surat

The reaction to this severely restrictionist policy was sharp, at least at Surat. When passes for Aceh were refused, Mughal authorities banned the loading of Dutch ships at the port. That was not all: in April 1648, the local Dutch factory was stormed by a force of 150 men. One Dutchman was killed, two others wounded and goods worth f.27,000 plundered. The attackers were never identified, but it was a clear message signalling the displeasure of both the Mughal authorities as well as the local merchants. Johan Tack, the

[31] S. Arasaratnam, 'Some notes on the Dutch in Malacca and the Indo-Malayan trade 1641-70', *Journal of South East Asian History*, vol. X(3), 1969, pp. 480-90.

Company's man at Agra, sought the Court's intervention in the restitution of the plundered goods. With the help of one of the *umara* at the Court, Haqiqat Khan, who was generally favourably inclined to the Company, an audience with Shahjahan was obtained. The emperor promised to grant a farman directing the *mutasaddi* of Surat to compensate the Company for the plundered goods. But before the farman could be issued, a delegation of Surat merchants arrived at the Court. They could not prevent the grant of the farman, but ensured that it was a very different kind of document. All that the farman did was to say that the local authorities at Surat would do their best to trace the plundered goods. The factors saw no point in even bringing the document to the attention of the *mutasaddi*. The Company then decided to retaliate at sea. A fleet sent from Batavia for the purpose arrived too late in 1648 to attack the Indian ships returning from Mocha. But the following year, two Gujarati ships on their way back from Mocha and carrying a cargo worth more than one and a half million guilders were seized just outside Surat. Following negotiations between the Company, the local authorities, and some of the leading merchants of the city, the Company's two-fold demand for compensation for the plundered goods and a promise to stop the Surat ships' attempted voyages to Aceh, Perak, Kedah and Phuket, etc. was accepted. In return, the Company released the seized ships and the cargo to the lawful owners.[32]

Coromandel

The implications of the Company's pass policy during these years were somewhat less severe on the Coromandel coast. The problems there revolved mainly around the issue of the refusal of passes for the ships of the all-powerful noble, Mir Jumla. Following the seizure in 1647 of tin worth 2,000 rials off Perak, from a ship of the Mir because it did not carry a Dutch pass, the governor of Masulipatnam, a subordinate of Mir Jumla, asked for restitution. Peace was bought temporarily by a promise to do the needful and by agreeing to sell the entire stock of cloves in the Company's

[32] H.W. van Santen, *De Vernidge Oost-Indische Compagnie*, pp. 21-4.

warehouses in Coromandel together with a certain amount of copper to the Mir. But the tin had not been returned by 1651 leading to obstruction of the Company's textile trade in the region. It was only after Commissioner Dirck Steur went to see Mir Jumla that an agreement emerged. The Company reiterated its promise to return the tin, besides undertaking to buy its textiles, at specified places only, from the representatives of the Mir. But problems surfaced again following the seizure of one of Mir Jumla's ships, the *Nazareth*, off Malacca, for flying the Portuguese flag after the Dutch-Portuguese truce had ended. Matters came to a head in 1653 when Mir Jumla threatened to attack Fort Geldria unless the *Nazareth* and its cargo were released immediately and passes granted for the Portuguese controlled ports in Sri Lanka. It was then decided to meet a part of the Mir's claims in respect of the goods carried by the *Nazareth*. Besides, passes were to be issued to all subjects of Golconda for ports under the jurisdiction of the king of Kandi and for Aceh. The only stipulation made regarding the latter was that in the event of the blockade of the port by the Dutch, ships sailing for Aceh would agree to proceed to another destination approved by the Company. It was, however, only at the end of 1655 that compensation in respect of the *Nazareth* was paid. The Company also conceded the Mir's right to trade with Makassar, Bantam and Kedah, as well as to send goods to Malacca aboard the Company's ships. In return, Mir Jumla agreed not to send ships to Jaffanapatnam in view of the ongoing Dutch-Portuguese struggle there.[33]

ECONOMY-WIDE IMPLICATIONS OF EUROPEAN TRADE

Trade as an instrument of growth

It, however, bears repetition that the occasional areas and phases of conflict notwithstanding, the overall relationship between the European corporate enterprises on the one hand, and the Indian and other Asian authorities they were obliged to deal with on the

---

33 Tapan Raychaudhuri, *Jan Company in Coromandel, 1605-1690*, The Hague, 1962, pp. 48-51.

other, was essentially an amicable one based on a perception of mutual advantage.

What was the situation like at an economy-wide level? In other words, what implications did the Europeans' trade have for the economies of the countries/regions where this trade was carried on? In so far as a country is relatively more efficient in the production of export goods than in that of import goods, an increase in trade between nations is ordinarily to the advantage of both the trading partners, involving an increase in the value of the total output in each of the two economies. The 'gains from trade' tend to become much more substantial in special situations such as in the case of the Euro-Asian trade in the early modern period. This is because the decline in the domestic production of import-competing goods, which would usually accompany an increase in the output of export goods in an ordinary trade situation involving the exchange of goods against goods, would be avoided when the imports consisted not of goods but of precious metals (which in any case were not produced domestically in countries such as India). An increase in the output of export goods attendant upon an increase in trade would then involve a net increase in total output and income in the economy. This would be so irrespective of whether the imported precious metals are treated as a commodity import or as a mechanism for settling trade balances.

The increase in the output of export goods in the Indian subcontinent in response to the secularly rising demand for these goods by the Europeans would seem to have been achieved through a reallocation of resources, a fuller utilization of existing productive capacity and an increase over time in the capacity itself. A reallocation of resources in favour of the production of export goods such as raw silk and particular varieties of textiles would have been signalled, among other things, by a continuous rise in the prices of these goods in the markets where they were procured. Evidence regarding such a rise is available in plenty in the European company documentation. The available evidence also suggests both a fuller utilization of existing capacity as well as expansion thereof over time. In the case of textile manufacturing, for example, artisans engaged in the activity on a part-time basis seem to have increasingly found it worth their while to become full-time producers and to relocate themselves in the so-called aurungs – localized centres of manufacturing production, where the Europeans were increasingly concentrating their procurement through the intermediary merchants. Among the other factors of production required, land was clearly in abundant supply practically all over the subcontinent at this time. As far as the necessary capital resources needed for the production of new spindles, wheels and looms etc. was concerned, given the extremely small amounts involved, and the fact that the European companies were ever willing to advance the necessary sums, the availability of funds also is highly unlikely to have been a constraining factor. It need hardly be stressed that across a country of the size of the Indian subcontinent, there are likely to have been regional variations with regard to the degree of dynamism, flexibility and potential for continuing expansion in the scale of production that this scenario envisages. However, evidence available at least in respect of regions such as Bengal, which was by far the most important theatre of company activity on the subcontinent, would generally seem to confirm the presence of such attributes in ample measure.

In this scenario, the Europeans' trade would have become a vehicle for an expansion in income, output and employment in the subcontinent. As far as additional employment generated in the textile manufacturing sector as a result of European procurement is concerned, an exercise carried out in respect of the average annual procurement of textiles and raw silk in Bengal by the Dutch East India Company over the period 1678-1708 suggested that a total of 33,770 to 44,364 additional full-time jobs would have been created by the Company's procurement of these two items. If one extended the exercise to cover the English East India Company, but considered only the early years of the eighteenth century between 1709 and 1718, the number of additional jobs created was estimated at 86,967 to 111,151. The probable total size of the workforce in the textile manufacturing sector in the province of Bengal was estimated at one million. The full-time jobs associated with the Dutch Company's trade thus accounted for between 3.37 per cent and 4.43 per cent of the total workforce in the sector: the proportion went up to between 8.69 and 11.11 per cent when the trade of the Dutch and the English East India Companies was considered together.[34]

The fact that the rate of growth of the Europeans' demand for goods such as textiles and raw silk was almost always greater than the rate at which their output increased turned the market increasingly into a sellers' market. This was reflected in the growing bargaining strength of the merchants vis-à-vis the companies. For example, in 1709 a number of textile suppliers dealing with the Dutch Company in Bengal refused to accept fresh contracts unless the Company gave them an assurance that henceforth in the event of only a limited variation between the quality of the sample given out and that of the pieces actually supplied by them, there would be no deduction made from the price mutually agreed upon at the time of the contract. The suppliers even insisted upon a refund of the price deductions made on this count on textiles supplied during the preceding season. A similar distinct improvement would also seem to have taken place in the bargaining strength of the weavers vis-à-vis the textile suppliers ensuring that the 'gains from trade' indeed percolated all the way down. Writing in 1700, for example, the Dutch factors at Hughli made the following observation. "The merchants inform us (and on investigation we find that they are speaking the truth) that because of the large number of buyers in the weaving centres and the large sale of textiles, the weavers can no longer be coerced. They weave what is most profitable for them. If one does not accommodate oneself to this situation, then one is not able to procure very much and the supplies go to one's competitors."[35]

The monetary domain

Quite apart from the implications of European trade for real variables such as income, output and employment, there was an

---

[34] This is based on a more detailed analysis carried out in Om Prakash, *The Dutch East India Company and the Economy of Bengal*, Ch. 8.

[35] N.A., Explanation by the Dutch factors of why the orders were not supplied in full, 1700, VOC, 1638, ff. 17-19, II Section.

important range of issues in the monetary domain which were affected by this trade. The import of large quantities of precious metals by the European companies into India on a continuing basis would have had certain consequences for the economy of the subcontinent. There is a considerable body of literature that assigns an important role to the imported American silver in shaping the growth of a number of European economies in the early modern period. According to Immanuel Wallerstein, for example, without the American silver, "Europe would have lacked the collective confidence to develop a capitalist system, wherein profit is based on various deferrals of realized value. This is *a fortiori* true given the system of a nonimperial world-economy which, for other reasons, was essential. Given this phenomenon of collective psychology, an integral element of the social structure of the time, bullion must be seen as an essential crop for a prospering world-economy."[36]

This is what made South America so valuable. In Wallerstein's words, "The production of gold and silver as a commodity made the Americas a peripheral area of the European world-economy in so far as this commodity was essential to the operation of this world-economy, and it was essential to the extent that it was used as money. In short, they [the Europeans] incorporated the Americas into their world-economy, primarily because they needed a solid currency base for an expanding capitalist system and secondarily to use the surplus in trade with Asia."[37]

But according to the proponents of this position, Asia was different. To quote Wallerstein once again, "At this epoch, the relationship of Europe and Asia might be summed up as the exchange of preciosities. The bullion flowed east to decorate the temples, palaces, and clothing of Asian aristocratic classes and the jewels and spices flowed west. The accidents of cultural

---

[36] Immanuel Wallerstein, *The Modern World-System: Capitalist Agriculture and the Origins of the European World-Economy in the Sixteenth Century*, New York, 1974, p. 46.

[37] Immanuel Wallerstein, *The Modern World-System II: Mercantilism and the Consolidation of the European World-Economy, 1600-1750*, New York, 1980, p. 109.

history (perhaps nothing more than physical scarcity determined these complementary preferences."[38]

Another western scholar, Rudolph Blitz, makes essentially a similar point: "In the Orient, much of the specie went promptly into hoards or was demonetized and became a commodity satisfying the oriental penchant for ornaments."[39] The otherness of Asia in this view thus derives essentially from the fact that while, in the case of Europe, the imported silver involved an accretion to the supply of money in the system, in Asia this valuable asset was frittered away by being used "for hoarding or jewelry?"[40]

There is reason to believe that such a clear-cut dichotomy between Europe and Asia is indeed quite untenable and does not conform to a wide body of evidence available to us. By far the most concrete of the effects associated with the import of American silver into Europe was the so-called 'price revolution' of the sixteenth century. A similar response is ruled out in the case of Asia for the simple reason that the first link in the chain, namely an increase in the supply of money, would not have come about in the Asian economies. But such a position is demonstrably false. In the case of Mughal India, for example, the treasure brought in by the European companies was intended for investment in Indian silk, textiles and other goods. In so far as foreign coins were not allowed to circulate locally, the very first step that would need to be taken by these companies in the matter of raising the necessary purchasing power would be the conversion of imported bullion and coins into Mughal Indian rupees. This could be done either through professional dealers in money known as *sarrafs* or by recourse to one of the imperial mints in the empire. In either event, there would be an automatic and correponding increase in the supply of money in the economy. It is, of course, perfectly possible that a part of the increased money supply might eventually have been hoarded or withdrawn from

---

[38] Wallerstein, *The Modern World-System: Capitalist Agriculture*, p. 41.

[39] Rudolph C. Blitz, 'Mercantilist policies and the pattern of world trade', p. 40.

[40] J. Sperling, 'The international payments mechanisms in the seventeenth and eighteen centuries', *Economic History Review*, 2nd series, vol. 14(3), 1962. Quoted in Wallerstein, *The Modern World System II*, p. 109.

active circulation. But in the present state of our knowledge, it would probably be futile to surmise how significant or marginal this phenomenon might have been. Some observations could nevertheless be made in this behalf. In any society, hoarding of precious metals in the form of bullion or coins would be a function of the structure of asset preferences. Given the virtual absence of deposit banking facilities in India, hoarding on a reasonable scale can very well be interpreted as a perfectly legitimate and rational form of holding liquidity. The point is that the implied irrationality in the 'Oriental penchant for hoarding' kind of story might in fact never have been there except perhaps at the margin.

A growing supply of money in response to a continuing import of precious metals would presumably have had implications for the functioning of an Asian economy along lines not necessarily very different from those in Europe. In relation to late Ming China, this is what William Atwell has to say, "Japanese and Spanish-American silver may well have been the most significant factor in the vigorous economic expansion which occurred in China during the period in question. This is true not only because of its direct impact on the silk and porcelain industries, although this clearly was of great importance; but also because an increase in the country's stock of precious metals upon which economic growth and business confidence seem to have depended would have been determined almost entirely by how much silver entered the country through foreign trade."[41]

The situation is unlikely to have been different in Mughal India, where it would seem that the rising supply of money was leading to a significant acceleration in the process of monetization in the economy. The well-known growing monetization of the land-revenue demand during the period was clearly a part of this larger process. Another significant feature of the Mughal Indian economy was the rise of banking firms all over the empire dealing in extremely sophisticated instruments of credit. Many of these firms had enormous resources at their command. Probably the best known of these was the house of the Jagat Seths operating

---

41 William S. Atwell, 'Notes on silver, foreign trade, and the late Ming economy', *Ching-Shih Wen-t'I*, vol. (3), 1977, p. 5.

from its headquarters at Murshidabad in Bengal. Along with its other activities, the firm organized the transfer of Delhi's share in the land revenues collected in the province. It need hardly be stressed that there was an important organic link between the rise in the money supply and the growth of the banking firms in the Mughal Indian economy.

What about the relationship between a rise in the money supply and the notional general price level in the economy? In other words, was there a counterpart in India to the European price revolution of the sixteenth century? A considerable body of work donc over the past quarter of a century or so on the history of prices in different regions of India during the seventeenth and the first half of the eighteenth century has consistently negated the possibility of a general price rise (as opposed to a rise in the prices of goods procured by the Europeans). This includes my own earlier work on the price history of Bengal based mainly on the evidence available in the records of the Dutch East India Company. The evidence regarding movements in the prices of wage-goods such as rice, wheat, sugar and clarified butter, which I had argued could indeed be treated as proxies for movements in the notional general price level in the economy, suggested considerable fluctuations in the prices of these goods but no statistically significant upward or downward trend.[42]

How does one reconcile the phenomenon of a rise in the supply of money with the absence of a rise in the notional general price level? While no definitive answer is possible, we might consider the following. Together with looking at the supply of money, we ought also to look at the demand for it. We have already noted that the 'bullion for goods' character of the Euro-Asian trade in the early modern period turned the foreign trade sector into an instrument of growth with the savings, investment and production in the economy registering an increase. The rising supply of money

[42] Om Prakash, 'Precious metal flows, coinage and prices in India in the 17th and the early 18th century', in Eddy H.G. van Cauwenberghe (ed.), *Money, Coins, and Commerce: Essays in the Monetary History of Asia and Europe (from Antiquity to Modern Times)*, Leuven University Press, 1991, pp. 55-74. Reprinted in Om Prakash, *Precious Metals and Commerce: The Dutch East India Company in the Indian Ocean Trade*, Aldershot, 1994.

in the system would then have been absorbed by rising output, essentially obviating the need for the general price level necessarily to go up. This process would be further reinforced by the increasing monetization in the economy whereby monetized transactions as a proportion of total transactions in the economy would have gone up. Finally, over the fairly long period with which we are concerned, natural increases in population would also have necessitated a secular rise in output and transactions if the per-capita output and availability were not to go down. All these factors would tend to check a general rise in prices consequent upon an increase in the supply of money caused by an increased inflow of precious metals.

Certain deviations from the above scenario across both space and time must be noted. Across space, the above analysis will not be fully applicable to the Malabar coast, for example. The Portuguese had enjoyed special rights in pepper procurement in parts of the region until 1663 when they were thrown out of Cochin by the raja with the active assistance of the VOC. But then the VOC got its pound of flesh consisting, among other privileges, in a monopsony in the procurement of pepper in the area between Purakkad and Cranganur, and a monopoly in the sale of opium. Given the terrain, it was impossible to prevent large-scale smuggling by Indian merchants, which substantially limited the scope of the Dutch monopoly privileges. But even so, in respect of that part of the total marketed output of pepper that the Dutch East India Company procured, the price paid to the intermediary merchants, which eventually also determined the return reaching the producers, was lower, possible substantially lower, than what the free market forces of demand and supply would have dictated. The macro-economic implications of the European procurement would thus have been grossly vitiated.

THE EARLY COLONIAL PERIOD

Across time, the situation during the second half of the eighteenth century was very different from that in the preceding period. The death of the Mughal emperor Aurangzeb in 1707 was the symbolic beginning of the process of the collapse of the centralized Mughal empire, the rise of the so-called successor states in provinces such as Awadh, Hyderabad and Bengal, and eventually the takeover of large parts of the country by the English East India Company, beginning with Bengal, where it was officially recognized by the Mughal emperor as the diwan of the province in 1765. Aurangzeb was followed in quick succession by Bahadur Shah (1707-12), Jahandar Shah (1712-13), Farrukhsiyar (1713-19) and Muhammad Shah (1719-48). The Emperial fabric was subjected to serious strain during the early part of the century marked by disaffection of the Rajputs, growing militancy among the Sikhs and Jats in the north, and continuing Maratha insurgency in the south. Weakened central authority encouraged governors in several provinces to establish near-autonomous regional states only paying lip-service to the emperor's authority. The financial bankruptcy of the central government – dramatized by episodes such as Jahandar Shah's own troops remaining unpaid from the time of his accession – was further accentuated by the increasing irregularity and default in the receipt of the imperial government's share in the land revenues due from the newly emerging successor states.

The rapid deterioration in the state of law and order seriously affected the flows of long-distance overland trade within the empire. An important route that suffered particular damage was the one that connected the heartland of the empire to Gujarat. Caravans organized by private merchants, even though protected by hired guards, could no longer travel safely from Agra to Surat. In view of the problems faced in the procurement and the transportation of textiles and Bayana indigo from Agra to Surat, the VOC was obliged to close its factory at Agra in 1716. The cost of the bills of exchange between these two cities, which ordinarily used to be no more than 1 to 2 per cent, now shot up to as much as 12 per cent. In Surat, the imperial mint was shut down for several years and numerous dealers in money were reported to have gone bankrupt.[43]

---

[43] Ashin Das Gupta, *Indian Merchants and the Decline of Surat, 1700-1750*, Wiesbaden, 1979, p. 142; John F. Richards, *The Mughal Empire*, Vol. I.5 in the *New Cambridge History of India series*, Cambridge, 1993, pp. 278-9.

The nature and the extent of the dislocation described above should, however, be kept in perspective and care taken that its negative implications for the overall standard of economic performance are not overstated. Research done over the past two decades or so suggests the strong possibility of various sectors in the Indian economy continuing to perform well during the course of the century. In the words of Burton Stein, scholars maintaining this position "agree that the rural economy over most of the 18th century India enjoyed substantial, if uneven, growth notwithstanding both the destructive wars culminating in those which won the subcontinent for the British, and the supposed political disorder in many areas. It is claimed that new, smaller states with efficient tax-gathering procedures replaced the Mughal military imperial order, that market networks proliferated and became to a degree interlinked, that a more prosperous agriculture came into being with increased commodity production as a result of rural investments by the revenue farmers of the time, that all of this was buoyed up by an ever-increasing level of international trade in which Indian artisans, merchants and especially bankers played key and lucrative roles, and that this phase of political economy obtained until the first quarter of the 19th century."[44]

From the perspective of the European trading companies, the most crucial developments were those taking place in Bengal, by far the most important of the Asian trading regions, supplying at the turn of the eighteenth century as much as 40 per cent of the total Asian cargo that the Dutch and the English East India companies imported into Europe each year. It is vitally important to note that as far as this province was concerned, the situation over the greater part of the eighteenth century was not materially different from that in the heyday of the Mughal empire in the seventeenth. The man mainly responsible for this in the early part of the century was Murshid Quli Khan, who dominated the history of the province between 1701, when he was sent there as the imperial diwan with a specific brief to try and increase the flow of revenues due to the imperial government from the province,

[44] Burton Stein, 'A decade of historical efflorescence', *South Asia Research*, Vol. 10(2), November 1990, pp. 132-3.

and his death in 1727. By scrupulously ensuring that the annual flow of the *khalisa* revenues to Delhi not only continued uninterrupted but in fact registered an increase over time, Murshid Quli succeeded in creating a mutually beneficial working partnership with the imperial government. In the domain of political stability and the state of law and order, the first four decades of the eighteenth century were certainly no worse than had been the case during the seventeenth. It is true that a certain amount of dislocation was caused in the early 1740s as a result of the Maratha incursions into the province. But that was essentially a temporary phase and things were by and large back to normal by the end of the decade. In brief, the picture of political confusion and unrest usually associated with the declining power of the Mughals in the first half of the eighteenth century is certainly not applicable to Bengal. In fact, the growing weakness of the centre, particularly in the wake of Nadir Shah's invasion during 1739-43, further strengthened regional polities, and successor states such as Bengal, Hyderabad and Awadh stopped paying their customary tribute to Delhi on a regular basis making larger resources available for internal deployment. The Europeans' trade from Bengal also registered a significant increase during the period. Thus of the rising total Dutch exports from Asia to Europe amounting to £19.24 million over the triennium 1738-40 as against £15 million during 1698-1700, the share of goods procured in the province had gone up to 47 per cent as against 41 per cent at the turn of the century. The corresponding figures in the case of the English East India Company were £23 million as against £13.79 million with the share of the Bengal goods being at the all-time peak of 66 per cent during 1738-40 as against 42 per cent during 1698-1700.

The second half of the eighteenth century witnessed a fundamental alteration in the nature of the Indo-European encounter. The takeover of Bengal by the English East India Company following the battle of Plassey in 1757 marked the inauguration of the colonial phase in this encounter. The nawab's army, though ten times the size of Clive's 2,000 sepoys and 900 Europeans, was routed providing the English Company its first foothold in the subcontinent. The formal acquisition of diwani rights in 1765 provided it with access to the province's revenues. These were used in part to strengthen further the Company's military strength. By 1782, the Company was able to maintain 115,000 men in India (90 per cent of them sepoys) enabling it to intervene effectively in other parts of the subcontinent such as the Deccan.

A part of the surplus from the Bengal revenues was also used to finance the procurement of goods for export to Europe. To that extent, these exports now became 'unrequited' involving a drain of resources from the country – a theme that has legitimately attracted a great deal of attention in the Indian nationalist historical writings of the nineteenth century. The bulk of the English Company exports during this period, however, were financed by the rupee receipts obtained by the Company locally against bills of exchange issued to English and other European private traders on London and other European capitals enabling these traders to transmit their Indian earnings home. Between the Bengal surplus revenues and the rupees receipts obtained against the bills of exchange, the Company found itself in a position to suspend altogether the import of treasure from home for nearly a quarter of a century. It was only in 1784 that these imports were resumed partly for investment in the procurement of export goods and partly to strengthen further the Company's military presence – a necessary prelude to the conquest of other parts of the subcontinent.

The altered situation held important consequences for the economy of the province. For one thing, the substantial reduction in the silver imports would seem to have been an important element behind the shortage of money that several contemporaries noted and commented upon. More importantly, there was a marked deterioration in the relative share in the total value of the output produced as far as the Bengali artisanal and the mercantile groups engaged in business with the English East India Company were concerned. This was a necessary corollary of the replacement of a market-determined relationship between the Company and these groups until about 1760 by a relationship marked by a clear-cut domination by the Company in the decades that followed. On the basis of its political muscle power, the Company now enforced unilaterally determined below-market terms on the producers of and the dealers in commodities such as textiles and opium. The blatant manner in which this was done, robbing in the process the producers and the merchants of a good part of what was legitimately due to them, would, in turn, have introduced distortions in the incentive structure in the domain of manufacturing and other production in the province. This, combined with the official Company and unofficial private English traders' monopolies in commodities such as salt and opium, is likely to have brought about a certain amount of decline in the value of the total output produced in the province, though in the present state of our knowledge it is not possible to indicate even broadly the extent of this decline.

There is a distinct possibility, however, that this decline was not altogether massive or irreversible and that the structure of both agricultural and non-agricultural production in the province continued to be marked by a reasonable degree of vitality and capacity to deliver. An important, though by no means conclusive, index suggesting this scenario is the continuing growth of both the Euro-Asian and the intra-Asian trade from the province. It is true that, under the pressure of the increasingly monopsonistic policies adopted by the English Company, the trade of the rival companies operating in the region was on the decline. Thus in the case of the VOC, although the overall value of its Asian exports to Europe between the trienniums of 1738-40 and 1778-80 went up from £19 million of £21 million, the average annual value of the Company's exports from Bengal came down from the all-time peak of £5 million in 1751-2 to a measly £1.32 million in 1784-5. But such a decline was much more than made up for by the English Company's own total exports to Europe going up from £23 million in 1738-40 to £25 million in 1758-60 and to an almost incredible figure of £69 million in 1777-9 giving us an annual average figure of £23 million. Bengal accounted for as much as half of this value. In intra-Asian trade, the decline in the Dutch Company exports as well as in those by the Indian merchants engaged in this trade was similarly much more than made up for by the spectacular rise in the English private merchants' trade with China.

CONCLUSION

The Euro-Asian, and more specifically the Indo-European, encounter over the three hundred-year period between 1500 and 1800 was a historical process with extremely significant and wide-ranging implications for both sides. Within the overall rubric of the desire to procure Indian goods, the precise motivation and mechanism behind the arrival of each of the European trading groups into the subcontinent was different. The Portuguese came basically for pepper, and throughout the sixteenth and the early part of the seventeenth century India provided an overwhelming bulk of the total pepper supplies reaching Lisbon. The Bay of Bengal figured prominently in the intra-Asian trading network of the Estado da India, and later also in the trading operations of the private Portuguese merchants both within Asia as well as between Asia and Europe. The Dutch East India Company, on the other hand, procured its pepper and other spices in the Indonesian archipelago and came to India looking mainly for the relatively inexpensive mass-consumption cotton textiles produced on the Coromandel coast, and to a smaller extent in Gujarat, with a view to using them as a medium of exchange to procure the Indonesian spices. This became the first link in a chain that eventually developed into a massive involvement in intra-Asian trade with other Indian commodities such as Bengal raw silk and opium also playing a critical role in the successful functioning of the complex network. In the last quarter of the seventeenth century, the fashion revolution in Europe put Indian textiles and raw silk at the head of the imports from Asia catapulting India into the position of being by far the most important supplier of goods for Europe. The key role of India in the Dutch East India Company's overall framework of trade continued well into the early years of the second half of the eighteenth century when the English East India Company, on the strength of its newly acquired special status in Bengal, overwhelmed the Dutch and forced them into reducing the scale of their operations in the subcontinent substantially. The French were late-comers on the scene having set up an East India Company only in 1664. In fact, it was only from the beginning of the second quarter of the eighteenth century onward that the French trade in the subcontinent became quantitatively significant. They were engaged in an almost continuous conflict with the English in south India, but like the Dutch were eventually unable to withstand the English hostility.

The English involvement in the trade of the subcontinent became significant only from the second quarter of the seventeenth century, after they had found it impossible to carry on profitable trade in the Indonesian archipelago due in part to the opposition by the Dutch. From this point on, India figured even more prominently in the total English exports to Europe than was the case with the Dutch. With the English Company's takeover of Bengal in the second half of the eighteenth century, India assumed an altogether new role for Britain. Bengal revenues provided an indirect subsidy to the British exchequer and the enormous opportunities – legal and clandestine – for private gain now available to the Company servants in their personal capacity created a whole new class of the new-rich 'nabobs' returning to England with fortunes unheard of before. It is, however, highly unlikely that these private fortunes constituted an element of any importance in the financing of the Industrial Revolution in Britain which was then getting under way.

As far as India was concerned, the substantial amount of trade carried on from her ports by the Europeans, both with Europe as well as with other parts of Asia, particularly from the early part of the seventeenth century onward, served to strengthen her status considerably as a premier trading and manufacturing nation in Asia. At the turn of the eighteenth century, India was probably the largest and the most cost-competitive textile-manufacturing country in the world. An increase in trade being beneficial for a country is an axiom: in India's case the 'bullion for goods' character of the European trade considerably enhanced its positive implications and indeed turned it into an important instrument of growth in the Indian economy. The gold and silver the Europeans imported from Europe and other Asian countries such as Japan led to a substantial increase in the supply of money in the country. The growing level of monetization in the economy, in turn, facilitated reform measures such as the growing conversion of the land revenue demand from kind into cash, which led to a further increase in market exchange and trade. The growing availability of precious metals in the system also helped the rise of banking firms, and generally became an important factor in facilitating the expansion of the Mughal empire.

By not involving a decline in the domestic output of import-competing goods, the 'bullion for goods' character of the European trade also implied that the positive implications of the growth in trade for the level of income, output and employment in the economy were considerably more substantial than would have been the case if this trade had been of the ordinary 'goods for goods' variety. In the agricultural sector, there was an increase in the acreage under cultivation, particularly in the case of high-value commercial crops such as cotton and opium. The increase in output and employment in the manufacturing sector was clearly on a scale that was not entirely insignificant. Job opportunities in several segments of the services sector such as that providing brokerage services would also have gone up. Besides, the fact that, on average, the rate of growth of the European demand for Indian goods such as textiles and raw silk was greater than the rate of growth of their supply, increasingly turned the market into a sellers' market. The fact that this involved not only an increase in the bargaining strength of the intermediary merchants vis-à-vis the Europeans but also a continuous improvement in the bargaining strength of the weavers vis-à-vis the intermediary merchants, implied that the benefits of the continuing rise in the level of output, income and employment were not confined to the intermediary groups but percolated all the way down to the weavers and the other constituents of the producing groups.

During the early colonial phase in the post-1760 period, this situation continued unaltered in many respects but underwent major modification in others. The composition of the trade with Europe remained unchanged, and except for the 'unrequited' part of the exports financed through the investment of the Bengal surplus revenues, the 'bullion for goods' character of the trade continued to be valid, though in a more restrictive and limited way. From the point of view of the English Company, the suspension of silver imports for a while and the financing of the exports mainly through the bills of exchange only meant that the payment in silver was now made in Europe rather than in India. But of course, this silver never reached India. Also, in so far as the relationship between the English East India Company on the one hand and the Indian intermediary merchants and producers on the other was no longer governed by the market but was dictated by the Company, a good part of the legitimate share of the producers and the merchants in the total output was now appropriated by the Company. As the Industrial Revolution began to mature in Britain, more fundamental changes followed. From the second quarter of the nineteenth century onward, India began to lose the European market for its textiles. Later in the century, the so-called colonial pattern of trade came into operation in a full-fledged manner and India was converted into an important market for textiles manufactured in Manchester and Lancashire.

BIBLIOGRAPHY

Arasaratnam, S., *Merchants, Companies and Commerce on the Coromandel Coast 1650-1740*, Delhi, 1986.

Bowen, H.V., Margarette Lincoln, Nigel Rigby (eds.), *The Worlds of the East India Company*, Woodbridge, 2002.

Chaudhuri, K.N., *The Trading World of Asia and the English East India Company 1660-1760,* Cambridge, 1978.

Chaudhuri, K.N., *Trade and Civilization in the Indian Ocean: An Economic History from the Rise of Islam to 1750*, Cambridge, 1985.

Das Gupta, Ashin, *Indian Merchants and the Decline of Surat C 1700-1750*, Wiesbaden, 1979.

Das Gupta, Ashin and M.N. Pearson (eds.), *India and the Indian Ocean 1500-1800*, Calcutta, 1987.

Kling, B.B., and M.N. Pearson (eds.), *The Age of Partnership: Europeans in Asia before Dominion*, Honolulu, 1979.

Marshall, P.J., *East India Fortunes: The British in Bengal in the Eighteenth Century*, Oxford, 1976.

Nightingale, Pamela, *Trade and Empire in Western India, 1784-1806*, Cambridge, 1970.

Prakash, Om, *The Dutch East India Company and the Economy of Bengal 1630-1720*, Princeton, 1985.

Prakash, Om, *Precious Metals and Commerce: The Dutch East India Company in the Indian Ocean Trade*, Aldershot, 1994.

Prakash, Om, *European Commercial Enterprise in Pre-Colonial India*, Vol. II.5 in the *New Cambridge History of India series*, Cambridge, 1998.
Prakash, Om and Denys Lombard (eds.), *Commerce and Culture in the Bay of Bengal 1500-1800*, Delhi, 1999.
Ptak, Rederich and Dietmar Rothermund (eds.), *Emporia, Commodities and Entrepreneurs in Asian Maritime Trade 1400-1450*, Stuttgart, 1991.
Raychaudhari, T. and Irfan Habib (eds.), *The Cambridge Economic History of India*, Vol. 1, Cambridge, 1982.
Richards, J.F. (ed.), *The Imperial Monetary System of Mughal India*, Delhi, 1987.
Steensgaard, Niels, *The Asian Trade Revolution of the Seventeenth Century: The East India Companies and the Decline of Caravan Trade*, Chicago, 1974.
Subrahmanyam, Sanjay, *The Political Economy of Commerce, Southern India, 1500-1650*, Cambridge, 1990.
Subrahmanyam, Sanjay, *The Portuguese Empire in Asia 1500-1700: A Political and Economic History*, London, 1993.
Subramanian, Lakshmi, *Indigenous Capital and Imperial Expansion: Bombay, Surat and the West Coast*, Delhi, 1996.

II

India in the Indian Ocean Trading Network on the Eve of the Europeans' Arrival in the Asian Seas

Among the historic consequences of the discovery by the Portuguese at the end of the 15th century of the all-water route to the East Indies via the Cape of Good Hope was the overcoming of the transport technology barrier to the growth of trade between Asia and Europe. The volume of this trade was no longer subject to the capacity constraint imposed by the availability of pack animals and river boats in the Middle East. Also, it was only after the discovery of the Cape route that the procurement of Asian goods as well as their transportation to Europe was organised by the Europeans themselves, who had travelled to the East in any number for the first time. What kind of trading network did the Portuguese find in operation on their arrival in the Indian Ocean? This paper analyses the central elements of this network from the vantage point of India, which was at the centre of the Portuguese – and later of the other Europeans' trading activities in Asia.

An analysis of the structure and the mechanics of the early modern Indian Ocean trade, alternatively referred to as Asian trade, ought perhaps to start with a recognition of the simple fact that this trade transgressed the boundaries of both the Indian Ocean as well as those of Asia. While in the east, it intruded prominently into the South China Sea, in the west, it embraced maritime trade with East Africa. Traditionally, the great arc of Asian trade included the Persian Gulf and the Red Sea in the northwest. The principal natural divisions of this huge area were the Arabian Sea, the Bay of Bengal and the South China Sea. Within each of these zones, there were important blocks of ports across which a large amount of trade had traditionally been carried on. The western or the Arabian Sea zone included ports in the Persian Gulf, the Red Sea, those on the East African coast and on the west coast of India. The Bay of Bengal network included ports in Sri Lanka, the Coromandel coast, Bengal, Burma, Thailand, Malaya and Acheh in Sumatra. Ports such as Canton and Zaiton in the South China Sea had extensive contacts both with the Indonesian ports as well as with ports in the straits of Malacca. Within each of these zones, there were also clearly identifiable sub-zones. To take an example, in the west, the ports of Aden, Hormuz, Cambay and Calicut formed one such sub-zone, while those of Kilwa, Mogadishu, Aden and Jiddah constituted another. Needless to emphasise, in terms of the ability of different constituents of a given zone to put important tradeable goods on the market, for which there was adequate demand elsewhere in the zone, there was a very definitive basis for trade within each of the zones. Such a basis also existed to an important degree across zones leading to the creation of significant long-distance trade flows in the Indian Ocean and beyond. By far the longest distance was covered by the route that connected Aden to Canton traversing a very large part of the total area covered by the great arc of Asian trade. There is evidence to suggest that this route was in regular use at least from the 7th century on. The principal group which had initiated trade on the route was the Persian merchants who had, however, been supplanted by and large by Arab merchants since about the 9th century on. The principal stops on the way were either Cambay or Calicut on the Indian west coast and a port such as Palembang in Sumatra. It would seem that sometime during the 12th century, Chinese junks also began operating on this route. There is evidence that the Chinese merchants established commercial contacts with places such as Sri Lanka, Quilon on the Malabar coast and with Hormuz in the Persian Gulf. The Chinese participation in trade on this route would appear to have reached important levels by the early years of the 15th century. Between 1404 and 1433, a series of seven commercial-cum-naval expeditions were dispatched from China under the command of Admiral Cheng Ho. The first of these expeditions is believed to have consisted of as many as 62 ships and 28,000 men. The fourth voyage is reported to have reached Hormuz and Aden, while those that followed claimed to have touched even the East African ports of Mogadishu and Malindi. But in 1433, the Chinese authorities abruptly withdrew from these ventures and, indeed, there is no record of these long distance voyages having ever been resumed. The precise circumstances behind this development are not quite clear but it would seem that the depredation of pirates infesting the South China Sea and the criticism that the profit earned from these voyages was not sufficiently attractive contributed to the decision of the Chinese authorities. In the meantime, the Arabs had also gradually pulled out of this long-distance route.

Whatever the reasons behind the Chinese and the Arab withdrawal from long-distance trade, it signalled a basic alteration in the organisational structure of Asian trade. The new structure was based on the segmentation of the great arc of Asian trade into the three divisions mentioned earlier – the Arabian Sea, the Bay of Bengal and the South China Sea. The ports of Cambay or Calicut and Malacca (founded at the beginning of the 15th century), which had until then served essentially as victualling and stopping points on the long route between West Asia and China, now became terminal ports. The role of these ports in providing a reasonably assured market in the goods brought in, as well as in making available those sought after by the visiting ships, besides offering facilities such as anchorage, warehousing and banking cannot be overemphasised. In the course of the 15th century, Malacca became a truly major centre of international exchange and a meeting point of traders from the east and the west. Allegedly, as many as 84 languages were spoken at this port. Also, each of the four major communities of merchants resident in and operating from Malacca – the Gujaratis, other 'western' merchants mainly from India and Burma, the merchants from Southeast Asia up to and including the Philippines, and finally the East Asians including the Chinese, the Japanese and the Okinawans – were allowed to have *shahbandars* of their own who managed the affairs of their communities autonomously of the local authorities.

India played a central role in this structure of Asian trade. In part, this indeed was a function of the mid-way location of the subcontinent between West Asia on the one hand and Southeast and East Asia on the other. But perhaps even more important was the subcontinent's capacity to put on the market a wide range of tradeable goods at highly competitive prices. These included agricultural goods, both food items such as rice, sugar and oil as well as raw materials such as cotton and indigo. While the bulk of the trade in these goods was coastal, the high seas trade component was by no means insignificant. The real strength of the subcontinent, however, lay in the provision of large quantities of manufactured goods, the most important amongst which was textiles of various kinds. While these included high value varieties such as the legendary Dhaka muslins and the Gujarat silk embroideries, the really important component for the Asian market was the coarse cotton varieties manufactured primarily on the Coromandel coast and in Gujarat. There was a large scale demand for these varieties both in the eastern markets of Indonesia, Malaya, Thailand and Burma as well as in the markets of the Red Sea, the Persian Gulf and East Africa. While it is impossible to determine precisely what proportion of total domestic demand for mass consumption textiles in these societies was met by imports from India, the available evidence would seem to point in the direction of this not being altogether insignificant. India's capacity to manufacture these textiles in large quantities and put them on the market at highly competitive terms made it in some sense the 'industrial' hub of the region surrounded by West Asia on one side and Southeast Asia on the other.

This circumstance also determined to a large extent the nature of India's demand for imports from the rest of Asia. This demand consisted essentially either of consumption goods which were not produced domestically for soil, climatic or other reasons, or of minerals and metals of various kinds whose domestic supply was either nil or substantially below the total demand. In the first category were items such as fine spices like cloves, nutmeg and mace from Indonesia, and horses and rose water from West Asia. The second category included rubies and other precious stones from Burma, as well as metals – both precious and non-precious. By far the most important non-precious metal imported was tin from Malaya. Precious metals, mainly silver, were imported overwhelmingly from West Asia. It was for this reason that from the 16th century onward, the port of Mocha was repeatedly referred to as the "treasure-chest" of the Mughal empire. It is really immaterial for our purposes whether the imported precious metals are treated as a commodity import or as a means of settling the adverse balance of trade that the concerned trading partner of the subcontinent had with it. The important point to emphasise is that by virtue of her relatively more advanced structure of manufacturing production and her capacity to provide large quantities of a basic manufactured consumption good such as inexpensive cotton textiles at highly competitive terms, India significantly enhanced the basis of trade in the Asian continent. She not only provided the textiles and, on a more modest scale, the food grains and the provisions in great demand in the neighbouring societies but also provided an important outlet for their specialised agricultural, mineral and other products. Trade satisfied different kinds of consumption needs for India as compared with her numerous trading partners in the Indian Ocean region. This by itself provided an excellent basis for a significant and growing level of trade. It is really in this sense that the critically important role of India in the structure of early modern Asian trade needs to be assessed.

The key position of India in the structure of Asian trade was also reflected in the important role of the Gujarati and other Indian trading groups in the actual conduct of this trade. This role, if anything, was strengthened in the course of the 15th century which, as we have seen above, witnessed the fragmentation of Asian trade into well defined segments. The participation of the Arab merchants got more and more confined to the trade between West Asia and the west coast of India. This left the trade between the west and the east coasts of India on the one hand, and the eastern Indian Ocean region on the other, almost exclusively in Indian hands – the Gujaratis more than any one else, but also the Chettis, the Chulias and other groups from the Coromandel coast, besides the Oriyas and the Bengalis. The participation of the Chinese merchants was now restricted by and large to controlling the trade between China and Malacca, while the Indonesian and the Malay merchants hardly seem to have ventured beyond the inter-island and the port to port trade in the Malay-Indonesian region. In sum, Indian merchants from different regions of the country constituted an important trading group operating in the Ocean.

From the vantage point of India, the two principal segments of maritime Asian trade were the western Indian Ocean and the Bay of Bengal. In the west, the link through the Red Sea and the Persian Gulf extended overland to the southern coast of the Mediterranean. The Bay of Bengal littoral extended through the straits of Malacca to the South China Sea going all the way to Japan. In the west, the area of operation of the Indian merchants stopped at the Red Sea and the Persian Gulf ports, while in the east it extended as far as Malacca. While there were clear-cut and by and large autonomous areas of operation and linkage in each of these two broad segments and there is a certain amount of merit in analysing each of these separately, it must be recognised that there was a considerable amount of interdependence and interaction across the two segments and that neither of the two should be regarded as a fully autonomous and self-contained system. One only needs to refer to the large volume of direct trade between Gujarat and Indonesia to realise the significance of this caution. This was equally true at the level of coastal trade as well, and one only has to remind oneself of the regular trade links in the 15th century between the ports of Bengal on the one hand and those of the west coast – both in Malabar and Gujarat – on the other.

In both the Arabian Sea and the Bay of Bengal, a considerable amount of trade was carried on both on the high seas as well as on the coastal trade circuits. The coastal circuits were often dominated by trade in agricultural products such as food grains and other bulk goods, and were usually characterised by the use of relatively small craft which would ordinarily not be useable on the high seas runs. Also, in comparison to the high seas connections, the role of the monsoon winds was comparatively limited in determining the rhythm of trade on the coastal circuits.

1. The West Coast

The west coast of India could conveniently be conceived of as consisting of four distinct segments divided roughly at the ports of Chaul, Karwar and Cannanore. To the north of Chaul lay the Gujarat coast, from Chaul to Karwar was the Konkan coast, south of Karwar until Mt. Eli immediately to the north of the port of Cannanore the Kanara coast, and to its south the Malabar coast. During the 15th century, the ports of Cambay in Gujarat and Calicut in Malabar were the two major international ports on the west coast of India, and between themselves handled a considerable amount of re-export trade. Gujarat was a major trading area in the subcontinent and the Gujaratis – mostly Muslims but also including Hindu traders – had traditionally been a dominant group amongst the Indian mercantile communities. Over the course of the 15th century, the trading activities of this group increased to a point where it emerged probably as the largest of all the groups engaged in trade in the Indian Ocean. This development would seem to be related to the cessation of the long distance trade between west Asia and China, and the rise of segmented Asian trade. The most important of the new ports to emerge during the 15th century was Malacca to which the Gujarati merchants shifted their trade from the Javanese and the Sumatran ports on which they used to concentrate until then in their eastern trade. The growth of Malacca continued in the second half of the 15th century, and so did the Gujarati share in the trade of the port. According to Tomé Pires, writing at a somewhat later date, about a thousand Gujarati merchants travelled each year to Malacca together with 4,000–5,000 sailors. It is true that the ships that left Cambay for Malacca each year included many owned and operated by Arab, Persian, Turkish, and other merchants from West Asia, but all these groups together were overshadowed by the Gujaratis who controlled the bulk of the trade on the route. The goods that the Malacca bound ships leaving Cambay carried were, in part, coloured woollen clothes and glassware from the Mediterranean, and items such as rosewater, opium, indigo and silver from west Asia. But a large part of the cargo would seem to have consisted of textiles manufactured in Gujarat – mainly of coarse cotton, though more expensive varieties including those manufactured from fine quality cotton and silk also seem to have figured in the list. The cargo obtained in exchange at Malacca included Chinese goods such as silk and porcelain, Indonesian spices such as pepper, cloves, nutmeg and mace, besides woods and aromatics, and precious and non-precious metals such as Malayan tin. In addition to Malacca, the Gujarati ships from Cambay called at ports such as Acheh, Kedah, Tenasserim/Mergui and Pegu. The goods carried to these ports were broadly similar to those carried to Malacca: the goods brought back were largely of local origin, rather than cosmopolitan as in the case of Malacca.

There was also a large amount of coastal trade carried on between Cambay and other smaller ports of Gujarat on the one hand, and ports on the Konkan, Kanara and the Malabar coasts to the south, and those in Bengal on the other. The principal commodity procured in the Konkan ports of Chaul and Dabhol was textiles, while the main item procured in Kanara and Malabar was pepper. A certain amount of rice was also procured in Kanara. At Calicut, limited quantities of Chinese and Indonesian goods were also picked up. Bengal provided food grains and provisions such as sugar, butter and oil in addition, of course, to textiles of different varieties.

A part of the large conglomerate of goods brought to Cambay was obviously destined for consumption in Gujarat, as well as the large north Indian hinterland supplied by it. But a good proportion would seem to have been re-exported mainly to West Asia, the most important ports in the region at this time being Aden and Jiddah. The other important constituent of the cargo to West Asia was textiles manufactured in Gujarat. These were predominantly those manufactured from coarse cotton and intended for mass consumption, though superior varieties manufactured from fine cotton and silk also figured in the list. The route from Cambay to Aden would seem to have been dominated by the Arab, Persian and other West Asian merchants, though the Gujarati merchants also operated on this route in an important way.

The Indonesian spices and other items imported from Cambay into Aden and other West Asian ports found their way in significant quantities in addition to the markets of West Asia to Europe via the Mediterranean. The two routes used for the purpose were those via the Red Sea and the Persian Gulf. While the Red Sea route terminated at the Egyptian port of Alexandria on the southern coast of the Mediterranean and involved only a small stretch of overland transportation, the Persian Gulf route made use of the Tigris or the Euphrates rivers and a fair amount of caravan transportation across Iraq and the Syrian desert. Important among the Mediterranean destination ports on this route were Tripoli (of Syria) and Beirut. This traffic was handled exclusively by the west Asian merchants. At the Mediterranean ports, the goods were procured mainly by the merchants from Venice and Genoa. While both the Red Sea and the Persian Gulf routes had been in use since antiquity, the relative amount of traffic on either at any given point in time depended partly on political circumstances. While during the 8th and the 9th centuries, the Persian Gulf route was the dominant one, the decline of the Abbasid Caliphate and the rise of the Fatimids in Egypt tilted the balance from the 11th century onward significantly in favour of the Red Sea route. This was also the period which witnessed a significant expansion in the volume of Euro-Asian trade. Evidence from the end of the 14th and the early years of the 15th century suggests that volume-wise the Alexandria trade was considerably larger – nearly double on an average – than the one via Beirut. However, since the latter handled the expensive spices much more, the difference between the two ports was much smaller in terms of value.[1]

Another direction in which the cargo arriving at Aden – particularly the coarse cotton textiles from Gujarat – moved was southwards to the East African ports of Mogadishu, Malindi and Kilwa through the agency of the West Asian merchants. There was also a certain amount of direct trade between Cambay and the East African ports carried on by the Gujarati merchants, but the extent of this trade was perhaps quite small.

On the southwest coast, the main ports in Konkan were Chaul and Dabhol. The principal orientation of these ports was towards West Asia, though the merchants of Dabhol are also known to have gone on to Bengal to join the fleet to Malacca. The volume of the latter traffic would, however, seem to have been quite small. The ports on the Kanara coast included Mirjan, Honawar, Bhatkal, Barkur, Basrur, Mangalore and Kumbla. Bhatkal was the principal port, the others being relatively minor and catering only to the coastal trade. Bhatkal was oriented exclusively to the west with connections to the Persian Gulf and the Red Sea. The principal exports from the port were white rice, sugar, iron, textiles, ginger and pepper, while the imports included copper, gold and horses from Arabia and Persia. The non-Islamic components of the trading community operating from the region consisted of Jains and the Saraswats, while the Muslims, who seem to have constituted the dominant group, included both the Navayat Muslims who claimed origins in Persia, as well as the so-called *pardesi* Muslim merchants, who were temporary residents in the area and came from the Arabian peninsula, Cairo, Turkey, Iraq and Persia.

[1] C. H. H. Wake, "The Changing Pattern of Europe's Pepper and Spice Imports, c. 1400–1700," *The Journal of European Economic History* 8, 1979, p. 364–9.

The principal port on the Malabar coast was Calicut followed by smaller ports such as Cannanore, Cochin and Quilon. The principal orientation of the high seas trade from the coast was westward with the Red Sea and the Persian Gulf, though a fair amount of trade was also carried on with the eastern littoral of the Bay of Bengal and with Malacca. The coastal connections stretched both northwards up to Gujarat as well as around the Cape with Sri Lanka, and via Coromandel as far north as Bengal. The principal exports from the coast were pepper, other spices such as ginger and cardamon, textiles, coconut and its ancillary products. The principal imports from West Asia were gold, silver and horses and from the east spices and aromatics. The *pardesi* merchants dominated the trade to the west, while the coastal trade and the high seas trade to the east was controlled by the local Mappila merchants.

2. The East Coast

The two principal trading regions on the east coast of India were the Coromandel coast and Bengal. The Coromandel coast is conventionally defined to include the stretch between Point Godavari and the island of Mannar, south of which lies the Fishery coast. To the north of Point Godavari is the Gingelly coast which is sometimes also included in the Coromandel coast. For our purposes, Bengal would be defined to include the Orissa ports of Pipli and Balasore. There was a fair amount of coastal trade between the ports of the two regions dominated, it would seem, by the merchants of Bengal. At the beginning of the 16th century, the principal Coromandel port was Pulicat linked via Tirupati and Penukonda to the imperial city of Vijayanagar to the northwest. The port next in importance was that of Nagapattinam in south Coromandel, which also had two minor ports at Kunjimedu and Naguru. The northern Coromandel port of Masulipatnam was of little consequence at this time. In Bengal, by far the most important port was Chittagong which was linked to the capital city of Gaur. Satgaon was next in importance until about 1580 when due to the silting up of the waterway on which it was situated, it was succeeded by Hugli. Pipli and Balasore in Orissa were the other important ports in the region.

The high seas trade from Pulicat was basically in two directions: to Mergui and the ports of the Irrawaddy delta in southern Burma on the one hand, and to Malacca and ports further east in the archipelago on the other. While the trade with Mergui was marginal, that with Pegu and lower Burma, in particular the ports of Martaban and Cosmin was more substantial. The principal exports from Pulicat consisted of textiles produced all over the Coromandel coast and red yarn from the Krishna delta. The imports into Coromandel included items such as gold, rubies, timber, tin, ivory and copper. In 1516, Antonio Dinis, sometime Portuguese factor at Martaban, reported that on an average four or five ships were engaged each year in the trade between Cosmin and Coromandel. The link to Malacca was perhaps even more important. Until its capture by the Portuguese in 1511, the annual traffic to the port from Coromandel usually consisted of one big ship and as many as five smaller ships. The average annual value of the textiles cargo imported into Malacca from Pulicat in the early years of the 16th century has been put at 175,000 cruzados. There usually was also an annual ship to Pidie in northern Sumatra, as well as traffic from Pasai to Coromandel. The principal items imported into Pulicat included Indonesian spices, various kinds of woods, Chinese silk and other goods, gold and non-precious metals such as tin, copper, quicksilver and vermilion. A major trading group at Pulicat was that of Muslims, a few of Arab origin, but mainly members of the Muslim communities of coastál south-eastern India, known as Chulias in parts of Southeast Asia and Marakkayars on Coromandel. The trading community also included Telugu speaking Chettis of the Balija and Komatti communities as well as Armenians. At the Malacca end, the mercantile community consisted largely of the so-called *keling* merchants of Tamil and Telugu origin led by people like Nina Chatu and Nina Suryadev. The sultan of Malacca himself is also known to have participated in this branch of commerce.

In addition to the high seas trade carried on from Pulicat and other Coromandel ports, there was also a fair amount of coastal trade carried on with the Bengal ports in the north, the Sri Lankan and other ports in the south, and with ports on the Malabar coast. The precise position at the beginning of the 16th century remains somewhat obscure for the available data pertain mainly to the sixteenth and the early 17th centuries. The changes, if any, over the intervening period, however, do not appear to have been particularly marked, except in the matter of the growing role of Masulipatnam through the 16th century in the coastal, as in the high seas, network. The available information suggests that there was regular trade between Bengal and Coromandel based on the import into ports such as Masulipatnam of rice, gram, wheat, long pepper, opium, clarified butter and Bihar saltpetre by an annual coastal fleet from Bengal. In the late sixteenth and early 17th century, the number of vessels in the fleet was between thirty and forty. While the ships from Bengal usually returned from north Coromandel itself, those from the Gingelly coast went further south to supply central Coromandel as far as Pulicat and Sao Tomé. The Coromandel cargo carried back to Bengal was raw cotton, tobacco, iron and crucible steel and some textiles, but the profit seems to have been made largely on the outward journey. The pattern of coastal trade originating in southern Coromandel, however, was quite different. The ports of the Kaveri delta were all rice exporters, but this trade was directed southwards rather than towards the deficit pockets to the north. Nagapattinam supplied rice to the west coast of Sri Lanka, Jaffna and on a more limited scale, to southern Malabar in addition to Acheh, on which route rice was used mainly as a ballast item. The principal items brought back from Sri Lanka were areca, cinnamon, timber and elephants. It is somewhat intriguing that the sources do not mention any coastal contacts between the Coromandel ports on the one hand and the Kanara, Konkan and the Gujarat ports on the other.[2]

As far as Bengal was concerned, in addition to the coastal trade with south-eastern India, the major commercial links extended to the eastern littoral of the Bay of Bengal and Malacca, to Sri Lanka, the Maldives, and Malabar and finally to the Gujarat, the Red Sea and the Persian Gulf complex. The eastward trade was dominated by the trade to Malacca. According to Meilink-Roelofsz, five to six ships sailed on an average each year in the early part of the 16th century from Bengal to Malacca and ports such as Pasai and Pidie. Most of these were rather small vessels but they did include one or two larger ones whose cargoes may have been worth as much as 80,000–90,000 *cruzados*. The exports from Bengal included textiles, rice, sugar and conserves, while the imports were a variegated lot. These included Borneo camphor, Moluccan spices, pepper, sandalwood, Chinese porcelain and silk, precious metals – perhaps mainly silver –, as well as base metals such as copper, tin, lead and mercury. The connection with Burma was mainly through the ports at Martaban, Dagon and Cosmin. According to the 1516 testimony of Dinis, four to five Bengal ships visited Cosmin each year carrying mainly textiles which were exchanged primarily against silver made into rings or small hoops.

The exports to Sri Lanka, the Maldives and the Malabar coast were again mainly textiles and foodstuffs, including large quantities of rice. Indeed, besides Kanara, Bengal was the principal rice surplus area in the entire region and areas such as the Maldives depended mainly on Bengal for their rice requirements. The principal item brought back by the Bengal vessels were cinnamon and areca from Sri Lanka, *cauris* used extensively in Bengal both for ornamental purposes as well as in the form of low denomination currency from the Maldives, and pepper, of which again Bengal was an important consumer, from Malabar. The trade to Gujarat was carried on primarily through Cambay, while the trips to Mocha in the Red Sea were often made after a stop over at the Maldives. The principal goods carried were textiles, sugar and long pepper, while the principal item brought back from Mocha was silver. The evidence regarding the Persian Gulf connection is, however, somewhat ambiguous.

The accounts of Tomé Pires and Barbosa also enable one to decipher the principal components of the mercantile community operating from Bengal. The indigenous merchants of Bengal are described as "merchants with great fortunes" and were an important constituent of the trading community. But a large part of the trade would seem to have been controlled either by merchants based at the partner ports or by foreign merchant groups settled in the Bengal ports. Thus the trade with Malacca was dominated by the *keling* merchants settled there. The pepper trade with Pasai and Pidie was carried on by Persian merchants settled at the Port of Chitta-

[2] Sanjay Subrahmanyam, *The Political Economy of Commerce. Southern India 1500–1650*, Cambridge 1990, p. 50–3, 93–8.

gong. This last mentioned group would seem to have also dominated the trade to the middle and the western Indian Ocean ports, though the traders on these routes also included Turks, Arabs, Rumis, Abyssinians and merchants from Chaul, Dabhol and Goa.[3]

To sum up, around the time the Europeans' participation in the maritime trade of India started at the beginning of the 16th century, India occupied a position of key importance in the structure of Indian Ocean trade. Of the three principal segments of this trade, the western Indian Ocean, the Bay of Bengal and the South China Sea, the first two were dominated by India. This domination was accounted for by India's mid-way location only in part. Perhaps more important was her capacity to put on the market a wide range of tradeable goods – particularly manufactured goods, the most important amongst which was coarse cotton textiles – at highly competitive prices. In the process, she helped expand the basis of trade in the region. This was a structure of trade in which the Europeans – of whom the Portuguese were the first – had no problem in finding a niche for themselves.

[3] Sanjay Subrahmanyam, "Notes on the Sixteenth Century Bengal Trade," *The Indian Economic and Social History Review* 24, No. 3, 1987, p. 265–89.

III

Asian Merchants and the Portuguese Trade in Asia

Om Prakash, Delhi School of Economics

In addition to major developments in the domain of renaissance, religion, and culture, the transition from the late medieval to the early modern world was marked by equally epoch-making changes in the field of economics. Probably the most wide-ranging of these was the rise of an early modern world economy facilitated by the two great maritime discoveries of the last decade of the fifteenth century – the discovery of the Americas and of the all-water route linking Europe and Asia via the Cape of Good Hope. An important element in the rise of this economy was the integration of the Indian Ocean into the larger framework of a developing world trade. Not only were the three principal segments of the early modern world economy – the New World, Europe, and Asia – now drawn into the vortex of world trade but there emerged also an organic and interactive relationship across the three segments whereby the growth of trade in one direction became critically dependent on the growth of trade in the other. The critical link was provided by the silver of South American origin, the growing availability of which became a pre-condition for the growth of the Euro-Asian trade. This was the earliest, if somewhat limited, incarnation of globalization.

Since it was the Portuguese who had discovered the Cape route, they promptly monopolized it and even asked the Pope to legitimize the arrangement. The result was that for a whole century, the only merchant group engaged in trade between Europe and Asia along the all-water route were the Portuguese. This situation, however, came to an end in the early years of the seventeenth century with the chartering of the English East India Company on the last day of the year 1600, and of the United Dutch East India Company on 20 March 1602. The last of the major European chartered monopoly trading companies engaged in Euro-Asian trade was the French East India Company founded in 1664.

This paper analyses the relationship between the Portuguese trade in Asia and the Asian merchants engaged in various branches of the Indian Ocean trade. It is useful to begin by drawing attention to the fact that this was an extraordinarily complex relationship allowing no simple propositions or answers. This complexity derived from a whole host of factors at work across both time and space. The Portuguese were admittedly the only European merchant group functioning in the Indian Ocean through the sixteenth century, but even so their presence had a multiplicity of facets. In its economic dimension, there was in the first place the official presence in the form of the Estado da India, which was supposed to run the commercial interests of the Crown. But the employees of the Estado from the Viceroy down simultaneously engaged extensively in trade on their private accounts, under a variety of arrangements. And then there were the private Portuguese traders who operated either under the protection of the Estado or outside of it. All these components of the Portuguese enterprise in Asia engaged in varying degrees in both the Euro-Asian and the intra-Asian trade.

Another complicating circumstance that explicitly needs to be taken into account is that Asian merchants per se were a highly diverse category with widely varying patterns of relationships with the different components of the Portuguese enterprise operating in Asia. A major determinant of these differences was the nationality or regional affiliation of the relevant Asian merchant group. In addition, during the sixteenth century, the relationship with the various components had an evolutionary character depending upon specific circumstances at a given point of time, or over a period of time. Thus given the politically dominant position of the Estado da India in places such as Sri Lanka, Cochin on the Malabar coast of India and in Malacca, the Asian merchants operating from ports in these regions had a very different kind of relationship with the Portuguese than, say, the Japanese merchants. Indeed, in the Japanese case the relationship of domination was simply reversed. One only has to remind oneself of the pancado arrangement under which foreign merchants including the Portuguese had to sell the Chinese raw silk they imported into Japan to a guild monopsony of ten merchants consisting of two from each of the five imperial cities of Edo (Tokyo), Osaka, Sakai, Nagasaki and Kyoto at a unilaterally determined price. As the Dutch East India Company factors had occasion to point out in the seventeenth century to the Japanese Shogunate, nowhere else in Asia were they subjected to a system where the buyer fixed the price. The Japanese pattern was thus clearly that of domination in reverse, a pattern for which it is difficult to find a parallel in early modern Asia.

Even though quantitative information is hard to come by for the sixteenth century, the broad contours of the implications of the arrival of the Portuguese into the Indian Ocean for Asian, in particular Indian, maritime merchants can nevertheless be deciphered. The Portuguese intrusion into the western Indian Ocean at the end of the fifteenth century initially created a situation of utter chaos. The Portuguese attempt to monopolize the spice trade called for a total exclusion of Asian shipping from the Persian Gulf and the Red Sea. This involved frequent raids on ships departing from Calicut with pepper for the Red Sea. But this phase was a rather short-lived one and the financial compulsions of the Estado da India soon made it opt for taxing Asian shipping in the area rather than trying to smother it. This was done by requiring all Asian ships to ask for and carry a *cartaz*. In the event of noncompliance, the vessel ran the risk of being seized by the Portuguese cruisers. The document authorized the vessel concerned to embark upon a specific trip and prohibited it from carrying goods monopolized by the Portuguese. The ports of call were specified and generally included a visit to a Portuguese-controlled port to pay duties on its cargo before proceeding to its destination. The fee charged for the grant of a cartaz was quite small and the principal pecuniary advantage derived by the Portuguese was the duties collected. The Portuguese were able to enforce such an arbitrary and high handed requirement essentially because of the virtual absence of an effective naval capability on the part of the Indian and most other Asian states at this time.

In order to ensure that the Indian vessels carrying the cartazes were not able to evade calling at the Portuguese-controlled ports and paying duties there, as well as to obviate the risk of Malabari pirate attacks on these vessels, the Portuguese introduced in the second half of the sixteenth century on the west coast of India the so-called *qafila* or caravan system. Under this system, Asian vessels operating between specified points were encouraged to sail in a group escorted by a Portuguese fleet. The practice was reasonably well-established by the 1570s: in 1596, sailing in a qafila was made obligatory. Apart from the Cambay – Diu qafila and a more spasmodic one centred at Ormuz, all the qafilas went to Goa. The escorting vessels themselves also carried goods. For example, the private cargoes for the homeward-bound fleet were normally carried by such vessels. Two or three qafilas left Goa each year for Cambay via Chaul, Bassein, Daman and in the seventeenth century, Surat as well. The Kanara qafila was also a regular one and made two to four voyages each year to Basrur, Mangalore and Honawar to fetch rice for the city of Goa. Yet another qafila travelled from Cape Comorin, via Cochin and Cannanore, to Goa. It included larger ships from Malacca, Siam, Bengal and Coromandel which were met by the guard fleet at Cape Comorin. In Cochin many smaller ships were assembled, and they all proceeded together to Goa[1].

What implications did the Portuguese trade and policies have for the coastal and the high-seas trade carried on by the Indian merchants? Given the significant differences in this regard between one part of the subcontinent and another, an answer to this query is best attempted at a regional level. To begin with let us take the western Indian Ocean, one finds that in Gujarat, after some initial resistance, the response of the local merchants was one of acquiescence in the Portuguese system. By the middle of the sixteenth century, all Gujarati ships leaving the ports of the Gulf of Cambay were obliged to call at Portuguese-controlled Diu and pay duties there. This involved an additional fiscal burden of around 5 percent of the value of the goods carried. The sixteenth century also witnessed a certain amount of reorientation of the Gujarati merchants' trade, with the share of the Red Sea sector in the total trade perhaps increasing substantially. It is significant that the English and the Dutch documentation of the 1620s relating to Surat stresses the important dependence of the merchants of the city upon the Red Sea trade. If this assessment is correct, Gujarat's trade with its other major trading partner, namely southeast Asia, would possibly have suffered a severe decline. What is likely to have been the role of the Portuguese in this process? Since a growth in the textile trade with the Red Sea would have brought them higher customs revenues at Diu, they would probably have welcomed this development and assisted it in whatever way they could. The picture is somewhat more complex in respect of the trade with southeast Asia. As Charles Boxer has shown, the pepper shipments originating at Aceh and destined for the Red Sea operated in an important way through the half century starting around 1540. He has also pointed to the continuing important role of Gujarati shipping in this trade. If the Gujaratis increasingly withdrew from the spice trade from the end of the sixteenth century onward, this probably had more to do with the growing substitution of the old water-cum-land route to the Mediterranean by the Cape of Good Hope route after the appearance on the scene of the Dutch and the English East India companies, than with any specific Portuguese policies.[2]

As for the Kanara coast, from about 1510 on, the Portuguese are known to have attacked the shipping from Bhatkal, particularly that bound for the Red Sea. But between 1518 and 1530, this port figured in the network of Portuguese Crown shipping, and annual voyages were organized to Ormuz with pepper and other goods such as iron, rice, sugar and ginger. In theory, the Indian merchants were not allowed to export pepper or import horses into Bhatkal which goods could only be sold at Goa, but the restrictions do not seem to have always been observed. The sailings to the Red Sea and South Arabia often seem to have been carried out even without a cartaz. From about 1530 onwards, the amount of pepper exported from Bhatkal to the Red Sea increased considerably. Of the huge quantities of pepper reaching Jeddah in the 1560s, a large part would seem to have been from Kanara, the other part having originated in Aceh and the Sunda straits. But by about 1575, Bhatkal had suddenly disappeared from the Indian Ocean trading network. This would seem to be the combined outcome of the decline of the Vijayanagar empire and of Portuguese policies. Goods from west Asia designed for sale in the capital city of the empire no longer had a market, and the horse trade was also adversely affected. As for the Portuguese, the establishment of three fortresses – two to the south and one to the north of Bhatkal – in 1568-9 had resulted in a considerable tightening up of the vigil against the transportation of pepper to the Red Sea. The Kanara port that took over the role of Bhatkal as the leading port of the coast from the late sixteenth century onward was Basrur. A Saraswat-dominated mercantile community referred to by the Portuguese as 'chatins de Barcelor' had traditionally carried on a fair amount of trade in rice, pepper and other goods from the port. By the early years of the seventeenth century, Basrur had become the leading rice-trading port of the Kanara coast. The rice was sent to Muscat, the Red Sea and the Persian Gulf, as well as to Goa and the Malabar ports. A Portuguese fort had been set up at Basrur in 1569 and a small settlement of white and black casados had come up there in the 1570s. The 'chatins de Barcelor' resisted the setting up of a customs house at the fort, which was eventually removed. There is evidence that the chatins' trade continued into the seventeenth century and, in addition to the rice trade, increasing amounts of pepper were now carried to Konkan and the Gujarat ports.

Given the Portuguese policy of monopolizing the trade in pepper, it is not surprising that a situation of conflict with the pardesi merchants developed very early in the history of Portuguese contact with the Malabar coast. The pepper fleets from Calicut, Kollam and Cannanore to the Red Sea were systematically attacked by the Portuguese squadrons both off the Malabar coast as well as at the entrance to the Red Sea. The relations with the Mappilas, however, were generally cordial at this time, and they were indeed used as intermediaries and brokers in the procurement of pepper. But the resistance to, and the successful evasion of Portuguese control by the Mappilas of Cannanore under the leadership of their chief, Mamale, an ancestor of the Ali Rajas, must be recorded. They had resented, among other things, the enforced diversion of the trade in horses and ginger from their port to Goa. By taking advantage of a palace revolution in Male, Mamale claimed sovereign rights in the Maldives and began collecting duties from ships calling there. The importance of this development lay in the fact that the Gujarati and other ships on their way from southeast Asia to the Red Sea carrying pepper and other goods could now call at the Maldives and evade the Portuguese on the Malabar coast. Malabarese pepper, Sri Lankan cinnamon and other goods were brought to these ships at the Maldives by the merchants of Bengal and Cannanore. The Portuguese attempts to disrupt this arrangement by operating from their fortresses at Pasai, Colombo, Male and Kollam were not particularly successful. With the cooperation of the Mappila traders from Calicut, who had put together an armed fleet under the command of the Kunjalis, spice shipments were also sent clandestinely to the Gujarat ports. This trade received a setback after the Portuguese gained control of the Gulf of Cambay. But a certain amount of spices continued to be smuggled, hidden in the bales of textiles.

By about the middle of the sixteenth century, a change in the relative stature of different Malabar ports became evident. Both Calicut and Cannanore were on the decline, while the rising port was that of Cochin which was now handling more and more of the trade both with Gujarat and the Persian Gulf as well as with southeast Asia. Clearly, the Portuguese were largely responsible for this. Indeed from the very beginning of their contacts with the Malabar coast, they had consciously promoted Cochin at the expense of both Calicut and Cannanore. Before they had moved on to Goa in the second decade of the sixteenth century, the headquarters of the Portuguese administration was at Cochin and in the course of time an important Portuguese settlement had arisen there. Quite early in the century, Cochin had also occasionally figured in the Crown shipping network.

In the second half of the sixteenth century, the trade from Cochin extended in both directions. There was, in the first place, the trade to the west coast north of Goa, mainly to Chaul, Surat and Diu. The goods exported were mainly pepper, ginger and other spices, as well as the goods brought in from Malacca and China. The imports were mainly opium, raw cotton and textiles, together with some grain. Since both pepper and opium were prohibited goods, it would seem that the trade was carried on with the connivance of the Estado. The other important trading link in the west was with Ormuz, while a relatively minor trade was also carried on with the Red Sea. Eastward, the principal links of Cochin were with the Coromandel coast, Malacca, Macao, Manila and, most important of all, Bengal. The trade to Malacca and to Macao was essentially a re-export of timber, pepper, areca and other spices against the import of textiles and rice. Ships from Goa to Macao called at Cochin on both the outward and the return voyages to take in or to offload goods belonging to the casado merchants at Cochin. As for Bengal, Antonio Bocarro estimated that, in its heyday, the total value of the trade in this branch was as much as 400,000 xerafins per annum, amounting perhaps to half of the total trade from Cochin. The exports to Bengal consisted above all of pepper, though some minor drugs and other spices also formed part of the cargoes. The main items imported were opium, foodstuffs, rice and textiles. The textiles included mainly khasas and malmals which often found their way into the liberty-chests of the carracks bound for Lisbon. The Cochin-Bengal link, however, nearly snapped after the Mughal expulsion of the Portuguese from Hughli in 1632, and this accounted in large measure for the decline of Cochin in the subsequent period.[3]

The Portuguese involvement in the trade of the Bay of Bengal began almost immediately after the capture of Malacca in 1511. As far as Bengal was concerned, the initial phase of Crown shipping was replaced from the 1560s onward by concession voyages. In addition, there were a certain number of private Portuguese individuals – traders and mercenaries – living in and operating from Bengal. Soon after the Mughal takeover of the province in 1576, the Portuguese settlement at Hughli was legitimized by a farman granted by Emperor Akbar in 1579. By the end of the sixteenth century, however, the Portuguese were expelled from Chittagong by Arakan's rulers. As noted above, the Mughals took similar action at Hughli in 1632.

Neither the *Carreira* nor the concession routes to Bengal were monopoly routes and the Indian merchants' trade is known to have co-existed together with that of the Portuguese. There was, however, a certain amount of reorientation of the Bengal trade in the process. In the Bay of Bengal, the trade with Aceh increased substantially at the expense mainly of that with Malacca, which registered a progressive decline from the 1540s onward. The trade with the Coromandel coast, however, continued uninterrupted. As far as the trade with the ports west of Cape Comorin was concerned, one finds that by the middle of the sixteenth century,

Indian merchants' trade with Gujarat and the Red Sea had ceased altogether. The only link with the region that survived at the end of the century was the casado merchants' trade between Hughli and Ormuz. It was only around the middle of the seventeenth century that the link between the Bengal ports and those in Gujarat and the Red Sea was revived.[4]

The situation was somewhat more complex on the Coromandel coast. Casado and other private Portuguese trading groups had already begun to settle down at Pulicat and the neighbouring port of Sao Tome de Mylapore in the second decade of the sixteenth century. In the 1530s, another important Portuguese settlement had been established at Nagapattinam. The monopolistic nature of some of the carreira routes to Coromandel notwithstanding, private Portuguese merchants' as well as Indian merchants' trade between Pulicat and Malacca is known to have continued on an important scale throughout the 1520s, 1530s and 1540s. But as Crown shipping gave way to the concession voyages to Coromandel on a reserved-route basis, the Indian merchants found themselves almost totally excluded from the Pulicat-Malacca run. They were now obliged to hire freight space aboard the concession holders' ships. An increase in the import duty at Malacca, combined with a rise in the freight charges, created further problems. This situation, together with the decline of the imperial city of Vijayanagar, led to an irreversible decline in the fortunes of the port of Pulicat. By the end of the sixteenth century, the port was only a shadow of its former self.

The port that succeeded Pulicat as the premier port of the Coromandel coast was that at Masulipatnam which, until the middle of the sixteenth century, was a relatively minor port. The rise of Masulipatnam was in part related to the consolidation of the Sultanate of Golconda under Ibrahim Qutb Shah (1550-80). But it also had a good deal to do with the emergence of an alternative network of trade in the Bay of Bengal. This basically represented the Indian merchants' response to the Portuguese stranglehold over the Pulicat-Malacca sector. The other constituent ports of the newly emerging network were Aceh, Malay peninsular ports such as Perak and Kedah, and the Burmese ports of Pegu, Bassein, Tavoy and Martaban, all of which had taken on an anti-Portuguese character. In the 1590s, two or three ships regularly left Masulipatnam for Pegu laden with textiles and yarn. The links with Aceh were even stronger. In exchange for Coromandel textiles and rice, Aceh provided horses and elephants, southeast Asian pepper and spices, and the gold and copper of Minangkabau and the Far East. Aceh had turned out to be a worthy successor to Malacca as a major entrepôt port in the region. The other Coromandel port that traded extensively with Aceh was that of Nagapattinam.

The rise of the alternative network greatly alarmed the Estado which made evry attempt to destroy it. Through official or unofficial armadas, attempts were made to disrupt the trade both at Aceh and at Masulipatnam. To counter the merchants of the latter port, who freely navigated the seas without the Portuguese cartazes, the Estado granted even licenses to privateers to lie in wait outside Masulipatnam with a view to capture the local shipping. But these attempts were not particularly successful at any point: there were even occasions when Portuguese captives from such attempts had to be ransomed from Masulipatnam by private Portuguese citizens. However, while the Portuguese authority could be ignored in the Bay of Bengal, it would have been dangerous to ignore them in the western Indian Ocean. Thus when a new link was established between Masulipatnam and the Red Sea in the 1580s in which Sultan Muhammad Quli Qutb Shah also participated, accommodation with the Portuguese became necessary. An agreement concluded between the Sultan and the Estado in 1590 provided for cartazes to be issued for the Mecca-bound shipping in exchange for 300 khandis of rice to be delivered to the Portuguese annually at Malacca or Sri Lanka. In 1598, it was decided to appoint a captain at Masulipatnam for the purpose of issuing cartazes. But while the Portuguese kept their part of the agreement by and large, the rice was never handed over to them. By the time the Dutch arrived at Masulipatnam in 1605, the Portuguese captain probably had already been withdrawn from the port.[5]

With the coming of the English and the Dutch East India companies into the Indian Ocean at the beginning of the seventeenth century, the nature of the relationship between European traders and Asian merchants was subjected to further complexity. This was particularly so in the case of the Dutch East India Company which participated in intra-Asian trade on an extensive scale as an integral part of its overall trading strategy. The wresting of extensive monopsonistic and monopolistic privileges by the Company from local rulers in the Indonesian archipelago and Sri Lanka subjected the Asian merchants trading from and to these regions to an enormous amount of unfair competition. Even in the specific context of the relationship between the Portuguese traders and the Asian merchants, the existence of a multiplicity of European trading bodies operating in the Indian Ocean had significant implications. Probably the most important of these was that Asian merchants who were denied permission by the Portuguese to operate in particular branches of trade through the instrument of the cartaz could now apply to the English or the Dutch for such permission. Strictly speaking, the Portuguese were not obliged to honor permissions given by rival European trading companies, but in practice this was done except in very special situations.

It should also be realized that the Portuguese trade in Asia was by no means an exclusively sixteenth century affair. Indeed, the establishment of the Portuguese India Company in 1628 represented in some sense the last desperate attempt to make the Portuguese Euro-Asian pepper trade viable. But the experiment was not particularly successful and as early as April 1633 it was decided to dissolve the Company. The last batch of cargo on the account of the Company left Goa in 1634. The Crown monopoly of pepper was partially relaxed in 1642 with the rights of the Casa da India being confined to purchasing the pepper on arrival in Lisbon at a pre-determined price. But the arrangement failed to stimulate the trade to any significant extent. The tonnage leaving Asia for Lisbon which had stood at 13,710 tons during 1631-40 increased during 1641-50 to only 16,030 tons. In the second half of the seventeenth century, it was only during 1671-80 that this figure exceeded 10,000 tons. The greater part of the eighteenth century also saw the Euro-Asian trade of the Portuguese languish at a relatively low level. The closing decades of the century, however, witnessed a striking revival of this trade mainly because of Portuguese neutrality in the European wars of the period. Until the French invaded Portugal in 1807, and indeed until the end of the wars in 1815, Lisbon was revived as a major entrepôt for the import of Asian goods into Europe, particularly Chinese tea and Indian textiles.

The Portuguese private traders engaged in intra-Asian trade had continued to operate on a reasonably vigorous basis through the seventeenth and the eighteenth centuries. A case in point is the private Portuguese trade from the Coromandel coast. The loss of Nagapattinam to the Dutch in 1658 indeed constituted a setback to the Portuguese trade from the coast. But their response was to relocate themselves in large numbers at the port of Porto Novo to the north, which over the last quarter of the seventeenth century emerged as a major country – trading port. An analysis, on the basis of information available in the Dutch shipping lists, of the ownership pattern of the ships, excluding Company ships and small coastal craft, that left this port between 1681-82 and 1685-86 for various Asian destinations shows that the Portuguese were a major group of merchants owning ships and operating from this port. By far the most important port of destination for the Portuguese shipping from Porto Novo was Aceh, followed by Pegu, Malacca, Goa and Manila.

Elsewhere in Asia, by far the most vibrant and prosperous group of private Portuguese traders was the one based at Macao. The Dutch East India Company records pertaining to foreign shipping movement at Batavia, for example, establish beyond any doubt the relative importance of Portuguese shipping from Macao in the pepper trade between Batavia and China. The Portuguese shipowners also carried substantial quantities of freight cargo belonging to English, French, Armenian and other merchants trading in the Indian Ocean/South China Sea complex. In the 1720s, the Portuguese from Macao are known to have even bought ships at Batavia to enhance their fleet's total cargo capacity. From the Chinese merchants at Canton they demanded and received exorbitant freight rates and the purchase of some of the ships by the Portuguese was made possible, it was claimed, by capital advanced by Chinese merchants, some of whom had moved to Macao.

With the resumption of the Dutch East India Company's direct trade to China in the 1730s, the Portuguese and the Chinese merchants operating at Batavia faced increasing problems. This obliged the Macao Portuguese to concentrate on specific sources of supply as well as markets in the Indian Ocean. An analysis of the Dutch shipping lists, as well as the information available in the English Company records for the period 1719 to 1754, shows that Portuguese ships called with varying frequency at the ports of Bengal, at Madras and Nagapattinam on the Coromandel coast, at Cochin, Tellicherry and Anjengo on the Malabar coast, and at Surat. Some of these ships, particularly those calling at Surat, are known to have in fact been owned by Asian merchants, flying the Portuguese flag for convenience. By far the most important ports of call for the genuine Portuguese shipping were Cochin, Tellicherry, and Madras.

Turning next to the specific question of what the Portuguese trade in Asia – both official and private – meant to the Asian merchants, it is important to realize that the nature of the Portuguese documentation does not allow a detailed quantitative analysis of this issue in the same manner as, for example, the Dutch documentation does. Given the enormous stakes the Dutch East India Company had in intra-Asian trade, instructions had been issued to its establishments all over Asia to keep track of the shipping movements of rival Asian merchants from and to the ports under their respective jurisdiction. This resulted in an enormous body of data that could be compiled from the local customs-house registers on the Asian merchants' trade over the seventeenth and the eighteenth centuries. This material is usually referred to in the literature as the "shipping lists". While an overwhelming bulk of the material has yet to be explored, the little that has been put to use has given extremely rich dividends. I might refer here to a study I did almost thirty years ago using this material relating to the trade carried on by Asian merchants from the ports of Bengal to ports of south-east Asia as well as the Maldive islands. Major limitations in the quality and the quantity of the material notwithstanding, a careful analysis of the material provided evidence which was absolutely unrivalled facilitating the arrival at reasonably definitive conclusions. To the extent that this material also covers the trade carried on by private Portuguese traders, it also helps us, as we have already seen, to form a broad idea of the movements in the trade of these merchants. But as this material is only available as from about 1630 onward, it is of no particular help in looking at the impact of the policies of the Estado da India as an important element in the movements in Asian merchants' trade in the sixteenth and the early years of the seventeenth century when the Estado was at the height of its power.

To sum up, from the standpoint of the Indian maritime merchant, the Portuguese cartaz system, in so far as it entailed only a small additional fiscal burden, was indeed no more than a minor irritant. But to the extent that this device was used to keep the Indian merchants out of trade in specific commodities or on specific routes, the Portuguese were indeed at least partly instrumental in forcing certain changes in the structure of Indian maritime trade. One such change was an alteration in the relative stature of various Indian ports. Striking cases include the decline of Bhatkal in Kanara, that of Calicut and Cannanore in Malabar accompanied by the rise of Cochin, and the replacement of Pulicat by Masulipatnam as the principal port of the Coromandel coast. The Indian merchants, however, generally adjusted quite well to the evolving situations and did not allow the enforced changes to overwhelm them. Probably the best example of this resilience is the emergence of an alternative network of trade in the Bay of Bengal centred on Masulipatnam, Aceh and several Malay and Burmese ports which had assumed an anti-Portuguese character.

It is also worth remarking that the experience of the Indian maritime merchants vis-à-vis the Portuguese in the sixteenth century was a true precursor of what awaited them in the seventeenth and the eighteenth centuries. The scale of operation of the new European entrants into the Indian Ocean viz. the English, the Dutch and the French East India Companies was much larger than that the Portuguese alone had been able to achieve. Quite often this meant new kinds of pressures being generated on the Asian maritime merchants. Even at the risk of oversimplification, however, I would like to end this brief essay by suggesting that the Asian maritime merchant – and particularly the Indian maritime merchant – indeed turned out to be resourceful enough not to succumb to these pressures and allow the Europeans to monopolize the intra-Asian trade.

Notes

1. M.N. Pearson, Merchants and Rulers in Gujarat, The Response to the Portuguese in the Sixteenth Century, Berkeley, 1976, pp.39-47.
2. M.N. Pearson, The Portuguese in India, vol. 1.1 in The New Cambridge History of India, Cambridge, 1987, pp.52-5; C.R. Boxer, "A note on the Portuguese reaction to the revival of the Red Sea spice trade and the rise of Atjeh, 1540-1600; Journal of Southeast Asian History, vol. 10(3), 1969, pp.415-28; Ashin Das Gupta, Indian Merchants and the Decline of Surat C1700-1750, Wiesbaden, 1979, pp.4-5.
3. Sanjay Subrahmanyam, The Political Economy of Commerce Southern India 1500-1650, Cambridge, 1990, pp.137-42.
4. Sanjay Subrahmanyam, 'Notes on the sixteenth century Bengal trade', The Indian Economic and Social History Review, vol. 24(3), 1987, pp.265-89.
5. Sanjay Subrahmanyam, The Political Economy of Commerce, pp.155-66.

IV

THE ECONOMIC DIMENSION OF THE PORTUGUESE ENTERPRISE IN ASIA

While by no means the only circumstance behind the Portuguese efforts of the latter half of the fifteenth century to establish a direct all-water link with Asia, the economic motive, and more specifically the desire to have a first-hand and exclusive access to pepper and other Asian spices, was clearly the dominant element characterizing the process. Once this objective had been achieved with the successful completion of the 1498 voyage of Vasco da Gama to Calicut and the procurement of the papal bull legitimizing the Portuguese monopoly of the Cape route, a decision regarding the precise mechanism to be followed in running the new enterprise had to be taken. Partly because of the absence of a strong mercantile tradition among the Portuguese comparable in any sense to that of the north-western Europeans, and partly because it had taken the lead in providing finance and the infrastructural support to the efforts which had culminated in the discovery of the Cape route, the Crown became an important component in the Asian enterprise from the very beginning. The principal organizing unit at the Lisbon end was the Casa da India, a royal trading firm entrusted with the overall charge of the trade with Asia. The Asian end of the enterprise was supervised by an administrative set-up described from the 1560s onwards as the Estado da Índia. This had its headquarters theoretically in Lisbon but for all practical purposes in Goa under the charge of a Viceroy nominated by the Crown. The Viceroy was assisted by, among others, informal Councils which by 1563 had evolved and become more institutionalized as the Council of State. The Viceroy had command over all Portuguese posts as well as military and naval forces from the Zambezi valley in Africa to Macao in China. The subordinate settlements followed the structure of control established in Goa.

In keeping with the traditional composition of the Asian imports into Europe, the principal item sought by the Portuguese Crown in Asia was spices-overwhelmingly pepper-though some other goods were also procured. The pepper was procured almost exclusively in the Malabar region (and later Kanara as well) on the southwest coast of India. The procurement of pepper was organized by the Estado while the sales in Europe were through contract sales based until the middle of the century at Antwerp and thereafter at Lisbon. While the principal economic activity carried on by the Estado on behalf of the Crown was the procurement of pepper for Europe, it also engaged in a certain amount of trade within Asia, again on the account of the Crown. The latter activity, however, was confined to the first half of the sixteenth century. Because of the radically different ways in which these two types of trade were carried on by the Estado, the nature of its relationship with the Indian/Asian merchants also varied considerably as between these two activities.

An important circumstance that made the Portuguese enterprise in Asia a rather complex affair wholly unsuited to characterization by an overall blanket label was the fact that the Portuguese Crown – or the Estado da Índia acting on its behalf – was not the only, or for that matter even the most important, component of this enterprise. As far as Euro-Asian trade was concerned, another major component engaged in the activity was that of the New Christian merchants who were descendants of Iberian Jews forcibly converted to Christianity at the end of the fifteenth century. This group also engaged in an important way in trade within Asia partly in order to feed its Euro-Asian trade. Many other segments of the Portuguese community in Asia operating under the jurisdiction and patronage of the Estado also engaged in a fair amount of intra-Asian trade on their respective private accounts. At a settlement such as Goa, these categories included, in addition to the New Christians already mentioned, government officials, soldiers, ecclesiastics, and the *Casados moradores* or married settlers. Finally, there was the group derisively called *chatins* consisting of individuals who had broken away from the Estado and no longer recognized its jurisdiction over them.

This paper will briefly analyse the pattern of functioning and, wherever possible, the scale of operations of the major components of the Portuguese enterprise in Asia engaged in Euro-Asian and/or intra-Asian trade. It will also go into the question of the extent to which these various components together anticipated in any way the functioning of the northwestern European trading companies that operated in Asia during the seventeenth and the eighteenth centuries as also the extent to which the Portuguese enterprise remained unique in its operations.

II

On the return of Vasco da Gama to Lisbon in 1499, the Portuguese government formed a syndicate for trade with Asia, in which both the Crown and certain private interests participated. In the voyage of Pedro Alvarez Cabral which left Lisbon on 9 March 1500 with thirteen ships, for example, ten were on the account of the Crown, while the remaining three belonged to different syndicates of Portuguese noblemen and Italian financiers. But from 1506 onward, the trade in precious metals from Portugal to India, and that in pepper and other major spices in the reverse direction, was reserved as a royal monopoly. However, the participation of private enterprise in the role of financiers continued. On occasions this could be quite important. Thus the fleet of 1510 under the command of Diogo Mendes de Vasconcelos was largely staffed and financed by the Florentine commercial house of Sernigi and its associates.

The mounting liquidity problems of the Crown forced a major reorganization of the trade in 1564 when the first of a series of contracts giving over trade on the Cape route to private parties was concluded. The remaining part of the sixteenth century witnessed a variety of experiments carried out in an attempt to identify the optimal strategy that would ensure the Crown maximum monopoly revenue without obliging it to be directly involved in the conduct of the trade with Asia. The Asian contract system was introduced in 1575. The first beneficiary of the new arrangement was the Augsburg merchant, Konrad Rott, together with his associates who included the Milanese merchant, Giovanni Batista Rovalesca. Under this arrangement, Rott received intact the royal monopoly of the Cape route – the procurement of spices in Asia, their shipment to Europe, the provisioning of the carracks in Lisbon and Goa, and the distribution of pepper in Europe. Just before his death in 1580, Dom Henrique renewed the Rott – Rovalesca contract for another five years. Under the terms of the contract, the contractors were supposed to purchase each year in India a total of 30,000 quintals of pepper – 15,000 on their own account and 15,000 on the king's account. The contractors were free to sell their half of the pepper as they chose; the king would also sell all of his 15,000 quintals (which cost him nothing) to the Rott – Rovalesca consortium at 32 cruzados per quintal. The consortium thus enjoyed exclusive European distribution of Portuguese pepper[1]. A sharp decline in the European price of pepper, however, forced Rott out of business. In February 1586, a new Asian contract was concluded for a period of six years with Rovalesca in association with Giraldo Paris. The contract system continued until 1598 when private enterprise was no longer willing to take up the pepper contracts. In any event, the experiment with the contract system had not been particularly satisfactory for either side. The syndicates were consistently unable to import the quantities specified in the contracts and never managed to make adequate profits. The bankruptcy of Rott has already been noted: his Milanese counterpart was also forced to follow suit.

In the context of the continuing problem of liquidity, the formation of the English and the Dutch East India companies would seem to have been instrumental in spurring the Portuguese Crown to consider the establishment of a Portuguese India Company. The Company was finally founded in 1628, but the experiment was not particularly successful, and as early as April 1633 it was decided to dissolve the Company. The last batch of cargo on the account of the Company left Goa in 1634. the Crown monopoly of pepper was partially relaxed in 1642 with the rights of the Casa da Índia being confined to purchasing the pepper on arrival in Lisbon at a pre-determined price. But the arrangement failed to stimulate the trade to any significant extent.

Throughout the sixteenth and the first half of the seventeenth century, an overwhelming proportion of the pepper imported into Lisbon was procured on the southwest coast of India. In the early part of the seventeenth century, the significance of Malabar/Kanara pepper increased even further. Thus between 1612 and 1634 pepper procured at Malacca, the only source other than the southwest coast of India, accounted for only 3.26 percent of the total amount of pepper shipped to Lisbon[2].

On the southwest coast of India, the procurement of pepper was begun at Calicut on the Malabar coast, where the Portuguese had first arrived. But relations with the *pardesi* merchants of the town as well as the Samudri raja

---

[1] James C. Boyajian, *Portuguese Trade in Asia under the Habsburgs 1580-1640*, Baltimore and London, 1993, p. 20.

[2] Calculated from A. R. Disney, *Twilight of the Pepper Empire, Portuguese Trade in Southwest India in the Early Seventeenth Century*, Cambridge, Mass., 1978, Appendix 2.2, p. 162.

deteriorated fast. The conflict with the merchants had its origin mainly in the Portuguese insistence on being provided with pepper before the Red Sea merchants had been served. The Portuguese attack on a *sambuk* was retaliated by their factory being looted which, in turn, led to an attack on the port and a bombardment of the town in 1501 that lasted for two days. The era of peaceful trading which, occasional instances of violence notwithstanding, had been the norm in the Asian waters for centuries, had finally been shattered by the Portuguese. At any rate, it was found more expedient to shift the centre of pepper procurement to Cochin where the more cooperative Mappila and the Syrian Christian merchants were used as brokers and intermediaries. The friendly relationship between the Estado and the Mappila merchants at Cochin, however, did not last very long. By the end of the third decade of the century, the merchants had declared a holy war – *jihad* – against the Estado. The hostility continued in one form or another into the seventeenth century. In the second half of the sixteenth century, in addition to Cochin, Kollam and marginally Cannanore on the Malabar coast, the Estado also began procuring pepper on the Kanara coast. Shipments from the mid-1560s onward generally included some Kanara pepper and from the last decade of the century onward, Kanara definitely outstripped Malabar as a source of pepper. Information available for the period 1612 to 1634 suggests that, roughly speaking, Kanara provided two-thirds of the total Indian supplies as against Malabar's one-third[3].

How important was the Cape route in relation to the total import of Asian pepper into Europe in the sixteenth century? It was Frederic C. Lane who had first talked in the 1930s of the revival of the Levantine trade to Europe and suggested that the economic importance of the Cape route in the sixteenth century may have been seriously exaggerated. According to him, Venice imported as much or more pepper from Alexandria in the 1560s as it had done in the late fifteenth century[4]. In his 1974 book, Niels Steensgaard argued that in the 1570s and the 1580s the Portuguese average annual import of about 20,000

[3] Calculated from Disney, *Twilight of the Pepper Empire*, Appendix 2.2, p. 162.

[4] Frederic C. Lane, «Venetian shipping during the commercial revolution», *American Historical Review*, vol. 38, pp. 228-229; «The Mediterranean spice trade, further evidence on its revival in the sixteenth century», *American Historical Review*, vol. 45, p. 586.

quintals would have accounted for only about 40 percent of the total amount of pepper brought into Europe. In the decade of the 1590s marked by unprecedented shipping losses, this would have been halved to about 20 percent[5]. In a paper published in 1979, C. H. H. Wake maintained that the Steensgaard scenario needed a drastic revision because he had both overestimated the size of the European market and underestimated the extent of the Portuguese imports. On the basis of his reinterpretation of the Magalhães Godinho data on pepper imports, Wake argued that until 1550, and again in the 1570s and the 1580s, the Portuguese accounted for upward of 75 per cent of Europe's pepper imports. Regarding the role of the Levant trade, Wake emphasized the existence of an important spice market in West Asia itself and the consequent need to distinguish between the total Asian supplies entering the Red Sea and the Persian Gulf, and the part that eventually reached Europe. He then argued that the supplies bought by the Venetian and other European merchants in the Levant were regulated strictly in accordance with the quantities brought to Lisbon earlier in the year by the Cape route. As a result, «the Levantine trade ebbed and flowed with the changing fortunes of the Portuguese enterprise». In the 1560s, for example, when the Portuguese imports are known to have been limited, the Venetian imports from Alexandria are generally believed to have been very large. The Venetian revival was cut short by the Cyprus war of 1570-1573 which, in the analysis of Wake, coincided with the recovery in the Portuguese trade. Finally, when Portugal's imports were marked by unprecedented maritime disasters in the 1590s, the Venetian trade again enjoyed a revival[6].

But then how important was pepper itself in the total Portuguese imports from Asia into Europe? Traditional wisdom on this subject suggests a figure (weightwise) of between 80 and 89 percent in the first half of the sixteenth century going down to under 70 percent in the second half of the century[7]. The Moluccan spices and ginger also became proportionately less important

[5] Niels Steensgaard, «The return cargoes of the Carreira in the 16th and early 17th century», in Teotonio R. de Souza (ed.), *Indo-Portuguese History, Old Issues, New Questions*, New Delhi, 1985, p. 22.

[6] C. H. H. Wake, «The changing pattern of Europe's pepper and spice imports Ca. 1400-1700», *The Journal of European Economic History*, vol. 8(2), 1979, pp. 385-387.

[7] Steensgaard, «The return cargoes of the Carreira in the 16th and early 17th century».

over time. Sri Lankan cinnamon, on the other hand, became increasingly more important. Also, indigo emerged in the cargoes in the second half of the century in a reasonably important way: the same was even more true of textiles, though one has to be particularly careful while interpreting weight figures in relation to textiles.

James Boyajian has recently argued the case for an almost revolutionary revision of the orthodoxy in relation to Portuguese Euro-Asian trade during the period 1680 to 1740. The three inter-related themes that are at the core of Boyajian's analysis are (a) a major upward revision in the volume and value of the Portuguese Euro-Asian trade during this period, (b) the relative insignificance of pepper in the total Asian cargo imported into Portugal and (c) the overwhelmingly important role played by private enterprise, mainly the New Christian merchants, in conducting the Portuguese Euro-Asian carreira trade. It has traditionally been conceded that the carreira ships operated on the account of the Estado da Índia did indeed transport on a regular basis a certain amount of private cargo belonging to naval personnel and to certain privileged institutions and individuals allowed to import under royal license. The novelty of Boyajian's estimates consists in his view of the magnitude of the private cargoes carried aboard these ships overwhelmingly on the account of the New Christian merchants. According to Boyajian, private cargoes accounted for an almost unbelievable 90 per cent of the total value imported over the period 1580-1640 from Asia. These merchants did not trade in pepper which continued to be handled by the Estado. But by virtue of the fact that the value of their trade in goods other than pepper was so large, the share of pepper in the total Portuguese imports into Europe shrank to a mere 10 percent or so. By far the most important constituent of the private cargo was textiles, accounting for as much as 62 percent of the total imports valuewise, followed by items such as precious stones (14 per cent), indigo (6 per cent) and spices other than pepper (5 percent)[8].

What is the statistical basis of Boyajian's estimates? As the 1755 Lisbon earthquake destroyed the Casa da Índia's records, Boyajian is obliged to use other evidence. According to him, Luis de Figueiredo Falcao's data and a few manifests from 1586-1598 indicate that total shipments of royal pepper and pri-

[8] Boyajian, *Portuguese Trade in Asia*, p. 44.

vate goods of the Carreira da Índia (excluding privileged cargo not subject to duties) amounted to 67 million cruzados, giving an average of 5.1 million cruzados for each of the thirteen years. Of this total, private cargo constituted almost 60 million cruzados, or just about 90 per cent, averaging 4.6 million cruzados annually. The inclusion of additional shipments of non-dutiable liberties and unregistered private cargo would raise the total value of the private cargo to well above 5 million cruzados per annum[9]. I have argued elsewhere in some detail that a close examination of the Boyajian estimates suggests that the picture is indeed not quite as straightforward and unambiguous as he would have us believe[10]. The problems with these estimates, however, raise questions only about the precise extent of the private Portuguese merchants' inter-continental trade between Europe and Asia, not about their considerably more important role in this trade than has traditionally been believed. Boyajian's significant upward revision of this role is certainly in the right direction and must be duly taken note of.

It would thus seem that from about the beginning of the last quarter of the sixteenth century onward, the Crown had been altogether marginalized in its role in conducting the Portuguese Euro-Asian trade. The spectacular rise of private enterprise, mainly the New Christian merchants, had cut deep into the relative share of the Crown in the volume and value of this trade, though the extent of this decline was almost certainly less, probably substantially less, than the estimates of Boyajian suggest. Also, even in respect of the relatively shrunk pepper trade, the Crown had now become essentially a *rentier*, handing over the actual conduct of business to private enterprise against a monopoly rent.

III

If the Crown had initiated the process of the Portuguese participation in Euro-Asian trade, it did precisely the same in the matter of the intra-Asian trade,

---

[9] Boyajian, *Portuguese Trade in Asia*, pp. 41-44.

[10] Om Prakash, «Was the Portuguese Asian enterprise redistributive?» in Teodoro de Matos and Luís Filipe F. R. Thomaz (ed.), *A Carreira da Índia e as Rotas dos Estreitos, Actas do VIII Seminario Internacional de Historia Indo-Portuguesa*, Angra do Heroísmo, 1998, pp. 551-562.

or what the Portuguese termed «trade from India to India». The Crown's involvement in this trade began in the second decade of the sixteenth century when it used the expertise of the so-called *keling* merchants of Tamil and Telugu origin who had long been settled at Malacca to get initiated into the intricacies of the trade of the Bay of Bengal. But this involvement, a part of which was in the form of collaborative ventures with members of the *keling* community had, however, been rather short-lived. From the beginning of the second half of the sixteenth century onward, the Crown involvement was indirect and confined essentially to giving benefices to private traders as rewards for service. Thus was born the so-called system of concession voyages, which eventually came to constitute the backbone of the Portuguese private merchants' trade within Asia.

A concession conferred on the grantee the right to make a voyage between two specified ports in the Indian Ocean and/or the South China Sea. A concession route could either be to a so-called «reserved» port in which case the concession holder had, in principle, the exclusive right to operate on the route. Or, alternatively, it could pertain to an «open» route in which event the grantee was designated the Captain-major of the fleet (including both Portuguese and non-Portuguese ships) operating on the route. The concession system which had begun in the 1550s had by the 1580s become a major component of the Portuguese trading network in Asia. Luís Filipe Thomaz has listed a total of thirty-four concession voyages in operation in the 1580s covering the China Sea, the Indonesian archipelago and the Bay of Bengal[11].

Many of the concession voyages covered fairly long distances and at least one of them, namely the voyage between Goa-Malacca-Macao-Nagasaki, started in the 1550s, was indeed instrumental in the resumption of the practice of a single voyage traversing all the three geographical segments of Asian trade, namely the Western Indian Ocean, the Bay of Bengal and the South China Sea – a tradition that had been lost ever since the cessation of the Cheng-Ho voyages in the 1430s. Until 1618, the annual voyage consisted of a single large carrack of between 1,200 and 1,600 tons, making it one of the largest ships engaged in intra-Asian trade. The voyage consisted of three segments

[11] Luís Filipe F. R. Thomaz, «Les Portugais dans les mers de l'Archipel au XVIe siècle», *Archipel*, 18 (1979).

– Goa-Malacca, Malacca-Macao and Macao-Hirado/Nagasaki. Different rates of return marked the three segments, often a characteristic feature of long distance trade. By far the most profitable segment was that between Macao and Nagasaki. This segment was, in principle, a monopoly segment, but other vessels are known to have plied this route, probably with the permission of the concession holder. It has been estimated that in the 1580s, Goa's merchants shipped about 250,000 cruzados in silver and other goods each year to Macao on the China-Japan carracks. They extracted from Japan more than 500,000 cruzados of silver annually, much of which returned to Goa and Cochin as silk, musk oil, porcelain and gold coin, after yet another exchange in Macao[12].

It is vitally important to realize that unlike in the case of the official Portuguese enterprise in Asia, the private enterprise continued to do well in the first half of the seventeenth century and in many cases even beyond that. To go back to the Goa-Malacca-Macao-Nagasaki voyage, for example, the chief of the Dutch factory at Hirado, Jacques Specx, had this to say in 1610: «The ship coming from Macao has about 200 or more merchants on board who go ashore at once, each one of them taking a house wherein to lodge with his servants and slaves; they take no heed of what they spend and nothing is too costly for them; and sometimes they disburse in the seven or eight months that they stay in Nagasaki more than 250,000 or 300,000 taels, through which the populace profit greatly; and this is one of the reasons why they are still very friendly to them.»[13] In 1618, António d'Oliviera de Moraes captained the Japan voyage consisting of six galliots. The galliots averaged about three hundred tons and their cargo of Japanese silver must have equalled that carried by the great carracks such as the *Santa Catarina* – that is, in excess of one million cruzados worth. During the 1620s, seven successful voyages consisting of 36 galliots were organized to Nagasaki. A series of nine successful voyages ensued during 1630-1638[14]. Evidently, the Dutch were not as yet in a position to interfere with the Portuguese private trade between Macao and

[12] Boyajian, *Portuguese Trade in Asia*, p. 84.

[13] Quoted in C. R. Boxer, *The Great Ship of Amacon, Annals of Macao and the Old Japan Trade, 1555-1640*, Lisbon, 1959, pp. 15-16.

[14] Boyajian, *Portuguese Trade in Asia*, p. 233.

Nagasaki: it would be highly risky to offend the many influential Japanese, including the Shogun, who invested in the cargoes carried by the Portuguese Japan ships. It was indeed this prosperity of the private Portuguese trade with China and Japan which had persuaded the Portuguese India Company to propose in February 1630 that a trade link be established between Lisbon and Macao, via Mozambique and Malacca. This would have bypassed Goa, normally the compulsory entrepôt for all Portuguese seaborne commerce between Europe and Asia. The move was firmly opposed by Viceroy Linhares and his council at Goa. Linhares pointed out that the large Company vessels would be too slow to evade the Dutch cruisers in the China Sea. More important from Linhares' viewpoint, direct trade with Macao would reduce customs returns at Goa and create unwelcome competition for local merchants engaged in the trade between Goa and the Far East[15]. The lucrative Japan connection, however, effectively came to an end following the expulsion of the Portuguese from Nagasaki in 1639 in pursuance of the new closed-country policy of the Japanese authorities. It is true that through the 1640s, merchants of Macao continued to trade on Chinese vessels between Canton and Nagasaki and other ports. For example, Manuel Dias de Silva indicated that he was investing in Japan trade in 1645, and in one year he spent upwards of 7,500 cruzados preparing the year's sailing to Japan[16]. But the prosperity enjoyed in the period until the close of the 1630s was a thing of the past.

In terms of profitability, the private Portuguese merchants' trade with China and Japan in the first four decades of the seventeenth century almost certainly was at the upper end of the spectrum and was, therefore, not quite representative of the overall performance level in intra-Asian trade taken as a whole. But as the recent detailed work by James Boyajian suggests, the overall position was not altogether too bad either. The kind of desperation and falling average profitability that marked the official Portuguese enterprise during these decades was absent from the private sector. It is also critically important to realize that at least in the case of one major group, namely the New Christians, there was an interactive and dynamic relationship between their intra-Asian trade and their Euro-Asian trade. The goods

[15] Disney, *Twilight of the Pepper Empire*, p. 101.

[16] Boyajian, *Portuguese Trade in Asia*, p. 236.

that formed part of the private cargo put aboard the returning carriera fleet at Goa were procured overwhelmingly through participation in intra-Asian trade which covered the coastal and overland *qafilas* as well as trade on the high seas. Equally importantly, a very substantial part of the capital invested in the intercontinental trade represented the profit earned through an extensive participation in intra-Asian trade. A part of this profit was earned in the form of precious metals-mainly silver-which were critical to the procurement of goods for Europe in places such as parts of the Indian subcontinent. The original investment funds brought from home were thus augmented considerably, accounting in a substantial measure for the overall success of the New Christian merchants' enterprise. The key to the success achieved by these merchants was the interdependent and the complementary character of their Euro-Asian and intra-Asian enterprises. It has, for example, been suggested that in the relevant decades, the Portuguese Crown and private merchants transferred 1-1.5 million cruzados in silver and a few other commodities from Lisbon to Goa each year. To sustain a carreira trade with five million cruzados and more in Lisbon, carreira merchants invested 1.5-2 million in Indian commodities. Therefore, the Portuguese investment in Goa and Cochin consistently exceeded exports to Asia by as much as 500,000 cruzados a year. The principal source of this additional sum was evidently the profit earned in intra-Asian trade[17].

IV

What the above analysis establishes quite conclusively is the complexity and the multi-facedness of the Portuguese enterprise in Asia in its economic dimension. The two principal components of this enterprise – official and private – engaged in a wide range of commercial activities with a fair amount of interlinkage between the two. The following stand out as the principal distinguishing features surrounding these commercial activities. In relation to Euro-Asian trade carried on by the Estado da Índia on behalf of the Crown, the key word was monopoly. Starting with exclusive access to the all-water route

[17] Boyajian, *Portuguese Trade in Asia*, p. 82.

to Asia via the Cape of Good Hope, the notion of monopoly embraced both the procurement as well as the trade in pepper and other spices both within Asia as well as between Asia and Europe. It is another matter that the situation on the ground did not permit a wholesale exclusion either of rival buyers in Malabar or of rival traders operating in the Asian waters or on the intercontinental water-cum-land route via the Middle East. The other outstanding feature of the Portuguese Euro-Asian trade was the enormously important role played in this trade from about 1580 onward by private enterprise, mainly the New Christian merchants. Even after an appropriate adjustment is made in the figures to allow for the admittedly severe methodological problems in Boyajian's estimates, the message is still loud and clear. Private enterprise was not to play such a critical role in intercontinental trade in respect of any of the other European enterprises that succeeded the Portuguese in the seventeenth and the eighteenth centuries. The New Christians also contributed significantly to the diversification of the Portuguese Euro-Asian trade in the matter of the goods exported to Europe as well as the point of their origin in Asia. The success of the New Christian merchants was largely ascribable to their extensive participation in intra-Asian trade which contributed significantly to their overall resource base including supplies of precious metals so critical for conducting business in several parts of Asia. The integrated view that they took of their intra-Asian as well as their Euro-Asian trade was evidently the key to their excellent performance.

Given this complex and multifaced character of the Portuguese enterprise in Asia, it should be obvious that any one label would not capture the totality of its operations. I have argued elsewhere, for example, that the most well-known of these labels, namely that of redistributive enterprise, does not quite fit the bill, though in part it is indeed an appropriate description. Also, if one briefly analyses the functioning of the European enterprises that succeeded the Portuguese in the seventeenth and the eighteenth centuries, it turns out that in many ways the Portuguese had indeed anticipated the commercial strategies of these enterprises further eroding the case for Portuguese exclusivity.

The largest of these enterprises was the Dutch East India Company (VOC) established in 1602 closely followed by the English East India Company which had received its charter from Queen Elizabeth I two years earlier. The notion of monopoly was in many ways even more central to the VOC than it had been to the Portuguese and certainly more effective. In the matter both of the procurement of spices other than pepper in the Indonesian archipelago and Sri Lanka as well as their transportation to and sale in the Netherlands, the Dutch were able to exercise an unprecedentedly effective monopoly control. In its trade within Asia as well, the Dutch East India Company took extensive steps to obtain exclusive rights in particular products and markets and minimize competition by indigenous merchants, making a judicious use of violence in the process. The Company also made an optimal use of the pass system to keep Asian competitors out of the trade in monopoly products such as spices and regulate their trade in several others, such as Malayan tin. If some violation of the prescribed policies and procedures, say by the Indian traders, was tolerated, it was only because the cost of unlimited conflict in the form of possible disruptions to its trade in the Indian subcontinent would have been unacceptably high for the Company[18].

Much as they would have wished to have access to comparable monopoly privileges, the other European enterprises were not particularly successful in this regard. The only exception to this was the English East India Company in relation to its trade in Bengal, and to a smaller extent in other parts of the subcontinent, in the latter half of the eighteenth century. The wresting of political control by the English Company in Bengal involved the substitution of a market-determined relationship between the Company on the one hand and the producers and merchants doing business with it on the other to one of utter domination of the former over the latter obliging them to accept terms substantially below the market. Because of the close nexus between the Company in its corporate dimension and its employees to whom it had left a free field to engage in intra-Asian trade on their private account, the control by proxy over Indian producers and traders was fully exploited by the employees as well. Such a nexus was nowhere more explicit and at times even damaging to the corporate interests of the Company than in the employees' private trade with China[19].

---

[18] Om Prakash, «Asian trade and European impact: A study of the trade from Bengal 1630-1720», in Blair B. Kling and M. N. Pearson (ed.), *The Age of Partnership: Europeans in Asia Before Dominion*, Honolulu, 1979, pp. 43-70.

[19] The details of this argument can be followed in Om Prakash, *European Commercial Enterprise in Pre-colonial India*, Cambridge, 1998, Chapter 7.

The other major area in which the Portuguese had provided a lead was participation in intra-Asian trade. We noted above that the English East India Company left the exploitation of this particular source of profit to its employees operating on their private account. But the Dutch East India Company fine-tuned its participation in what I have elsewhere described as the «great arc of Asian trade» stretching from Persia in the extreme northwest to Japan in the extreme northeast of Asia to a point of near-perfection. Indeed if there is one characteristic feature that distinguished the Dutch East India Company from the other European enterprises was the large scale participation in its corporate capacity in intra-Asian trade as an integral part of its overall commercial strategy. The two principal elements that contributed significantly to the phenomenal success achieved by the Company in its intra-Asian trading network were its spice monopoly and the exclusive access amongst the Europeans to the Japan trade during the latter's «closed-country» era.

While no other European corporate enterprise approached anywhere near the scale and sophisticatedness of the Dutch Company participation in intra-Asian trade, there were interesting variants tried by the French and the minor companies. Soon after the newly organized Compagnie des Indes decided to participate in intra-Asian trade in 1719, it was obvious to the factors at Pondicherry that the Company's financial and other resources were simply not adequate to allow a meaningful participation in this trade entirely on its own. A decision was, therefore, taken to invite the Company's employees as well as other traders, both Indian and European, to collaborate with the Company in the venture. The life span of this unique venture lasted for about twenty years between 1722 and 1741. During the 1720s, the Company took the lead in organizing voyages out of Pondicherry, but the sums invested on the account of the Company were strictly limited. By the end of the decade, French Company employees operating in their private capacity would seem to have become the dominant element in the enterprise[20]. The most well-known of the French private traders, though not the one to have made most money, was Joseph François Dupleix, the head of the Chandernagore factory between 1731 and 1741.

---

[20] Catherine Manning, «French country trade on Coromandel (1720-50)», *Revista de Cultura*, Macao, n.ºs 13/14, January-June, 1991, p. 168.

Between 1726 and 1730, the Ostend Company also engaged in a certain amount of intra-Asian trade. The Company was formally dissolved in 1731, but François de Schonamille, an Antwerp merchant who had served the Company for many years and had been appointed governor after Alexander Hume had deserted to the English in December 1730, stayed on at Bankibazar and kept the factory going until 1744. This he was able to do by engaging in a certain amount of trade on his own account often in collaboration with other important private European traders operating in Bengal at the time[21].

Finally, we might take note of the case of the Danish East India Company as yet another variant on the theme of the European Companies' participation in intra-Asian trade. The Company had been chartered in 1616 and the first fleet on its account consisting of two men-of-war and three merchantmen had left Copenhagen in August 1618 to explore the possibilities of trade in Sri Lanka, the Coromandel coast and the Indonesian archipelago. Given the grossly inadequate support in ships and capital from home, the Danish venture derived its real sustenance from participation in a limited range of coastal as well as high-seas trade within Asia. The coastal trade from Trancquebar southwards extended as far as Sri Lanka. The first high-seas connection developed was that with Tenasserim, where the principal competition was provided by the Portuguese operating from Nagapattinam. The shortage of capital soon forced the conversion of this particular activity into essentially one of a freight service which too was terminated in the early 1630s. The arrival of capital and ships from Copenhagen in April 1624 had in the meantime facilitated the establishment of a more substantive link between Trancquebar and Makassar, the principal outlet for cloves smuggled out of the Moluccas. By the late 1620s, the Danes were sending on a regular basis two ships per annum from Trancquebar to Makassar. They had emerged as reasonably important buyers of cloves in exchange mainly of coarse cotton Coromandel textiles causing a good deal of embarrassment and concern to the VOC.

To conclude, a disaggregation of the economic dimension of the Portuguese enterprise in Asia between its official and private components seri-

[21] Jan Parmentier, *De Holle Compagnie, Smokkel en Legale Handel onder Zuidernederlandse Vlag in Bengalen, Ca. 1720-1744*, Hilversum, 1992, pp. 45, 53-54.

ously discounts the validity and the usefulness of an overall blanket label for this enterprise. Being the first amongst the European enterprises to operate in Asia, while it certainly had features unique to itself such as an extremely large private sector participation in Euro-Asian trade, in many other ways it anticipated what its successors would try to do with varying degrees of success during the seventeenth and the eighteenth centuries.

V

Cooperation and conflict among European traders in the Indian Ocean in the late eighteenth century

The principal agencies instrumental in the running of the Euro-Asian commercial network in the early modern period were the European corporate enterprises—the Portuguese *Estado da Índia* and *Casa da Índia* in the sixteenth century, and the Dutch, the English and the French East India Companies in the seventeenth and the eighteenth centuries. A certain amount of Euro-Asian trade was also carried on by private European traders, though it was probably quantitatively significant only in the case of the Portuguese private traders. As far as European participation in intra-Asian trade was concerned, the only corporate enterprise engaged in it in an important way was the Dutch East India Company. For the rest, it was left overwhelmingly to private traders—the Portuguese (the most important component of the group being the so-called 'New Christian' converts from Judaism), the Dutch (VOC [Verenigde Oost-Indische Compagnie] employees who carried on private trade on a substantial but clandestine basis), the French, and most important of all the English who were allowed to engage in trade on their private account while continuing to be in the service of the Company. Many of these traders used their intermediary role in the Euro-Asian diamond trade (which was outside the East India Company's monopoly) as commissioners to raise the necessary capital resources for investment in trade on their private account.

The afore-mentioned entities—whether corporate or private—operating in the Indian Ocean-South China Sea complex had an extremely variegated relationship both among themselves as well as with the Indian maritime merchants engaged in intra-Asian trade, and competing with them along routes common to both. A key element that permeated all these relationships for a long time was the relative absence of coercive authority available to any one of the players over another. This scenario, however, underwent a fundamental alteration in the second half of the eighteenth century when the English East India Company gained political authority in several parts of the Indian subcontinent. The most far-reaching changes occurred in Bengal following the assumption by the Company in 1765 of *diwani* rights in the province. Fellow corporate enterprises functioning in the province such as the Dutch and the French East India Companies were among the principal victims of the newly found authority of the English East India Company. For example, the growing English stranglehold over the textile weavers, obliging an increasing proportion of them to work exclusively for the English Company, made it difficult for the Dutch and the French to procure an adequate quantity of textiles. In 1767, the Dutch proposed to the English that they should be assigned weavers in the various production centres who would then be allowed to work for them without hindrance. Since the English formally took the position that the Dutch, as indeed all other Europeans, were perfectly free to carry on their trade in the province, this was agreed to in principle but eventually nothing came of the proposal.[1] A Fort William public notification dated 28 April 1775 even asserted 'that the weavers of the province of Bengal and Bihar should enjoy a perfect and entire liberty to deal with any persons whom they pleased and that no person should use force of any kind to oblige the weavers or other manufacturers to receive advances of money or to engage in contracts for the provision of clothes against their will, and that all persons offending against this order should suffer severe punishment'.[2] The charade was continued in the English response dated 8 September 1785 to a Dutch memorandum: 'Under your agents, they [the weavers] may work more freely perhaps than under our own, and you may rest assured that we shall not countenance the servants or gomastahs of our own Board of Trade in any attempts that they may make to oppress the natives who work for you and not us, or prevent your employment of their industry. The weaver who works for your Company contributes equally to pay the revenue, with the weaver who works for our own Board of Trade, and perhaps more so. And an extension to the sale of Bengal manufacture is more profitable to Great Britain than a monopoly in the purchase of such goods as would restrain the manufacture'.[3] The truth, however, was otherwise and the Dutch procurement continued to suffer heavily.

The coercive authority available to the English Company (and by extension to its servants engaged in trade on their private account) was used not only in respect of the rival European corporate enterprises and private European traders but also in relation to the Indian merchants engaged in intra-Asian trade. Apart from textiles, the most widespread misuse of this authority took place in the procurement of

[1] Algemeen Rijksarchief, The Hague (henceforth ARA), Memoir prepared by Dutch director, George Louis Vernet, and submitted to the English on 10 May 1768, Hooge Regeering Batavia (henceforth HRB) 247; J.M. Ross at Khirpai to Director at Hugli, 8 July 1767, Appendix D, HRB 247.

[2] ARA, the notification was signed by J.P. Auriol, Assistant Secretary, HRB 253.

[3] ARA, the English Company reply dated 8 September 1785 to the second Dutch memorandum, Macpherson and Council to Eilbracht and van Citters, HRB 211.

and trade in opium. Soon after the take-over of Bengal, English Company servants stationed in Bihar established private monopolies in the drug. From 1765 onward, the factors at Patna decided to operate jointly and divide the profits from the venture on the basis of each person's status in the hierarchy. In 1773, the Company decided to assume monopoly rights in the drug for itself. The arrangement was for the Company to organise the procurement of the drug on an exclusive basis and then arrange for its sale to prospective traders through public auctions held at Calcutta. The adverse effect that this had on the trade of the rivals including the Dutch East India Company—its servants engaged in trade in the drug on a clandestine basis—and the Indian merchants trading with the eastern sections of the Indian Ocean, was quite substantial.

While it is true that the impact of the altered status of the English East India Company was felt most acutely in Bengal, the other regions of the subcontinent were by no means immune from it. On the Coromandel coast, for example, the 1750s and the 1760s witnessed the acquisition by the Company of extensive land-revenue collection rights in key textile-producing districts in the Northern Circars and central Coromandel, giving it an unprecedented degree of control over the textile merchants and weavers in the area. The Company even demarcated looms on which textiles would henceforth be produced exclusively for itself.

The situation was not very different on the west coast after the English takeover of the Surat castle in 1759. The Mughal notable 'Meah Achan' was allowed to continue as the Nawab but was made subordinate to the authority of the new English *qiladar*. The English also appropriated to themselves the right to mediate in all disputes between the local merchants and the rival European Companies. While the Dutch Company was formally assured both before and after the takeover that its right to trade in the province unhindered would in no way stand compromised, the facts were different. The real whipping boys of the English in Gujarat, however, were the Portuguese and not the Dutch.

The last quarter of the eighteenth century had witnessed a striking revival of the Portuguese Euro-Asian trade. In the preceding century, the establishment of the Portuguese India Company in 1628 had represented in some sense the last desperate attempt to make the Euro-Asian pepper trade conducted on the Crown's account viable. But the experiment had not been particularly successful, and as early as April 1633 it had been decided to dissolve the Company. The last batch of cargo on the account of the Company left Goa in 1634. The Crown monopoly of pepper was partially relaxed in 1642 with the rights of the *Casa da Índia* being confined to purchasing the pepper on arrival in Lisbon at a pre-determined price. But the arrangement failed to stimulate the trade to any significant extent. The tonnage leaving Asia for Lisbon which had stood at 13,710 tons during 1631–40 went up during 1641–50 only to 16,030 tons. In the second half of the seventeenth century, it was only during 1671–80 that this figure exceeded 10,000 tons.[4] The

[4] T. Bentley Duncan, 'Navigation between Portugal and Asia in the Sixteenth and Seventeenth Centuries', in E.J. van Kley and C.K. Pullapilly, eds, *Asia and the West: Encounters and Exchanges from the Age of Explorations*, Notre Dame, 1986, p. 22.

greater part of the eighteenth century also saw the Euro-Asian trade of the Portuguese languish at a relatively low level. The closing decades of the century, however, witnessed a striking revival of this trade mainly because of Portuguese neutrality in the European wars of the period. Until the French invaded Portugal in 1807, and indeed until the end of the wars in 1815, Lisbon was revived as a major entrepôt for the import of Asian goods into Europe, particularly Chinese tea and Indian textiles. Between 1780 and 1788, as many as 41 ships are recorded as having arrived at Goa from Lisbon. In a good year such as 1785, this number could be as many as nine.[5] This growth continued in the 1790s, with particular emphasis on textiles procured at Surat. The arrival of the *Rainha dos Anjos* at Bombay in 1796 with several lakhs of rupees worth of capital for investment in Surat textiles, together with the news that the Company that had sponsored this trip intended to appoint a consul-general and resident at Surat, alarmed the English East India Company enough to enforce Bengal-like restrictions on the Portuguese procurement of textiles at Surat. The Nawab was persuaded to extract a penalty bond from the principal brokers of the city to the effect that they would not sell goods to anybody without his consent. At the same time, agreements were made with the principal manufacturers and weavers by the English Company brokers obliging the former to produce textiles only for them. Sepoys were deployed in the streets and over looms to deter the Portuguese from buying up the piece goods on which the Company had advanced money. When the Portuguese protested against such coercive measures, the Bombay Council instructed the Nawab to withdraw the embargo. The Commercial Board at Surat, however, defied Bombay and argued that the system followed by them was only 'restrictive' rather than 'coercive'.[6] In January 1798, the Board reported that it had been forced to use the Nawab's authority to compel the *khatri* weavers to fulfil their engagements, as the contractors declared that they could do nothing without the intervention of government. In February 1798, the Supreme Government at Calcutta reviewed all the reports from Surat which it had received through Bombay and announced its conclusion that the Company must assume more authority.[7]

No such problems, however, had to be faced by the Portuguese private merchants engaged in intra-Asian trade. Unlike the trade with Europe, this trade had continued on a reasonably vigorous basis through the seventeenth and the eighteenth centuries, though there obviously were ups and downs. A case in point is the private Portuguese trade from the Coromandel coast. The loss of Nagapattinam to the Dutch in 1658 had indeed constituted a setback to the Portuguese trade from the coast. But their response was to relocate themselves in large numbers at the port of Porto Novo to the north, which over the last quarter of the seventeenth century emerged as a major country-trading port. An analysis on the basis of information

[5] Celsa Pinto, *Trade and Finance in Portuguese India*, Delhi, 1994, Appendix 4, p. 270.

[6] Lakshmi Subramanian, *Indigenous Capital and Imperial Expansion, Bombay, Surat and the West Coast*, Delhi, 1996, pp. 260–62.

[7] Pamela Nightingale, *Trade and Empire in Western India 1784–1806*, Cambridge, 1970, pp. 162–63.

available in the Dutch shipping lists of the ownership pattern of the ships, excluding Company ships and small coastal craft, that left this port between 1681–82 and 1685–86 for various Asian destinations shows that the Portuguese were a major group of merchants owning ships and operating from this port. The number of ships departing and owned by this group was seven out of a total of 19 in 1681–82, six out of 14 in 1682–83, six out of 10 in 1683–84 and 1684–85, and seven out of 14 in 1685–86. The single most important shipowner among the Portuguese was one Manuel Teixeira Pinto. By far the most important port of destination for the Portuguese shipping from Porto Novo was Aceh, followed by Pegu, Melaka, Goa and Manila.[8]

Elsewhere in Asia, by far the most vibrant and prosperous group of private Portuguese traders was the one based at Macao. The Dutch East India Company records pertaining to foreign shipping movement at Batavia, for example, establish beyond any doubt the relative importance of Portuguese shipping from Macao in the pepper trade between Batavia and China. The Portuguese shipowners also carried substantial quantities of freight cargo belonging to English, French, Armenian and other merchants trading in the Indian Ocean/South China Sea complex. Indeed, in the 1720s, the Portuguese from Macao are known to have bought ships at Batavia to enhance their fleet's total cargo capacity. At Canton, they demanded and received exhorbitant freight rates from Chinese merchants. The purchase of some of the ships by the Portuguese was made possible, it was claimed, by capital advanced by Cantonese merchants, some of whom had moved to Macao.[9]

With the resumption of the Dutch East India Company's direct trade to China in the 1730s, the Portuguese and the Chinese merchants operating at Batavia faced increasing problems. This necessitated growing concentration by the Macao Portuguese on specific sources of supply as well as markets in the Indian Ocean. An analysis of the Dutch shipping lists, as well as the information available in the English Company records for the period 1719 to 1754, shows that Portuguese ships called with varying frequency at the ports of Bengal, at Madras and Nagapattinam on the Coromandel coast, at Cochin, Tellicherry and Anjengo on the Malabar coast, and at Surat. Some of these ships, particularly those calling at Surat, are known to have in fact been owned by Asian merchants, flying the Portuguese flag for convenience. By far the most important ports of call for the genuine Portuguese shipping were Cochin, Tellicherry and Madras. Over the period 1719 to 1754, Portuguese shipping called at Cochin regularly between 1723 and 1742 except in 1733, with the number of ships each year varying between two and six. Between one and four of these ships were Macao-based. From the early 1740s onward, the main Malabar port of call was Tellicherry, with the number of ships in a year often being as many as six and reaching the top figure of eight in 1749. This shipping was also dominated by that from Macao. The principal commodity carried to

[8] Sanjay Subrahmanyam, 'Staying On: The Portuguese of Southern Coromandel in the Late Seventeenth Century', *The Indian Economic and Social History Review*, Vol. 22 (4), 1985, pp. 445–63.

[9] George B. Souza, *The Survival of Empire: Portuguese Trade and Society in China and the South China Sea 1630–1754*, Cambridge, 1986, pp. 128–32.

Malabar was Chinese sugar which was exchanged there mainly against pepper and sandalwood. In the case of Madras, the only years between 1719 and 1754 when Portuguese shipping did not call at the port were 1734, 1741, 1747 to 1749, and 1754. The numbers each year, however, were generally more modest than those at Cochin and later Tellicherry, varying between one and five. Most of these ships were also Macao-based.[10] The emergence in the second half of the eighteenth century of English private traders as major competitors in the Indian Ocean and the South China Sea undoubtedly affected the trade of the Macao merchants adversely. But this did not prevent them from continuing to be an important segment of the trading community in the region.[11] Thus, a 'list of ships and smaller vessels together with their cargo, weaponry and manpower aboard which arrived at and departed from Melaka in the year 1763',[12] records the arrival in the month of January of four Portuguese vessels, all from Macao on their way to Malabar with a cargo of sugar, spelter, radix China, alum and porcelain. The trip from Macao to Melaka had taken the four ships between 16 and 27 days. The 1780s also witnessed a certain amount of trade in Indian cotton and opium being carried on with China by the Portuguese traders, based mainly in Macao. In order to facilitate this trade, a Company was set up in Goa, in 1788 with 69 shareholders holding 200 shares collectively, each worth 2000 *xerafins.*[13]

The relationship of the Portuguese trading community with fellow Asian merchants as well as with the competing European private merchants and corporate enterprises operating in the Indian Ocean/South China Sea complex was essentially one of acute rivalry often bordering on unconcealed antagonism. But at the same time there were important and unexpected areas of cooperation between individual Portuguese traders on the one hand and individual Asian and non-Portuguese European traders and even European corporate enterprises on the other. At times, of course, what began as an episode of cooperation might eventually turn into one of conflict. The rest of this essay examines in some detail the nitty-gritty of such dealings in relation to two episodes in the 1780s against the backdrop of the Fourth Anglo-Dutch War. We are able to follow the two episodes in such close detail only because their growing complexity obliged the Batavia authorities of the Dutch East India Company, which was involved indirectly or directly in both the episodes, to bring the entire correspondence together with its enclosures to the attention of the Directors of the Company at Amsterdam. This correspondence has survived and is preserved at the *Algemeen Rijksarchief*, The Hague.

The first case I will take up for discussion involved a Portuguese merchant, João Barreto, based at Bombay, the supercargoes of the English East India Company at Canton, the second-in-command of the Dutch East India Company's

[10] *Ibid.*, pp. 156–68.

[11] The Dutch shipping lists for the 1760s, for example, record the continuing arrival of Macao shipping at Nagapattinam (See shipping list for 1764, ARA, VOC 3077, ff. 1139–40 and for 1766, VOC 3164, ff. 607–08).

[12] ARA, VOC 4877 (unfoliated).

[13] Pinto, *Trade and Finance in Portuguese India*, p. 36.

establishment at Surat, upper-merchant Abraham Josias Sluysken, and Muhammad Saleh Chellaby of a well-known Turkish merchant clan in Surat. The Chellabies had come to Surat probably from Iraq in the mid-seventeenth century. At the turn of the eighteenth century, the leading merchant of this clan, Muhammad Saleh Chellaby, was among the most important merchants of Surat. The sequence of events involving the four parties to the dispute was as follows.[14] In March 1781, Sluysken hired from Chellaby a ship called *Istanbul* for a return trip to Canton. The hire charges were agreed at the figure of Rs 3,101 per month with a minimum liability of Rs 31,010. In the event of the ship being retained by Sluysken beyond a period of ten months, additional hire charges would become due pro rata. All expenses of equipping and provisioning the ship as well as a salary of Rs 50 per month together with double ration for a representative of Chellaby who was to travel in the ship were to be borne by Sluysken. The representative was to be provided by Chellaby with pearls worth Rs 500 to be sold against goods at Canton on Chellaby's account. The cost of any repairs to the ship while in the custody of Sluysken was to be shared by Chellaby only to the extent of 10 per cent. In the event of an attack on the ship, the owner was to bear the cost of only half of the ammunition used in its defence. Finally, the ship was to be returned to the owner in the same condition in which it had been given to the freighter.[15]

After collecting the ship from Chellaby, Sluysken renamed it *De Goede Hoop* and dispatched it to Canton in April 1781. But before the ship could enter the port, it was seized by an English Company fleet under the command of one Captain McClary. This was a consequence of England having declared war on Holland on 20 December 1780, over secret Dutch trade and negotiations with the American colonies then in revolt against England. Information regarding the outbreak of the Fourth Anglo-Dutch War had since reached Asia and the ship was seized as enemy property. The Dutch factors in Surat including Sluysken as well as those at the other Dutch establishments in India were placed in detention and declared prisoners of war. On receipt of information regarding the seizure of the ship, Sluysken and Chellaby entered into an understanding on 8 June 1782 with the following stipulations. Considering that the war might well be a prolonged one and the ship would in all probability be subject to damage and deterioration while in detention at Canton, Sluysken agreed to instruct his factors on the ship to hand it over to anybody named by the owner. The liability of Sluysken would be limited to the payment of the hire charges for the minimum period of ten months besides the salary of Chellaby's representative travelling on the ship, till such time as the ship was released by the English. In the event of Sluysken being eventually compensated by the English for the losses suffered by him, he would share the proceeds

[14] Details of this case are available in a volume entitled 'Stukken betreffende in het 1782 te Canton in China gehuurde en aan een Engels onderdaan verkogte schip "De Goede Hoop" door den Ondercoopman en Secunde te Souratte Sluysken 1782–1790', ARA, HRB 864. The volume is not foliated.

[15] Agreement between Sluysken and Chellaby dated 24 March 1781 regarding the hiring of the *Istanbul* by the former, ARA, HRB 864.

with Chellaby by suitably enhancing the hire charges payable by him. Having obtained Sluysken's consent to relinquish any claim to the ship, Chellaby entered into an arrangement with João Barreto who agreed to buy the ship from Chellaby for a sum of Rs 86,000 and collect it from Sluysken's men at whatever port near Canton the ship happened to be berthed at. In order to facilitate the transfer, Sluysken agreed to the request of Chellaby to sign a sale-deed stating that the ship belonged to him and that he was selling it to Barreto. Sluysken also committed himself to compensating Chellaby suitably in the unlikely event of his factors aboard the ship not obeying his instructions to hand the ship over to Barreto or his nominee. On his side, Chellaby stated explicitly that notwithstanding the fact that Sluysken had stated in writing that he had received an advance payment of Rs 86,000 from João Barreto for the ship, Sluysken had indeed received no such payment and owed nothing on this account to Chellaby. Chellaby further stated that he had received adequate assurance regarding the payment by Barreto of the sum of Rs 86,000 and an additional further sum mutually agreed upon between them. As soon as news was received at Surat that the ship had been handed over to his nominee, Barreto would make the payment at Surat. All these details were included in an agreement signed between Sluysken and Chellaby at Surat on 22 June 1782.[16]

On being approached for the release of the ship, the English supercargoes at Canton refused to oblige, making the plea that the sale of the vessel was illegal in as much as a Dutch national could not be permitted to sell ships or war ammunition to an English subject (Barreto) while the two countries were at war. A formal resolution to this effect was adopted by the English Commercial Council at Canton on 1 November 1782. On 2 January 1783, a copy of the resolution was sent to the Governor-General and Council at Batavia in the form of a letter of protest against the proposed sale of the vessel. The letter was forwarded to Van der Graaf, extraordinary member of the Batavia Council in Sri Lanka, for the observations of Sluysken. In his letter of 15 October 1783, Sluysken maintained that since he had hired the ship from Chellaby in March 1781 before news regarding the outbreak of the Fourth Anglo-Dutch War had reached Asia, he had done nothing illegal. Also at no point in time had he owned the ship and had nothing to do with its sale to Barreto except for lending his name to the transaction.[17]

The Fourth Anglo-Dutch War ended in May 1784 but the matter of *De Goede Hoop* was still pending. On 30 July 1784, the Batavia Council noted that the English supercargoes at Canton had in the meantime brought the matter directly to the attention of the Board of Directors in Amsterdam, the *Heeren XVII*. In their letter of 12 December 1786, the *Heeren XVII* rebuked the Batavia Council for treating the matter as being beyond its jurisdiction and asked it to take appropriate action. However, the only action Batavia took was to send the entire

[16] Agreement between Sluysken and Chellaby dated 22 June 1782, ARA, HRB 864.

[17] Letter from Sluysken to Governor-General Altine and Council at Batavia dated 15 October 1783, ARA, HRB 864.

correspondence pertaining to the case over to the *Heeren XVII*. But the matter was still pending in 1788 and the final outcome of the case is not recorded.[18]

The other case on which we have a considerably greater degree of detail available in a manuscript volume of several hundred folios,[19] pertains to the dealings in the 1780s between a Portuguese private trader, José Ribeiro de Macedo based on the west coast of India and active in the trade with Southeast Asia as well as China on the one hand and the Sri Lanka and Batavia establishments of the Dutch East India Company on the other. It is remarkable how a relationship that began on the most positive of notes soon evolved into one of bitter conflict with factions within the VOC playing distinctly partisan roles.

In common with many other establishments of the Company, the Dutch East India Company establishment at Sri Lanka with its headquarters at Colombo was afflicted with a serious liquidity crisis in the early 1780s. Batavia had been unable to send the promised f. 600,000 needed there and it was getting nearly impossible to raise resources locally. The community of Dutch burghers on the island was not in a position to lend any more to the Company; the establishment at Malabar was itself in difficulty and had already approached Colombo for assistance.[20] On 28 January 1783, therefore, at a secret meeting of the Colombo Council, a resolution was adopted to try and raise a sum of Rs 200,000 in the Surat market from Nanabhai, the second son of the renowned Bania merchant of Surat, Bhai Shah.

Considering that the Company's own factors at Surat were under detention by the English East India Company ever since news regarding the outbreak of the Fourth Anglo-Dutch War had reached India, it was decided to raise the loan through José Ribeiro de Macedo who would then make the amount available to the Company at Colombo. The Company would be willing to pay the usual 0.75 per cent monthly rate of interest as also stand surety for the repayment of the loan. The surety document would be signed by Governor Iman Willem Falck on behalf of the Company. The resolution went on to authorise Van der Graaf, extraordinary member of the Batavia Council at whose initiative the entire project had been undertaken, to tell Ribeiro that an incentive he could use to persuade Nanabhai to make the loan available was that if the latter were interested and made an appropriate request, he would be appointed the broker of the Company at Surat as soon as the Company's functioning was resumed there at the end of the war, in the vacancy caused by the death of broker Govind Ram. In case this inducement

[18] Extract from a resolution adopted by the Batavia Council on 30 July1784; Extract from a letter from Batavia to Surat, 10 August 1784; Extract from a letter from Batavia to *Heeren XVII*, 27 October 1784; Extract from letters from *Heeren XVII* to Batavia, 3 November 1785 and 12 December 1786; Extract from a letter from Batavia to *Heeren XVII*, 13 November 1787; Extract from the Batavia Council resolution of 29 January 1788. All these documents are in ARA, HRB 864.

[19] The volume is titled 'Kopie-verbaal betreffende de geldlening van een Portugese koopman in Goa aan het Nederlandse gouvernement van Ceylon, 1785–1786' and is available under ARA, VOC 10112. The volume is not foliated.

[20] Secret letter from Governor Iman Willem Falck and Council at Colombo to Batavia, 7 February 1783, ARA, VOC 10112.

was not found to be adequate, Nanabhai was to be further told that the Company would help him recover from the English Company the sum of Rs 100,000 together with the interest accrued on it. This amount had been given in loan by the firm of Bhai Shah to the VOC in March 1781. Bills of exchange negotiated against this sum and deposited with the firm for payment to the Company's textile suppliers had been confiscated by the English at the time of the takeover of the Dutch assets. In case the efforts to recover the sum from the English Company after the conclusion of peace were eventually unsuccessful, the Dutch Company would take over the liability of paying the firm.[21] Should such extraordinarily generous terms nevertheless be found wanting in persuading Nanabhai to loan the sum of Rs 200,000 to Ribeiro, the latter was to try and raise the loan from another creditor. The surety document signed by Falck and given to Ribeiro was therefore to include a clause that its validity would not be limited to the transaction concluded with Nanabhai but would cover a loan raised from anyone else. Should such a creditor happen to be a European who preferred to be repaid in Europe, the Company would arrange payment in Amsterdam within six weeks of the presentation of the necessary claim. The rate of conversion used would be 100 Surat or Bombay rupees as equivalent to 135 Dutch guilders. The surety document also provided that should the creditor choose to be repaid in terms of goods, then he would be free to collect the same in Sri Lanka or Batavia. The goods that would be offered for purchase by him, together with their prices, were specified in the document.[22] The only requirement imposed upon Ribeiro was that he had to ensure that the funds reached Sri Lanka before the onset of the south-west monsoon in mid-April. He was offered a commission of 2.5 per cent of the sum to be raised in loan as compensation for his efforts.[23] The proposal was approved by Batavia in their secret letter to Colombo dated 25 April 1783.[24]

Ribeiro carried out the commission successfully and delivered Rs 200,000 to the Colombo factors in April 1783. He, however, did not use the surety document 'because that might have brought him into problems with the English'. Also the money was raised not from Nanabhai but from a Parsi merchant of Bombay, Nausherwanji Manekji, at the usual rate of interest of 0.75 per cent per month. Colombo believed that the burden of interest payment would not have to be borne for a period of more than two months or so in so far as the loan could be repaid at Batavia in the form of goods in July.[25]

Since loans could be negotiated only against adequate security, Ribeiro had been obliged to insure two of his ships the *Esperança* and the *Flor de Goa* together

[21] Resolution adopted at the secret meeting of the Colombo Council, 28 January 1783, ARA, VOC 10112.

[22] Surety dated 29 January 1783 bearing the signature of Iman Willem Falck and the Company seal in red lac, ARA, VOC 10112.

[23] Resolution adopted at the secret meeting of the Colombo Council, 28 January 1783, ARA, VOC 10112.

[24] Secret letter from Batavia to Colombo, 25 April 1783, ARA, VOC 10112.

[25] Secret letter from Colombo to Batavia, 5 June 1783, ARA, VOC 10112.

with two smaller vessels against a sum of Rs 240,000 at an unusually high premium and deposit the insurance letters as security with Nausherwanji Manekji. Ribeiro was also obliged to employ the two ships on a trip to Batavia notwithstanding the fact that he had been planning to send the *Flor de Goa* to Bengal with cargo that he had already bought. Ribeiro also undertook to invest one-third of the total loan of Rs 200,000 in goods at Batavia on the account of Nausherwanji Manekji and transport the goods free of freight to Bombay. Ribeiro claimed that he was also not entitled to any commission or reimbursement of costs in relation to this obligation.[26]

In view of the special efforts and costs incurred in raising the loan for the VOC, Ribeiro requested that for a period of four to five years he be treated at par with burghers of Batavia and together with his nominees be exempted from the payment of harbour dues and other taxes there. Since Colombo was not authorised to take a decision in the matter, they referred it to Batavia with a strong recommendation that Ribeiro's request be granted. They were particularly encouraged to do so, they pointed out, by Ribeiro's offer to provide them with another Rs 200,000, an offer that had been readily accepted. This was done by giving the factors a bill of exchange for this amount payable at Goa forty days after sight. In addition, Ribeiro offered a sum of Rs 400,000–500,000 by December 1784 and collect in repayment goods at Batavia at prices specified in the surety document provided to him earlier by the Colombo factors. The loans raised by him would be at his own cost and risk, the only liability of the Company being the payment of interest at 0.75 per cent per month for the period between the receipt of the amount at Colombo and its repayment at Batavia.[27]

In their letter of 22 July 1783, Batavia informed Colombo that while they were unable to accede to Ribeiro's request for being treated at par with the burghers of Batavia for a period of four to five years, they would be willing in view of his services to the Company to extend to him during the current year the privileges that the merchants from Macao enjoyed at Batavia.[28] In the meantime, one of Ribeiro's ships, the *Esperança*, had reached Batavia from Goa via Sri Lanka. At Ribeiro's request, permission was granted for the ship to be repaired at the Company's shipyard on the island of Onrust.[29] However, when the person in charge of the shipyard reported that the vessel was leaking far too much and it was not entirely safe to have it repaired at the yard, Ribeiro was asked to divert the ship to another island, De Kuyper, for repairs.[30]

An important clause in the terms the factors at Colombo had offered to Ribeiro while requesting him to raise a loan for them was that the creditor would be entitled, if he so desired, to receive repayment of the loan in the form of goods at Sri Lanka or Batavia. These goods as well as the prices at which they would be offered

[26] *Ibid.*
[27] *Ibid.*
[28] Secret letter from Batavia to Colombo, 22 July 1783, ARA, VOC 10112.
[29] Resolution of the Batavia Council, 18 July 1783, ARA, VOC 10112.
[30] *Ibid.*, 22 July 1783, ARA, VOC 10112.

were specified in detail in the surety document the factors had provided to Ribeiro. This was something the Colombo factors had done on their own without prior authorisation from Batavia. As it happened, almost from the very beginning, this became a source of conflict between Ribeiro and Batavia, a conflict that eventually assumed serious proportions with other elements being introduced in it as time passed.

Being himself the creditor to the Company, Ribeiro asked for the first lot of goods, consisting of tin and sugar, at Batavia in July 1783. On the ground that the Company itself needed all the tin it had in stock for the two ships it planned to send to China soon, the request for tin was turned down. Japanese bar copper was offered instead. As for sugar, Ribeiro was authorised to buy the amount asked for from private parties at Batavia.[31] Ribeiro took up the offer in respect of the bar copper and was supplied with 400 *piculs* asked for, at the price agreed upon at Colombo.[32] The following month Ribeiro asked for spices. While his requirement of cloves was met in full, that of nutmeg and mace was accommodated only to the extent of 50 per cent.[33] Ribeiro then decided to write to the Batavia Council reminding it of the terms that had been offered to him at Colombo and reiterating his request to be treated at par with the burghers of Batavia for a period of four to five years. While the Council did not respond in the matter of the goods to be sold to Ribeiro, it extended the period over which the privileges usually made available only to the merchants from Macao would be available to Ribeiro by another year, in respect of a maximum of two ships that he might bring on his account into Batavia.[34]

In a strongly-worded confidential letter to Colombo in October 1783, the Governor-General and Council at Batavia admonished the Governor and factors there for exceeding their brief, and unauthorisedly promising to Ribeiro the sale of goods at Batavia at pre-determined prices, a promise to which he was now holding the Company. If fulfilled, it even held the risk of working against the Company's own trade on the west coast of India. Batavia went on to say that while it recognised the services rendered by Ribeiro, it did not believe his claim that while raising the loan for the Company, he had to insure his ships at an unusually high premium or that he had been obliged to undertake to invest one-third of the loan in buying goods at Batavia on behalf of the creditor and to transport them to Bombay free of freight-charges and without being recompensed for associated costs. But since they nevertheless felt committed to honouring a formal agreement, they had supplied Ribeiro with goods at prices agreed upon at Colombo. But it had been impossible to do so in respect of tin because of inadequate stocks. The factors were directed never to enter into such an arrangement in future.[35]

[31] *Ibid.*, 25 July 1783, ARA, VOC 10112.

[32] *Ibid.*, 29 July 1783, ARA, VOC 10112.

[33] *Ibid.*, 15 August 1783, ARA, VOC 10112.

[34] *Ibid.*, 26 August 1783, ARA, VOC 10112.

[35] Secret letter from the Governor-General and Council at Batavia to the Governor and Council at Colombo, 14 October 1783, ARA, VOC 10112.

On being thus chastised, Colombo immediately got in touch with Van Angelbeek, the Dutch governor of Malabar at Cochin, requesting that the processing of the bill of exchange for Rs 200,000 on Goa that had been given by Ribeiro to the Colombo factors, and which they had forwarded in June 1783 to Cochin for collection, be stopped immediately till such time as clearance for the same had been obtained from Batavia.[36] In March 1784, however, Cochin reported back to Colombo that already before the receipt of their letter of 25 November 1783, the document had been sent on to one Gracias at Goa for collection. Gracias had delayed the dispatch of the funds pending clarification on whose account the risk on the way from Goa to Cochin was to be assigned. No further progress in the matter had been made till Ribeiro himself came to Cochin and paid to the factors there a sum of Rs 140,000 mostly in gold coins. The remaining amount of Rs 60,000 was settled by a bill of exchange issued on the house of David Scott at Bombay. The Cochin factors gave this bill to an Englishman locally, in settlement of the cost of the 7,000 sacks of saltpetre bought from him eventually to be used as ballast on the return ships from Colombo to Europe. The Rs 140,000 received in cash were being sent on to Colombo with Ribeiro.[37]

Ribeiro reached Colombo with the *Minerva* on 29 March 1784 and presented a memorandum to Governor Falck and the Colombo Council on 3 April detailing the salient points in his dealings with the Company over the last year or so. He pointed out that it was Van der Graaf, the extraordinary member of the Batavia Council, who had approached him, as could be seen from his letter of 31 January 1783, with an urgent request to raise a sum of Rs 200,000 for the Company and have it delivered at Colombo by 15 April 1783. Ribeiro had to put in an extraordinary amount of effort to arrange the loan 'and I know of no other deal that has caused me as much inconvenience'.[38] Due to unavoidable circumstances, he had not been able to make use of the surety document provided to him and had to raise the loan against his personal credit. He had not charged the Company the 2.5 per cent commission (amounting to Rs 5,000) that he had been offered. He had also borne the cost of insuring the money on its way between Bombay and Colombo amounting to 4 per cent of the total sum. He had in addition provided a second loan of Rs 200,000 to the Colombo factors. His liability on that transaction was limited to arranging for the delivery of the amount at Goa. But he had himself delivered it to Van Angelbeek at Cochin again bearing the 2 per cent cost of insurance of the amount between Goa and Cochin himself. He had finally brought the amount in his own ship to Colombo charging the Company neither for the cost of transportation nor for the risk of loss of the amount on the way.[39]

[36] Letters from the Governor and Council at Colombo to Van Angelbeek and Council at Cochin, 14 June 1783 and 25 November 1783, ARA, VOC 10112.

[37] Letter from Van Angelbeek and Council at Cochin to the Governor and Council at Colombo, 21 March 1784, ARA, VOC 10112.

[38] Letter from Ribeiro at Colombo to Iman Willem Falck and the Colombo Council, 3 April 1784, ARA, VOC 10112; Letter from Colombo to Batavia, 9 April 1784, ARA, VOC 10112.

[39] Letter from Ribeiro at Colombo to Iman Willem Falck and the Colombo Council, 3 April 1784, ARA, VOC 10112.

It was thus clear, Ribeiro claimed, that he had more than fulfilled his part of the deal. When he had travelled from Colombo to Batavia in 1783, therefore, he had full expectations that the Governor-General and Council at Batavia would honour their side of the bargain. On arrival at Batavia, he had put in his demand for the delivery of goods but he had been told that the factors at Colombo had no authority to enter into such a deal with him. The authorities at Batavia were, therefore, not obliged to honour it and that he was free to buy goods wherever he wanted. At this point, he had told the Batavia Council that the surety document provided to him, as well as the formal agreement with him, had been signed by Falck on behalf of the States of the United Netherlands and the Dutch East India Company. It was no concern of his if Falck had exceeded his brief. Under the terms of the agreement, Batavia was obliged to supply him goods listed in the surety document at prices specified there up to the value of the loan given by him to the factors at Colombo together with the interest on it. Ribeiro reminded the Colombo factors of the sacred nature of a contract which must be fulfilled in all its aspects. He pointed out that he had a formal right to insist on being supplied with goods at Batavia up to a total value of Rs 400,000 plus interest, but that in a spirit of accommodation he would be satisfied if goods worth Rs 200,000 plus interest were made available to him there.[40]

The factors at Colombo forwarded Ribeiro's memorandum to Batavia on 9 April 1784 with a strong recommendation that his demands be accepted. They also pointed out that the prices specified in the surety document in respect of the goods that the creditor could ask for at Batavia were not at all unfavourable to the Company. To take an example, it was pointed out that the price of Rs 55 per 100 lbs. in the case of Japanese bar copper was but Rs 5 (or 8.33 per cent) lower than the sale price at Surat. Indeed, the money equivalent of the risk involved in sending this and other items to Surat by sea on the Company's own account was much greater. The letter closed by gently warning Batavia that in case the terms of the contract with Ribeiro were not fulfilled at the Company's end, the credibility of the Company in general and that of the establishment at Sri Lanka in particular would be damaged beyond repair.[41]

Batavia's response to these pleas was contained in the Council's resolutions of 15, 22 and 25 June 1784. With a view to avoiding possible complications arising out of non-fulfilment of the obligations enjoined by the Sri Lanka agreement, it was decided to supply to Ribeiro tin, sugar and other goods up to a maximum value of Rs 200,000 plus interest, at prices specified in the surety document subject to the availability of stocks in the Company's warehouses. Ribeiro was also to be permitted to unload and sell the freight cargo that his ships, the *Esperança* and the *Minerva,* had brought along provided the textiles were first brought into the Company's warehouse for the computation of the import duties payable and the

[40] *Ibid.*

[41] Letter from the factors at Colombo to the Governor-General and Council at Batavia, 9 April 1784, ARA, VOC 10112.

duties so computed actually paid. The Council also agreed to stock 75 cases of opium belonging to Ribeiro in its warehouses till such time as his ships were ready to depart from Batavia.[42] The Council was, however, very clear that Ribeiro's requests going beyond the Sri Lanka agreement would not be granted. Thus he was not allowed to return the sum of Rs 200,000 that had been paid to him earlier by the Council together with 4 per cent interest per annum by selling 75 cases of opium to the Company. He was also not to be favoured with the requested bill of exchange on the supercargoes at China to the amount of 85,000 Spanish *mats* to be paid at Batavia in cash.[43]

In its meeting of 12 August 1784, the Batavia Council decided to treat the loan of Rs 200,000 provided by Ribeiro at Colombo in April 1783 as having been settled by the sum of Rs 200,000 reimbursed to him at Batavia. The Colombo factors were directed to pay the interest due on this amount for the period the money was at the Company's disposal. The second loan of Rs 200,000 given at Cochin was to be treated as having been settled by the sale of goods to Ribeiro at Batavia. The interest on this amount would also be calculated and paid by the factors at Colombo thus closing both the transactions. The necessary instructions were sent to Colombo in the Council's letter dated 10 September 1784.[44]

The following few months witnessed a dramatic change in the situation. The Batavia Council suddenly became increasingly accommodative of the growing and, in many cases, unprecedented demands of Ribeiro in a manner unthinkable in the past. Ribeiro had clearly been working on individual members of the Council and had managed to win a sufficient number over to ensure decisions favourable to him, at times by majority vote.

On his return on 2 January 1785 from China, where he had gone with the *Esperança*, Ribeiro wrote to the Batavia Council a rather strongly worded letter on 22 January. He deplored the fact that the *Minerva* had been lying at Batavia for a period of 131 days between 11 June and 19 October 1784 (when it would seem to have been used for trade within the region) waiting for the cargo of sugar which had not been made available and which he had now been told was unlikely to be made available before May next. The resultant loss to him because of the overstay of the *Minerva* necessitated the payment of compensation to him 'because a contract could not work unless either both the parties strictly adhered to the terms or one of the parties causing damage to the other provided the necessary compensation'.[45] Since he was only looking for a fair settlement, he suggested that the Council nominate a person with whom he could thrash out the details. At its meeting on 28 January, the Batavia Council adopted an unusually conciliatory tone pointing out that it was indeed necessary to meet the obligations under the

[42] Resolution of the Batavia Council, 22 June 1784, ARA, VOC 10112.

[43] *Ibid.*, 15, 22 and 25 June 1784, ARA, VOC 10112.

[44] *Ibid.*, 12 August 1784; Letter from Batavia to Colombo, 10 September 1784, ARA, VOC 10112. Note that in its later deliberations it was the Cochin loan that the Council claimed to have repaid to Ribeiro in cash at Batavia.

[45] Resolution of the Batavia Council, 28 January 1785, ARA, VOC 10112.

agreement and to satisfy Ribeiro. It was, therefore, decided to nominate an extraordinary member of the Council, Adriaan Boesses, together with the *shahbandar* and license-master of Batavia, Lamarael van Gensau, to negotiate with Ribeiro.[46]

In the course of the negotiations that lasted three or four days, Ribeiro put forward the following claims: (*a*) a sum of 23,695 Ryx Dollars (1 R.D. = Rs 1.6) by way of compensation for the overstay of the *Minerva* at Batavia at the rate of R.D. 225 and 32 stuivers per day for a period of 105 days; and (*b*) a sum of R.D. 85,437 and 22 stuivers by way of the balance of the loan of Rs 200,000 together with interest until 18 October 1784 after adjusting the amount Ribeiro owed to the Company. These two amounts together totalled up to R.D. 109,132 and 22 stuivers. In addition, Ribeiro wanted R.D. 250 per day towards costs in respect of the *Esperança* starting 31 January 1785 until the time it got its full cargo of sugar from the Company. On top of all this, he also wanted an interest payment at the rate of 0.75 per cent per month on the entire amount due to him.[47]

In an unprecedented decision, the Council admitted the claim of R.D. 23,695 in respect of the *Minerva* in full. It also admitted the claim of R.D. 250 per day in respect of the *Esperança* modifying it only to the extent that the starting date of the claim would be 1 March rather than 31 January 1785. Ribeiro was also asked to see if he could reduce the daily cost of the upkeep of the ship from R.D. 250 by cutting down the size of the personnel etc. Finally, the claim of R.D. 85,437 and 22 stuivers in respect of the balance of the loan of Rs 200,000 plus interest was also admitted to be settled by the supply of the necessary amount of sugar.[48]

When Ribeiro expressed dissatisfaction even with this extraordinarily generous offer, the two negotiators were further authorised to inform him that he would also be allowed to buy sugar in the year 1786 at his option either from private suppliers or from the Company which would supply him at the price charged from other foreign merchants in 1785.[49]

The Batavia Council resolution of 8 March 1785 further approved the sale of another lot of 2,000 *piculs* of tin to Ribeiro at the specified price of R.D. 18 per *picul*. It also approved the payment of interest at the rate of 0.75 per cent per month on Ribeiro's total claim of R.D. 109,132 and 22 stuivers for the period starting 18 October 1784. The date of the start of the payment of the daily cost of R.D. 250 in respect of the *Esperança* was also advanced to 1 February 1785. Finally, starting 1 April 1785, Ribeiro would also be entitled to a daily payment of R.D. 220 in respect of the *Bellona*, a ship that he had brought from China.[50] These unusually extravagant terms clearly owed their origin to Ribeiro's friends in the Batavia Council, though in an effort to put a cloak of legitimacy on them, the factors at Colombo were sharply rebuked by the Council for having put the

[46] *Ibid.*, 28 January 1785, ARA, VOC 10112.
[47] *Ibid.*, 8 February 1785, ARA,VOC 10112.
[48] *Ibid.*, 8 February 1785, ARA, VOC 10112.
[49] *Ibid.*, 11 February 1785, ARA, VOC 10112.
[50] *Ibid.*, 8 March 1785, ARA, VOC 10112.

Company in a position where it had become necessary to make all these concessions available to Ribeiro.[51]

In April 1785, Ribeiro approached the Batavia Council yet again, this time asking for the daily costs of the *Luiza* that his factors in Malabar had sent to Batavia to collect the cargo that might be lying ready there. On the grounds that the *Esperança* and the *Bellona* were quite adequate to transport any cargo that might be provided to Ribeiro in accordance with the Colombo contract, this request, however, was turned down. Also in order to minimise the costs on account of the continued stay of the *Esperança* and the *Bellona*, it was decided to sell a part of the sugar cargo recently received at Batavia to Ribeiro notwithstanding the fact that it was otherwise needed for the Japan trade. The Council's decision not to reimburse Ribeiro for the daily costs of the *Luiza* was reiterated in its resolutions of 6, 13 and 24 May 1785.[52]

Ribeiro's response to the somewhat modified attitude of the Batavia Council was to become even more aggressive and unreasonable in his demands going to the extent of threatening legal action against the Company in the event of non-fulfilment of his financial claims. In a memorandum presented to the Council on 30 September 1785, Ribeiro submitted a detailed itemised account of what he claimed the Company owed him. This claim consisted of two parts, the first for a sum of R.D. 193,253 and 45 stuivers and the second for R.D. 65,821 and 30 stuivers. The first claim covered the two loans of R.D. 125,000 (Rs 200,000) each provided by Ribeiro in April 1783 at Colombo and in June 1783 in the form of a bill of exchange on Goa respectively and the interest thereon at the rate of 0.75 per cent per month. The amount of compensation due in respect of the overstay of the *Minerva*, the *Esperança*, and the *Bellona* was then added to this amount. The final figure of R.D. 193,253 and 45 stuivers was reached by deducting from the amount so calculated the value of the goods supplied by the Company to Ribeiro at Batavia on three occasions. At the price specified in the surety document, Ribeiro's claim would translate into 42,945 *piculs* and 14 lbs. of powder-sugar to be supplied by the Company.[53]

The other part of the claim amounting to R.D. 65,821 and 30 stuivers included items such as 2.5 per cent commission on the first loan of R.D. 125,000, a sum of R.D. 6,250 in respect of the transportation of the second loan of R.D. 125,000 from Goa to Cochin and then on to Colombo, and interest on both these amounts calculated at 0.75 per cent per month. Next was an item of R.D. 19,800 on account of Ribeiro's expenses at Batavia during his forced stay there over a period of nine months. But probably the most curious of all was an item of R.D. 43,650 including an interest component of R.D. 3,650 on account of the loss allegedly suffered by

[51] Letter from the Governor-General and Council at Batavia to the factors at Colombo, 5 April 1785, ARA, VOC 10112.

[52] Resolution of the Batavia Council, 24 April 6, 13 and 24 May 1785, ARA, VOC 10112.

[53] Memorandum submitted by Ribeiro to the Batavia Council, 30 September 1785, ARA, VOC 10112.

Ribeiro on the sale value of the cargo loaded on the *Minerva* because of its overstay at Batavia.[54]

It is not surprising that on the receipt of this claim, the Batavia Council felt utterly outraged describing it as 'unheard of and captious'. The Council was particularly concerned that Ribeiro had not taken into account the sum of Rs 200,000 (R.D. 125,000) given to him on 10 September 1783 at Batavia on behalf of the Company by Adriaan Boesses, the extraordinary member of the Batavia Council, in repayment of the principal amount of the loan provided by Ribeiro at Cochin. The *shahbandar* of Batavia, N. Lacle, was therefore summoned to the Batavia Council meeting of 4 October 1785 and asked to check this particular detail with Ribeiro. On being contacted, Ribeiro admitted that the amount had indeed been paid to him but that he had not taken it into account because he did not accept the Company version that he was not entitled to get goods at Batavia against the Cochin loan in the same manner as against the earlier one made available by him at Colombo. He agreed that he indeed owed this amount to the Company together with interest starting 10 September 1783 provided the Company was willing to meet his overall claims on it.[55]

At the time of filing his claim with the Batavia Council, José Ribeiro de Macedo had threatened the Council that in the event of his claim not being met, he would initiate legal action against the Company. It was in this context that the Council resolved to put all papers pertaining to this affair together and send them in a separate volume to the *Heeren XVII* for information and use if and when necessary. That is how the large volume enabling us to follow this fascinating case in such great detail came into being. It is, however, not clear whether the threatened process against the Company was in fact initiated by Ribeiro or indeed how the case was eventually settled.

To conclude, the two cases discussed in this paper provide important information on the mechanics of trade in the Indian Ocean-South China Sea complex in the late eighteenth century. The deal between Chellaby and Sluysken provides insights into the whole question of the use of hired vessels in trade in the region. The second case discussed in the paper draws attention to a number of intriguing issues. The first of these was the offer of unprecedentedly generous terms without prior clearance from Batavia by the Colombo factors of the Dutch East India Company to José Ribeiro, a private Portuguese trader, to mediate in raising a loan in the Surat market. The deal between Ribeiro and the Surat creditor, Nausherwanji Manekji, was also highly unusual in so far as it obliged the former to invest one-third of the total loan in goods at Batavia on the latter's account and transport them free of cost to Bombay. Finally, the case draws attention to the functioning of the Batavia Council and the way in which its members could be influenced ostensibly through money power.

[54] *Ibid.*

[55] Letter from *Shahbandar* N. Lacle to the Batavia Council, 6 October 1785, ARA, VOC 10112; Resolution of the Batavia Council, 18 October 1785, ARA, VOC 10112.

VI

Financing the European Trade with Asia in the Early Modern Period: Dutch Initiatives and Innovations

One of the principal outcomes of the great discoveries of the closing years of the fifteenth century was the rise of a pre-modern world economy. It was the almost simultaneous discovery of the Americas and of the all-water route to the East Indies via the Cape of Good Hope that had brought the three potential constituent segments of this economy, namely Europe, the New World and Asia, together for the first time. By providing a wide range of goods for both Europe and the New World, and by absorbing in return an important segment of the New World output of silver, Asia played a key role in the creation and the subsequent successful functioning of this global network of exchange.

The principal agencies instrumental in the running of the Euro-Asian commercial network in the early modern period were the European corporate enterprises - the Portuguese *Estado da Índia* in the sixteenth, and the Dutch, the English and the French East India companies in the seventeenth and the eighteenth centuries. A certain amount of Euro-Asian trade was also carried on by private European traders, though it would seem to have been quantitatively significant only in the case of the Portuguese private traders. The seventeenth century was marked by a fundamental change in the character of the Euro-Asian commercial encounter. The 'Asian trade revolution', to use the terminology of Niels Steensgaard, of the early seventeenth century, however, consisted only to a certain extent in the Portuguese 'redistributive enterprise' giving way to the pursuit by the Dutch and the English companies of rational and productivity-maximising commercial policies. From the vantage point of India, the 'revolution' consisted even more in the extension of the trading links established by the Europeans to all major segments of coastal India, an enormous increase in the volume and value of their trade in the subcontinent in the course of the century, its diversification to include a whole range of new trade goods for the European and various Asian markets and, perhaps most important of all, the manner in which the procurement of goods for trade was organised.

But if between the sixteenth and the eighteenth centuries, Euro-Asian trade witnessed profound changes in a variety of directions, its central characteristic feature remained unchanged. This was the necessity for the Europeans to pay for the Asian goods overwhelmingly in precious metals. This particular phenomenon has sometimes been ascribed to the rigidity of consumer tastes in the East, which rendered the Asian markets for European goods extremely small and static. Alternatively, it has been suggested that the absorption of precious metals by India or China reflected the hoarding habits in these societies.[1] But perhaps a more convincing explanation of this phenomenon is the inability of Europe to supply western products with a potential market in Asia at prices that would generate a large enough demand for them to provide the necessary revenue for the purchase of the Asian goods. Europe at this time had an overall superiority over Asia in the field of scientific and technological knowledge but as yet did not have the cost advantage that came with the Industrial Revolution in the nineteenth century. This put the Asian, and particularly the Indian, producers, with their considerably lower labour costs and a much longer history of sophisticated skills in handicrafts of various kinds, in a position of advantage over their European counterparts in the production of a variety of manufactured goods. The only major item Europe was in a position to provide to Asia was precious metals. The growth of the Euro-Asian trade, therefore, was critically dependent upon an increase in the availability of these metals. In

[1] See, for example, Rudolph C. Blitz, 'Mercantilist policies and the pattern of world trade,1500-1750,' *Journal of Economic History*, 27 (1967), pp. 39-55.

this context, the working of the South American silver mines and the enormous import of American silver into Europe during the sixteenth and the early seventeenth century was a development of critical significance. Although the American silver initially arrived in Spain, a large part of it eventually found its way to Amsterdam, mainly via Hamburg. In fact, from the early years of the seventeenth century onward, the Dutch were the undoubted masters of the European bullion trade and Amsterdam the leading world centre of the trade in precious metals.[2] It is an indication of the international standing of this city as a market for precious metals that the English East India Company also obtained a large part of its requirements of these metals in Amsterdam. An important implication of this "bullion for goods" model of Euro-Asian trade was that as far as the Europeans were concerned, the profit from the trade was derived almost entirely from the sale of Asian goods in Europe rather than also from the sale of European goods in Asia.

The bullion-based character of the Euro-Asian trade is brought out unambiguously in the overwhelming domination of precious metals in the exports of each of the principal European corporate enterprises to Asia. One of these enterprises, however, went a step further and significantly augmented the purchasing power taken from Europe by resources raised in Asia itself. This enterprise was the Dutch East India Company (VOC), by far the largest carrier of Asian goods into Europe well into the eighteenth century. This paper analyses the principal mechanisms evolved by the Company to enhance its resource base in Asia during the seventeenth and the eighteenth centuries. A part of this enhancement essentially represented only a change in form in so far as the equivalent of the resources raised in Asia had to be reimbursed in Europe. The Company resorted to this method, which was later emulated by other enterprises also, essentially in the interest of both greater convenience and reduced risk of loss on the way in physically transporting the precious metals to Asia.

[2] J.G. van Dillen, 'Amsterdam als wereldmarkt der edele metalen in the 17de en 18de eeuw,' *De Economist*, 72 (1923), pp. 538-550, 583-598, 717-730.

But a large part of the resources raised in Asia represented not a transfer but sums of money earned there essentially through a highly organised and effective participation in intra-Asian trade. The Dutch East India Company was the only European enterprise to undertake this major innovation.

1. The unquestioned domination of precious metals in the total export bill from Europe comes out unambiguously in the case of each of the major European corporate enterprises engaged in the trade with Asia. In the case of the English East India Company, for example, treasure accounted approximately for between 65 and 90 percent of the total value exported to Asia between 1601 and 1760.[3] In respect of the French *Compagnie Perpetuelle des Indes* (1725-69), this proportion varied between 55 and 86 percent.[4] The story was not very different for the Dutch East India Company. The goods the Company exported to the East included woollen, silk and other textiles manufactured mainly at Leiden, and non-precious metals such as lead, iron, vermilion and mercury, besides sundry items such as wines and beer. Since the Company's accounts do not permit a clear-cut distinction between the cost of these goods and that of the equipment and consumption goods also sent along, a systematic analysis of the proportion that trade goods (and by implication, precious metals), formed of the total exports is not feasible. But some information available for the eighteenth century in respect of the Amsterdam chamber alone suggests that this proportion was usually between 10 and 20 percent.[5] The information base for the seventeenth century is much more fragmentary. But on the whole, it would seem to suggest a somewhat higher average figure for this century. According to the information available in the *Generale*

[3] Calculated from K.N. Chaudhuri, *The English East India Company: the Study of an Early Joint-Stock Company, 1600-1640,* (London, 1965), Table II, p. 115 and *The Trading World of Asia and the English East India Company, 1660-1760,* (Cambridge, 1978), Appendix 5, Tables C1 and C4, pp. 507,512.

[4] Calculated from Philippe Haudrère, *La Compagnie française des Indes au XVIIIe siècle 1719-1795,* (Paris, 1989), vol. 4, Tables IIE and F, pp. 1196-98.

Missiven, there were even some years in the second half of the seventeenth century when the value of trade goods exported matched that of the precious metals.[6]

The data on the Dutch Company exports of precious metals refer in fact to the totals of the allotments made to individual chambers each year, but these corresponded closely to the actual amounts exported. The decennial totals are set out in Table 1.

Table 1. The export of precious metals (coined and uncoined) by the VOC to Asia, 1602-1794

(Decennial totals in million florins rounded off to the nearest thousand)

1602 - 10	5.207	1700 - 10	39.275
1610 - 20	10.186	1710 - 20	38.827
1620 - 30	12.360	1720 - 30	66.030
1630 - 40	8.500	1730 - 40	40.124
1640 - 50	9.200	1740 - 50	38.275
1650 - 60	8.400	1750 - 60	58.958
1660 - 70	12.100	1760 - 70	53.542
1670 - 80	11.295	1770 - 80	48.317
1680 - 90	19.720	1780 - 90	47.896
1690 - 1700	28.605	1790 - 94	16.972
		Total	573.789

Source: J.R. Bruijn, F.S. Gaastra and I. Schöffer, *Dutch-Asiatic Shipping in the 17th and 18th Centuries* (The Hague, 1987), vol. I, table 39, p. 187.

[5] J.R. Bruijn, F.S. Gaastra and I Schöffer, *Dutch-Asiatic Shipping in the 17th and 18th op. cit.*, p. 183.

[6] This assumes that the term *koopmanschappen* (merchandise) has been used carefully to include only trade goods. (F.S. Gaastra, "The exports of precious metals from Europe to Asia by the Dutch East India Company, 1602-1795" in J.F. Richards (ed.), *Precious Metals in the Later Medieval and Early Modern Worlds*, (Durham. 1983), p. 461.

It will be seen from the table that a relatively high figure of f. 12 million had already been reached by the decade 1620-30. The big increase took place from about 1680 with an all-time peak of f. 66 million being reached during 1720-30. A generally very high level was maintained throughout the second half of the eighteenth century. It should, of course, be realised that the decennial totals smooth out enormous annual fluctuations so characteristic of the entire period. To take an extreme example, the decade 1740-50 with an annual average of f. 3.82 million included a year such as 1742-43 when the figure was no more than f. 1.6. million, and the preceding one of 1741-42, when it was as high as f. 7 million. [7]

2. In addition to the goods and precious metals they made available, the Directors of the Dutch East India Company also authorised the factors in Asia to raise resources locally, the equivalent of which would be duly reimbursed in the Netherlands to the rightful claimants. This arrangement was referred to as "assistance received from Holland" (*secours uit het lieve vaderland*) and amounted in the course of the seventeenth century to a modest f. 30 million. The situation, however, had altered radically by the eighteenth century when the sum under this head amounted to a whopping f. 207 million.[8] In order to put the latter figure in perspective, one might note that over the same period, the value of the precious metals exported by the Company to Asia amounted to f. 448 million (Table I).

The "assistance received from Holland" consisted of several components. Until the middle of the eighteenth century, the principal source of funds the Company tapped in Asia was its own employees desirous of transmitting funds home. The source of these funds, in turn, was essentially two-fold: money made locally

[7] J.R. Bruijn, F.S. Gaastra and I Schöffer, *Dutch-Asiatic Shipping*, vol. I, table 46, p. 240.
[8] Femme Gaastra, 'De Verenigde Oost-Indische Compagnie in de 17de en 18de eeuw: de groei van een bedrijf. Geld tegen goederen', *Bijdragen en Mededelingen betreffende de Geschiedenis der Nederlanden*, 89 (2), (1976), pp. 244-72; Femme Gaastra, 'Private money for Company trade: the role of the bills of exchange in financing the return cargoes of the VOC', *Itinerario*, 18, 1 (1994), pp. 65-76.

through clandestine private trade and funds smuggled in from the Netherlands to take advantage of a higher exchange rate. The latter was done either on the employees' own account or on that of others against a fee. In the latter half of the eighteenth century, a part of the individual savings made available to the Company factors had taken on a legitimate character. This was the result both of the partial opening up of the intra-Asian trade to the Company servants as well as of the setting up of the Opium Society which enabled the employees to participate in the opium enterprise legally. With the English take-over of Bengal in the 1760s, the situation with respect to that province changed dramatically. An important source now tapped by the Company was the servants of the English East India Company anxious to remit home their enormous savings made in a variety of ways under the new dispensation. The efforts of the Company's factors in Bengal in this regard were supplemented by those of the Directors in Amsterdam at whose initiative an altogether new arrangement for getting hold of a part of these funds was worked out.

Until the middle of the eighteenth century, an overwhelming bulk of the transactions with the Company's own employees were carried out at the eastern headquarters of the Company at Batavia, though, in principle, the factors in Bengal and Sri Lanka were also authorised to carry them out. The mechanism was indeed quite simple. Against cash received, the factors issued a bill of exchange to the employee concerned. The latter, in turn, could carry it home in person if he was returning at the end of his engagement, or send it to a relative, an agent, or a banker, who would claim reimbursement on his behalf from the Amsterdam or another Chamber of the Company. In addition to the principal amount, the Company also paid interest at the rate of 4 percent per annum for the period that it had held the amount with itself. Another attraction from the point of view of the employees was the large differential in the exchange rate used. At the beginning of the eighteenth century, a silver ducaton could be bought in Holland at 63 stivers and converted into a bill at Batavia at 78 stivers, involving a net profit of 24 percent in addition to the 4 percent interest. It was this particular consideration that encouraged the smuggling out of large sums of money from Holland with the express intent of making it available to the Company at Batavia against bills of exchange. In 1735-36, for example, a sum of as much as f. 4.5 million is believed to have been smuggled out. In 1740, the Directors issued instructions that the exchange rate at Batavia be reduced to 72 stivers. Three years earlier, the Company had also stopped paying interest.[9] The transaction was nevertheless still quite profitable and large sums of money continued to be smuggled out of Holland.

The mechanism of raising resources in Asia by issuing bills of exchange redeemable in Holland witnessed substantive modifications in the second half of the eighteenth century. For one thing, from 1745 onwards, bills presented in the Netherlands for payment were honoured only after the auction of the return cargo had been completed. This procedure was modified yet once again in 1760 whence two thirds of the obligations were discharged after the autumn sales and one-third after the spring sales. In the 1760s and the 1770s, a limit was also prescribed on the amounts that Batavia and other factories in Asia could accept against bills of exchange in the course of a year.[10] In 1763, for example, the limit for Batavia was put at f. 2 million which was subsequently raised in 1778 to f. 3 million. The most important development of the period, however, was the emergence of Bengal as a major source of funds for investment in the procurement of the return cargo. This money came from the Company's own employees, but much more importantly, it came from the servants of the English East India Company, who were experiencing an unprecedented phase of prosperity (acquired largely through the use of unethical means) in the wake of the English Company take-over of the province. In 1768, the English East India Company had imposed a limit of £ 70,000 on the value of the bills it would itself issue besides fixing the rate of exchange at the highly disadvantageous figure of 2 shillings to a rupee. This

[9] Femme Gaastra, "Private money for Company trade".
[10] Femme Gaastra, "Private money for Company trade".

made the VOC a highly attractive alternative. The administrative mechanism followed in the dealings with the English servants was not very different from that followed in respect of the dealings with the Company's own servants except that in many instances of dealings with the English servants, the Dutch director of the Bengal factory collected an unauthorised commission on the deal. The most notorious of the directors in this respect was one Johannes Mathias Ross. Also, quite often, individual English servants bought bills not only in respect of their own remittances but also on behalf of fellow servants. Probably the most important of such agents was one William Paxton who bought twelve bills in 1778/79 amounting to f. 130,521 on behalf of nine clients.[11]

From about 1770 onward, the process of raising resources in Bengal through the medium of bills of exchange was marked by an important innovation. In addition to the usual mechanism of funds being collected in Asia through bills of exchange issued locally, the Directors of the Company now also began operating at the European end. This was done by negotiating in Amsterdam the procurement of bills of exchange drawn by Englishmen resident in England on their correspondents in Calcutta, directing the latter to pay to the local Dutch Company factors the sum of money specified in the bill. Many of these Englishmen had earlier bought bills from the Dutch Company factors in Bengal and were now on the other side. The transactions in these bills were intermediated by some of the leading Anglo-Dutch banking firms such as Hope and Co. and Pye Rich and Wilkieson who guaranteed timely payment against them. During the 1770s, this particular method became an important avenue for raising resources in Bengal. In a transaction entered into with Pye Rich and Wilkieson in 1773, for example, the Directors bought four such bills, each of the value of f. 125,000. The rate of exchange agreed upon was 26 stivers to a rupee. In the

[11] Femme Gaastra, "British capital for VOC in Bengal: private fortunes and financial transactions by servants of the Dutch and English East India Companies in Bengal, C. 1760-1790", in Om Prakash and Denys Lombard (eds.), *Commerce and Culture in the Bay of Bengal,. 1500-1800*, forthcoming.

event of the bills not being honoured in Bengal, the banking firm was liable to pay a 12 percent compensation to the Company. The payment due to the firm against the bills was to be made only after the receipt of information that the money had in fact been collected in Bengal.[12] The Directors were able to negotiate such a favourable package evidently because of the large sums of money waiting in Calcutta for being remitted home. The parties interested in effecting the remittances were not particularly keen to use the offices of the English East India Company for the purpose for reasons that are not hard to fathom. This arrangement, however, did not last very long and for all intents and purposes was terminated following the outbreak of the Fourth Anglo-Dutch War in 1780.

Looked at from the point of view of the Dutch East India Company, the large amount of resources raised in Asia through the mechanism of bills redeemable in Europe and issued to its own employees or to that of the English India Company essentially represented a device to minimize the risk of loss of treasure by shipwreck while being transported from Europe to Asia. But the unusually large premium in the form of a differential rate of exchange offered in respect of funds smuggled into Asia from Europe can perhaps be fully rationalized only in terms of the highest ranking officials in the Company's hierarchy, perhaps including the Directors themselves, collaborating with the employees in Asia in defrauding the Company. The precise nature and the mechanism of this highly probable process of collaboration, however, remains unclear.

If we shift the focus from the Company to the regional economies in Asia where the Company conducted its trade, the various mechanisms of raising resources through bills of exchange need to be distinguished from each other. Bills bought in Asia against money smuggled in from Europe were exactly at par with precious metals imported by the Company itself in so far as both represented a net addition to the availability of precious metals and

[12] Femme Gaastra, "British capital for VOC in Bengal".

consequently the supply of money in the regional economies concerned. But this was not the case in respect of bills bought against sums of money made through a clandestine or legitimate participation in intra-Asian trade. Matters got even worse in respect of the bills bought by the employees of the English East India Company. Not only were the funds used for the purpose made in India, but as Peter Marshall has described graphically, these were made by resorting to all forms of unethical and illegal use of the English East India Company's, and by extension of the English factors', newly acquired political leverage in the province.[13]

3. If the raising of resources in Asia by issuing bills of exchange was a device the Dutch East India Company resorted to in common with the other major European corporate enterprises functioning in the East, an extensive participation in intra-Asian trade was a feature unique to the VOC. Also, if the bills represented only a mechanism facilitating the transfer of purchasing power from Europe to Asia, participation in intra-Asian trade was a device to earn huge sums of money, partly in the form of precious metals, constituting a substantial net addition to the total purchasing power in Asia available for investment in goods for Europe.

In so far as the crown had initiated and then sustained for a while the Portuguese involvement in intra-Asian trade in the early part of the sixteenth century, one could perhaps discern in the Portuguese case some kind of a precedent for the Dutch Company involvement in Asian trade. But after a brief phase of active participation, the crown had withdrawn from the trade to become basically a dispenser of patronage through the concession system. More importantly, there was no specific commercial strategy involved in the way the Portuguese crown had gone about participating in the intra-Asian trade. By and large, the Portuguese had simply become yet another group to participate in an existing framework of trade, and initially at least operated with the

[13] P.J. Marshall, *East Indian Fortunes: The British in Bengal in the Eighteenth Century* (Oxford, 1976).

assistance of and in collaboration with Indian and other Asian merchant groups. The Dutch pattern of involvement in intra-Asian trade, on the other hand, had a definitive logic behind it besides involving the forging of important new commercial links across the Indian Ocean and the South China Sea.

The starting point of Dutch participation in the trade of the East Indies was, of course, the procurement of pepper and other spices for the European market. They realized from the very beginning that if the spice trade was to continue to be highly profitable, they must strive to gain control of both the total amount reaching Europe and the cost price in the Indies. The 1602 merger of the pre-companies into the United Company was only the first step in this direction. The ultimate aim was to eliminate the rivals in this trade – the Portuguese, the English, and the Asian merchants. Between 1605 and 1609, the Company managed to wrest from the authorities in Amboyna and Ternate agreements obliging the producers to supply their cloves exclusively to the Dutch. A similar agreement was concluded in 1605 with the Banda group of islands regarding the procurement of nutmeg and mace. The latter agreement was renewed after the conquest of the islands by the Company in 1621.

The control exercised by the Company on the Spice Islands enabled it to procure spices other than pepper at incredibly low prices. This ensured a very high rate of gross profit on these spices, often exceeding 1,000 percent. Before the arrival of the Dutch, the spice growers had been used to exchanging their wares for Indian cloth, rice and other necessities brought to them by Indian and other Asian merchants as well as the Portuguese. The Company could have obtained the Indian textiles – by far the most important medium of exchange in the Spice Islands – at Acheh and other places in Indonesia, but its acute business instinct drove it to their source, the Coromandel coast, where four factories were established between 1606 and 1610 covering both the northern and the southern stretches of the coast. Gujarat, on the west coast of India, the other major Indian region supplying textiles to the

Indonesian archipelago, was reached in 1618 with the establishment of a factory at Surat. Within a few years, subordinate factories had been opened at Cambay, Broach and at Agra in Northern India. Thus began the Company's participation in intra-Asian trade, which in course of time assumed important proportions and became an object of as much concern as the Euro-Asian trade itself.

It is important to realize that the idea of extensive participation in intra-Asian trade had originated not with the Company's Board of Directors, the Heren XVII, but with the officials at the Company's eastern headquarters established at Bantam in 1609 and shifted in 1618 to Jacatra, renamed Batavia in 1621. The driving force behind the project was a remarkable man, Jan Pietersz. Coen, who was named governor-general of the East Indies in April 1618 at the young age of 31 years. The way Coen went about the whole thing displayed a remarkable grasp of the realities of Asian trade. He devised a carefully worked out strategy and followed it up with great tenacity. In 1619, he sent to the Directors a blueprint of the Company's intra-Asian trade: cloth from Gujarat (obtained against spices, other goods and Spanish rials) to be exchanged against pepper and gold in Sumatra; cloth from Coromandel (obtained against spices, Chinese goods and gold, and rials) to be exchanged against pepper at Bantam; sandalwood, pepper and rials to be exchanged against Chinese gold and goods, the latter also being used to obtain silver from Japan. Finally, rials of eight could be obtained at Arabia against spices and other sundry items. Since the Company already had spices available to it, all that was needed to turn this blueprint into reality was an adequate number of ships and enough capital for some time to establish the intra-Asian trading network – "a little water to prime the pump". The Company already had a permanently circulating capital of between f. 2.5 and f. 3.5 million in the East Indies at this time, but Coen wanted more. The Directors, however, expressed their inability to do much in this regard and Coen realized that resources for the development of intra - Asian trade had to be found largely within Asia.

In addition to pepper and other spices, the key commodity in

Coen's blueprint was Indian textiles, which had to be paid for in Coromandel mainly in gold and in Gujarat mainly in silver. It was, therefore, imperative to establish trade relations with Asian sources of precious metals – whether they be themselves producers of these metals or be obtaining them through trade. By far the most important Asian producer of precious metals at this time was Japan. The discovery and working of new silver mines in the sixteenth century had turned Japan into the second largest producer of silver in the world next only to the Spanish American mines in the New World. In addition to its own output, Asia also received considerable quantities of the New World silver through trade. In addition to the lots brought in by the Portuguese and the European companies via the Cape of Good Hope, large quantities of this silver also reached the Red Sea and the Persian Gulf region via the Levant. Another route through which American silver reached Asia was the galleon trade between Acapulco and Manila. Since the Manila trade, controlled by the Spanish, was out of the reach of the Dutch, the two principal areas of interest to them were Japan and the Middle East.

A factory was established at Hirado in southwestern Japan in 1609. Although items such as fine quality cotton textiles, spices, sugar, lead, quicksilver, and musk could be sold in Japan, the principal items in demand there during the early period of Dutch trade were Chinese silk, silk textiles, and other Chinese goods. The Dutch initially tried to obtain Chinese goods in the Indonesian archipelago and the Malay peninsula. Indeed, the establishment of trade relations with places such as Patani and Siam, and later with Cambodia, Annam, and Tonkin was partly in the quest of Chinese goods. But success was limited, and attempts were made almost from the very beginning of trading relations with Japan to establish a trading post, by force if necessary, on the coast of China or its immediate vicinity. The efforts to blockade Chinese trade with Manila were followed by an attack on Macao in 1622 and the subsequent occupation of the Pescadores. But soon thereafter, in 1624, the Dutch were persuaded to move to

Taiwan in return for an informal agreement that Chinese merchants would be allowed to go there to trade with them. The principal commodities procured by the Company in Taiwan were Chinese silk and silk textiles for the Japanese market. A part of the silver obtained from Japan in exchange for the Chinese goods was then invested not only in getting the next round of silk in Taiwan but also gold needed chiefly for the crucial Coromandel trade. Gold was procured in Taiwan rather than directly in Japan until the former was lost to the forces of Coxinga in 1662. This was done chiefly to take advantage of the very different gold silver parity in the two places until 1637 favouring the procurement of gold in Taiwan. From 1641 in any case the export of gold from Japan was banned. This was a sequel to the 1639 closure of the country to all foreigners except the Chinese and the Dutch, the latter being required in May 1641 to move to the islet of Deshima off Nagasaki harbour.

In the meantime, efforts had been going on to further widen the supply base of the raw silk and the silk textiles required for the Japan trade. From the early 1640s on, Bengal emerged as a major supplier of raw silk for Japan. Ever since 1615, the factors at Coromandel had been trying to find a foothold in Bengal, which at that time was looked upon basically as a potential source for textiles, sugar and saltpetre. But in so far as the Bengal goods could be procured at Coromandel itself, where they were regularly imported by the Indian merchants, the efforts to establish a factory in Bengal lacked intensity and seriousness of purpose. It was only after the factors at Agra drew Batavia's attention in 1630 to the import by Indian merchants of a large quantity of relatively inexpensive raw silk from Bengal into Agra each year and enclosed a sample of the product with their report that the requisite urgency was imparted to the Bengal project. The expulsion of the Portuguese from Hugli in 1632 helped. A factory was established at Hariharpur in Orissa in 1633, and another at Hugli in 1635. Bengal raw silk was included in the Dutch cargo for Japan for the first time in 1640 and soon became a major constituent item of this cargo.

Efforts to reach the other major Asian source of precious metals, namely the Red Sea and the Persian Gulf region at the other extremity of the great arc of Asian trade, had also been initiated quite early, using the Company's establishment at Surat as the base. As early as 1616, attempts were made to establish trade relations with Mocha. But in 1624, following problems arising out of the seizure of two ships belonging to the port of Dabhol, the Company had no option but to abandon the factory for good. As far as Persia was concerned, a factory was established at Gombroon in 1623. Initially, Persia was in fact a net absorber of precious metals rather than a net supplier. The principal item procured there at this time was raw silk in exchange for goods such as pepper and other spices, Japanese copper and Indian textiles, and precious metals. Between 1622 and 1634, several of the ships from Holland were sent directly to Surat and Persia with fair amounts of capital. In 1624-25, for example, three of these ships carried f. 600,000 to these factories, constituting nearly one-third of the total precious metals sent to Asia that year.[14] But this pattern lasted only for a brief while, and from 1643 on Persia emerged as a net supplier of silver abassies and gold ducats, which were smuggled out on a regular basis, often by concealing them in cavities made into the bales of raw silk.[15] The resultant loss in the value of silk was evidently an acceptable price to pay for getting hold of the silver and gold coins. From a comparatively modest sum of f. 235,000 in 1642-43, the value of these coins came to exceed a million florins in 1649-50. The average annual value of the coins smuggled out over the following decade was f. 660,712.[16] But over the rest of the seventeenth century, the sums involved were extremely modest, if they were at all positive, and it was only around 1700 that for a

[14] F.S. Gaastra, "De VOC in the 17de en de 18de eeuw; de groei van een bedrijf. Geld tegen goederen", p. 261.
[15] K. Glamann, *Dutch Asiatic trade, 1620-1740*, (Copenhagen, The Hague), 1958, p. 120.
[16] F.S. Gaastra, "The exports of precious metals from Europe to Asia," Appendix 4, Table 1.

few years, Persia again became a major – in fact the most important – provider of precious metals in Asia.[17]

What the above analysis establishes quite definitively is that by about the middle of the seventeenth century, the Dutch East India Company had become a major participant in intra-Asian trade with trading links all along the great arc of Asian trade. The crucial role played by this trade in the overall commercial strategy of the Company was summed up neatly by the Heren XVII in 1648 as follows: "The intra-Asian trade and the profit from it are the soul of the Company which must be looked after carefully because if the soul decays, the entire body would be destroyed."[18] Three years later, the Directors even expressed the hope that at some point it would be possible for Batavia not only to finance the exports to Europe (which in 1650-51 amounted to f. 2.49 million) wholly out of the profits from intra-Asian trade, but also to send to them in addition some Asian precious metals. Although such extravagant hopes were never realized, the fact remains that through the seventeenth century, participation in intra-Asian trade was of great advantage to the Company. Note that between 1640 and 1688, the invoice value of the return cargo from Asia amounted to approximately f. 150 million as against f. 120 million worth of precious metals and goods exported to Asia over the same period. Thus about 20 percent of the return cargo represented the profits from intra-Asian trade. Considering that the total proceeds from the sale of the return cargo amounted to f. 420 million, the sales value of 20 percent of the cargo would amount to f. 84 million. This amount was more than sufficient to cover the sum of f. 67 million paid out as dividend by the Company over the period.[19]

The expansion of trade into vitally important areas was

[17] The average annual sum exported between 1700-01 and 1703-04 was f. 873, 560 (calculated from F.S. Gaastra, "The exports of precious metals from Europe to Asia", Appendix 4, Table 2, p. 475).

[18] Algemeen Rijksarchief (ARA), Heren XVII to Batavia, 22.9.1648, Verenigde Oost-Indische Compagnie (VOC) 317, f. 120vo.

[19] F.S. Gaastra, *Bewind en Beleid bij de VOC. De Financiele and Commerci(le Politiek van de Bewindhebbers 1672-1702 Commerciele* (Zutphen, 1989), p. 205.

critically dependent on the growing availability of precious metals, a large amount of which was found through the greater part of the century within Asia. Evidence available in the Company's archives, including the "General journals kept by the Bookkeeper-General at Batavia for the period 1700-01 to 1789-90" enables one to partially reconstruct the resource flows to the Indian factories over the two centuries of the Company's trade in the region. The findings are summarized in Table 2. It need hardly be emphasized that there are significant gaps in the information available. The non-availability of the regional distribution on a systematic basis of the origin of the precious metals the Company brought into Gujarat and Bengal during the seventeenth century is only one of these. Even when such a distribution is available for the eighteenth century, and in the case of Coromandel also for the seventeenth, the degree of precision one can achieve is limited. This is because the precious metals exported from Batavia included lots received from Holland as well as from sources within Asia. The figures in column 5 of the table, therefore, constitute only the lower limit of the amounts originating within Asia. But even if one took into account only the figures in this column, the overwhelming role of Asia in the precious metals brought into Coromandel right through 1680 is established conclusively. For Bengal, the occasional and non-systematic information available also underscores the important role of Asia, particularly Japan, in the mix of precious metals sent to the region in the seventeenth century. Finally, as far as Gujarat is concerned, the available information suggests a pattern where the precious metals imported until the 1630s originated mainly in Holland, and thereafter increasingly in Japan and the Middle East. The domination of Japan was particularly marked between 1638-39 and 1644-45, as was that of Persia over the following fifteen years or so.[20]

The two key factors that enabled the Dutch to achieve an

[20] H.W. van Santen, *De Verenigde Oost-Indische Compagnie in Gujarat en Hindustan 1620-1660*, (Leiden, 1982), Table 2, p. 37.

Table 2. Value and regional distribution of precious metals imported by the VOC into India, 1640-1785

Year[1]	COROMANDEL					GUJARAT					BENGAL					MALABAR				
	1[2]	2	3	4	5	1	2	3	4	5	1	2	3	4	5	1	2	3	4	5
1640-50	1,846,411 (8yrs)	NA	zero	36.8	63.2	700,500 (6yrs)	87.6	NA	NA	NA	NA					NA				
1650-60	1,755,449 (5yrs)	NA	zero	24.4	75.6	438,000 (3yrs)	61.8	NA	NA	NA	NA					NA				
1660-70	1,482,339 (4yrs)	NA	zero	36.3	63.7	66,872 (10yrs)	15.2	NA	NA	NA	1,225,741 (7yrs)	87.7	NA	NA	NA	NA				
1670-80	1,882,547 (1yr)	NA	zero	24.0	76	zero (10yrs)	zero	zero	zero	zero	1,090,386 (6yrs)	77.8	NA	NA	NA	NA				
1680-90	NA					17,935 (10yrs)	3.1	NA	NA	NA	1,167,630 (10yrs)	74.6	NA	NA	NA	NA				
1690-1700	NA					zero (10yrs)	zero	zero	zero	zero	2,120,169 (10yrs)	85.1	NA	NA	NA	NA				
1701-02	905,929	73.7	zero	84.2	17.8	zero	zero				2,046,197	82.9	zero	62.0	38.0	81,198	50.2	zero	100.0	zero
1711-12	1,012,326	75.4	zero	100.0	zero	zero	zero				2,979,992	87.1	zero	100.0	zero	12,923	7.1	zero	100.0	zero
1722-23	1,180,714	75.4	zero	100.0	zero	1,502,875	85.1	zero	100.0	zero	3,834,482	95.5	zero	100.0	zero	zero	zero			
1731-32	561,689	58.8	zero	77.8	22.2[3]	zero	zero				1,781,999	84.9	zero	100.0	zero	zero	zero			
1741-42	zero	zero	zero			200,582	53.0	zero	100.0	zero	4,735,089	90.7	zero	68.3	31.7 (Coromandel)	870,167	69.3	zero	71.0	29.0 (Coromandel)
1751-52	1,005,067	42.2	zero	73.0	27	99,094	19.8	zero	zero	100.0 (Persia)	4,729,994	86.6	7.6	88.4	3.9	422,362	54.4	zero	5.3	94.7 (Surat)
1761-62	1,370,763	78.1	zero	100.0	zero	zero	zero				2,634,282	86.3	11.5	88.5	zero	150,000	23.0	zero	zero	100.0 (Surat)
1770-71	1,330,185	71.6	39.1	39.0	21.9	zero	zero				397,183	55.9	83.3	16.7	zero	179,535	83.6	zero	100.0	zero
1784-85[4]		zero	zero			zero	zero									zero	zero			

Note:
[1] Until 1700, the figures are on an average annual basis.

[2] Explanation of numbers heading columns:
1. Value of treasure imported in florins. The figures in parenthesis in this column for the period 1640-1700 refer to the number of years in a decade for which information is available.
2. Proportion of treasure to total value imported (%).
3. Proportion of treasure directly imported from Europe (%).
4. Proportion of treasure imported from Batavia (%).
5. Proportion of treasure imported from the rest of Asia (%).

[3] This is the amount of bills of exchange (wissels) issued at Coromandel and honoured by Sri Lanka.
[4] The funds invested in Bengal during this year were raised by issuing bills of exchange locally which were payable in Europe.
NA stands for not available.

Source: For the seventeenh century, the figures for Coromandel are based on information available in T. Raychaudhuri, *Jan Company in Coromandel, 1605-1690,* (The Hague, 1962); for Gujarat in V.B Gupta, *The Dutch East India Company in Gujarat Trade, 1660-1700: A study of Selected Aspects*, unpublished Ph D. Thesis, University of Delhi, 1991, and for Bengal in Om Prakash, *The Dutch East India Company and Economy of Bengal, 1630-1720,* (Princeton, 1985). The eighteenth century evidence is from the "General Journals kept by the Bookkeeper-Generaal at Batavia for the period 1700-01 to 1789-90" ARA, *Boekhouder-General Batavia (BGB)*, 10751-10801.

enviable position in intra–Asian trade during the seventeenth century were the spice monopoly and the exclusive right to trade with Japan. The spice monopoly provided the Company with a staple item of trade in demand all over Asia and entailing an extraordinarily high rate of return. The Japan trade brought in large quantities of precious metals, mainly silver until 1668 and gold thereafter. The relative position of Holland and Japan in the matter of the supply of precious metals is set out in Table 3.

What this table suggests quite unambiguously is a clear and substantial lead for Japan between the late 1630s and the end of the 1670s. There were two further advantages associated with the procurement of precious metals in Japan as compared to Holland. In the first place, the Japanese supplies were obtained in exchange for commodities that were themselves sold at a good profit. Second, the cost per unit of silver procured seems to have been lower in Japan. If one assumed that the value that the factors in Batavia assigned to a *tael* of Japanese *schuit* silver in their books correctly

Table 3. The Dutch East India Company's import of precious metals from Holland and Japan into Batavia, 1621-1699. (Annual average in florins)

Period	Holland	Japan
1621-1624	1,215,000	157,924
1628-1632	1,240,000	–
1633-1636	1,075,000	921,044
1637	1,000,000	3,029,550
1640-1649	940,000	1,518,871
1650-1659	840,000	1,315,121
1660-1669	1,200,000	1,454,913
1670-1679	979,500	1,154,148
1680-1689	1,972,000	298,383
1690-1699	2,691,000	228,952

Source: The years included in the table are those for which information regarding Japan is available. Until 1637, the figures for Japan are based on Oscar Nachod, Die Beziehungen der Niederländischen Ostindischen Kompagnie zu Japan im Siebzehnten Jahrhundert, (Leipzig, 1897), Appendix, Table E. pp. cc vii - cc viii. The figures for 1621-1624 are given in Nachod directly in florins but those after 1624 are in teals. The rate of conversion used here is the same as that used by the Company: 615 stivers to a teal until 1636 and 57 stivers to a teal for 1637. The figures for 1640-1699 are based on Kristof Glamann, Dutch-Asiatic Trade, Table III, p.51, who based himself on Nachod and other sources. Until 1662, the imports from Japan were entirely in silver, and from 1668 entirely in gold. For the period 1660-1669, the component of gold in the average annual figure of f. 1,454,913 was f. 406.902 (or 28 percent). The figures for Holland have been calculated from Bruijn, Gaastra. Schöffer, Dutch-Asiatic Shipping, vol. 1. Appendix 4, Table 46 with one year lag.

represented its cost price, the cost of the Japanese silver works out to be 24.75 percent lower that in Holland until 1636 and 35.58 percent lower thereafter.[21] One might also add that, in addition to the precious metals, Japan also provided large quantities of bar copper which sold at a good profit in both Asia and Europe.

In the course of the last quarter of the seventeenth century, however, things became increasingly difficult for the VOC in Japan.

[21] Om Prakash, *The Dutch East India Company and the Economy of Bengal 1630-1720*, (Princeton, 1985), p. 21.

As table 3 shows, there was a steep decline in the Dutch import of precious metals from Japan from about 1680. This was the cumulative outcome of the ban on the export of silver in 1668, the introduction of the appraised trade system in 1672 and of the limited trade system in 1685, and finally the debasement of the gold koban in 1696 with its gold content being reduced from 85.69 to 56.41 percent without any reduction in its silver price of 6.8 taels.[22] In the absence of a major alternative Asian source of gold, the Company did continue to procure small quantities of gold koban occasionally until the middle of the eighteenth century, but the critical role of Japan in promoting the Company's intra-Asian trade had come to an end in 1696.

The declining volume as well as the profitability of intra-Asian trade in precious metals was perhaps an important element in the changing fortunes of the Company in the matter of the profitability of the intra-Asian trade in general as between the seventeenth and the eighteenth centuries. It has been estimated that while in the seventeenth century as much as 90 percent of the total income earned by the Company in Asia was derived from trade, the proportion came down over the eighteenth century to around 60 percent, the remainder of the income being contributed by items such as taxes and tolls.[23] Of course, as the work of de Korte on the Company's finances shows, the eighteenth century also was not a homogeneous unit in this respect. Indeed, in the course of the century, the Company's Asian income from trade (*generale winsten*) fluctuated a great deal with a significant and irreversible decline being registered only from 1768-69 onward. The average annual income earned by the Company from Asian trade, calculated on a decennial basis, was over f. 4 million during the first four decades of the century, over f. 6 million during the 1740s and the 1750s, f. 4 million during the 1760s, and a little over f. 2.5 million during the 1770s and the 1780s.[24]

[22] Om Prakash, *The Dutch East India Company and the Economy of Bengal*, Ch. 5.
[23] F.S. Gaastra, *De Geschiedenis van de VOC*, (Zutphen 1991), p. 133.

Another index that suggests a relatively declining participation by the VOC in Asian trade is the lower absorption rate of shipping coming in from Holland into intra-Asian trade in the eighteenth century. The relevant information is summarized in Table 4. Before we draw our conclusions from the table, however, it might be useful to note the limitations of this data base. For one thing, the absorption rate in the Asian trade worked out on the basis of the difference between the number of ships (and the volume of tonnage) arriving into and leaving Asia would overstate the real absorption rate for several reasons. In the first place, by virtue of its age or for other reasons, a ship might simply be pulled out of service after arrival in Asia. It would then not be included in the shipping returning to Europe, but at the same time would not have been available for use in intra-Asian trade. Also, of the shipping pressed into service in Asia, a certain amount was not used for purposes of trade but for patrolling, armed combat and so on. Besides, in the eighteenth century, the apparently high absorption rate of the 1780s is likely to have been related to the problems in sending ships back to Europe because of the Fourth Anglo-Dutch War. An acute shortage of sailors would have produced a similar result in the 1790s. On the other hand, in so far as the Company occasionally bought vessels in Asia which were used exclusively in intra-Asian trade, the absorption rate suggested by the table would understate the real absorption rate of shipping in Asian trade. In the absence of the relevant information, the bias in neither direction can be corrected, though perhaps it was not particularly pronounced in either and was in part at least self-cancelling. The other

[24] J.P. de Korte, *De Jaarlykse Financiele Verantwoording in de Verenigde Oost Indische Compagnie*, (Leiden, 1984), Appendix 10. The precise average annual figures on a decadel basis were as follows:

1700/01-1709/10 *f.* 4,192,286
1710/11-1719/20 *f.* 4,487,979
1720/21-1729/30 *f.* 4,287,878
1730/31-1739/40 *f.* 4,514,343
1740/41-1749/50 *f.* 6,081,362
1750/51-1759-60 *f.* 6,267,012
1760/61-1769/70 *f.* 4,086,227
1770/71-1779/80 *f.* 2,537,701
1780/81-1789/90 *f.* 2,768,002

problem with the data pertains to the fact that the ships permanently absorbed in intra-Asian trade might very well have had very different working lifespans depending partly upon which stage of their life they had been kept back in Asia. This would necessarily leave a certain margin of error in the conclusions drawn from the table.

Subject to these limitations, the main conclusions suggested by the table are as follows. In terms of the absolute number of ships

Table 4. Dutch/East India Company shipping arriving at and leaving Asia, 1602-1794

Years	No. of ships arriving in Asia	Tonnage arriving in Asia	No. of ships leaving Asia	Tonnage leaving Asia	Proportion of arriving ships absorbed in Asia	Proportion of arriving tonnage absorbed in Asia
1602-10	69	33,370	47	20,100	31.9	39.8
1610-20	114	55,410	46	26,590	59.6	52.0
1620-30	130	50,960	68	35,280	47.7	30.8
1630-40	154	62,640	72	38,890	53.2	37.9
1640-50	165	100,950	92	73,740	44.2	27.0
1650-60	196	118,341	102	84,200	48.0	28.8
1660-70	228	125,186	115	79,313	49.6	36.6
1670-80	218	142,289	129	91,975	40.8	35.5
1680-90	196	126,619	133	98,165	32.1	22.5
1690-1700	223	138,827	145	100,697	35.0	27.5
1700-10	271	180,620	188	133,437	30.6	26.1
1710-20	297	220,074	240	182,164	19.2	17.2
1720-30	353	272,103	308	243,314	13.7	10.6
1730-40	363	270,095	290	221,205	20.1	18.1
1740-50	307	246,565	215	170,155	30.0	31.0
1750-60	287	276,295	234	227,650	18.5	17.6
1760-70	288	287,845	223	222,450	22.6	26.7
1770-80	287	287,190	231	230,670	19.5	19.7
1780-90	288	233,850	197	144,093	31.6	38.4
1790-94	106	84,943	85	66,370	19.8	21.9

Source: Calculated from J.R. Bruijn, F.S. Gaastra, I. Schöffer, *Dutch-Asiatic Shipping*, vol. 1, tables 35 and 36, pp. 174-176.

absorbed in Asian trade there was a decline from 744 in the seventeenth century (98 years) to 640 in the eighteenth (94 years). In terms of tonnage, however, the volume had gone up over the same period from 305,642 tons to 518,072 tons. But in relative terms, the decline between the seventeenth and the eighteenth centuries is unambiguous and fairly significant in terms of both the number of ships as well as the volume of tonnage. Thus the proportion of ships absorbed in Asian trade came down from an average of 44 percent in the seventeenth century to 23.5 percent during the eighteenth. The corresponding values for the volume of tonnage were 32.1 percent and 22 percent respectively. A relative reduction in participation in intra-Asian trade between the seventeenth and the eighteenth centuries, however, does not by any means detract from the exceptionally important role that such participation played in enhancing the net resource base of the Company in Asia for investment in goods for Europe without imposing a corresponding burden on the Board of Directors at home.

4. The Euro-Asian encounter over the three-hundred year period between 1500 and 1800 had at its heart a fast-growing volume and value of trade between the two continents. While Asia provided an increasingly diverse range of goods over this period to Europe, the latter continued to be obliged to pay for these goods overwhelmingly in the form of precious metals which were physically transported in large quantities to Asia. A supplementary mechanism devised was to raise resources in Asia mainly from the European Company employees against bills of exchange which were subsequently redeemed in Europe.

By far the most innovative of the European corporate enterprises engaged in Euro-Asian trade during the seventeenth and the eighteenth centuries was the Dutch East India company. In the matter of the raising of resources in Asia through the mechanism of the bills of exchange, for example, the Board of Directors of the Company managed to raise large sums of money in Bengal in the second half of the eighteenth century by securing the intermediation of leading Anglo-Dutch banking firms in the transactions. But what put the Company in a class by itself was its participation in intra-Asian trade on a truly large scale as an integral part of its overall commercial strategy. More than anything else, it was this particular strength of the Company that enabled it to dominate Euro-Asian trade well into the eighteenth century.

VII

Seventeenth-Century India as Seen by the Dutch

The European perception of India as a distinct geographic and political entity probably does not go back to a time earlier than the late eighteenth, if indeed not the nineteenth century. This is certainly true of people of countries such as Netherlands whose historical association with India was entirely commerce-based and who regarded different regions of India essentially as constituent elements of a larger geographical area they described as the East Indies. This area embraced not only South Asia and Southeast Asia but also parts of the Middle East, and in a loose sense even the Far East. The relevant area of operation for the Dutch East India Company was what I have elsewhere described as the Great Arc of Asian Trade, extending from the Persian Gulf in the north-west to Japan in the north-east.

India had traditionally occupied a position of central importance in this trading network. In part, this was a function of the midway location of the subcontinent between West Asia on the one hand and Southeast and East Asia on the other. But perhaps even more important was the subcontinent's capacity to put on the market a wide range of tradable goods at highly competitive prices. These included agricultural goods, both food items such as rice, sugar and oil and raw materials such as cotton and indigo. While the bulk of the trade in these goods was coastal, the high seas trade component was by no means insignificant. The real strength of the subcontinent, however, lay in the provision of large quantities of manufactured goods, the most important amongst which were textiles of various kinds. While these included high value varieties such as the legendary Dhaka muslins and the Gujarat silk embroideries, the really important component for the Asian market was the coarse cotton varieties manufactured primarily on the Coromandel coast and in Gujarat. There was a large-scale demand for these varieties in the eastern markets of Indonesia, Malaya, Thailand and Burma as well as in the markets of the Red Sea, the Persian Gulf and East Africa. While it is impossible to determine precisely what proportion of total domestic demand for mass-consumption textiles in these societies was met by imports from India, the available evidence would seem to indicate that it was not insignificant. India's capacity to manufacture these textiles in large quantities and to put them on the market at highly competitive terms made it in some sense the 'industrial' hub of the region surrounded by west Asia on one side and southeast Asia on the other.

This circumstance also determined to a large extent the nature of India's demand for imports from the rest of Asia. This demand consisted essentially either of consumption goods which were not produced domestically for climatic or other reasons, or of minerals and metals of various kinds whose domestic supply was either nil or substantially below the total demand. In the first category were items such as fine spices like cloves, nutmeg and mace from Indonesia, and horses and rosewater from west Asia. The second category included rubies and other precious stones from Burma, as well as metals — both precious and non-precious. By far the most important non-precious metal imported was tin from Malaya. Precious metals, mainly silver, were imported overwhelmingly from West Asia. It was for this reason that, from the sixteenth century onward, the port of Mocha was repeatedly referred to as the 'treasure-chest' of the Mughal empire. It is really immaterial for our purpose whether the imported precious metals are treated as a commodity import or as a means of settling the adverse balance of trade that the concerned trading partner of the subcontinent had with it. The important point to emphasize is that by virtue of her relatively more advanced structure of manufacturing production and her capacity to provide large quantities of basic manufactured consumption goods such as inexpensive cotton textiles, India significantly enhanced the scale of trade in the Asian continent. She not only provided textiles and foodgrains and other provisions in demand in the neighbouring countries but also provided an important outlet for their specialized agricultural, mineral and other products. Trade satisfied different kinds of consumption needs for India as compared with her numerous trading partners in the Indian Ocean region. This by itself provided an excellent basis for a significant and growing level of trade. It is really in this sense that the critically important role of India in the structure of early modern Asian trade needs to be assessed.

The key position of India in the structure of Asian trade was also reflected in the important role of the Gujarati and other Indian trading groups in the conduct of this trade. This role, if anything, was strengthened in the course of the fifteenth century which witnessed the fragmentation of Asian trade into well-defined segments. Increasingly, the participation of the Arab merchants became confined to the trade between West Asia and the west coast of India. This left the trade between west and the east coasts of India, on the one hand, and the eastern Indian Ocean region, on the other, almost exclusively in the hands of Indians — the Gujaratis more than anyone else, but also the Chettis, the Chulias and other groups from the Coromandel coast, besides the Oriyas and the Bengalis. The participation of the Chinese merchants was now restricted by and large to the trade between China and Malacca, while the Indonesian and the Malay merchants hardly seem to have ventured beyond the inter-island and the port-to-port trade in the Malay-Indonesian region. In sum, Indian merchants from different regions of the country constituted an important trading group operating in the Indian Ocean.

It is critically important to realize that among the European corporate enterprises engaged in Euro-Asian trade between the sixteenth and the eighteenth centuries, which included the Portuguese Estado da India and the English, the Dutch, the French and the Danish East India Companies, it was the Dutch East India Company more than anyone else which truly realized the potential of exploiting the opportunities of trading within Asia with India as a key area of operation, in addition to trading between Asia and Europe. To a certain extent, the richness of this potential had also been recognized by the Portuguese in the sixteenth century, but in their case the bulk of the participation in intra-Asian trade was at the level of private Portuguese traders under the patronage of the Estado da India rather than by the Estado itself.

Over centuries, and indeed millennia, the principal commercial interest of the Europeans in Asia had been the procurement of spices such as pepper, cloves, nutmeg, mace and cinnamon and other luxury goods such as Chinese silk and Indian textiles. For the simple reason that Europe had traditionally been unable to supply western products with a potential market in Asia at prices that would generate a large enough demand for them to provide the necessary revenue for the purchase of the Asian goods, these goods had always been paid for overwhelmingly in precious metals. Considering that wealth had traditionally been associated exclusively with precious metals, this particular pattern of trade had persuaded authors such as

Gibbon to complain that in return for trivialities, Europe was allowing itself to be bled by Asia. This perception lasted for a long time and indeed assumed a great deal of respectability under the vulgar bullionist version of Mercantilism in the early modern period.

By far the most important item traditionally figuring in the Euro-Asian spice trade was pepper whose major centres of production in Asia were the island of Sumatra in the Malay-Indonesian archipelago and the south-west coast of India comprising the Malabar and Kanara coasts. The Portuguese landed at Calicut in 1498 and through the sixteenth and the early part of the seventeenth century, the Malabar and Kanara coasts remained nearly the sole providers of pepper to the Estado da India. In order to avoid conflict with the Portuguese as also to be able to procure at source other spices such as cloves, nutmeg and mace, grown exclusively in the Moluccas at the eastern extremity of the archipelago, both the English and the Dutch East India Companies in the early years of the seventeenth century reached out to Java in the archipelago rather than to India. As it turned out, the larger resource base of the Dutch East India Company together with other factors combined to give it a distinct edge in the archipelago over its English rival. Regional authorities in the Spice Islands were successfully coerced into granting to the Dutch exclusive monopsony rights in all the three spices grown in the area — cloves, nutmeg and mace. In this context, a situation of armed conflict between the English and the Dutch was becoming inevitable. The hostilities erupted in 1618, and the English emerged distinctly the worst of the two. The London agreement of 1619 provided for an English share of one-third in the trade of the Spice Islands, and of one half in the pepper trade subject to the English contributing one-third of the cost of maintaining the Dutch garrisons in the area. But due to both to Dutch hostility and the shortage of resources with the English, the arrangement did not quite work. The 1623 incident at Amboyna led to a recall of English factors from the shared centres in the archipelago to Batavia and hastened the process of the English withdrawal from the Spice Islands. This made them turn to India where they had first appeared at Surat in 1608 (though it was not until 1612 that formal trading rights were obtained there, followed by the establishment of a factory in 1613) on an almost full-time basis.

The position of the Dutch East India Company was very different. Having obtained the exclusive monopsonistic rights in the Spice Islands, they wanted to make the best of the situation. This was done by the creation over a period of time of an extensive network of participation in intra-Asian trade on a large scale. This eventually became by far the single most distinguishing element of the Dutch East India Company's trading strategy among all the European corporate enterprises as also the principal factor explaining their domination of intra-Asian as well as Euro-Asian trade throughout the seventeenth century. The control exercised by the Company on the Spice Islands enabled it to procure spices other than pepper at incredibly low prices. This ensured a very high rate of gross profit on these spices, often exceeding 1,000 per cent. Before the arrival of the Dutch, the spice growers had been used to exchanging their wares for Indian cloth, rice and other necessities brought to them by Indian and other Asian merchants. The Company could have obtained the Indian textiles — by far the most important medium of exchange in the Spice Islands — at Acheh and other places in Indonesia, but its acute business instinct drove it to their source, the Coromandel coast, where four factories were established between 1606 and 1610, covering both the northern and the southern stretches of the coast. Gujarat, the other major Indian region supplying textiles to the Indonesian archipelago, was reached in 1618 with the establishment of a factory at Surat. Within a few years subordinate factories were opened at Cambay and Broach, and at Agra in northern India. Since the textiles bought on the Coromandel coast had to be paid for mainly in gold, and those in Gujarat mainly in silver, the next stage in the expansion of the Company's participation in intra-Asian trade was to reach out to areas providing gold and silver. By far the most important Asian producer of precious metals at this time was Japan. A factory was established at Hirado in southwestern Japan in 1609. Since Chinese silk was the principal commodity in demand in Japan, trade relations were established with Taiwan in 1624. From the early 1640s Bengal emerged as a major supplier of raw silk for Japan. The last of the major Indian regions figuring in the Company's intra-Asian trade was Malabar, where it established itself in 1647. However, it was only in 1663 when the Dutch, collaborating with the Raja of Cochin, managed to throw the Portuguese out that the Dutch trade in Malabar began on a regular and substantive basis. Efforts to reach the other major Asian source of precious metals, namely the Red Sea and the Persian Gulf at the other extremity of the great arc of Asian trade, had also been initiated quite early, using the Company's establishment at Surat as the base. Indeed, from 1643 onward Persia emerged as an important supplier of silver *abassies* and gold *ducats*, which were smuggled out on a regular basis, often by concealing them in cavities made into bales of raw silk. By about the middle of the seventeenth century, then, the Dutch East India Company had become a major participant in intra-Asian trade with trading links all along the great arc of Asian trade. The two key factors that enabled the Dutch to achieve this enviable position were the spice monopoly and the exclusive right to trade with Japan in the 'closed country' era of its history, extending from 1639 to 1854.

While extensive participation in intra-Asian trade was the principal feature that distinguished it most from its fellow European corporate enterprises throughout its trading history, the Euro-Asian trade was by no means neglected at any point in time. As we saw above, the principal constituent of the cargo procured in Asia for Europe in the initial stages consisted of pepper and other spices. The proportion of spices in the total invoice value was thus as high as 74 per cent in 1619-21 and 68 in 1648-50. By 1698-1700 this figure had come down to a mere 23 percent. This was essentially an outcome of the fashion revolution in Europe which resulted in a dramatic increase in the demand for Asian finished textiles and raw silk. From 16 percent of the total exports in 1619-21, the share of this group went up to as much as 55 percent by the end of the seventeenth century. The fact that India was by far the most important supplier of this commodity group put her at the very centre of the Euro-Asian trade of the Company. At the end of the seventeenth century, goods procured in Bengal alone — the principal Asian supplier of textiles and raw silk sent to Europe — accounted for as much as 40 percent of the total Dutch exports to Europe valuewise. If goods procured in the three other principal Indian regions — Gujarat, the Coromandel coast and the Malabar coast — are added to the Bengal cargo, this proportion goes up to as much as around 70 percent.

This extended discussion of the trading strategy of the Dutch East India Company, while not entirely germane to the theme of this chapter which is a discussion of the Dutch perception of seventeenth-century India, must nevertheless be regarded as crucial in order to place the rest of our discussion in perspective. More than any other major European corporate enterprise at work in India between the sixteenth and the middle of the eighteenth century, the Dutch East India Company was the largest in terms of the volume and value of trade carried on in and from the subcontinent. This would include the Portuguese in the sixteenth and the English and the French in the seventeenth and the first half of the eighteenth century. But even more importantly, the nature of the Dutch Company's relationship with the subcontinent was qualitatively very different from that of any of its fellow enterprises. The Company's connection with India started in 1606, i.e. within four years of its establishment in 1602 and lasted all the way until its liquidation in the 1790s. The Dutch connection with India formally came to an end in 1825 when the remaining Indian establishments were handed over to the English East India Company in exchange for the latter's establishments in Southeast Asia. Throughout this long period, the sole interest of the Company in the subcontinent was commerce with no involvement whatever in political processes. The only exception to this was Cochin on the Malabar coast where the Company did, indeed, enjoy a certain amount of political power and patronage in alliance with the Raja of Cochin. But the role of Cochin in the Company's overall profile in the subcontinent was of no particular significance at any point in time.

This unidimensional involvement of the Company with India throughout its history ensured that for all purposes India was to be looked upon simply as a provider of goods for other parts of Asia as well as for Europe and, on a more limited basis, as an absorber of goods from other parts of Asia and, on a negligible scale, from Europe. The country had no other attraction or significance for the Company, which was only interested in interacting with groups and institutions that were inseparably linked with the successful conduct of its trade. An example would be the Mughal Indian as well as South Indian coinage and minting and monetary systems in general. Neither the Mughals nor the South Indian rulers allowed the circulation of foreign coins in their dominions. Since the principal import of the Company into the subcontinent consisted of gold and silver bullion and coins of foreign origin, it was critically important that the conversion of these into Indian coins was done quickly, knowledgeably and as cost-effectively as possible. So one finds a great deal of commentary on and analysis of Mughal Indian as well as South Indian coinage systems in the Company's documentation. Another example would be the commercial activities of the Indian mercantile classes engaged in coastal and overseas trade. Given the enormous interest of the Company in intra-Asian trade, Indian merchants engaged in this trade were regarded as important rivals whose activities needed to be constantly watched and monitored. This attempt at monitoring resulted in the compilation of by far the largest and the most detailed body of both quantitative and qualitative information regarding Indian merchants' coastal and overseas trade from different regions of India available in any primary source — Asian or European — that is available today.

So this was the India that the Dutch were interested in and which they commented upon and recorded extensively. By the same token, they were not interested in reaching out to other spheres of activity involving access to power or authority which were regarded essentially as projects involving avoidable expenditure and shifting the focus away from the central concerns of trade. An example of this was the passing over of an opportunity to fortify the factory at Hugli in the 1690s. The context was the revolt by the Zamindar, Sobha Singh of Chatwa-Barda in Midnapore district in Bengal, which kept the province in a state of serious disorder for nearly two and a half years between the middle of 1695 and the close of 1697. Initially, the Dutch factors turned down the request by the provincial administration for assistance in crushing the revolt. But in August 1696 the rebels succeeded in capturing the fort at Hugli, exposing the local Dutch factory to grave danger. It was then decided to disregard the standing instructions by Batavia to maintain strict neutrality in situations of this sort, and steps were taken to restore the control of the fort to the Mughal authorities. A contingent of Dutch soldiers was deployed to sorround the fort, and the *Berkensteyn* was stationed in the Hugli river at a point from which its guns could cover the fort. The known superiority of European weaponry persuaded the rebels not to put up a fight. The fort was promptly vacated and the Dutch restored it to the Bakhshi, Mirza Hasan Ali's control. Needless to emphasize, the Dutch action was in response to compelling local circumstances and did not represent a shift from the basic policy of neutrality. This is borne out by the Company's reluctance to take advantage of the permission given by the Subahdar Ibrahim Khan to all the European Companies to strengthen their defences and even fortify their settlements. In fact, once the revolt had been crushed, the temporary measures taken to strengthen the defences of the Hugli factory were rescinded.

If its naval superiority enabled the Dutch Company to oblige the Mughal authorities in times of need (another example was the naval assistance provided in the Mughal campaign against

Chatgaon in 1665-66), it was also its strongest weapon to fight the authorities when its central concerns were threatened. A case in point was the demand the Mughal authorities made on the Dutch, the English and the French in the 1690s to provide protection to Indian shipping against the depredations of European pirates operating mainly from their bases in Madagascar. The plunder of the *Ganj-i-Sawai* in 1695 was instrumental in the introduction of the system of Dutch and English convoys to the Red Sea. A large ship of 1,000 khandies paid a fee of Rs.20,000 for a round trip while a smaller vessel qualified for Rs.15,000. Half the sum was found by the *mutasaddi* of Surat from the customs duties, while the rest was jointly subscribed by the merchants whose ships were to make the trip. The Company was allowed to carry its own cargo or freight goods on the escort vessels it made available. This arrangement worked well until 1698, when a Surat merchant Hasan Hamadani lost a richly laden ship. The ship had not formed part of the convoy, but each of the three Companies was nevertheless obliged in February 1699 to give a bond (*muchalka*) accepting responsibility for any losses that vessels from Surat might in future sustain at the hands of the pirates. The English were made responsible for the vessels going to the southwest coast of India, the Malay peninsula and the Indonesian archipelago, the French for those going to the Persian Gulf, and the Dutch for vessels going to the Red Sea. Abdul Ghafur and other merchants interpreted the *muchalkas* as implying the Companies' responsibility for losses whether or not a particular ship that might be captured formed part of the convoy, an interpretation that the Europeans contested.

An occasion for testing the enforceability of the *muchalkas* arose in September 1701, when news reached Surat that one of Abdul Ghafur's ships from the Red Sea, the *Husaini*, had been plundered. The Dutch refused to pay compensation, claiming that this was one of the ships that had broken convoy. Ghafur organized his fellow merchants, who decided that until the Dutch paid the compensation, no one would fit out a ship. They also demanded suspension of the Company's trade until a settlement was reached. The imperial court decreed in favour of the merchants, and ordered the Dutch to pay the compensation claimed. Pending this, their trade was banned throughout the Mughal empire. As was usual in such situations, however, the ban was only partially enforced. The demand for compensation was met, but it was only in November 1702 that the ban on trade was withdrawn.

In August 1703, yet another of Abdul Ghafur's ships was attacked and captured while it was anchored at the Surat bar. The Dutch refused to pay compensation, as the piracy had not occurred on the high seas. They also decided to use their naval muscle power to find a long-term solution to this problem. A strong Dutch naval force arrived from Batavia off Surat in September 1703 and blockaded the port, cutting off the port's life line. This was repeated a year later. The Company, of course, recognized that from the perspective of the Indian maritime merchant, Surat at this time was by far the premier port of the subcontinent linking the west coast of India to the Red Sea and the Persian Gulf. It was also perhaps the most cosmopolitan of the Indian ports attracting a large number of merchants who were the subjects of the Persian or the Turkish monarchs. Being mindful of not jeopardising the Company's relations with these countries, the commander of the blockading fleet decided to exempt these merchants from the blockade. But that led to the problem of defining precisely as to who was an Indian merchant and which was an Indian ship. To take advantage of the exemption, many of the Muslim merchants of Surat claimed foreign connections. Using his discretion, the commander released a ship saying that it was an Arab rather than a Mughal vessel. It belonged to Haji Muhammad Ali of Kung in the Persian Gulf and the *nakhuda* (captain), the sailors and the soldiers on board were mostly Arabs. The factors at Surat disagreed and pointed out that it was without any doubt a Gujarati ship and that it was a common practice to employ Arab sailors and even claim Arab ownership. At any rate, the Dutch strategy of putting the Mughal authorities under severe pressure by blockading the port worked in its entirety. At the suggestion of the new governor of Surat, Najabat Khan, the Emperor agreed to relieve the Dutch of the 1699 *muchalka*, thereby restoring the *status quo ante* of 1696 stipulating only the provision of convoy to the Surat ships. This was in January 1705, but the Dutch blockade of Surat was lifted only in 1707.

It need hardly be stressed that the relationship between the Dutch and the other European Companies on the one hand and the Mughal Indian authorities on the other was a delicately fine tuned one based on a perception of mutual benefit. An increase in the volume and value of foreign trade brought about by the functioning of the Companies in the Empire was highly welcome. In particular this was related to (a) the accretion to the customs revenues at the Empire's ports which accrued directly to the imperial exchequer and (b) the fact that the Companies' imports consisted overwhelmingly of precious metals which were not produced domestically but were nevertheless needed in large quantities to run the empire's monetary system as well as to cater to other needs. On their part, the Companies fully realized the critical significance and value of their Indian operations and would always be wary of using their naval superiority except under the most pressing circumstances.

II

On the specific question of the Dutch perception of seventeenth-century India, the bulk of the massive documentation of the Dutch East India Company is understandably devoted to issues related to trade and commerce. On the more general questions of polity and society, unfortunately, there is not very much available. I would, however, like to deal in some detail with one specific set of documents available for the Mughal empire for the 1620s. Indian historians working on the seventeenth century have for long been familiar with *Jahangir's India* translated and edited by W.H. Moreland and Pieter Geyl, and published by Cambridge University Press way back in 1925. This is a small part of the set of documents that I will analyse in the rest of this paper. In this endeavour, I will draw heavily on D.H.A. Kolff and H.W. van Santen (ed.), *De geschriften van Francisco Pelsaert over Mughal Indie, 1627: Kroniek en Remonstrantie.*

Jahangir's India was one part of Francisco Pelsaert's two-part account of Mughal India written at Agra in the 1620s. Several other accounts of a similar nature have been published over the years in the Linschoten Society series, the Dutch counterpart of the English Hakluyt Society. These include the two-volume W.Ph. Coolhaas (ed.), *Pieter van den Broecke in Azie*, W. Caland (ed.), *De Remonstrantie van W. Geleynssen de Jongh*, W. Caland (ed.), *De Open-deure tot het Verborgen Heydendom door Abraham Rogerius*, A.J. Bernet Kempers (ed.), *Journaal van Dircq van Adrichem's Hofreis naar den Groot-Mogol Aurangzeb, 1662* and J.Ph. Vogel (ed.), *Journaal van J.J. Ketelaar's Hofreis naar den Groot Mogol te Lahore 1711-1713*. The two last mentioned are accounts of the embassies to the Mughal emperor's court in 1662 and 1711-13 respectively. The account of Abraham Rogerius is almost a theological work regarding the Hindus of South India. Of the two part journal of Van den Broecke, the second part deals with the Surat factory of the Dutch East India Company between 1620 and 1629. The account of Geleynssen de Jongh basically analyses the commercial possibilities in Gujarat around 1630, but it also contains a good deal of information on the various Hindu sects and castes to which the Gujarati merchants belonged.

As far as the writings of Francisco Pelsaert, a Dutch factor at Agra in the 1620s, himself are concerned, the two parts, viz. the chronicle and the *Remonstrantie* (Report or Relation), indeed together comprise a single unified account. The first part of the *Remonstrantie* which deals with trade has a good deal in common with Geleynssen's *Remonstrantie* except that while Geleynssen confines himself to Gujarat, Pelsaert claims to write about the Mughal empire as a whole. The latter part of the Pelsaert's *Remonstrantie* where he talks about the customs of the land follows logically from his chronicle. In addition to Moreland and Geyl, Pelsaert's writings have in the past found other editors. In 1631, Ioannes de Laet included portions of the *Remonstrantie* and nearly the whole of the chronicle in his Latin work *De Imperio Magni Mogolis sive India Vera Commentarius, etc.*, dealing with the Mughal empire. An English version appeared in Bombay in 1928 as J.S. Hoyland (translator) and S.N. Banerjee (annotator), *The Empire of the Great Mogol: A Translation of De Laet's "Description of India and Fragment of Indian History"*. Parts of the *Remonstrantie* appeared in French in 1664 in Melchisedech de Thevenot, *Relations de Divers Voyages Curieux*. The Chronicle, translated and edited by Brij Narain and Sri Ram Sharma, appeared in book form as *A Contemporary Dutch Chronicle of Mughal India* in 1957, after having been published in parts in *The Journal of the Bihar and Orissa Research Society* (1942 and 1943) and *The Journal of the Bihar Research Society* (1946). The translation unfortunately was rather defective and the annotation did not do justice to the text. As a result, the Chronicle has not really received the attention of the historians of India to the extent that it deserves.

The Chronicle basically deals with the political and military history of the Mughal empire between 1537 and 1627. After a short introduction, Pelsaert begins his account with Humayun's campaign of 1537. In 11 folios, Pelsaert describes Humayun's defeat by Sher Shah Sur in 1540, his subsequent wanderings in Western India, his trip to Persia, the campaign that led to his return to the throne of Delhi in 1555 and finally his demise in 1556. Akbar's reign is then taken up in great detail in 42 folios. A very lively account of the 1606 rebellion by Khusro follows.

All this takes up about 40 percent of the chronicle. The years between Khusro's rebellion and 1621 when Pelsaert arrived in Agra are then commented upon in great detail, though the chronology is not always faultless. It is unlikely that this section was based on a proper evaluation of the existing chronicles with the help of knowledgeable experts. The last part of the chronicle — again occupying nearly 40 percent of the total — covers the last seven years of Jahangir's reign when Pelsaert was himself present in the empire. Personal observations come through very richly in this part of the account. The campaign of Shahjahan against the Centre receives much attention. The part dealing with the conflict that reached out to Gujarat is particularly rich in detail and perhaps deserves to be regarded as an important historical document.

In order to convey an idea of the richness of the contents of the Chronicle, let me in conclusion draw attention to three quantitative accounts that the Chronicle provides. The first of these details the treasure left behind by Akbar at his death in 1605. The second is a list of the empire's umara and mansabdars while the third catalogues the various animals probably belonging to the emperor. It is for the specialists of Akbar's reign to determine the reliability of these accounts.

List 1

The value of the treasure left behind by Akbar is stated to be 34 crores, 82 lakhs and 26386 3/4 rupees as follows:

Coins	*Rs.*
6,970,000 gold muhrs reckoned at Rs. 14 per piece	97,580,000 3/4
Silver rupees	100,000,000
230,000,000 copper paisas	766,666
Total	198,346,666 3/4

Precious stones etc.	
Diamonds, rubies, emeralds, pearls and other precious stones	60,520,521
Silverware such as jars, plates, cups, vessels, candleholders, pedestals, beds, etc.	2,225,838
Clothing using gold	19,006,745
Golden pots, plates, spoons and figures of elephants, camels, horses, etc.	9,507,992
Copper plates, pots, pans, cups, etc.	51,225

Fine porcelain consisting of large plates, cups, bottles etc. of extraordinary curiosity	2,507,747
Total	93,820,068

Fine Persian carpets, etc. Gold and silver sheets from Persia, Turkey, Gujarat and Christendom together with silk textiles, etc., from Bengal and other places	15,509,979
Woollen stuffs from Christendom, Persia and Kashmir, etc.	503,252
Tents etc. for the palaces	9,925,545
Books written by great masters of which 24,000 volumes are bound in costly material	6,463,731
Guns, firelocks, lead for ammunition, etc.	8,575,971
Harnesses, shields, swords, daggers and other weapons	7,555,525
Gold and silver saddles, bridles for horses etc.	2,525,646
Carriages for use in war etc.	5,000,000
Total	56,059,649
Grand Total	348,226,383¾

List II

The second quantitative account deals with the Mughal *umara* and *mansabdars* who were inherited by Jahangir from Akbar and were listed in the king's register.

	Rank	*Number of horses (these are seldom maintained in full)*
8 umara	5,000	40,000
9 gentlemen	4,500	40,500
25 umara	4,000	100,000
30 "	3,500	105,000
36 "	3,000	108,000
42 "	2,500	105,000
45 "	2,000	90,000
51 "	1,500	76,500
55 "	1,000	55,000
58 "	700	40,600

80 mansabdars	500	40,000
73 "	400	29,200
58 "	350	20,300
72 "	300	21,600
85 "	250	21,250
150 "	200	30,000
242 "	150	36,300
300 "	100	30,000
245 "	80	19,600
397 "	60	23,820
298 "	40	11,920
240 "	30	7,200
232 "	20	4,640
110 "	10	1,100
741 ahadis	4	2,946
1,332 "	3	3,966
1,428 "	2	2,856
950 "	1	950
7,281 umara, mansabdars and ahadis		1,068,248

LIST III

Then follows a list of elephants, horses, camels, mules, oxen, etc. (probably belonging to the emperor)

		Number
a.	Elephants, big and small, male and female, of whom 100 are particularly large and handsome	6,751
b.	Horses	
	Persian of particularly good breed and beauty	3,200
Turkish		5,970
From Kutch		2,500
From the mountains of Gond		210
	Mares from all over	120
	Total of horses	12,000
c.	Camels	6,223
d.	Mules	260
e.	Oxen	7,000
	Total	32,234

VIII

The English East India Company and India

It was on the last day of the year 1600 that a charter granted by Queen Elizabeth I incorporated some 219 members under the title of 'The Governor and Company of Merchants of London Trading into the East Indies': this was the body that came to be known as the English East India Company. Along with its rival organization in the Netherlands, the Dutch East India Company chartered just over a year later, it stood out as the most remarkable contemporary edifice of commercial capitalism. The process which had culminated in the establishment of these two organizations which dominated trade between Asia and Europe during the seventeenth and the eighteenth centuries had indeed started with the discovery by the Portuguese at the end of the fifteenth century of the all-water route to the East Indies via the Cape of Good Hope. Among the historic consequences of the discovery was the overcoming of the transport-technology barrier to the growth of trade between Asia and Europe. The volume of this trade was no longer subject to the capacity constraint imposed by the availability of pack animals and riverboats in the Middle East. Both the old and the new routes were in use throughout the sixteenth century, but by the early years of the seventeenth, when the English and the Dutch companies had successfully challenged the Portuguese monopoly of the all-water route, the new route had almost completely taken over the transportation of goods between the two continents. In addition to transportation, the procurement of Asian goods was also organized from the sixteenth century onward by the Europeans themselves, who were then arriving in the East in significant numbers. The goods procured had to be paid for overwhelmingly in precious metals. This was essentially an outcome of the inability of Europe to supply goods that could be sold in Asia in reasonably large quantities at competitive terms. The new vistas of the growth of trade between the two continents opened up by the overcoming of the transport-technology barrier could have been frustrated by the shortage of silver for export to Asia that the declining, or at best stagnant, European output of this metal might have occasioned, but fortunately, the discovery of the Cape route had coincided with that of the Americas. The working of the Spanish American silver mines had tremendously expanded the European silver stock, a part of which was available for diversion to Asia for investment in Asian goods. A continued expansion in the volume and the value of the Euro-Asian trade could now take place.

In the last quarter of the sixteenth century, the Portuguese Crown faced a growing range of problems in its Euro-Asian pepper trade. These, coupled with the loss in 1585 of Antwerp's position as the staple market for Asian spices in north-western Europe as a result of the blockade of the Scheldt, gave the merchants from the northern Netherlands a strong incentive to challenge the Portuguese monopoly of the Cape route and to participate directly in the Euro-Asian spice trade. In April 1595, the Amsterdam based 'Company of Far Lands', which was the first among the so-called Dutch 'precompanies', sent out four ships to the East Indies under the command of Cornelis de Houtman. One of the ships was lost but the remaining three came back in August 1597 with a cargo of pepper, nutmeg and mace. In the meantime, a number of new 'precompanies' had been organized for trade with the East Indies. One of these was in Amsterdam, two in Zeeland and another two in Rotterdam. The two Amsterdam companies were merged in 1598 and came to be known as the 'Old Company'. It was on the account of this Company that eight ships were sent out to the East in the spring of 1598. The ships returned safely in 1599, and the profit on the voyage was estimated at around 400 percent. This caused great consternation among the English merchants engaged in the spice trade from the Levant where supplies of Asian spices were brought in regularly via the water-cum-land route passing either through the Red Sea and Egypt or through the Persian Gulf, Iraq and the Syrian desert. The fear of Dutch domination of the spice market in north-western Europe thus served as the catalyst that led a group of London merchants to apply to the Crown for a monopoly charter for the East India trade. The birth of the English East India Company on 31 December 1600 was followed by that of the Dutch East India Company on 20 March 1602 on the strength of a charter granted by the States-General, the national administrative body of the Dutch Republic. In so far as this Company brought the existing 'precompanies' together under one umbrella, it was christened the United East India Company (Verenigde Oost-Indische Compagnie).

Between 1601 and 1612, the 12 voyages organized by the English East India Company to the East were on separate and terminable account. The period between 1613 and 1642 witnessed the operation of three successive joint stocks. In the meantime, in 1637, Charles I had granted a patent to the so-called Courteen's Association to trade to those parts of the East Indies where the Company had not established a factory. But the Association turned out to be a dismal failure and constituted no real threat to the monopoly of the Company. The outbreak of the civil war in the 1640s caused a certain amount of dislocation for the Company's trade, but matters improved considerably after the charter of 1657 which provided for a permanent joint stock. The monopoly privileges of the Company were threatened yet again in July 1698 when a rival body – usually described as the New English East India Company – received a charter from the Crown. But in April 1702, the two companies agreed to have a joint Board of Directors, the final amalgamation coming in 1709 under an award by the Earl of Godolphin. From this point on there was no further challenge to the Company's monopoly until 1813, when the new charter legalized the entry of private traders into the East Indian trade. Twenty years later, the Company ceased to be a trading body and was entrusted solely with the running of the colonial administration of India, a process that had started in 1765 with the Company wresting from the Mughal Emperor Shah Alam the *diwani* (revenue collection) rights in the province of Bengal. The Company was liquidated in 1858 following the assumption by the British Crown of direct responsibility for Indian affairs.

Like other Europeans, the principal interest of the English in the East, initially at least, was in the procurement of pepper and other spices for the European market. The first two voyages were directed at Bantam in Java where a factory was established in 1602. From 1613, Sumatra became the chief supplier of pepper to the Company. The crucial importance of the Coromandel textiles in facilitating this trade and making it more profitable had also been brought home to the Company quite early. A factory was established at Masulipatnam in 1611, though the first Company voyage to the Coromandel coast was not organized until 1614. In the meantime, given the Dutch monopsonistic designs in the Indonesian archipelago in the matter of the procurement of spices such as cloves, nutmeg and mace, a situation of armed conflict with the VOC was becoming inevitable. The hostilities erupted in 1618, and the English emerged distinctly the worse of the two. The London agreement of 1619 provided for an English share of one-third in the trade of the Spice Islands, and of one half in the pepper trade of Java subject to the English contributing one-third of the cost of maintaining the Dutch garrisons in the area. The English headquarters in the region were moved to Batavia in 1620, and the two companies shared garrisons in Banda, Moluccas and Amboyna, but due both to Dutch hostility as well as the English shortage of resources, the arrangement did not quite work. The 1623 incident at Amboyna led to a recall of the English factors from the shared centres in the archipelago to Batavia, and hastened the process of the English withdrawal from the Spice Islands.

While the English had come to Coromandel in search of textiles for the south-east Asian markets, their attempts to penetrate the Gujarat trade were linked directly to their Euro-Asian trade. Because of the possibility of a military engagement with the Portuguese and/or the Dutch, each of the English voyages to the East consisted of a certain minimum number of ships. But on the return voyage, a cargo consisting of pepper and other spices alone would fill perhaps only one of these ships. Hence the urgent need to diversify the return cargo by including in it items such as Indian textiles and indigo. Gujarat textiles could, of course, also be used for the south-east Asian trade to the extent necessary. The third voyage sent out in 1607, therefore, carried instructions to explore the commercial possibilities of the western coast of India. William Hawkins reached Surat in 1608 and went on to Agra the following year but was unable to obtain formal trading rights. Henry Middleton, the Commander of the sixth voyage, was also refused permission to trade at Surat. Thomas Best, the Commander of the tenth voyage, who reached Surat in September 1612, however, finally managed to obtain an imperial edict conferring formal trading rights on the Company. A factory was established at Surat in 1613, and regular trade started there and at Ahmedabad, Burhanpur and Agra, with a ship being sent back directly from Surat for the first time in 1615. Between 1616 and 1617, while only four small ships were dispatched directly to Bantam from London, nine ships of large tonnage were sent to Surat. The President at Surat was also placed in charge of the Company's trade in Persia. The Crown leased Bombay to the Company in 1668, and in 1687 Bombay superseded Surat as the headquarters of the Company in western India. In the meantime, the Company's trade had extended into Bengal in the early 1650s with the establishment of a factory at Hugli.[1]

Though items such as indigo and saltpetre figured in the Company's exports from India, the most important commodity the Company procured there was textiles. Initially, a part of these textiles was carried to the Indonesian archipelago to pay for the pepper and spices bought there. After 1624 when the Company's procurement of cloves smuggled by Asian merchants into Makassar became important, the volume of Coromandel textiles carried to Makassar via Batavia and later Bantam became fairly large. But this trade declined rather sharply from 1643 as Dutch efforts to plug the smuggling into Makassar became increasingly more successful. The only other Asian market to which the Company carried Coromandel textiles was Persia, but the quantities involved were never large. In view of the continuing poor performance in this area, the Company decided in 1661 to withdraw from participation in intra-Asian trade and concentrate its energies and resources on Euro-Asian trade.

From about this time onward, the English participation in intra-Asian trade was confined to private traders, and these included senior Company employees engaged in this activity on their private account. Among the important private English traders operating from Coromandel during the second half of the seventeenth century were the governors of Madras. Two of these, Elihu Yale and Thomas Pitt, were particularly active and are known to have amassed huge fortunes, estimated in the case of Yale at a massive £200,000. Other governors with significant private trading interests included Edward Winter, William Langhorn, Streynsham Master, Gulston Addison, Edward Harrison and Joseph Collet.[2] Most, if not all of these individuals were also diamond commissioners. Diamonds were an important item of trade not covered by the Company's monopoly and figured prominently in English Euro-Asian trade on private account. The diamond trade was controlled basically by Jewish merchants, many of whom had migrated from Portugal to England around the middle of the seventeenth century. This migration had led to a shift in the axis of the diamond trade from Goa–Lisbon to Madras–London. The diamond merchants operated mainly by appointing commissioners in India to whom funds were dispatched regularly and who looked after the procurement and shipment of the rough stones. In recompense for their labours, the commissioners were entitled to a 7 percent commission on the value of the investment. The accounts of a leading

1 K.N. Chaudhuri, *The English East India Company: The Study of an Early Joint-Stock Company 1600–1640* (London, 1965); K.N. Chaudhuri, *The Trading World of Asia and the English East India Company, 1660–1760* (Cambridge, 1978).

2 P.J. Marshall, 'Private British Trade in the Indian Ocean before 1800', in *India and the Indian Ocean, 1500–1800*, eds Ashin Das Gupta and M.N. Pearson (Calcutta, 1987).

diamond merchant in London, John Chomley, provide for some years information on the total amount of funds remitted annually from London to Madras for investment in rough diamonds. While this amount fluctuated a great deal between one year and another, an exceptionally good year such as 1676 witnessed the remittance of as much as £100,000 on this account.[3] There ordinarily was a gap, sometimes as long as six months, between the receipt of the funds by the commissioner in Madras and their actual investment in the purchase of the diamonds. The resultant additional liquidity available at no extra cost often constituted a major contributory element to the commissioner's success in the trading ventures he carried on on his private account. The group of Company servants engaged in private trade, of course, also included many who did not occupy senior positions in the Company's hierarchy. In addition, there were the so-called free merchants settled in India who were an important constituent of the group of English private traders engaged in intra-Asian trade.

The trading strategy followed by the Company's principal rival, the Dutch East India Company, was quite different. By far the most distinctive characteristic feature of this strategy was a large-scale participation in intra-Asian trade as an integral part of the Company's overall trading operations. By the middle of the seventeenth century the range of the Company's intra-Asian trading network covered practically all major points along the great arc of Asian trade extending from Gombroon in the Persian Gulf to Nagasaki in Japan. The two principal factors contributing to the great success achieved by the Dutch East India Company in this endeavour were the spice monopoly in the Indonesian archipelago and the exclusive access amongst the Europeans to the Japan trade following the closure of the country to the rest of the world in 1639. It should also be realized that the extensive as well as highly profitable participation in intra-Asian trade, which contributed a great deal to the Company's dominant position in Euro-Asian trade through at least the seventeenth century, would have been impossible without the coordinating role played by the office of the Governor-General and Council at Batavia, the intermediate high-ranking agency in Asia with extensive decision-making powers. But at the same time it must be recognized that there were other dimensions of Batavia's intermediate role, all of which were not necessarily to the Company's advantage in the long run. Take, for example, the procurement of Indian textiles for the European market following the fashion revolution of the last quarter of the seventeenth century, when trade in these textiles became the single most important component of the English and the Dutch East India companies' Euro-Asian trade. By the turn of the eighteenth century, Bengal emerged as the single largest provider of these textiles. The Bengal–Europe trade in textiles was essentially a luxury trade in which exclusiveness and novelty in designs and patterns mattered a great deal. In 1681, for example, the English Court of Directors had written to their factors in Bengal:

[3] Søren Mentz, 'English Private Trade on the Coromandel Coast, 1660–1690: Diamonds and Country trade', *Indian Economic and Social History Review*, 33 (1996), 155–74.

> Now this for a constant and generall Rule, that in all flowered silks you change ye fashion and flower as much as you can every yeare, for English Ladies and they say ye French and other Europeans will give twice as much for a new thing not seen in Europe before, though worse, than they will give for a better silk for [of] the same fashion worn ye former yeare.[4]

Later the same year, they wrote: 'Of all silk wares, take it for a certain rule that whatever is new, gaudy or unusual will always find a good price at our candle.'[5] This exclusiveness, coupled with the intense competition among the Europeans for limited supplies, put a large premium on quick decisions by the local European factors. Such a decision might pertain to the purchase of a textile with a new pattern or a colour combination or a textile whose quality or size specification was substantially different from that stated in the relevant orders list. In this kind of a situation, the English factors were able to score a great deal over their Dutch counterparts. Given the distance between England and India, the English Directors really had no option but to allow a considerable amount of discretion in such matters to factors in Calcutta and elsewhere on the subcontinent. The result was a constant flow of new varieties, colour combinations and patterns in the textiles sent by Calcutta to London, though in the process the prices paid for these textiles continuously went up. The Dutch factors, on the other hand, were systematically denied such discretionary powers. The reason was the belief that, considering that Batavia was only a few weeks away from Hugli or for that matter any other Asian chief factory, such discretion was best left only to the Governor-General and Council. But the fact of the matter was that Batavia was never really able to help the Bengal factors effectively in deciding what to buy. The net result was that the Dutch factors in Bengal were at no time able to match the initiative and drive of their English counterparts. It was this more than anything else that enabled the English Company to almost catch up with the VOC by the turn of the eighteenth century in the matter of the average annual value of its imports from Asia. This process continued in the eighteenth century, and by 1740 the English had actually forged ahead of the Dutch.

The increase in the output of textiles and other export goods in the subcontinent in response to the secularly rising demand for these goods by the English and the Dutch East India companies would seem to have been achieved through a reallocation of resources, a fuller utilization of existing productive capacity and an increase over time in the capacity itself. A reallocation of resources in favour of the production of export goods such as raw silk and particular varieties of textiles would have been signalled, among other things, by a continuous rise in the prices of these goods in the markets where they were procured. Evidence regarding such a rise is available in plenty in the European company documentation. The available evidence also suggests both a fuller utilization of existing capacity as well as expansion thereof over time. In the case of textile

4 Quoted in V. Slomann, *Bizarre Designs in Silks* (Copenhagen, 1953), p. 114.
5 Quoted in Slomann, *Bizarre Designs in Silks*, p. 114.

manufacturing, for example, artisans engaged in the activity on a part-time basis seem to have increasingly found it worth their while to become full-time producers and to relocate themselves in the so-called *aurungs* – localized centres of manufacturing production, where the Europeans were increasingly concentrating their procurement through the intermediary merchants. Among the other factors of production required, land was clearly in abundant supply practically all over the subcontinent at this time. As far as the necessary capital resources needed for the production of new spindles, wheels and looms etc. were concerned, given the extremely small amounts involved and the fact that the European companies were ever willing to advance the necessary sums, the availability of funds also is highly unlikely to have been a constraining factor. It need hardly be stressed that across a country the size of the Indian subcontinent there are likely to have been regional variations with regard to the degree of dynamism, flexibility and potential for continuing expansion in the scale of production that this scenario envisages. However, evidence available at least in respect of a region such as Bengal, which was by far the most important theatre of company activity on the subcontinent, would generally seem to confirm the presence of such attributes in ample measure.

In this scenario, the English and other European companies' trade would have become a vehicle for an expansion in income, output and employment in the subcontinent. As far as additional employment generated in the textile manufacturing sector as a result of European procurement is concerned, a recent study of the trade of the English and the Dutch East India companies in the early years of the eighteenth century, estimated the number of additional full-time jobs created at approximately 100,000, accounting for around 10 percent of the total workforce in the sector.[6]

Our information on the distribution of the gains accruing from a growing foreign trade among the various sections engaged in productive activity is extremely limited. The two major groups directly affected by the growth in the volume of the European trade were the merchants dealing with the companies and the artisans who manufactured the export goods. The intense and growing competition among the English and the Dutch for goods such as textiles and raw silk increasingly created a sellers' market. This was reflected in the growing bargaining strength of the merchants vis-à-vis the companies. The position is somewhat less clear in relation to the textile weavers and other producing groups supplying to the merchants where, in principle, one would expect that at least a small part of the gain would have been transmitted to the producers in the form of increased employment and better returns, and there is some evidence that this indeed happened. On the whole, then, there can be very little doubt that the English East India Company and other European trading companies' commer-

6 Om Prakash, *The Dutch East India Company and the Economy of Bengal, 1630–1720* (Princeton, 1985), Chapter 8.

cial operations in the subcontinent represented a distinctly positive development from the perspective of the Indian economy.[7]

This scenario, however, underwent a substantive modification during the second half of the eighteenth century. The starting point was the assumption of political leverage by the English East India Company in different parts of the subcontinent. The process began in south-eastern India where the English and the French became allies of contestants for the succession of the Nawab of Arcot and the Nizam of Hyderabad. War ebbed and flowed across southern India with little intermission from 1746 until complete English victory brought the fighting to an end in 1761. British victory meant that the territories of the English-backed Nawab of Arcot became a client state of the English East India Company. Much more fundamental in importance was the incorporation of Bengal as a province under actual British rule. The 1765 Treaty of Allahabad was an outcome of the battle of Plassey in 1757 and that of Buxar in 1764. According to this treaty, the Mughal emperor conferred on the East India Company the *diwani* or the responsibility for the civil administration of Bengal; at the same time the *wazir* of Awadh accepted a British alliance and a British garrison. This settlement gave the British rule over some 20 million people in Bengal together with access to a revenue of about £3 million, and it took British influence nearly up to Delhi.

What the availability of substantive political leverage to the English East India Company in a province such as Bengal did was to bring to an end the level playing field that the intermediary merchants and artisans doing business with it had hitherto enjoyed. The relationship between these groups and the European companies had generally been free of coercion and determined by the market forces of supply and demand. That was now a thing of the past. Through an extensive misuse of its newly acquired political power, the Company subjected suppliers and artisans to complete domination, imposing upon them unilaterally determined terms and conditions which significantly cut into their margin of profit. For the procurement of textiles, for example, the province was divided into a number of segments each under the authority of a Commercial Resident. This Resident then arranged for information to be collected regarding the number of weavers, looms, pieces of textiles of different kinds manufactured in each *aurung* in his area in a year, the number ordinarily procured by rival European trading companies as well as private merchants each year, and so on. Since the Company's textile requirements took precedence over everyone else's, individual suppliers of the Company were allotted weavers who were banned from working for anyone else till such time as they had met their contractual obligations towards the Company. The terms offered by the Company to the suppliers, and in turn, by the latter to the weavers, were extraordinarily poor. The perennial complaint of the weavers was that the price allowed them by the Company hardly enabled them to cover the cost of the raw materials. In 1767, the weavers of the Khirpai division went so far as to send a delegation to Calcutta with a peti-

7 Prakash, *The Dutch East India Company and the Economy of Bengal*, Chapter 8.

tion requesting that the prices offered to them be increased by at least so much as to afford them a subsistence wage. They did manage to obtain an order directing the Commercial Resident, identified as one John Bathoe, to do the needful. But this evidently was no more than eyewash because Bathoe not only openly disregarded the order but indeed threatened to have the weavers arrested in the event that they continued with their claims.[8]

The woes of the intermediary merchants and the artisans were further aggravated by the complete marginalization of the rival European trading companies by the English. Indeed, within a few months of the takeover of the province after the battle of Plassey, the English factors were reported to be forcibly taking away pieces woven for the Dutch. In the early 1760s, the Commercial Residents at Malda and Midnapur were instructed to ensure that the best weavers of Jagannathpur, Olmara and the neighbouring *aurungs* worked exclusively for the English. This was at complete variance with the public posture that the English East India Company took. A Fort William public notification dated 28 April 1775, for example, asserted

> that the weavers of the province of Bengal and Bihar should enjoy a perfect and entire liberty to deal with any persons whom they pleased and that no person should use force of any kind to oblige the weavers or other manufacturers to receive advances of money or to engage in contracts for the provision of clothes against their will, and that all persons offending against this order should suffer severe punishment.[9]

The charade was continued in the English response dated 8 September 1785 to a Dutch memorandum:

> Under your agents, they [the weavers] may work more freely perhaps than under our own, and you may rest assured that we shall not countenance the servants or gomastahs of our own Board of Trade in any attempts that they may make to oppress the natives who work for you and not us, or prevent your employment of their industry. The weaver who works for your Company contributes equally to pay the revenue with the weaver who works for our own Board of Trade, and perhaps more so. And an extension to the sale of Bengal manufacture is more profitable to Great Britain than a monopoly in the purchase of such goods as would restrain the manufacture.[10]

The truth, however, was otherwise. The marked decline in the relative share in the total value of the output produced as far as the Bengali artisanal and the mercantile groups engaged in business with the English East India Company were

8 Algemeen Rijksarchief (ARA), J.M. Ross at Khirpai to Directors at Hugli, 16 May 1767, Appendix C2, Hooge Regering Batavia (HRB), 247.

9 ARA. The notification was signed by J.P. Auriol, Assistant Secretary, HRB 253.

10 ARA. The English Company reply dated 8 September 1785 to the second Dutch memorandum, Macpherson and Council to Eilbracht and van Citters, HRB 211.

concerned might, in turn, have introduced distortions in the structure of incentives in the domain of manufacturing and other production in the province.

Totally unjustified and distressing as such an erosion into the relative share of the mercantile and artisanal groups in the total output produced was, it is nevertheless important to distinguish between this range of implications of the altered status of the English East India Company as a trading body and the changes, if any, in the broad macroeconomic implications of its trading operations. There is a strong likelihood that the structure of manufacturing production in the province continued to be marked by a reasonable degree of vitality and capacity to deliver. An important, though by no means conclusive, index suggesting this scenario is the continuing growth of both the Euro-Asian and the intra-Asian trade from the province. It is true that under the pressure of the increasingly monopsonistic policies adopted by the English Company, the trade of their rival companies operating in the region was on the decline. But such a decline was much more than made up for by the English Company's own total exports to Europe going up from an annual average of under £700,000 during 1758–60 to as much as £1.92 million during 1777–79. Bengal accounted for as much as half of this value.[11] In intra-Asian trade, the decline in the Dutch Company exports as well as in those by the Indian merchants engaged in this trade was similarly much more than made up for by the spectacular rise in the English private merchants' trade with China.

Seemingly paradoxically, while the English East India Company's exports from India were undergoing a substantial increase during the second half of the eighteenth century, the import of bullion by the Company into the subcontinent was practically coming to an end. Thus against the annual average of £650,000 for the decade of 1751–60 as a whole, the annual average for the last two years of the decade was under £160,000. Such detailed information is unfortunately not available for the post-1760 period, but an appendix to the Ninth Report from the Select Committee of the East India Company entitled 'An account of the quantity of silver exported by the East India Company to Saint Helena, India and to China' from 1758 to 1771 lists only Mocha and Benkulen under India.[12] There is some evidence, however, which suggests that the import of treasure into India was resumed on a limited scale and on an occasional basis from 1784 onward.

Before we go into the question of how the export of goods was financed in the absence of the import of treasure, a comment on the resultant perceived shortage of circulating medium in the province would seem to be in order. The classic statement drawn upon in this context is the one made by James Steuart in 1772: 'the complaints of a scarcity of coin in Bengal, once so famous for its

[11] Om Prakash, *European Commercial Enterprise in Pre-Colonial India*, vol. II, no. 5, in the *New Cambridge History of India* series (Cambridge, 1998), p. 348.

[12] This statement is available in Appendix 5 to the 'Ninth Report from Select Committee appointed to take into consideration the state of the administration of justice in the provinces of Bengal, Bihar and Orissa', 25 June 1783, BL, OIOC, L/Parl/2/15.

wealth, are so general that the fact can hardly be called into question.'[13] Considering that there is no evidence on the stock of coined money or the amount of *sicca* rupees in circulation in the province at any point in time during the eighteenth century, there is no way the fact of shortage of money can be established or disputed in an objective manner. However, the relatively low rate of agio (*batta*) that was charged on Arcot *sicca* rupees at Dhaka between 1769 and 1773 would strongly discount the likelihood of any serious shortage of money being there in the region at this time.[14]

That still leaves the question of how the Company managed to increase its exports from India significantly during this period in the context of the virtual stoppage of the import of bullion unanswered. The explanation lies in good measure in the substantial quantities of rupee receipts obtained by the Company locally against bills of exchange issued to English and other European private traders payable in London and other European capitals. In so far as this procedure provided a safe channel to a whole host of European individuals to remit home savings made in India by participation in private trade and through other means, the amounts available under this arrangement were usually quite large. Even the procurement of tea at Canton was organized partly on the basis of the funds made available at Calcutta by Englishmen in exchange for bills to be issued at Canton on London.[15] Between 1757 and 1784, the value of the bills issued on the East India Company headquarters in London, including those drawn at Canton, has been estimated at a little over £11.8 million.[16] For the period between 1785 and 1796, the figure suggested is £5.7 million.[17] From the perspective of the Company as a corporate enterprise, the financing of the procurement of the export goods in India through rupee receipts obtained against bills of exchange payable in London or elsewhere as against through bullion shipped from home only represented a change of form, but from the perspective of the economy of the regions in which the Company functioned, this represented a substantive change.

Another source of funds for investment in export goods that the Company had access to after obtaining the *diwani* of the province of Bengal in 1765 was the surplus from the provincial revenue that it now collected. Such a diversion of the revenue was obviously unethical, and indeed the Parliamentary Select Committee of 1783 indicted the Company in no uncertain terms for having done this. The Committee observed that:

In all other Countries, the Revenue following the natural Course and Order of

[13] 'Memoirs of Coinage in Bengal', 1772, OIOC, Home Miscellaneous, vol. 62, p. 163.

[14] Rajat Datta, *Society, Economy and the Market: Commercialization in Rural Bengal, c.1760–1800* (Delhi, 2000), pp. 348–50.

[15] For an example of this kind of transaction, see a Company advertisement from Fort William dated 30 July 1781, Appendix 12 to Ninth Committee Report, OIOC, L/Parl/2/15.

[16] Calculated from P.J. Marshall, *East Indian Fortunes: The British in Bengal in the Eighteenth Century* (Oxford, 1976), p. 255.

[17] Rajat Datta, *Society, Economy and the Market*, p. 353.

> Things, arises out of their Commerce. Here, by a mischievious Inversion of that Order, the whole Foreign, Maritime Trade, whether English, French, Dutch or Danish arises from the Revenues; and these are carried out of the Country, without producing any Thing to compensate so heavy a Loss.[18]

But ethics had never been the weakness of the likes of Robert Clive who predicted to the Directors in September 1765 that in the forthcoming year there would be a 'clear gain' to the Company of £1.65 million which would serve to 'defray all the expense of the investment [in goods for export], furnish the whole of the China treasure, answer the demands of all your other settlements in India, and leave a considerable balance in your treasury besides'.[19] Such extravagant hopes were in fact never realized because a large part of the Bengal revenues had to be diverted to wars and other uses. With the return of peace in the 1780s and the 1790s, hopes were raised yet once again, and in 1793 Henry Dundas produced figures to show that a clear £1.4 million a year would be available for investing in goods for Europe.[20] His prophecies, like those of Clive and his contemporaries in 1765, were again brought to nothing by war. A Select Committee of the House of Commons reviewing the years 1792 to 1809 was obliged to point out that instead of the surpluses promised by Dundas, there had indeed been an overall deficit in India of some £8 million.[21] This, of course, does not mean that a part of the Bengal revenues would not have been diverted to the procurement of goods for export to England and there would clearly have been years when the sums so diverted would have been substantial. But it would seem impossible to work out on a systematic basis what proportion of the total exports of the English East India Company in the post-1765 era would have been financed from the Bengal revenues and qualifying for the category of 'unrequited' exports.

'Unrequited' exports represented the principal constituent element in the rubric of 'drain' of resources from India to Britain by the English East India Company in its corporate dimension. But there was in addition a private dimension to this phenomenon effected partly through the purchase of bills of exchange issued by the Company. The practice was by no means confined to the English Company. The Dutch East India Company was an equally important channel used for the transmission of private savings to Europe. Indeed, from about 1770 onward the process of raising resources in Bengal by the Dutch East India Company for investment in goods for export was marked by an important innovation. In addition to the usual mechanism of funds being collected in Asia through bills of exchange issued locally, the Directors of the Company now also began operating at the European end. This was done by negotiating in Amsterdam the procurement of bills of exchange drawn by Englishmen resident

[18] Ninth Report from Select Committee, OIOC, L/Parl/2/15.

[19] *Fort William–India House Correspondence and Other Contemporary-Papers Relating Thereto*, IV (Public Series), ed. C.S. Srinivasachari (New Delhi, 1962), pp. 338–9.

[20] P.J. Marshall, *Problems of Empire: Britain and India, 1757–1813* (London, 1968), p. 84.

[21] Marshall, *Problems of Empire*, p. 84.

in England on their correspondents in Calcutta, directing the latter to pay the local Dutch Company factors the sum of money specified in the bill. Many of these Englishmen had earlier bought bills from the Dutch Company factors in Bengal and were now on the other side. The transactions in these bills were intermediated by some of the leading Anglo-Dutch banking firms such as Hope & Co. and Pye Rich & Wilkieson who guaranteed timely payment against them. During the 1770s, this particular method became an important avenue for raising resources in Bengal. In a transaction entered into with Pye Rich & Wilkieson in 1773, for example, the Directors bought four such bills, each of the value of a little over £10,000. In the event of the bills not being honoured in Bengal, the banking firm was liable to pay a 12 percent compensation to the Company. The payment due to the firm against the bills was to be made only after the receipt of information that the money had in fact been collected in Bengal.[22] The Directors were evidently able to negotiate such a favourable package because of the large sums of money waiting in Calcutta to be remitted home. The parties interested in effecting the remittances were not particularly keen to use the offices of the English East India Company for the purpose, because the savings sought to be remitted home often contained a part – at times a rather large part – that the person concerned would be hard put to justify as legitimately made through participation in private trade or other authorized avenues of earning money.

In his *John Company at Work* published more than half a century ago, Holden Furber was the first professional historian to try to quantify the size of the annual drain of wealth from India to Britain. For the years between 1783 and 1793, he put this figure at £1.8 million.[23] For Bengal alone, which was by far the most important single Indian region to contribute to this phenomenon, a recent study puts the figure at £1 million for the years between 1757 and 1794.[24] Given the nature of the data, it is indeed quite impossible to attach any degree of precision to such estimates. All that one can say is that Bengal revenues provided an indirect subsidy to the British exchequer, and the enormous opportunities for private gain now available to the Company servants in their personal capacity created a whole new class of new-rich 'nabobs' returning to England with fortunes unheard of before. It is, however, highly unlikely that these private fortunes constituted an element of any importance in the financing of the Industrial Revolution in Britain which was then getting under way.

The rise of the China trade, which was by far the most important source of private trading fortunes, led to what Holden Furber has termed a 'commercial revolution' involving a clear domination of trade in the Indian Ocean and the South China Sea by the private English traders. Such a domination would almost certainly have had a certain amount of adverse impact on the trading operations

22 Femme Gaastra, 'British Capital for the VOC in Bengal', in *Commerce and Culture in the Bay of Bengal, 1500–1800*, eds Om Prakash and Denys Lombard (Delhi, 1999).

23 Holden Furber, *John Company at Work, A Study of European Expansion in India in the Late Eighteenth Century* (Cambridge, Mass., 1948), p. 310.

of the Indian merchants engaged in trade in the Eastern Indian Ocean. It is, however, important to keep the matter in perspective. The overall adverse impact on the fortunes of the Indian merchants engaged in intra-Asian trade would not seem to have been anything like catastrophic. The direct involvement of the Indian merchants in the China trade had never been of any significance, and to that extent, a growth in the English private trade in the sector had no specific and immediate implication for these merchants except that English ships also did a fair amount of business in south-east Asia on the way to and from China. It would seem that initially the increased competition by the English was injurious to the Indian merchants engaged in trade with this region. But over time the volume and value of trade on the India–south-east Asia sector would in fact seem to have registered a significant increase, with the Indian merchants getting their due share in the rising volume of trade.

As far as the English East India Company in its corporate dimension was concerned, an analysis of the implications of the grant of the *diwani* to the Company for the prosperity or otherwise of the agricultural sector of the province is perhaps more promising than trying to work out what part of the total Bengal revenues drained away to Britain.

The agrarian counterpart of the aggrieved Bengal textile weaver was the opium peasant who was similarly subjected to significant non-market pressures by the English East India Company, as well as by its employees operating in their private capacity. Soon after the takeover of the province, Company servants tried to establish private monopolies in the drug. These individuals generally did not engage in internal or international trade in the item on their own but would sell it on a monopoly basis to the prospective traders in the drug who would include Indian merchants, other private English traders and the Dutch East India Company. The gross profit earned in the process has been estimated to be quite high. This situation was altered radically in 1773 when the English Company decided to assume monopoly rights in the drug for itself. The arrangement was for the Company to organize the procurement of the drug on an exclusive basis and then arrange for its sale to prospective traders through public auctions held at Calcutta. In principle, the monopoly implied that the entire output of the drug would have to be handed over to the Company through a contractor at a price determined unilaterally for the year. In 1797, the contract system was abolished in favour of an agency system involving direct control by the Company of the cultivation of opium. If a peasant decided to be in the business of producing opium, he had no option but to deal with the Company. But in principle, he had the right not to be in the business of producing opium and to reject the offer of a cash advance in return for pledging his crop to the English Company agent.[25]

The opium enterprise was clearly of great advantage to the English East India Company, the contractors and other intermediaries participating in the enter-

24 Datta, *Society, Economy and the Market*, p. 57.

25 Extract, Bengal Revenue Consulations, 23 November 1773, Appendix 57, Ninth Committee Report, OIOC.

prise as well as to the private English traders engaged in the opium trade. As for the peasants participating in the opium enterprise, the position was more complex. There can be no question that the opium monopoly involved a certain amount of coercion over the peasants, and it is likely that the degree of this coercion exceeded the officially stipulated limits. What can one say about the overall implications of the English Company's opium monopoly? Was the expansion in output over time solely a function of the coercion to which the peasant was subjected? Or is it possible that the peasant found even the monopoly price, particularly after it was periodically increased between 1823 and 1838, preferable to the option of growing alternative crops? While no definitive answers to these questions are as yet possible, certain tentative suggestions may be made. The cultivation of opium did involve a four- to five-month commitment to demanding arduous work. The reason the acreage still went on increasing was because of the liberal policy the government followed in the matter of giving advances to the actual and prospective opium growers. These advances came in handy for meeting the peasants' land rent obligations and were extremely welcome. The fact that the government monopoly provided an assured market for the peasants' output at a predetermined price not subject to alteration by the size of the crop also worked as a positive factor. The cash advances involved the injection of fairly large sums of money into the commercial agricultural sector of the region directly through the peasants. The crop that this helped the expansion of was both of high value as well as being intended entirely for the market.

At a more general level, how did the functioning of the Company as the *diwan* affect the state of the agricultural sector in the province? The most basic element of state policy, of course, was the size and the pattern of land revenue demand made on the sector. On an average, 40–45 percent of the agricultural output was collected as land revenue. There was an almost continuous increase in both the amount of revenue assessed as well as that collected. With 1755 as base equal to 100, the index of the amount assessed stood at 135 in 1770, 155 in 1778 and 168 in 1783. The amount of revenue collected also went up but by a somewhat smaller margin. The collection was made exclusively in cash, significantly furthering the process of monetization in the province. There is evidence, for example, that in 1769 even sharecroppers in an extended *zamindari* of Burdwan were obliged to sell the crop and then pay the *zamindar* in cash, a process which seems to have intensified in subsequent years. During periods of price slumps, the Mughal revenue officials often used to accept payment of revenue in kind in order that the real burden on the peasantry was reduced. That element of flexibility was now done away with altogether.[26]

The major famine that hit the province in 1769–70 is conventionally believed to have caused as many as 10 million deaths, accounting for a third of the total population. Recent research, however, suggests that devastating as the famine was, the death toll is unlikely to have been anywhere near this figure. The dura-

26 Datta, *Society, Economy and the Market*, pp. 333–4.

tion of the famine at its peak was a maximum of six months, and the worst affected were six districts in western and north-eastern Bengal. It is nevertheless true that the role of the English East India Company in alleviating the misery caused by the famine was practically nil. The collection of revenue was strictly enforced throughout the famine: indeed, more revenue was collected at its height than in the subsequent year. Also, the Company failed to provide any form of institutional relief. Up to April 1770, the Company had advanced only Rs100,000 'for the purchase of rice on account of a charitable distribution made to the poor in and around Murshidabad'. An amount of Rs400,000 was all that was provided by way of financial aid from the Murshidabad treasury between April 1769 and May 1770 to help the cultivators to organize production during the ensuing agricultural season.[27]

An area in which the Company was more effective was in intervening in the market as a device to free it of the major internal restrictions imposed by *zamindari* control during the period of the *nizamat*. The fact that merchants were able to carve out petty domains of privileged trade, and that *zamindars* and other landed proprietors were the prime agents for the establishment of these markets, jointly militated against the development of an unfettered system of markets in the province. What this had involved was the proliferation of *zamindari* outposts (*chowkies*) to collect tolls at various rates dictated by the financial predilections of an individual *zamindar* and continuous conflicts between merchants and *zamindars* over the rate of tolls, over market jurisdictions and the movement of commodities. What the East India Company was able to do was to take a body of steps between 1773 and 1790 to rectify this situation. These included the abolition of all duties levied upon grain while being transported from one place to another. It was only at the final point of destination that a duty was to be charged. The management of such duties was to be under five customs houses to be established at Calcutta, Hugli, Murshidabad, Dhaka and Patna. The other problem, of the control exercised by the *zamindars* and the *talluqdars* over markets, was found more difficult to address. Finally in 1790 the Board of Revenue decreed a separation between rent collected in the markets so controlled and the taxes collected there on trade. While rent could continue to be collected on a private basis, the right to tax was henceforth to be vested in the Company. The combined result of these policies was a proliferation of market places all over Bengal. The increase in their numbers or their establishment in previously deficient areas enabled the peasantry to relate more easily to wider commercial networks.[28]

This profile of a reasonably vibrant agricultural sector and rural economy in the second half of the eighteenth century seeks to revise substantially the orthodoxy in the historiography on the subject. It has traditionally been held, for

27 Datta, *Society, Economy and the Market*, Chapter 5.

28 Datta, 'Markets, Bullion and Bengal's Commercial Economy: An Eighteenth-Century Perspective', in *Commerce and Culture in the Bay of Bengal, 1500–1800*, eds Om Prakash and Denys Lombard (Delhi, 1999).

example, that because of the revenue policy of the East India Company, there was a large-scale distress sale of *zamindaris* in the province which had rendered the land market highly depressed. Specific evidence now available regarding the generally buoyant state of the land market during this period suggests the strong need of giving up such stereotypes and having a fresh look at this phase in the history of Bengal. Such an enterprise will fit in quite well with the work that has now been under way for two decades or more seeking to view Indian history in the eighteenth century in a new light.

IX

Alternative Trading Strategies: The Dutch and the English East India Companies in Asia, 1600-1650

The most outstanding feature revealed by an analysis of the two largest European trading companies operating in Asia in the seventeenth and the eighteenth centuries, namely the Dutch and the English East India Companies, in a comparative perspective is the very different trading strategies followed by them in their trading operations in the East. Very early in its career, the Dutch Company realized the enormous potential of participating in trade within Asia in addition to trade between Asia and Europe. Participation in intra-Asian trade as an integral feature of its overall commercial strategy soon became by far the most important distinguishing characteristic feature of the Company. Indeed, it was the only European corporate enterprise to participate extensively in intra-Asian trade on its official account. The English East India Company, on the other hand, never really got into intra-Asian trade on any significant scale at any point in time. Indeed, in 1661, it consciously withdrew from even its marginal involvement in this trade leaving it entirely to its employees operating in their private capacity. It was, however, not for lack of trying that the English had been denied their share of the pie. They were as aware of the potential of participation in intra-Asian trade as their Dutch rivals. But an acute shortage of resources in money, men and ships coupled with the absence of a long term vision entailed by the absence of an organization marked by permanent joint stock that made it impossible for the English to make successful inroads into the emerging Dutch monopoly in this area. Indeed, the complexity of the relationship between the two companies in the East in the first half of the seventeenth century can best be analysed in terms of the unconcealed hostility of the Dutch towards the English efforts to partake in the fruits of the intra-Asian trade.

The Dutch East India Company was founded in 1602 by a charter granted by the States-General, the national administrative body of the Dutch Republic. The Euro-Asian trade in pepper carried on by the Portuguese Estado da India was running into serious problems in the last quarter of the sixteenth century. This coupled with the loss, in 1585, of Antwerp's position as the staple market for Asian goods in North-western Europe as a result of the blockade of the Scheldt, gave the merchants from the northern Netherlands a strong incentive to challenge the Portuguese monopoly of the Cape route and participate directly in the Euro-Asian spice trade. In April 1595, the Amsterdam based Company of Far Lands, which was the first among the so-called 'precompanies' sent out four ships to the East Indies. One of the ships was lost but the remaining three came back in August 1597 with a cargo of pepper, nutmeg and mace. In the meantime, a number of new companies had been organized for the trade with the East Indies. The inevitable result of the competition among these companies was an increase in the cost price of the pepper and other spices and a decline in their sale prices. Mainly through the mediatory efforts of Johan van Oldenbarnevelt, the various companies agreed to come together, and the Verenigde Oost-Indische Compagnie (VOC) was chartered on 20 March 1602. The Company was given the sole right for a period of twenty-one years to sail east of the Cape of Good Hope and west through the Strait of Magellan.

The other major company engaged in the Euro-Asian trade was the English East India Company (EIC). The great success attendant upon the venture of the 'Old Company' of Amsterdam into the Euro-Asian trade with the successful return of its vessels in 1599 had caused great consternation among the English merchants engaged in the spice trade of the Levant. The fear of the Dutch domination of the spice market in Northwestern Europe thus served as the catalyst that led a group of London merchants to apply to the Crown for a monopoly charter of the East India trade. The request was granted and on 31 December 1600 was born the 'Company of Merchants of London trading into the East Indies'. Between 1601 and 1612, the twelve voyages organized by the Company were on separate and terminable account. The first joint stock lasted from 1613 to 1623, the second from 1617 to 1632 and the third from 1631 to 1642. It was only the charter of 1657, which provided for a permanent joint stock.[1]

The central characteristic feature of Euro-Asian trade was the necessity for the Europeans to pay for the Asian goods overwhelmingly in precious metals. This was an outcome essentially of the inability of Europe to supply western products with a potential market in Asia at prices that would generate a large enough demand for them to provide the necessary revenue for the purchase of the Asian goods. The only major item Europe was in a position to provide to Asia was precious metals. Indeed, an analysis of the Dutch and the English East India companies' exports to the East Indies over the seventeenth and the eighteenth centuries testifies to an unambiguous pattern where precious metals dominated the total exports throughout the period. In the case of the Dutch Company, the purchasing power made available to the factors in Asia did not consist only in the goods and precious metals sent aboard the outward-bound ships. A second component of the 'assistance received from Holland' (*'secours uit het lieve vaderland'*) as the funds raised locally by the factors in Asia (initially only at Batavia but later also by those at selected factors such as Bengal) by issuing bills of exchange (redeemable by the Company's Directors at Amsterdam), which generally carried a four per cent interest. The bills were bought predominantly by the Company's servants on the lookout for a safe channel to remit their savings home.[2]

The 'assistance received from Holland' was supplemented considerably by the profits earned by the company through participation in trade within Asia. Throughout the seventeenth century, not only were these profits considerable, but a large part of them was earned in precious metals. The starting point of Dutch participation in the trade of the East Indies was, of course, the procurement of pepper and other spices for the European market. They realized from the very beginning that if the spice trade was to continue to be highly profitable, they must strive to gain control of both the total amount reaching Europe and the cost price in the Indies. Between 1605 and 1609, the Company managed to wrest from the authorities in Amboyna and Ternate agreements obliging the producers to supply their cloves exclusively to the Dutch. A similar agreement was concluded in 1605 with the Banda group of islands regarding the procurement of nutmeg and mace. The latter agreement was renewed after the conquest of the islands by the Company in 1621.

By the early 1620s, then, the Dutch had acquired effective monopoly rights in nutmeg and mace. The case of cloves was somewhat more complex. There was a large scale smuggling trade carried on between the producing areas and Makassar, enabling the English, among others, to obtain large quantities of this spice. Though from 1643 onward the Company had managed to reduce such smuggling, it was only after the conquest of Makassar in 1669 that the Dutch fully controlled the trade in cloves. As for pepper – which was a substantially more important item for investment in the Indies that all the other spices put together – in spite of the availability of formal monopoly rights in a number of states in the region, the Company never acquired effective monopoly rights in the spice.

The control exercised by the Company on the Spice Islands enabled it to procure spices other than pepper at incredibly low prices. This ensured a very high rate of gross profit on these spices, often exceeding 1,000 per cent. Before the arrival of the Dutch, the spice growers had been used to exchanging their wares for Indian cloth, rice and other necessities brought to them by Indian and other Asian merchants as well as by the Portuguese. The Company could have obtained the Indian textiles – by far the most important medium of exchange in the Spice Islands – at Aceh and other places in Indonesia, but its acute business instinct drove it to their source, the Coromandel coast, where four factories were established between 1606 and 1610 covering both the northern and the southern stretches of the coast. Gujarat, on the west coast of India, the other major Indian region supplying textiles to the Indonesian archipelago, was reached in 1618 with the establishment of a factory in Surat. Within a few years, subordinate factories had been opened at Cambay and Broach, and at Agra in Northern India. Thus began the Company's participation in intra-Asian trade, which in course of time assumed important proportions and became an object of as much concerns as the Euro-Asian trade itself.

It is important to realize that the idea of extensive participation in intra-Asian trade had originated not with the Directors but with the officials at the Company's eastern headquarters at Batavia. As early as 1612, Hendrik Brouwer, a future Gouvernor-General of the East Indies, had described the Coromandel coast as the 'left arm of the Moluccas and the surrounding islands because without textiles that come from there, the trade in the Moluccas wil be dead'.[3] The driving force behind the project was a remarkable man, Jan Pietersz. Coen, who was named Governor-General of the East Indies in April 1618 at the age of twenty-one years. The way Coen went about the whole thing displayed a remarkable grasp of the realities of Asian trade. He devised a carefully worked out strategy and followed it up with great tenacity. In 1619, he sent to the directors a blueprint of the Company's intra-Asian trade: cloth form Gujarat (obtained against spices, other goods and Spanish rials) to be exchanged against pepper and gold in Sumatra; cloth from Coromandel (obtained against spices, Chinese goods and gold, and rials) to be exchanged against pepper at Bantam; sandalwood, pepper and rials to be exchanged against Chinese gold and goods, the latter also being used to obtain silver from Japan. Finally, rials of eight could be obtained in Arabia against spices and other sundry items. Since the Company already had spices available to it, all that was needed to turn this blueprint into reality was an adequate number of ships and enough capital for some time to establish the intra-Asian trading network – 'a little water to prime the pump'. The Company already had a permanently circulating capital of between *f* 2,5 million and *f* 3,5 million in the East Indies at this time but Coen wanted more.

Large quantities of this silver also reached the Red Sea and the Persian Gulf region via the Levant. Another route through which American silver reached Asia was the galleon trade between Acapulco and Manila. Since the Manila trade, controlled by the Spanish, was out of reach of the Dutch, the two principal areas of interest to them were Japan and the Middle East.

A factory was established at Hirado in South-western Japan in 1609. Although items such as fine-quality cotton textiles, spices, sugar, lead, quicksilver and musk could be sold in Japan, the principal items in demand there during the early period of Dutch trade were Chinese silk, silk textiles and other Chinese goods. The Dutch initially tried to obtain Chinese goods in the Indonesian archipelago and the Malay peninsula. Indeed, the establishment of trade relations with places such as Patani and Siam, and later with Cambodia, Annam and Tonkin, was partly in the quest for Chinese goods. But success was limited, and attempts were made almost from the very beginning of trading relations with Japan to establish a trading post, by force if necessary, on the coast of China or in its immediate vicinity. The efforts to blockade Chinese trade with Manila were followed by an attack on Macao in 1622 and the subsequent occupation of the Pescadores. But from thereafter, in 1624, the Dutch were persuaded to move to Taiwan in return for an informal agreement that Chinese merchants would be allowed to go there to trade with them. The principal commodities procured by the Company in Taiwan were Chinese silk and silk textiles for the Japanese market. A part of the silver obtained from Japan in exchange for the Chinese goods was then invested in getting not only the next round of silk in Taiwan but also gold needed chiefly for the crucial Coromandel trade. Gold was procured in Taiwan rather than directly in Japan until the former was lost to the forces of Coxinga in 1662. This was done chiefly to take advantage of the very different gold/silver parity in the two places until 1637 favouring the procurement of gold in Taiwan. From 1641 in any case the export of gold from Japan was banned. This was a sequel to the 1636 closure of the country to all foreigners except the Chinese and the Dutch, the latter being required in May 1641 to move to the islet of Deshima off the Nagasaki harbour.

In the meantime, efforts had been going on to further widen the supply base of the raw silk and the silk textiles required for the Japan trade. From the early 1630s, Bengal emerged as a major supplier of raw silk for Japan. Ever since 1615, the factors at Coromandel had been trying to find a foothold in Bengal, which at that time was looked upon basically as a potential source for textiles, sugar and saltpetre. But in so far as the Bengal goods could be procured at Coromandel itself, where they were regularly imported by the Indian merchants, the efforts to establish a factory in Bengal lacked intensity and seriousness of purpose. It was only after the factors at Agra drew Batavia's attention in 1630 to the import by Indian merchants of a large quantity of relatively inexpensive raw silk from Bengal into Agra each year and enclosed a sample of the product with their report that the requisite urgency was imparted to the Bengal project. The expulsion of the Portuguese from Hugli by the Mughals in 1632 helped. A factory was established in Hariharpur in Orissa in 1633, and another at Hugli in 1635. Bengal raw silk was included in the Dutch cargo for Japan for the first time in 1640 and soon became a major constituent item of this cargo.

The last of the major Indian regions figuring in the Company's intra-Asian trade was the southwest coast of India, comprising the Malabar and the Kanara coasts. After several abortive visits to the region by the Dutch factors, a treaty was signed between the Company and the Samudri raja of Calicut in January 1626. The treaty stipulated that all pepper and ginger grown in the region would be supplied to the Dutch at a fixed price,

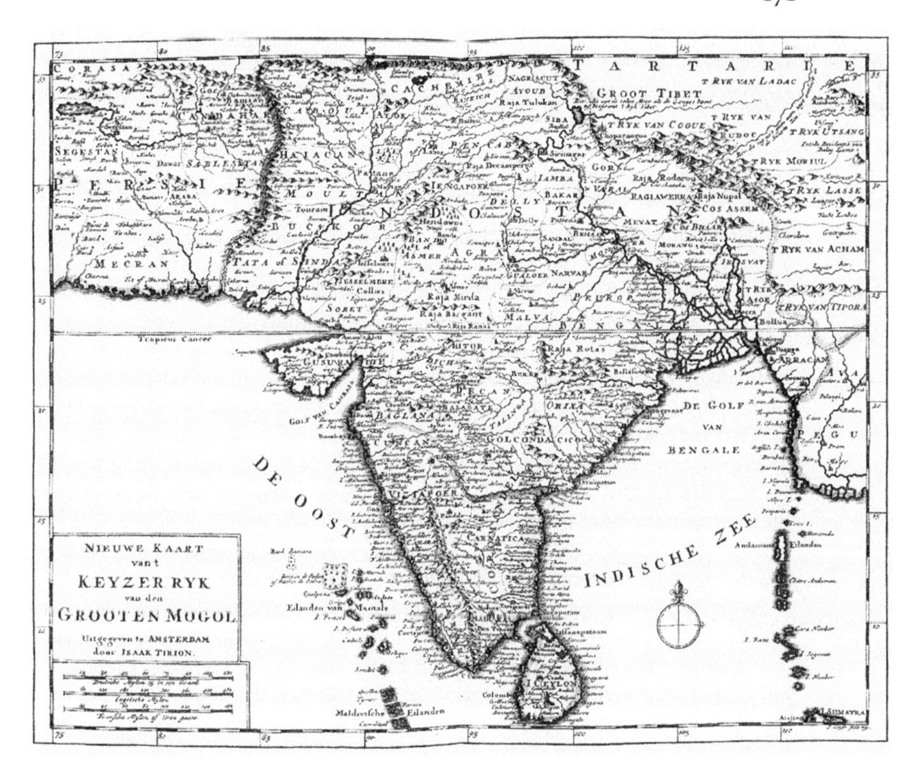

Map of the Moghul Empire, by Isaac Tirion in Amsterdam, 1754 (University Library, Ghent)

and that no export or import duties would be charged from the Company. But since no ships or capital could be spared for Calicut over the following several years, the treaty remained a dead letter. In 1633 and 1634, the fleets sent from Batavia to Surat were asked to call at the Malabar ports and trade there, without, however, setting up factories. Between 1636 and 1643, the Dutch fleet sent each year to blockade Goa also put in at Malabar and carried on a limited amount of trade there. In order to facilitate the blockade and generally to serve as a watchtower (*uitkijkpost*) over Goa, the Company established a small factory in 1637 at Vengurla in the kingdom of Bijapur on the Kanara coast under the direct jurisdiction of Batavia. In Malabar, a factory was eventually set up in Kayakulam in 1647. But the resumption of hostilities with the Portuguese after the end of the Ten Years' Truce in 1652 forced a withdrawal of the factory. It was only in 1663 when the Dutch, collaborating with the Raja of Cochin, managed to throw the Portuguese out that the Dutch trade at Malabar region began on a regular and substantive basis. The strategic role of the Vengurla factory now came to an end. It was placed under the charge of the chief factory at Surat in 1673 and for all practical purposes abandoned in 1685, though formal orders for its closure were not issued until 1692.

Efforts to reach the other major Asian source of precious metals, namely the Red Sea and the Persian Gulf region at the other extremity of the great arc of Asian trade, had also been initiated quite early, using the Company's establishment at Surat as the base. As early as 1616, attempts were made to establish trade relations with Mocha. But in 1624, following problems arising out of the seizure of two ships belonging to the port of Dabhol, the Company had no option but to abandon the factory for good. As far as Persia was concerned, a factory was established at Gombroon in 1623. Initially Persia was in fact a net absorber of precious metals rather than a net supplier. The principal item procured there at this time was raw silk in exchange for goods such as pepper and other spices, Japanese copper and Indian textiles, and precious metals. Between 1622 and 1634 several of the ships from Holland were sent directly to Surat and Persia with fair amounts of capital. In 1624-25, for example, three of these ships carried *f* 600 000 to these factories, constituting nearly one third of the total precious metals sent to Asia that year.[4] But this pattern lasted only for a brief while, and from 1643 Persia emerged as a net supplier of silver *abassies* and gold *ducats*, which were smuggled out on a regular basis, often by concealing them in cavities made into the bales of raw silk.[5] The resultant loss in the value of silk was evidently an acceptable price to pay for getting hold of the silver and gold coins. From a comparatively modest sum of *f* 235,000 in 1642-3, the value of these coins came to exceed a million florins in 1649-50. The average annual value of the coins smuggled out over the following decade was *f* 660,712.[6] But over the rest of the seventeenth century, the sums involved were extremely modest, if they were at all positive, and it was only around 1700 that, for a few years, Persia again became a major – in fact the most important provider of precious metals in Asia.[7]

What the above analysis establishes quite definitively is that by about the middle of the seventeenth century the Dutch East India Company had become a major participant in intra-Asian trade with trading links all along the great arc of Asian trade. The crucial role played by this trade in the overall commercial strategy of the Company was summed up neatly by the Directors in 1648 as follows: 'The intra-Asian trade and the profit from it are the soul of the Company which must be looked after carefully because if the soul decays the entire body would be destroyed'.[8] Three years later, the Directors even expressed the hope that at some point it would be possible for Batavia not only to finance the exports to Europe (which in 1650-1 amounted to *f* 2, 49 million) wholly out of profits from intra-Asian trade, but also send to them in addition some Asian precious metals. Although such extravagant hopes were never realized, the fact remains that, throughout the seventeenth century, participation in intra-Asian trade was of great advantage to the Company. Note that between 1640 and 1688 the invoice value of the return cargo from Asia amounted to approximately *f* 150 million as against *f* 120 million worth of precious metals and goods exported to Asia over the same period. Thus about 20 per cent of the return cargo represented the profits from intra-Asian trade. Considering that the total proceeds from the sale of the return cargo amounted to *f* 420 million, the sales value of 20 per cent of the cargo would amount to *f* 84 million. This amount was more than sufficient to cover the sum of *f* 67 million paid out as dividend by the Company over the period.[9]

The two key factors that enabled the Dutch to achieve an enviable position in intra-Asian trade during the seventeenth century were the exclusive right to trade with Japan and the spice monopoly. The Japan trade brought in large quantities of precious metals, mainly silver until 1668 and gold thereafter. It was pointed out earlier that in May 1641 the Dutch had been obliged to move to the islet of Deshima off the Nagasaki harbour. At the same time, their trade had been subjected to a variety of restrictions. For example, days were prescribed on which alone they could offer their goods for sale, until which time they had to be kept in sealed warehouses. Also the *pancado* system was extended to the entire lot of Chinese raw silk the Company imported into Japan. This system required the Company to sell the silk at a price determined by a guild monopoly consisting of a group of merchants from the five imperial cities of Edo (Tokyo), Osaka, Kyoto, Sakai and Nagasaki. Commercially injurious as these restrictions were, the Dutch meekly accepted them. The Directors, in fact, want so far as to instruct Batavia to maintain the trade, if necessary, 'even from the ships'. In a report submitted to the Directors in September 1652, Pieter Sterthemius, the chief of the Nagasaki factory during 1650-1 wrote: 'But I seem to hear a whisper in my ear, that some vexations can surely be endured for the sake of Japan's sweet gains, since Japan is the strongest sinew of the Company's inland trade and of the Indian profits; and this (in so far as our self-respect allows us to endure it) is true'.[10] The sweet gains, of course, were the precious metals the trade provided.

The other major differential advantage enjoyed by the Company was the spice monopoly. This monopoly provided the Company with a staple item of trade in demand all over Asia and entailing an extraordinarily high rate of return.

Indeed, it was the spice monopoly that brought the Company in direct conflict with its English rival eventually forcing it out of intra-Asian trade and adopting a commercial strategy which was totally different from that adopted by the VOC.

As in the case of the VOC, treasure accounted for approximately between 65 and 90 per cent of the total English exports to Asia.[11] Also, like the VOC, the principal interest of the English in the East, initially at least, was the procurement of pepper and other spices for the European market. The first two voyages were directed at Bantam in Java where a factory was established in 1602. From 1613, Sumatra became the chief supplier of pepper to the Company. Factories were established at Aceh, Tiku and Priaman, but the factory at Bantam remained the headquarters of the Company's trading organization in the region. The crucial importance of the Coromandel textiles in facilitating this trade and making it more profitable had also been brought home to the Company quite early. In 1606, therefore, it accepted the offer of two Dutchmen, Peter Floris and Lucas Atheunis, to set up a factory on the coast of Coromandel and supply textiles for the Southest Asian markets. Floris and Atheunis established a factory at Masulipatnam in 1611, though the first Company voyage to the coast was organized only in 1614.

In the meantime, given the Dutch monopolistic designs in the archipelago, a situation of armed conflict with the VOC was becoming inevitable. The hostilities erupted in 1618, and the English emerged distinctly the worse of the two. The London agreement of 1619 provided for an English share of one-third in the trade of the Spice Islands, and of one half in the pepper trade of Java subject to the English contributing one-third of the cost of maintaining the Dutch garrisons in the area. The English headquarters in the region were moved to Batavia in 1620, and the two companies shared garrisons in Banda, Moluccas and Amboyna. But due to the English shortage of resources, and more importantly the Dutch hostility towards the English, the London agreement of 1619 proved largely a failure. Jan Pietersz. Coen was determined not to allow the English to share in the Dutch spice monopoly and used all kinds of arguments and excuses to deny the English their due. In January 1622, he wrote to the Directors: 'It was impossible to deal with the English. They would do as much damage to the Dutch interests as they could, and then claim that it was they who were the aggrieved party. The jealousy, the distrust and the envy that these people had was unlikely to be neutralized by any regulations, agreements or orders. The more apart the two stayed from each other, the greater were the chances of continued friendliness between the two'.[12] A favourite refrain of Coen was that the English did not come up with their share of the costs of maintaining the garrisons as stipulated in the London agreement and therefore did not qualify for sharing in the spice and pepper trade. In May 1622, this is what Coen had to say: 'Regarding the costs at the Moluccas, Amboyna, Banda and Pulicat, the English had nothing but complaints to make. Their ambition and greed could never be appeased. In all matters, big and small, they found themselves cheated, sunk, affronted and despised so much so that it appeared that the entire means at the disposal of the Company would not be enough to meet their claims'.[13]

The 1623 incident at Amboyna led to a recall of the English factors from the shared centres in the archipelago to Batavia, and hastened the process of the English withdrawal from the Spice Islands. By 1624, the factories at Patani, Ayutthaya and Japan had also been abandoned. From this point on, pepper was procured mainly at Bantam to which the English had moved back from Batavia, and cloves at Makassar, where a factory had been established in 1613. As D.K. Bassett has demonstrated, the English were among the major buyers of the cloves smuggled in large quantities into this port until 1643 both by the merchants from Makassar as well as by those operating from several of the Malayan ports.

An important medium of exchange used in both Bantam and Makassar was the textiles from the Coromandel coast. The 1619 London agreement had a clause entitling the English Company to a share in the trade at Pulicat provided they shared one half of the cost and the maintenance of the Dutch fort and garrison there. To foreclose any English apprehensions in this regard, an agreement was concluded at Jakarta (the former name of Batavia) in April 1621 providing that in the event of the two companies wishing to buy identical varieties of textiles the procurement would be done jointly.[14] The VOC also undertook to provide accommodation to the English within the Fort Geldria against payment of rent till at least such time as alternative arrangements could be made.[15] But as in the archipelago, the cooperation between the two companies was more in name than in actual fact. Almost from the very beginning, the English complained both about the inadequacy of the accommodation provided to them in the fort as well as about the procedure adopted to work out their share of the cost of the maintenance of the garrison kept in the fort. The English also complained that the Dutch did not offer them half of the total textiles procured but insisted on dividing the lot in proportion to the capital invested by the two companies respectively. The English also found the burden of their share of the maintenance costs of the fort and the garrison at Pulicat crippling. In any event, all hopes of cooperation were doomed after the 1623 Amboyna massacre. The formal termination of the cooperation in textile procurement in Coromandel came to an end on 1 July 1623 with the English withdrawal from Pulicat. In the mid-1620s, the English established another factory on the Coromandel coast at Armagon.[16]

The other major consequence of the 1619 London agreement was the decision to equip a joint defence fleet to blockade the Portuguese possessions on the Malabar coast and to cruise against the Portuguese shipping on the west coast of India. The admiral of the fleet consisting of seven Dutch and four English vessels that left Batavia on 18 October 1621 was the Dutchman Jacob Dedel while the vice-admiral was the Englishman Humphrey Fitzherbert. But like the planned commercial cooperation at Pulicat, the venture of the defence fleet was also a dismal failure. On 18 November 1621, the fleet was driven by contrary winds to the Nassau Islands. The English then wanted to get back to Batavia but were prevented from doing so by Dedel by using his additional vote in the fleet's council. The fleet was unable to inflict any particular damage on the Portuguese and in July 1622, Coen advised Dedel to return to Batavia after leaving the Dutch ships of the fleet at Surat.[17]

The Anglo-Portuguese alliance made possible the establishment of an English factory in 1640 at Madras as well, which in September 1641 was designated as the chief factory of Coromandel. In 1682 the Dutch forced the English out of Bantam and from 1685 the only English establishment in the Indonesian archipelago was at Benkulen in Sumatra.

While the English had come to Coromandel in quest of textiles for the Southeast Asian markets, their attempts to penetrate the Gujarat trade were linked directly to their Euro-Asian trade. Because of the possibility of a military engagement with the Portuguese and/or the Dutch, each of the English voyages to the East consisted of a certain minimum number of ships. But on the return voyage, a cargo consisting of pepper and other spices alone would perhaps fill only one of these ships. Hence the urgent need to diversify the return cargo by including in it items such as Indian textiles and indigo. Gujarat textiles could, of course, also be used for the Southeast Asian trade to the extent necessary. The third voyoge sent out in 1608, thereforte, carried instructions to explore the commercial possibilities of the western coast of India. William Hawkins reached Surat in 1608 and went on to Agra the following year, but was unable to obtain trading rights. Henry Middleton, the commander of the sixth voyage, was also refused permission to trade at Surat. It was only in September 1612 that Thomas Best finally managed to obtain formal trading rights. A factory was established at Surat in 1613 and regular trade started there and at Ahmedabad, Burhanpur and Agra. A ship was sent back home directly from Surat for the first time in 1615. Between 1616 and 1617, while only four small ships were dispatched directly to Bantam from London, nine ships of large tonnage were sent to Surat. The President at Surat was also placed in charge of the Company's trade in Persia. The Crown leased Bombay to the Company in 1668: in 1687 it superseded Surat as the headquarters of the Company in western India. In the meantime, the Company's trade had extended into Bengal in early 1650s, with the establishment of a factory at Hugli.

To conclude, the first half of the seventeenth century (and particularly the first quarter) witnessed a tremendous amount of rivalry between the Dutch and the English East India Companies in Asia. At least in one instance this rivalry took the form of an actual armed conflict on the sea. That was the 1618 engagement between the ships of the two companies in the Indonesian archipelago. The principal aim of the Dutch was to keep the English out of the lucrative intra-Asian trade which they were able to do by closely guarding their spice monopoly. The releative shortage of resources with the English also contributed in a significant way to this outcome as it did in the matter of their voluntary withdrawal from the Japan trade. Access to exclusive participation in the latter eventually became the other principal circumstance accounting for the overwhelming Dutch success in the matter of intra-Asian trade.

NOTES

1 K.N. Chaudhuri, *The English East India Company: The Study on an Early Joint-stock Company 1600-1640* (London 1965), 22, 28 & 209.
2 F.S. Gaastra, 'De Verenigde Oost-Indische Compagnie in de 17de en 18de eeuw: de groei van een bedrijf. Geld tegen goederen', in *Bijdragen en Mededelingen betreffende de Geschiedenis der Nederlanden*, vol. 89 (2), 1976, 244-272.
3 J.E. Heeres (ed.), *Corpus-Diplomaticum Neerlando-Indicum* (The Hague 1907), vol. I, 154.
4 F.S. Gaastra, 'De Verenigde Oost-Indische...', 261.
5 Kristof Glamann, *Dutch Asiatic Trade 1620-1740* (Copenhagen/The Hague 1958), 120.
6 F.S. Gaastra, 'The exports of precious metals from Europe to Asia by the Dutch East India Company, 1602-1795', in J.F. Richards (ed.), *Precious Metals in the Later Medieval and Early Modern Worlds* (Durham 1983), Appendix 4, Table 1.
7 The average annual sum exported between 1700-1 and 1703-4 was *f* 873,650 (calculated from F.S. Gaastra, 'The exports..., Appendix 4, table 2, 475).
8 NA (Nationaal Archief)/ VOC nr. 317, f° 120v, Heren XVII to Batavia, 22/9/1648.
9 F.S. Gaastra, *Bewind en Beleid bij de VOC. De financiële en commerciële politiek van de Bewindhebbers, 1672-1702* (Zutphen 1989), 205.
10 Om Prakash, *TheDutch East India Company and the Economy of Bengal, 1630-1720* (Princeton 1985) 121.
11 K.N. Chaudhuri, *The English East India Company...*, Table II, 115; K.N. Chaudhuri, *The Trading World of Asia and the English East India Company, 1660-1760* (Cambridge 1978), Appendix 5, Tables C1 and C4, 507 & 512.
12 NA/ VOC nr. 1073., Coen to Heren XVII, January 1622.
13 NA/ VOC nr. 1074., Coen to Pulicat, May 1622.
14 Om Prakash, *The Dutch Factories in India, 1617-1623. A collection of Dutch East India Company documents pertaining to India* (Delhi 1984), 156-158.
15 Ibidem, 157.
16 Ibidem, 255.
17 Ibidem, 270.

X

European Private Traders in the Eastern Indian Ocean Trading Network in the Early Modern Period

It was with the discovery of the Cape route between Asia and Europe at the end of the fifteenth century that the European factor was introduced into the mechanics of Indian Ocean trade. The Portuguese, who had discovered the route and had monopolized it through the sixteenth century, were followed in the early years of the seventeenth by the English and the Dutch. Other European merchant groups, such as the Danes and the French, made their appearance later in the century. The Ostenders were the last of the lot to arrive in India in the second decade of the eighteenth century. Each of these groups consisted of two distinct entities – a corporate enterprise usually, though not in all cases, in the form of a national chartered monopoly company, and individual merchants engaged in trade on their private account. An overwhelming proportion of the latter had travelled to the East under the auspices of the relevant corporate group and engaged in private trade also, with or without the company's permission. Others engaged in private trade on a full time basis. The Euro-Asian trade was carried on overwhelmingly by corporate groups, leaving the trade within Asia by and large to individual traders, the most numerous amongst whom eventually were the English private traders. The only major exception to this pattern was the large scale and systematic participation in intra-Asian trade by the Dutch East India Company as an integral part of its overall trading strategy. In the sixteenth century, the Portuguese Crown had also participated in intra-Asian trade, but on a relatively limited scale and duration.

Throughout the sixteenth and the first half of the seventeenth century, the Euro-Asian trade of the Portuguese was centred on India. But since the Dutch and the English procured their pepper and other spices mainly in Indonesia, the Asian loci of the Euro-Asian sea-borne trade shifted at the beginning of the seventeenth century from India to the Indonesian archipelago. It was nearly three quarters of a century before the Asian loci shifted back to India. This was a consequence of a change in European fashions assigning an increasingly important role to textiles and raw silk in European imports. It was only in the second half of the eighteenth century that the growing role of Chinese tea in these imports again deflected somewhat the central position of India in Euro-Asian trade. India also played a key role in the Dutch intra-Asian trade. Indeed, it was a long-established pattern for Indonesian spice growers to demand Indian textiles in exchange for their wares, which had set thc VOC on the path of intra-Asian trade in the first place. Later in the seventeenth century, Bengal raw silk and opium played an extremely important role in the successful functioning of the Dutch intra-Asian trade network. Among the private European traders engaged in this trade, the largest group, namely the English private traders, also operated overwhelmingly from India.

In India, European corporate and private enterprise operated on the west and east coasts, but there can be very little doubt that the trade on the east coast, involving the use of the ports on the Coromandel and in Bengal, accounted for the bulk of the total trade. Thus, in the case of the Dutch East India Company goods procured in Bengal alone accounted for as much as 40 percent of the total Asian cargo sent to Europe at the end of the seventeenth century. This figure was not very different in the case of the English East India Company. If we were also to take into account the procurement on the Coromandel coast, the figure would go up substantially in both cases. In the case of the European private traders also, the trade conducted through the ports of the Bay of Bengal considerably overshadowed that of ports of the Arabian Sea or for that matter probably any other regional conglomeration of ports in Asia. This paper will examine some of the more important aspects of the private European merchants' trade in and from the Bay of Bengal from the first contacts established by the Portuguese in the early years of the sixteenth century to the closing years of the eighteenth, when English private trade had come to dominate several of the key branches of the Indian Ocean trading network. It is important to realize that the policy and attitude that different corporate enterprises adopted towards the private traders of their particular nationality differed dramatically from one to the other, from outright hostility at one end of the spectrum to formal collaboration at the other with a whole range of variation in between. Since this was an important factor determining the trading strategy adopted by a given private trading group, the commercial activities of such groups will be analysed in the context of the policies adopted towards them by the corporate enterprises of their respective nationalities.

The Dutch Private Traders

The prime example of sheer hostility by a corporate enterprise towards private trade by its employees was that of the Dutch East India Company. This was the direct outcome of the Company's own large scale involvement in intra-Asian trade from the very beginning as an integral part of its overall trading strategy. In order to prevent the employees from emerging as rivals, their participation in intra-Asian trade was banned. That, however, did not prevent them from engaging, mainly from the Bay of Bengal, in a substantial volume of highly lucrative trade on a strictly clandestine basis involving an unauthorized and blatant use of the Company's ships, and often also its capital resources. Given its clandestine nature, the goods figuring in this trade were principally high-value low-bulk items. By far the most important of these was Bengal opium, for which there was a highly lucrative and growing market in the Indonesian archipelago from about the middle of the seventeenth century onward. Pieter van Dam has suggested that at one stage the volume of clandestine private trade from Bengal was nearly as large as that on the Company's own account. As far as opium alone was concerned, in an unusually bountiful year such as 1676, the volume of opium smuggled into Batavia could be several times the amount imported on the account of the Company. An anonymous report submitted to the *Heren XVII* in 1684 contained a detailed description of the organizational structure of this trade at the Bengal end. In 1679 Director Jacob Verburg founded in the name of his wife a 'small company' with the specific purpose of carrying on private trade. To facilitate its operations, two of the share-holders in the 'company' – both nephews of Verburg's wife – were appointed to the key posts of the directorate's *fiscal* (the law-enforcement officer) and the Hugli factory's warehouse officer, respectively. In order to enable him to discharge his 'duties' properly, the *fiscal* was provided with a staff large enough to keep an eye on all Dutch Company ships entering or leaving the port of Hugli. As soon as a ship approached the port, the warehouse officer went aboard and offered to buy whatever private cargo might be on board. The prices offered were obviously considerably below the market, but usually the deals went through because it was known to all that in the event of an unsuccessful negotiation, the *fiscal* would be promptly informed and the goods confiscated. The goods obtained by the warehouse officer in this manner were then sold in the open market at substantially higher prices on the account of the 'small company'.

As far as goods procured in Bengal were concerned, the procedure was to buy them in the name of a non-existent Bengali merchant. These goods were then loaded on the Company's ships along with the regular cargo. Some time before the ships were due into the harbour at Batavia, the contraband was taken out in small boats. The watch and ward staff at Batavia at times managed to seize part of the smuggled goods, but that made only a very minor dent into the total profit from the smuggling operation. A rough idea of the magnitude of the profit earned could probably be formed by the fact that at Verburg's death in 1681, his wife carried with her to Holland a fortune running to f. 600,000. Even the warehouse officer had managed to save a sum of f.150,000 over a period of three to four years.[1] Insofar as the clandestine nature of this trade often obliged the servants to pay a price above the market in respect of goods procured and accept one below it for goods sold, their private trade tended to spoil both the buying and the selling markets for the Company. There was, however, very little the Company could do about this problem. One measure was to strengthen cruising watch-and-ward operations in Batavia. The other was to periodically issue proclamations reiterating the penalties, including dismissal from service and deportation to Holland, prescribed for those found engaging in private trade. This was done in 1677, 1678, 1680 and 1683. The last of these decrees went so far as to prescribe punishment by death. But the vested interests were far too entrenched to be dislodged easily and nothing changed.[2]

A major landmark in Company policy towards private Dutch participation in intra-Asian trade was the partial opening up of this trade in the early 1740s. The initiative had been taken by Gustaf Willem Baron van Imhoff, the governor-general-designate of the Dutch East Indies. In a memorandum submitted in 1741, van Imhoff argued that the Company's trade in the factories west of Malacca had been on the decline for some time and compared unfavourably with that of the English and French. He therefore suggested that it would be in the best interest of the Company to declare trade with that region, except in strategic commodities such as spices and Japanese copper, open to all Dutch nationals. Van Imhoff's recommendations were accepted by the Directors in 1742. The communication received by the Indian factories from Batavia in 1743 stipulated that 'the navigation and trade from and to Batavia both to the east as well as to

1 Anonymous report entitled 't Oostindische Sacspiegeltje', *Algemeen Rijksarchief* (hereafter ARA), VOC 4704.

2 Om Prakash, *The Dutch East India Company and the Economy of Bengal, 1630-1720*, Princeton, 1985, pp.86-9, 154-6.

the west of India has been declared open for everyone with the provision that the trade in spices, copper, tin, pepper as well as the import of opium will be reserved for the Company'.[3] In September 1745 van Imhoff further outlined the geographical extent of his free-trade area. It comprised China, Batavia, Malacca, all harbours from Acheh to Bengal, and Bengal to Nagapattinam, Ceylon, and from Cape Comorin to Persia, then along the African coast to Madagascar and Mozambique. Private trade under the new dispensation was to be carried on under the flag and the protection of the Company. Private traders were to pay customs duty to the Company at the rate of 4 percent at Hugli and 5 percent at Surat. On its part the Company would settle accounts with local authorities at established rates for its own goods. At Hugli, this would leave a surplus of 1.5 percent for the Company, of which 0.5 percent would be given to the *fiscal*. While it is quite clear that the 1743 provisions did indeed lead to a certain amount of additional Dutch private participation in intra-Asian trade, the scale of this participation, particularly from the Bay of Bengal, remains unclear.

The Portuguese Private Traders

The relationship between the *Estado da India* and private Portuguese merchants engaged in intra-Asian trade ranged from open hostility to substantive patronage. The group the *Estado* was hostile to was that operating outside its jurisdiction and derisively referred to as the *chatins*. It consisted mainly of deserters from the Portuguese garrisons in quest of fortunes that they could never visualize in the employment of the *Estado*. The principal region to which they spread out looking for opportunities to trade was the Bay of Bengal littoral. As early as the decade of 1511-20, there is evidence of fair numbers of these people making contact with Bengal ports such as Satgaon and Chatgaon, as well as Pulicat on the Coromandel coast. On the ground that 'one more merchant was one less soldier', the *Estado* invariably adopted a hostile attitude towards these people. As Luis Filipe Thomaz has pointed out, at Malacca, where Hindus and Muslims paid no more than 6 percent as customs duty, these Portuguese private traders were obliged to pay as much as 10 percent.[4] *Estado* hostility

[3] ARA, 'Consideratien over de opengestelde vrije Vaart en Handel-hoedanig die in Souratta sal kunnen gereguleert werden', by Director Jan Schreuder at Surat, 2 March 1746, HRB 837, paragraph 340.

[4] Luis Filipe F.R. Thomaz, 'The Portuguese in the Seas of the Archipelago during the 16th Century', p.78. Originally published as 'Les Portugais dans le mers de l'Archipel au XVIe siecle, *Archipel*, 18 (1979). Available in translation in *Trade and Shipping in the Southern Seas, Selected Readings from Archipel (18), 1979*, Paris, 1984, pp.75-91.

could take other forms as well, such as extending formal jurisdiction over such communities and subjecting them to taxes.

An overwhelming majority of the Portuguese private traders, however, operated within the *Estado* framework and under its patronage. While the group included government officials, soldiers, ecclesiastics, Jews, New Christians and others, its most important component was that of the *casados moradores* or married settlers. Some of these traders are known to have amassed enormous fortunes. Thus, four members of this group declared bankruptcy in 1633 in Japan in the amount of 1.25 million *taels* worth of silver.[5] The *casado* traders had extensive dealings with other European and Asian trading groups as well as the *Estado da India*, in relation to which it also constituted a kind of pressure group.[6] The privileges extracted from the *Estado* included occasional limited commodity monopolies and special rates of customs duties.

The *casado* traders were also a major, though by no means the only, beneficiary of the 'concession' system introduced in the 1550s. Following the conquest of Malacca in 1511, the Portuguese Crown had itself participated on a fair scale in intra-Asian trade. This was initially done in cooperation with the Tamil *keling* merchants settled at Malacca. Co-operation had stretched even to the organization of joint ventures in which private Portuguese merchants were also allowed to participate indirectly. Most of these ventures operated between Malacca and the Bay of Bengal and involved the creation of the so-called Crown-routes (*carreiras*). However, for a variety of reasons, the period over which direct participation by the Crown in intra-Asian trade lasted was rather brief. By the middle of the sixteenth century, Portuguese participation in intra-Asian trade had become essentially a private effort. The role of the Crown was now confined basically to the grant of benefices under the so-called concession system.

A concession conferred on the grantee the right to make a voyage between two specified ports in the Indian Ocean and/or the China Sea. A concession route could be to a so-called 'reserved' port, in which case the concession holder, in principle, had the exclusive right to operate on the route. Alternatively, it could pertain to an 'open' route

5 C.R. Boxer, *The Great Ship of Amacon, Annals of Macao and the Old Japan Trade, 1555-1640*, Lisbon, 1959, p.131; George B. Souza, *The Survival of Empire, Portuguese Trade and Society in China and the South China Sea, 1630-1754*, Cambridge, 1986, p.30.

6 One knows, for example, that Ferdinand Cron, an important *casado* trader lent his own money or money raised using his personal credit and standing on numerous occasions to the Portuguese State in Goa. Sanjay Subrahmanyam 'An Augsburger in Asia Portuguesa: further light on the commercial world of Ferdinand Cron, 1587-1624', in Roderich Ptak and Dietmar Rothermund, eds., *Emporia, Commodities and Entrepreneurs in Asian Maritime Trade, c. 1400-1750*, Stuttgart, 1991, p.405.

in which event the grantee was designated the captain-major of the fleet (including both Portuguese and non-Portuguese ships) operating on the route. The perquisites carried by this position included appointment as purveyor of the estates of the deceased in respect of all persons on the trading fleet, the right to buy and sell before anyone else, an occasional customs-concession, and so on. Important among the 'reserved' routes were those between Coromandel and Malacca and between Coromandel and Pegu. An example of an 'open' route was that between the ports of Orissa and Malacca. Some of the concession routes (*viagem*) were replacement for old Crown-routes (*carrieras*): others were newly created. Thus the voyage between Malacca and Pegu was a replacement: that to Pipli was a newly created one. In view of the privileges attached, all concession grants enjoyed a premium in varying degree and were fully transferable to another resident of the *Estado* settlements.[7]

The concession system began in the 1550s, and by the 1580s had become a major component of the Portuguese trading network in Asia. Thomaz has listed a total of 34 concession voyages in operation in the 1580s covering the China Sea, the Indonesian archipelago and the Bay of Bengal. In the Bay of Bengal, all the important concession voyages operating from Coromandel in the 1580s were, in principle, on reserved routes. These included two from Sao Tome (one each to Malacca and Pegu) and four from Nagapattinam (one each to Martaban, Mergui, Ujang Salang (Phuket) and Kedah). Since the concession to Malacca provided for only one ship in a year, usually a large carrack carried, inter alia, freight goods and about a hundred or more merchants. Given Portuguese control over Malacca, the concession holder on this route could be reasonably certain of enjoying a monopoly. But the same was not true of those operating between Coromandel and the Malayan ports, bringing down considerably the premium on the concession voyages to these ports.[8] The concession routes to Bengal were three in number. The ones to Chatgaon and Satgaon (later to Hugli) were replacements of Crown-routes, while the one to Pipli was new. None of these routes carried monopoly concessions.[9]

7 Sanjay Subrahmanyam, 'The Coromandel-Malacca trade in the 16th century: A study of its evolving structure', *Moyen Orient et Ocean Indien*, vol. 3, 1986, pp.55-80.

8 Sanjay Subrahmanyam, 'The Coromandel-Malacca trade'.

9 Sanjay Subrahmanyam, 'Notes on the sixteenth century Bengal trade', *The Indian Economic and Social History Review*, vol. 24 (3), 1987, pp.265-89.

The French and the Ostend Private Traders

The Portuguese concession system had entailed a fair amount of patronage by the *Estado da India* to private Portuguese trading ventures in Asia. The ultimate in formal co-operation and collaboration between a given corporate enterprise and the private traders of that nationality, however, was achieved by the French in the first half of the eighteenth century. In 1719, the newly organized *Compagnie des Indes* decided to participate in intra-Asian trade as well. It was, however, immediately obvious to the factors at Pondicherry, that the Company's financial and other resources were just not adequate to allow a meaningful participation in this trade entirely on its own. A decision was therefore taken to invite employees as well as other traders, both Indian and European, to collaborate with the Company. This unique venture lasted about twenty years between 1722 and 1741. During the 1720s, the Company took the lead in organizing voyages out of Pondicherry, but the sums invested on the account of the Company were strictly limited. By the end of the decade, French Company employees operating in their private capacity would seem to have become the dominant element in the enterprise. Thus, while in the *Soucarama* sent from Pondicherry to Manila in 1724, the contribution by the Company and the employees was 51.7 and 18.6 percent respectively (the remainder being put up by Indian and other European traders), the respective share of the two groups had altered to 9.4 and 65.6 percent in the *Pondicherry* sent to Mocha in 1729. The total capital invested in the *Soucarama* was 24,690 pagodas and in the *Pondicherry* 26,500 pagodas.[10] Company employees and other French traders also operated independently of the Company.

It was usual for the French to form 'societies' or 'associations' which undertook one or more voyages. Each participant in a venture, independent merchant or organization, put up a certain amount of money. The voyage of the *Pondicherry* mentioned earlier had been initiated in Pondicherry, but the shortage of capital there had persuaded the organizers to invite the employees and other traders at Chandernagore to participate. A sum of Rs.4,000 had also been subscribed on behalf of the Ostend Company on which a profit of 50 percent was reported to have been made.[11]

There was a great deal of co-operation between French shipping based at Chandernagore and that based at Pondicherry in organizing voyages both westward and east-

[10] Catherine Manning, 'French country trade on Coromandel (1720-50)', *Revista de Cultura*, Macao, nos. 13/14, January-June 1991, table on page 168.

[11] Jan Parmentier, *De Holle Compagnie, Smokkel en Legale Handel onder Zuidernederlandse Vlag in Bengalen, ca 1720-1744*, Hilversum, 1992, pp.53-4.

ward. The eastward destinations covered South-East Asia, the principal ports of call were Acheh, Mergui and Pegu. The principal goods carried there were Coromandel textiles and Bengal opium, saltpetre and firearms, exchanged against goods such as pepper, teak, eaglewood, rubies and rice. Further east, Manila was probably the most important eastward port of call for the French. Between 1720 and 1750 a ship from Pondicherry is known to have called at this port every year but four. Probably because of the larger capital investment required, trips to China were much less frequent. Thus, over the same period of thirty years, no more than seven voyages were made between Pondicherry and Canton and profits were not particularly high.[12]

At least some French private traders are known to have done very well for themselves. Mahe de la Boudonnais is believed to have left Asia with more than three million livre tournois (approximately f. 1.5 million) and Duvelaer more than five.[13] The most well-known of them, however (though perhaps not the one to make most money), was Joseph Francois Dupleix, the head of the Chandernagore factory from 1731 to 1741. Immediately on arrival in Chandernagore, Dupleix had established a 'society' for trade. His associates ranged from direct participants in his ventures to providers of loans on an ordinary or respondentia basis. His French associates included Costanier, one of the directors of the French Company and two successive governors of Pondicherry, Lenoir and Dumas. English merchants of Calcutta and Madras such as Eliot, W. Price, Benet, Court and Wycht also carried on trade in association with Dupleix. His principal Dutch associate was the chief of the Dutch factory in Hugli, Jan Albert Sichterman, who is reported to have invested no less than Rs. 87,000 in the *Francois* sent by Dupleix to Basra in 1736. In 1739, he owed a debt of Rs. 42,000 to Dupleix. Yet another group of European merchants deeply involved in Dupleix's venture were the employees of the dissolved Ostend Company including Pierre Strebel, John Ray, Leendeert Meynders and, above all, Francois de Schonamille. Schonamille had been a free trader on the Coromandel coast between 1719 and 1723 and had associated with the French at Pondicherry. Just before the dissolution of the Ostend Company in 1731, Schonamille had been appointed the chief of the factory at Bankibazar. It was on the basis of his private trading ventures, mainly in association with Dupleix, that Schonamille formally kept the Ostend factory going until 1744. Of the four voyages organized by Dupleix in 1731, Schonamille invested Rs. 7,000 on the trip to Acheh, Rs. 3,000 on that to Mahe and Rs. 2,000 on the trip to Surat.[14] In a subsequent venture

[12] Catherine Manning, 'French country trade', pp.165-6.

[13] Phillippe Haudrere, 'The French Company of the Indies in the 17th and 18th centuries success or failure', *The Indian Ocean Review*, vol. I (2), June 1988, p.11.

[14] Jan Parmentier, *De Holle Compagnie*, p.55.

to Manila, Schonamille put up Rs. 4,000 on respondentia at 50 percent interest. That Dupleix's own share in the capital investment in a particular voyage might not be very high is suggested by the break-up of the total investment made in the voyage by the *Balocopal* to Manila in 1738. Of the total sum of Rs. 243,000 invested, Dupleix's own share was only Rs. 30,000. Of the remainder, Rs. 105,000 was put up by Eliot, Rs. 40,000 by one of the Carvalho brothers, Rs. 30,000 by Dumas and Rs. 23,000 by Costanier, the balance being subscribed probably by smaller associates. The list of persons providing loans for Dupleix's ventures was a long one and included persons such as the *Jagatseth*. The respondentia loans carried a minimum of 18 percent interest, though it could be much higher. A major component of Dupleix's business was the carrying of freight cargo of mainly Armenian and Muslim merchants. The rate charged normally varied between 7 and 10 percent of the valuc of thc cargo.[15]

Between 1731 and 1741 Dupleix organized or participated in about 91 voyages. An overwhelming bulk of these – as many as 79 – went westward, including 16 to Surat and 14 to Basra. The other westward destinations included the Maldives and Mozambique, Malabar, Mocha and Jiddah and Bandar Abbas. The eastward destinations included Acheh (two), Pegu and Malacca (one each), Manila (six) and Canton (two). Steady profits were made on most of these trips. But Dupleix would seem to have had more than his share of misfortune in the form of shipwrecks. The loss of the *Amiable* in 1735 while returning from Jiddah with Rs. 500,000 worth of gold was a crippling blow. Fortunately for him, the loss he suffered in the disappearance of the *Balocopal* in the Bay of Bengal on its way back from Manila in 1739 amounted to no more than Rs. 40,000. Dupleix kept transferring his savings to France through both legitimate and unauthorized channels. In 1741, his capital in Pondicherry and Chandernagore was reported to have amounted to about Rs. 550,000.[16]

The withdrawal of the French East India Company from the intra-Asian trade in 1741, followed by the outbreak of hostilities between the English and French in 1744, practically put an end to French participation in trade within Asia. There was, however, a remarkable revival in the French private trade from Bengal in the 1750s. In the 1780s and the 1790s, French participation in Asian trade was based chiefly on Mauritius. While only six French vessels were recorded as having called at Cochin in 1785-6, the number had gone up to 17 in 1791-2. Nearly all these ships were trading between

15 Indrani Ray, 'Dupleix's private trade in Chandernagore', *The Indian Historical Review*, vol. 1 (2), 1974, pp.279-94.

16 Indrani Ray, 'Dupleix's private trade'.

Mauritius and Mahe, Pondicherry, the Maldives and Colombo. Only one had made a China voyage and only two had gone to Bengal.[17]

The English Private Traders

There can be little doubt that by far the most important of the European private traders operating in the Bay of Bengal, and indeed in the whole of Asia, particularly during the eighteenth century, were the English. Until about the 1760s, a very large proportion of them were employees of the English Company, thereafter, the so-called free merchants settled in India probably predominated. The Company itself had withdrawn in 1661 from its marginal participation in intra-Asian trade, and by a series of 'indulgences' issued in the late 1660s and the 1670s had formally allowed its servants to trade on their private account. While there never was any formal collaboration between the Company on the one hand and its servants and free merchants on the other on the French pattern, the English servants did indeed make full use of their official position to promote their private interests. At times this even involved manipulating official Company policy, involving loss to the Company in its corporate character.

The English private traders operated from ports on both the east and the west coasts of India. Over the seventeenth and the early years of the eighteenth century, Coromandel ports witnessed English private trading activity on a much larger scale than did ports in Bengal. Masulipatnam was the principal port used on the Coromandel coast but around the turn of the century, more and more private English shipping moved on to Madras. In Bengal, the principal port used was Hugli until it was replaced by Calcutta in the early years of the eighteenth century. In course of time, Calcutta emerged as the most important port of English private trade from India. On the west coast, English private trade began at Surat in the early years of the seventeenth century, but moved on to Bombay in the eighteenth.

Among the important private English traders operating from Coromandel during the second half of the seventeenth century were the governors of Madras. Two of them, Elihu Yale and Thomas Pitt, were particularly active and are known to have amassed huge fortunes, estimated in the case of Yale at £200,000. Other governors with significant private trading interest included Edward Winter, William Langhorn, Streynsham Master, Gulston Addison, Edward Harrison and Joseph Collet. Among the chiefs of the English factory at Masulipatnam, major private traders included William Jearsey,

[17] Holden Furber, *John Company at Work, A Study of European Expansion in India in the late Eighteenth Century*, Cambridge, Mass., 1948.

Richard Mohun and Robert Freeman. Most, if not all, of these individuals were also diamond commissioners, an activity that contributed handsomely to their prosperity. Diamonds were not covered by the Company's monopoly of Euro-Asian trade and could be freely imported into England against a 4 percent fee. The London diamond merchants operated mainly by appointing 'commissioners' in India to whom funds were despatched regularly and who looked after procurement and the shipment of the rough stones. By and large, these commissioners were chosen from amongst the senior officials of the Company based in Coromandel who were simultaneously engaged in intra-Asian trade in a substantial manner on their private account. As recompense the commissioners were entitled to a 7 percent commission on the value of the investment. There ordinarily was a gap, sometimes as long as six months, between the receipt of funds by the commissioner in Madras and their actual investment in the purchase of diamonds. The resultant additional liquidity available at no extra cost often constituted a major element in the commissioner's success in his individual country trading ventures.

While the bulk of the English private trade from Coromandel would seem to have been in the hands of individual merchants, there were several alternative patterns in use as well. Some of the governors of Madras organized 'joint stocks', that is, large syndicates of investors who would buy shares in one or more ships under the governor's management. A large segment of the English community had a stake in Madras's shipping, either as part owners or as lenders of respondentia loans. Such loans were secured on the cargo of a ship at a rate adjusted to the risk and the length of the voyage, the risk being on the lender.[18] Partnership ventures between two or more individual merchants were also quite common. Thus, Richard Mohun, Matthew Mainwaring and George Chamberlain are known to have been partners in trading ventures based on a 4:9, 3:9 and 2:9 share, respectively. Another noteworthy partnership was that between William Monson and Nicholas Morse, who traded on equal shares from Madras. On occasion a vessel was owned jointly by several persons, the profit earned from its trips being shared proportionately. Thus in 1675, the *Indulgence* was reported to have been owned to the extent of one third by Richard Mohun, and the remaining two thirds jointly by William Langhorn, Harris, Matthew Mainwaring and Robert Fleetwood.[19] In the case of voyages to China, large partnerships are known to have been formed to invest in the ships, including not only Englishmen

[18] P.J. Marshall, 'Private British trade in the Indian Ocean before 1800', in Ashin Das Gupta and M.N. Pearson, eds., *India and the Indian Ocean 1500-1800'*, Calcutta, 1987, p.287.

[19] Ian Bruce Watson, *Foundation for Empire, English Private Trade in India 1659-1760*, New Delhi, 1980, pp.122-3, 330-1.

at Madras, but also those in Surat, Bombay and the Malabar ports. Many of these voyages seem to have started and finished at Surat.[20]

Joint ownership, financing and management of ships occasionally also included Indian merchants. For example, in the trade between Madras and South-East Asia there was collaboration between Governor Harrison of Madras, Governor Joseph Collet of Benkulen (who had earlier been in Madras and after a few years returned there as governor) and Sunku Rama, the chief merchant of the English Company at Madras. In May 1713, Collet advised Sunku Rama as follows, 'In such an adventure as I propose I shall constantly continue to be concern'd with you One half, not doubting but that Governor Harrison will at your request, supply my Proportion in Respondentia'.[21] The private English trade with Manila and Macao often involved Armenian, Spanish and Portuguese intermediaries. The Madras merchant, John Scattergood, had as his business partners at Malacca the Captain China Chan Yungqua and the Portuguese Joao de Matta. Through them Scattergood arranged second stage investments in voyages to Trengganu, Siam, Acheh, Banjamasin and Java. In 1720, de Matta was entrusted with the goods shipped on the *Bonita* to sell as he thought fit in the straits of Malacca and adjacent ports in return for 5 percent commission.[22]

The eastward trade carried on by private English merchants from India consisted essentially of three segments – South-East Asia, the Philippines, and China. The first of these stretched from ports such as Pegu, Tenasserim-Mergui, Ujang Salang, Kedah and Acheh – all on the eastern littoral of the Bay of Bengal – to Ayuthya in the Gulf of Siam. The port frequented in the Philippines was Manila and that in China, Canton. In an analysis of the English private trade with the region, it is useful to distinguish between the period before about 1760 and that after. This is because the second half of the eighteenth century witnessed a substantive growth in the relative weight of the eastward trade in the overall trading operations of private English merchants from India. Holden Furber has ascribed this turning from the west to the east as an important element in the 'commercial revolution' in the Indian Ocean trade. The great expansion in the eastward trade in the post-1760 period, carried on by the free English merchants, was the outcome basically of a substantial growth in the trade with Canton which, in turn, was related in a large measure to the growth of the English power in the Indian subcontinent. The English had become the actual rulers of Bengal, they were the dom-

20 P.J. Marshall, 'Private British trade', p.285.

21 D.K. Basset, 'British "country" trade and local trade networks in the Thai and Malay States, C. 1680-1770', *Modern Asian Studies*, vol. 23 (4), 1989, p.635.

22 D.K. Bassett, 'British "country" trade', p.635.

inant power on most of the Coromandel coast, and they had strengthened their position in western India. The special position of the English Company, and by association of that of the private English merchants, vis-a-vis the suppliers and producers of goods in regions such as Bengal, significantly increased the margin of profit from private trade. This was reflected in a sharp increase in the volume of trade in high-value commodities such as Bengal opium, which together with Bombay cotton provided the basis of the large private English fortunes made in India. The newly found power and the expanded resource base had now enabled private English shipping to go beyond the Asian networks within which it had until then operated, and create new ones of its own.

The changing destination pattern of the eastward trade had its counterpart in the changing relative weight of the various Indian ports where English shipping directed at the region originated. Over the seventeenth and the first half of the eighteenth century, the bulk of the English trade with South-East Asia, which accounted for an overwhelming proportion of the total trade with the eastward region, was carried on from the Coromandel coast. This picture underwent a complete overhaul in the second half of the eighteenth century when the Madras shipping essentially took the back seat and the bulk of the eastward trade was carried on by the English shipping based at Calcutta and Bombay.

A rough idea of the growth as well as the changing destination pattern of the private English merchants eastward trade from India can be formed by reference to the fact that while in the first half of the eighteenth century, the Dutch at Malacca recorded a maximum of 10 English private ships heading east through the straits in any one year, the number had gone upto 24 in 1764, and as many as 50 in 1774. Simultaneously, more ships were going through the Sunda Straits.[23] While a large part of this would be ascribable to the growth of the China trade, it also reflects a more thorough penetration of the South-East Asian markets by English traders. The Dutch control of Malacca as of 1641 and their special position in the archipelago notwithstanding, it had always been possible to do a certain amount of trading in the region in items such as opium, tin and pepper which the Dutch by and large had sought to reserve for themselves. The Dutch control over the Malay sultans' trade had always been tenuous and English country captains, by paying higher prices and with the aid of some discrete bribery, had found it possible to trade even at Malacca itself. But in the post-1760 period, it was no longer necessary to be discreet and Dutch claims of monopoly could be countered quite openly.

23 P.J. Marshall, 'Private British trade', p.297.

Until the middle of the eighteenth century, by far the most important destination for private English shipping from India was South-East Asia, and the principal Indian port from which shipping was directed there, Madras. The principal ports called at were Pegu, Tenasserim/Mergui and Ayuthya, Kedah, Acheh and Malacca besides Bantam and Batavia. At Batavia, English ships were obliged to operate under stringent restrictions as to the commodities in which they traded, while the trade to Bantam was lost as of 1682 when the port was taken over by the Dutch and declared closed to others. Pegu remained an important destination, but trade with the port was subject to vigorous competition from Indian merchants. During the 1720s and the 1730s, between 6 and 12 ships left Madras for Pegu each year. In 1720, 1722 and 1737, the number of incoming ships from Pegu rose to 13-14 and in 1739, as many as 21 arrivals were recorded. The number of Indian ships in these lists often exceeded that of the private English merchants.[24] The principal items procured in Pegu were gold, timber and rice.

At the Siamese ports of Mergui and Tenasserim in the Bay of Bengal, and of Ayuthya in the Gulf of Siam, private English traders encountered the dynamic trading organization of the king of Siam. The trade between Madras and Mergui/Tenasserim was dominated throughout by Asian merchants. A large number of Chinese junks regularly called at Ayuthya, making it an important meeting point between the East and the West. Between October 1683 and November 1684 as many as 42 ships including 11 belonging to the English are recorded as having called at the port. At the beginning of 1685, more than a dozen English, French and Portuguese ships left Ayuthya westward with Japanese bar copper bought from the foreign trade minister of Siam, the Greek Constantine Phaulkon.[25] But the Mergui massacre of July 1687 followed by the Anglo-Thai war of 1687-8 put a temporary stop to English trade at the Siamese ports, and it was not until 1705-6 that Governor Thomas Pitt and associates reinstated this trade. Initially, they used ships with Asian or Portuguese title or captaincy but by 1708-9, English ships were being used again. In 1718, a private agreement was signed at Ayuthya promising favourable treatment for Madras ships. The English Madras-Ayuthya connection would seem to have continued on a regular basis in the 1720s and on a less regular basis in the 1730s. Occasionally, a Madras ship also called at Tonkin.[26]

Other important South-East Asian ports frequented by the English included Kedah and, above all, Acheh. Chinese junks regularly called at Acheh, making it yet another important source for Far Eastern goods. Exports to Acheh included Coromandel tex-

24 D.K. Bassett, 'British "Country" trade', p.636.

25 D.K. Bassett, 'British "Country" trade', p.628-9.

26 P.J. Marshall, 'Private British trade', p.286.

tiles, rice and slaves besides fair quantities of Bengal opium. Imports into Madras included camphor, Benzoin, wax and pepper besides goods of Far Eastern origin. A 1660 agreement between Acheh and the English Company had exempted ships flying English colours from customs duties, subject to the requirement that the English shippers would trade exclusively through the shahbandar and other royal officials. While that would almost certainly have cut into the profit margin, the turnover would have been rendered quicker. Indian ships visiting Acheh were not bound by this requirement, but paid 12 percent import duty. The attraction of Acheh for the English traders increased further in 1687 following their temporary exclusion from Siam. The years around the turn of the century witnessed a certain amount of dislocation involving even a private British naval blockade of the port in 1702 (organized by Alexander Hamilton) to enforce English exemption from customs duties. There was another blockade for a few weeks in 1706 organized this time by Delton and Griffith. Repeated invitations from the sultan to resume trade with the port did lead to a resumption of voyages to Acheh from both Madras and Bengal around 1715. But soon thereafter, some gold was seized from the Madras ship *Messiah* by the Acheh government. In retaliation, the sultan's ship was seized at Madras by Governor Joseph Collet in October 1717. Trade to Acheh under British colours did not resume apparently until the 1730s.[27]

From the 1760s onward, the British country traders operating from Madras began to organize themselves into powerful syndicates. This combined with the greater political and economic leverage available to the British all over India from about this time generally increased their competitive strength in Acheh and the South-East Asian market. The Gowan-Harrop syndicate significantly expanded its operations in Acheh from about 1766. The syndicate, taken over by Jourdan, Sulivan and De Souza in 1770, included several members of the Fort St. George council. It loaned mercenaries to the sultan and eventually dominated the port of Acheh. Kedah was also emerging as a major trading port for the English around this time. Indeed, in 1772, the Madras Presidency ranked Kedah above Acheh as an outlet for opium and piece-goods. Acheh was assumed to have a market for 150 chests of opium as against 250 chests in Kedah. The anticipated profit on the Acheh investment was 30,000 pagodas compared to 45,000 pagodas in Kedah.[28]

In addition to South-East Asia, private English shipping from Madras also went to Manila and China, the former from about the 1670s and the latter after about 1690s.

[27] D.K. Bassett, 'British "Country" trade', p. 629-32.

[28] D.K. Bassett, 'British "Country" trade', p. 639-40.

Trade with both these destinations seems to have been fairly regular, but relatively small-scale. Until 1789, the only European ships permitted into Manila were Portuguese. From 1674 English owned ships based at Madras began making regular trips to Manila under Portuguese colours. For most of the eighteenth century, an average of three ships a year went from Madras to Manila. The 1789 repeal of the restrictive Spaniard regulations enabled the private English vessels to go to Manila under their own colours.[29] As far as the Madras-Canton trade was concerned, it was based on the export of silver to Canton in exchange for gold and commodities such as tutenag, quicksilver, alum and sugar. The bulk of these goods were re-exported from Madras to western India. From about 1760 onward, the India-China trade assumed important proportions. But the share of Madras shipping in the revitalized China trade was negligible: that was a trade carried on mainly by the private English shipping based at Bombay and Calcutta.

Until the 1760s, the private English merchants' trade was practically nonexistent from Bombay and relatively quite small from Calcutta. The number of vessels going eastward from the latter port was reported to be four each in 1704-5 and 1705-6 and three in 1706-7. A large proportion of these vessels, if not all of them, had destinations in South-East Asia, mainly Malaya and Sumatra. The principal exports to the region were textiles and opium and the principal imports sandalwood, sappanwood, tin and pepper.[30]

Over the first half of the eighteenth century, Bengal shipping also went further east to Manila and Canton. Between these two destinations, the Manila connection was more regular. Bengal textiles were sold there mainly against Mexican silver. In the early part of the century, there was also a certain amount of co-operation with the Madras shipping in trips to Manila, though by 1727 Madras was beginning to complain of Bengal's competition at the port. In the 1720s, a total of 10 Calcutta ships are believed to have gone to Manila: in the 1730s, this number had come down to 6 or 7. Between 1740 and 1748, another 7 Bengal ships are reported to have called at Manila. After a gap until 1759, the arrival of Bengal ships was again recorded at Manila in 1760, 1764 and 1767. Thereafter, there is no evidence of shipping on this route until the late 1780s, when it was no longer necessary to operate under Portuguese or Asian colours. Contracts were now officially made between Calcutta merchants and the new Spanish Royal Philippine Company for Bengal goods to be delivered openly at Manila in English ships. The Canton connection was much more irregular until about 1760. Bengal

[29] P.J. Marshall, 'Private British trade', p.285.

[30] P.J. Marshall, *East Indian Fortunes, The British in Bengal in the Eighteenth Century*, Oxford, 1976, pp.85-8.

ships are known to have called at Canton only in 1725 and 1736, though another ship, the *Shah Alam*, the largest of the Calcutta fleet, was also reportedly being fitted for a voyage to Canton in 1730.[31]

The situation had, however, changed completely by the 1760s, when what Furber has termed the 'commercial revolution' in the Indian Ocean trade was well under way. This revolution, completed by the 1780s, consisted in the first place of a clear domination of trade in the Indian Ocean and the South China Sea by private English shipping based in Calcutta and Bombay, and in the second, of a increasingly central and indeed dominant position of the trade with China and Malaya in private English trade from India. This was the consequence of a variety of factors at work, both economic and political. These ranged from the growing popularity of Chinese tea in the European market and the growing prosperity of English merchants engaged in country trade, to the wresting of formal political control by the English East India Company in Bengal and of considerable political leverage in western India.

An approximate idea of the order of magnitude involved in the growth of the China trade could perhaps be formed by reference to the fact that between 1774-82 and 1785-6, imports by English country ships at Canton had doubled. By 1797-8, these had nearly trebled again.[32] The two principal items carried to Canton were Gujarat cotton and Bengal opium. In 1760, David Cuming had remarked that the only big Bombay ships he had noted at Canton were those belonging to the English East India Company. But in 1787, Cuming counted forty sails of large, privately owned ships from Bombay which had imported 60,000 bales of cotton. On an average, over the last quarter of the eighteenth century, cotton accounted for approximately half of the total English exports to China. In the early years of the nineteenth century cotton exports were marked by large annual fluctuations. Against the peak of Rs. 9 million worth in 1807-8, for example, exports in 1812-13 were worth only Rs. 2.3 million. The bulk of cotton exports from Bombay were on the accounts of private traders. Thus in 1810-11, these merchants accounted for as much as 91.4 percent of the total cotton exports from Bombay, the remainder being on the account of the English East India Company. A certain amount of Bengal cotton was also carried to China by the Calcutta shipping. Thus in 1810-11, the private Calcutta shipping carried nearly one third (31.3 percent) of the amount of cotton carried by Bombay shipping on the account of both the Company as well as the private traders.[33] The principal Bengal commodity carried to China

[31] P.J. Marshall, *East Indian Fortunes*, pp.89, 104.

[32] P.J. Marshall, 'Private British trade', p.297.

[33] Pamela Nightingale, *Trade and Empire in Western India, 1784-1806*, Cambridge, 1970, pp.23, 233.

was, of course, opium. As opposed to an average of one per season in the 1760s, the number of Bengal based ships to Canton had gone up by 1778 to as many as ten. Valuewise, Bengal opium did not overtake Indian cotton until 1823,[34] but from the perspective of private traders, opium had already superseded cotton as the most lucrative item by the early years of the nineteenth century.[35]

The starting point of the China trade was the growing involvement of the English East India Company in the import of Chinese tea into England. Since the British government levied duties of as much as 115 percent on all imports of tea, smuggling by rival bodies operating from the European continent was a highly profitable enterprise. This, however, ceased to be the case following the Commutation Bill of 1784 which reduced the duties to a mere 12 percent. The result was that the English Company was able to price the competitors out of the market and further increase its imports from China. As with most Asian commodities, however, Chinese tea had to be paid for mainly in specie. Once Bengal revenues became available to the Company, following the acquisition of *diwani* rights in 1765, the directors asked the Bengal Council to ship Rs. 4 million in cash annually to Canton. But this was not found feasible, and indeed after 1768 no specie could be spared from Bengal. As far as Indian goods were concerned, Gujarat cotton and Bengal opium were the only items with a large market in China. Opium was a contraband item and the Company obviously could not handle it on its own, but a certain amount of cotton was indeed carried by Company ships to Canton on a regular basis. The close collaboration between Company servants and private traders, however, ensured that the bulk of the cotton trade was left to the latter. This, together with a large and growing clandestine trade in opium, made the China trade by far the most lucrative branch of trade for the private English merchants operating from India.

By a curious intermingling of the private traders' interests with those of the Company, the China trade became not only an important vehicle for the generation of private European fortunes in India, but also the leading medium of the remittance home of these fortunes. The proceeds from the goods the private merchants sold in China invariably exceeded the value of goods like silk, sugar-candy, tea, mercury and camphor procured there by a considerable margin. It was in the mutual interest of these merchants as well as the Company for this surplus purchasing power to be put at the disposal of the supercargoes at Canton for investment in tea on the account of the Company. The Company would then be spared the necessity of carrying specie to China,

[34] Michael Greenberg, *British Trade and the Opening of China 1800-42*, Cambridge, 1951, p.81.

[35] Pamela Nightingale, *Trade and Empire*, p. 233.

and bills of exchange issued at Canton on the directors in London for the money received would ensure for the merchants a safe avenue for the transfer home of their fortunes on a regular basis. In the event they needed the money in India, the bills of exchange were made payable in Calcutta. The private traders were often able to expand the size of their outward cargoes by raising fairly large sums of money in respondentia from individuals who were looking for avenues to transmit their savings home. Between 1770-83, approximately £ 3 million worth of bills of exchange were issued at Canton: this figure would have gone up substantially with the striking growth of the China trade after 1784. The critical importance the Company attached to receiving purchasing power at Canton is further illustrated by the Bengal Governor-General John Macpherson making in May 1785 what he called a personal suggestion to Gregorius Herklots, the Dutch second-in-command at Hugli. Macpherson began by saying that as against the usual 400-450 chests in the 1770s, the Company had now agreed to provide 800 chests of opium to the Dutch. Since the English badly needed to finance their supercargo at Canton without having to send specie from Calcutta, they would appreciate if Batavia could arrange for the payment of the opium supplied to them in Bengal at Canton. The amount of opium mentioned was between 800 and 1,000 chests on a recurring annual basis. As a further incentive, the governor-general added that he was willing to give a guarantee that even in case of war, 'we should send the opium to Batavia under a flag of peace and leave you the full and secure preparation of it…it is immaterial to the English Company whether this trade is carried on by a foreign Company or by people living at Calcutta'. The letter went on to say that, 'I know not but many good consequences would arise to your Company from beginning to pay money in China for opium to be delivered to you in Bengal'. One of the potential good consequences hinted at was the restoration of Nagapattinam to the Dutch. Herklots sent a vague reply saying that he would get in touch with Batavia, but the arrangement did not appeal to the Dutch and was never put in practice.[36]

The fact that there was a great degree of collaboration between the private English traders and the governments of Bombay and Bengal is fully borne out in the case of both the cotton and the opium exports to China. In the case of cotton, this collaboration was at times even at the expense of the Company. Following the Commutation Act of 1784, the average annual sales of cotton in Canton had leaped from around 300,000 *taels* worth to as much 2.16 million *taels* within a period of three years. Private trading interests in collaboration with the Company officials, however, ensured that the Com-

[36] ARA, Correspondence between the English and the Dutch authorities in Bengal 1785-94, letter from Governor-General John Macpherson to Gregorius Herklots, 19 May 1785; letter from Herklots and Council at Hugli to John Macpherson and Council at Calcutta, 26 May 1785, HRB 212 (unfoliated).

pany itself was allowed to partake of this bounty only up to a point. In April 1789, for example, the directors deplored the fact that against a capacity of 1,500 to 2,000 bales Company ships carried at the most 800 bales for the Company and made the remaining space available to private traders. The factors were therefore instructed to send as much cotton as possible to Canton on the Company's own account. In April 1790, the Court even sent 600 chests of dollars to Bombay specifically for the purchase of cotton. Six years later, Bombay was ordered to send as many as 15,000 bales of cotton to China to repair the finances of the Company at Canton. But the factors by and large managed to disregard these instructions, and the Company's share in the total cotton exports to China never reached important proportions. Instead, the Company's power and authority at Surat and elsewhere was made available in ample measure to the private traders in their efforts to control the cotton dealers. Such control was deemed necessary to check the rise in price as well as the problem of adulteration in the cotton supplied. In December 1801, an agreement was concluded between the government on the one hand, and three agency houses of Bombay trading in cotton together with three Parsi merchants, on the other. The private traders and the government agreed to buy the cotton jointly, and to divide it amongst them. The Company's share was not larger than that assigned to each firm. It was also realized that the problem of adulteration could be tackled effectively and on a long term basis only if the Company extended its power in Gujarat. As Nightingale has emphasized, it was this consideration rather than the menace of French imperialism that spurred British territorial expansion in the region. But from about 1805 onward, the directors succeeded in obliging the Bombay government to substantially increase the Company's share in the cotton trade. The domination of the government by the private traders evidently was over, even if they continued to be important participants in the cotton trade with Canton.[37]

The principal item carried to China by the private English shipping based at Calcutta was opium. Being contraband, it was completely outside the Canton commercial system. It was not channeled through the Hong merchants but was smuggled to outside brokers against cash payment. In addition the Calcutta ships also carried to Canton commodities such as Malayan tin and Sumatran pepper purchased en route in Batavia and other Malay ports against items such as Bengal opium and textiles. On the return trip some of the China goods were sold in South-East Asia. The trade from Calcutta to Canton and South-East Asia thus became part of an integrated mechanism in which the export of opium played the central role. Ever since the middle of the seventeenth century, the opium trade between Bengal and South-East Asia had been handled pre-

[37] Pamela Nightingale, *Trade and Empire*, Chaps. 5-7.

dominantly by the Dutch East India Company. But the British conquest of Bengal had changed all that and the private English trader had emerged as the principal dealer in Bengal opium. In the 1760s the procurement of opium in Bihar had been monopolized by a succession of English Company servants operating in their private capacity. In 1773, the Company itself had taken over the monopoly and made opium available to private traders through public auction in Calcutta. To the great advantage of these traders, the amount made available to the Dutch Company under a newly introduced quota system was kept at the relatively low level of 450 chests per annum. The amount was later increased to 800 chests, but successively brought down again first to 700 and from 1787 onward to 500 chests a year.[38] English private traders operated with impunity in the former Dutch preserves in the archipelago and sold large quantities of Bengal opium in the region. Shipping records of Batavia show that British private tonnage calling at that port increased from 3,000 to 5,000 tons between 1784 and 1786.

Already in 1764 private British traders were believed to have brought in 500 chests of opium into the Straits of Malacca. In 1777 the value of Calcutta's trade with Malaya and Indonesia was estimated to match the trade with China. Upto 1500-2000 chests of opium could be sold in the port of Riau which the sultan of Johor had opened to the English around 1768, and a considerable amount of pepper and tin obtained there. The American war and a Dutch counteroffensive in the Malacca Straits which closed Riau in 1784, temporarily checked the commercial expansion of Calcutta shipping into Malaya, but in 1786 it took a more concrete form with the annexation of Penang, the first British settlement in Malaya. This was the culmination of the British private traders' search for a foothold in South-East Asia that could serve as a base for shipping and trade. Several places such as Acheh, Balambangan and Ujang Salang had earlier been explored for the purpose but without success. In March 1789 English traders were reported to be smuggling at least 2,000 chests of opium into China. Calcutta's eastward trade as a whole was estimated in 1793 at around Rs. 5 million, of which about Rs. 3 million worth consisted of opium. This sum would have bought about 4,500 chests of which around 2,000-2,500 seem to have reached China and a roughly similar amount sold on the way in the Malay archipelago.[39]

To conclude, over the three hundred year period between the beginning of the sixteenth century and the close of the eighteenth, Europeans played an increasingly important role in the functioning of the vast trading network originating in the Bay of

[38] Om Prakash, 'Opium monopoly in India and Indonesia in the eighteenth century', *The Indian Economic and Social History Review*, vol. 24 (1), 1987, pp.63-80.

[39] Holden Furber, *John Company at Work*, pp.174-5, 183.

Bengal. There were European corporate enterprises as well as private traders, many of them simultaneously employees of the corporate enterprises. The attitudes of the latter to the private traders differed a great deal depending largely on the degree of involvement of the enterprise in the intra-Asian trade. The Dutch East India Company which was the only corporate enterprise engaged in a substantive intra-Asian trade stood at one end of the spectrum and over the greater part of its existence was uncompromisingly hostile to employees illegally engaging in private trade. It is another matter that the employees nevertheless managed to do so. The brief involvement of the French East India Company in intra-Asian trade from the Bay of Bengal in the first half of the eighteenth century represents in some sense the other end of the spectrum involving a formal collaborative arrangement between the Company and its employees together with Indian merchants. English private merchants, who accounted for a very large proportion of the total European private contingent, particularly during the eighteenth century, were in the happy position of enjoying the patronage of the Company for their intra-Asian enterprises, as well as taking full advantage of its growing political power in the subcontinent. This contributed no small measure to their increasing domination of the trade in the Indian Ocean.

XI

English Private Trade in the Western Indian Ocean, 1720–1740 *

I

India and Indian merchants had traditionally played a central role in the successful functioning of the Indian Ocean trading network. In part, this, indeed, was a function of the midway location of the subcontinent between the Middle East on the one hand, and Southeast and East Asia, on the other. But perhaps even more important was the subcontinent's capacity to put on the market a wide range of tradable goods at highly competitive prices. By far the most **[p. 216]** important of these goods were textiles of various kinds. While these included high-value varieties such as the legendary Dhaka muslins and the Gujarat silk embroideries, the really important component for the Asian market was the coarse cotton varieties manufactured primarily on the Coromandel coast and in Gujarat. There was large-scale demand for these varieties both in the eastern markets of Indonesia, Malaya, Thailand and Burma as well as in the markets of the Red Sea, the Persian Gulf and East Africa.

The key position of India in the structure of Asian trade was also reflected in the important role of the Gujarati and other Indian trading groups in the actual conduct of this trade. This role, if anything, was strengthened in the course of the fifteenth century, which witnessed the fragmentation of Asian trade into well-defined segments. The trade between the Middle East and the west coast of India was shared between the Arabs/Persians and the Indians. As far as the trade between the west and the east coasts of India, on the one hand, and the Eastern Indian Ocean region, on the other, was concerned, it was now left almost exclusively in the hands of Indians – the Gujaratis more than anyone else, but also the Chettis, the Chulias and other groups from the Coromandel coast, besides the Oriyas and the Bengalis.

* First published in: *Journal of the Economic and Social History of the Orient*, 50 (Leiden: Brill, 2007), pp. 215–234. The original page numbers are shown in square brackets within the text.

I would like to thank the British Academy for inviting me as an Academy Visiting Professor in June-July 2002. This enabled me to work in the Oriental and India Office Collection at the British Library, London where material for this paper was collected. I would like to thank Peter Marshall for being an excellent host on behalf of the Academy.

Gujarat was a major trading area in the subcontinent and the Gujaratis had traditionally been a dominant group among the Indian mercantile communities. Over the course of the fifteenth century, the trading activities of this group increased to a point where it emerged probably as the largest of all the groups engaged in trade in the Indian Ocean. In the seventeenth and the early part of the eighteenth century, the ship-owning maritime merchant community operating from Surat – the principal port of the region – was in good measure Muslim, though by no means exclusively or even overwhelmingly so. The most important of the Surat maritime merchants at the turn of the eighteenth century was Mulla Abdul Ghafur, a Bohra Muslim owning as many as seventeen sea-going ships with a total dead-weight carrying capacity of well over 5,000 tons. The prosperity of this affluent merchant family lasted several generations.

In what way did the coming in of the Europeans into the Indian Ocean, following the discovery of the sea-route via the Cape of Good Hope at the end of the fifteenth century, alter the basic structure and dynamics of the Indian Ocean trade, with special reference to the trade to and from India? Stated very briefly and succinctly, the answer to this query has to be that nothing very much happened in that regard except that the volume and value of the trade in the Ocean registered a distinct increase. Given the fairly sophisticated and developed organization, as well as the structure of production and trade that the Europeans encountered on their arrival in the East, the only meaningful option available to **[p. 217]** them was to integrate themselves into the existing structure and become yet another unit operating within it. That is precisely what they did, except for occasional episodes of aberration which do not need to detain us here.

Each of the principal European corporate enterprises operating in the Indian Ocean, starting with the Portuguese Estado da India in the sixteenth century, and followed by the English, the Dutch and the French East India companies in the seventeenth and the eighteenth centuries, included a component consisting of employees and others belonging to that particular nationality and engaged in trade within Asia on their private account. It is useful to remember that the policy and attitude that different corporate enterprises adopted towards the private traders of their particular nationality differed dramatically from one to the other, from outright hostility at one end of the spectrum to formal collaboration at the other with a whole range of variation in between.

The prime example of sheer hostility by a corporate enterprise towards private trade by its employees was that of the Dutch East India Company.

This was the direct outcome of the Company's own large scale involvement in intra-Asian trade from the very beginning as an integral part of its overall trading strategy. In order to prevent employees from emerging as rivals, their participation in intra-Asian trade was banned. In the case of the Portuguese, the relationship between the Estado da India and private traders engaged in intra-Asian trade ranged from open hostility to substantive patronage in the form of the concession system. The ultimate in formal cooperation and collaboration between a given corporate enterprise and the private traders of that nationality, however, was achieved by the French in the first half of the eighteenth century. In 1719, the newly organized Campagnie des Indes decided to participate in intra-Asian trade as well. It was, however, immediately obvious to the factors at Pondicherry that the Company's financial and other resources were simply not adequate to allow a meaningful participation in this trade on its own. A decision was therefore taken to invite employees as well as other traders, both Indian and European, to collaborate with the Company. This unique venture lasted about twenty years between 1722 and 1741.

There can be very little doubt that by far the most important group of European private traders operating in Asia, particularly during the eighteenth century, was that of the English private traders. The English East India Company itself had withdrawn in 1661 from its marginal participation in intra-Asian trade, and by a series of 'indulgences' issued in the late 1660s and the 1670s had formally allowed its servants to trade on their private account. While there was never any formal collaboration between the English Company on the one hand and its servants and free merchants on the other, the English servants **[p. 218]** did indeed make full use of their official position to promote their private interests. At times, this even involved manipulating the official policy of the English Company to the detriment of the Company in its corporate character.

The fact that the extensive documentation of the English East India Company preserved at the Oriental and India Office Collection (OIOC) at the British Library, London, contains only a limited amount of material on the private trading activities of its servants, has been well-known and is reflected in the relatively limited amount of work done on this subject. What one ideally needs for this purpose are the private papers of major participants in the private trading endeavour. One such participant in the Surat-Red Sea trade in the 1720s and the 1730s was Sir Robert Cowan, governor of the English East India Company at Bombay between 1729 and 1734. This paper is based mainly on the private papers of this man. The original papers are available in the Public Record Office at Belfast. Microfilm copies available in the Oriental and India Office Collection at the British Library have been used for this paper. What makes the Cowan papers (to which the late Ashin Das Gupta had first drawn our attention in his seminal 1979 Surat book) quite unique is the fascinating level of detail available in them. The range of subjects touched upon in the papers is truly staggering, covering not only his own and his associates' private trading activities but also highlighting essentials of the entire trading network of the private English trading community of the period.

II

Robert Cowan had arrived in India from Portugal in about 1717 after being in private business there for several years. In February 1719 he was granted permission to reside in Bombay as a free merchant. In December 1720, he was sent to Goa as the chief of the factory there. Partly as a reward for the good work he did there in negotiating with the Portuguese authorities, he was appointed member of the Bombay Council in 1721. He was appointed chief of the Mocha factory in 1724, from where he returned to Bombay towards the end of 1728. On 10 January 1729, he took over as governor of Bombay succeeding William Phipps. Cowan was dismissed from service in 1734 for giving freedom of trade to a Portuguese vessel in Bombay. He died early in 1737, not long after his arrival in England. The Cowan papers deal with his trading and related activities essentially over the period 1724 to 1734. These activities covered a wide range from trading, freighting space on vessels owned by him wholly or in part, freighting space for his own cargo on other merchants' – both European and Indian – ships, loaning funds on respondentia, arranging insurance and **[p. 219]** money transfers, acting as attorney for fellow English private traders, recovering bad debts on their behalf and generally networking with them. In Surat, Cowan even participated in the revenue farming of tobacco cultivation. As mentioned above, between 1724 and 1728 he was located at Mocha and from 1729 onward at Bombay.

The Surat-Mocha trade consisted overwhelmingly of Gujarat textiles on the outward voyage and precious metals on the incoming one. Information available in respect of the textile cargo (which accounted for nearly the whole of the cargo) carried by the *Dolphin* from Surat to Mocha on the account of a private English merchant, John Hope – the English chief at Surat in 1721 – provides important details regarding the costs of the ship's cargo. Of the total proceeds of Mocha Dollars 35,463 realized by the sale of the ship's cargo, a sum of 22,819 dollars was remitted to Hope at Surat while another 8,612 dollars were retained at Mocha by the local corresponding trader pro rata to his investment in the. ship's cargo. The remaining sum of 4,032 dollars was accounted for by customs duties (1,063 dollars at 3 percent), brokerage (532 dollars at 1 ½ percent), commission presumably for the local corresponding trader (1,773 dollars at 5 percent), house rent for two seasons (300 dollars), servants' wages (17 dollars), presents to the local governor (300 dollars) and a small amount of 45 dollars towards *shiffage* (?). Since the cost price of the textile cargo is not specified, unfortunately the earned profit cannot be calculated.[1]

A letter from Francis Dickinson at Mocha to Robert Cowan at Bombay dated 29 April 1729 contains further interesting details regarding the private English Surat-Mocha trade. Dickinson reported that the bulk of Cowan's cargo that he had brought with him, as well as the lot that had arrived with the *Fateh Baksh*, had already been sold at terms much better than what the Surat merchants, who had arrived later, managed to get. The fall in the cost price of the Surat textiles, brought about by a fall in the price of cotton, had been of great help. The country was in a state of peace and quiet and all routes were open. It was, however, important that the cargo arrived on time (i.e. by late December) and was of the right specifications. It was further noted that if the textiles carried the stamp of the Company and carried the legend *Surkah Angrezi* in the Devanagari script, they were likely to do better. The varieties bought at Dholka by Haridas Govindjee had done well. Further instructions for Govindjee from Purushottam (the local expert) were enclosed. It would also be desirable to have these varieties manufactured at Cambay. In order to facilitate that, one Gondy **[p. 220]** Shakar Moor was being sent to supervise this. It would be appreciated if the Company's man at Cambay, Innes, was duly directed to assist in this process and to receive the goods in the Company's factory as they were delivered. Cowan was also requested to arrange for a bill of exchange on Surat for fifteen thousand rupees payable on sight. In order to minimize dependence on Surat brokers who charged a two percent brokerage, and occasionally cheated the private traders, Purushottam together with another person was sent along from Mocha. These persons were familiar with the varieties in demand in Mocha and would charge a 2 percent commission on the actual cost.[2]

---

[1] Letter from Mocha to Surat dated 15 June 1722, Microfilm number IOR Positive 11613 containing D654/Bl/5B, entitled "Pauws, Annesleys and Curgenvens papers", document no. 3.

[2] Microfilm number IOR Positive 11616, Part II 654/Bl/5H, document No.6 in collection 23 entitled "Messers Dickinson, Robinson and Ramsden papers".

While holding the office of chief of the English factory at Mocha, Cowan engaged in a variety of other activities in his private capacity, in addition to engaging in trade on his private account. One of these activities involved acting as the local agent of private English traders based elsewhere. In this role he sold goods on their behalf, recovered overdue debts and so on, all at an appropriate commission. An example of the former is the shipment of 1,120 bales of dates that Thomas Smith, Martin French and William Cordeaux sent to Cowan at Mocha from Gombroon in November 1724. Each of the three merchants had an equal share in the shipment sent aboard the *Success Franky* freighted from one Francis Walker, private merchant at Basra. The charter party of the vessel provided that it would be equipped with masts, sails, guns and ammunition as well as mariners at the cost of the owner. Half the total freight was to be paid in advance while the other half was to be paid on arrival at Mocha by Cowan on behalf of the merchants. Any unnecessary delay on the way was to be penalized by a fine of 50 percent on the total freight charges payable. The proceeds from the sale of the dates were to be remitted in the case of William Cordeaux to Messrs Massey and Draper at Bombay, and in that of Thomas Smith to William Phipps. Unfortunately, the rate of the commission payable to Cowan is not mentioned.[3]

An episode relating to the recovery of outstanding debts pertains to 1723-24 when John Hope of Bombay requested Cowan to recover a debt of 7,454 Mocha Dollars due from one Muhammad Yasin and of 8,204 dollars due from Sheikh Haji Muli, both merchants at Mocha. In the first instance, Cowan managed to recover 2,500 Spanish Dollars from the former but nothing from the latter. Both, however, provided to Cowan fresh letters acknowledging the balance amounts and promising to clear them the following season together with **[p. 221]** the interest. Hope also acknowledged the receipt of 1,000 Spanish Dollars from Cowan which he had recovered from Nihalchand Lakhimchand in partial payment of the debt of 5,085 Spanish Dollars owed by kinsman Munji Tesung, loaned to him in respondenting on the *Prince Augustus*. Should Nihalchand fail to clear the balance within the stipulated period, Cowan was to sell off the goods deposited with him as security. Hope suspected that the reason the respondentia bill was not being cleared was that the sale of the goods was unlikely to generate the necessary amount of funds. Ragoes, the broker through whom the loan had been negotiated, had since had several meetings with Munji Tesung who was currently in Surat. While the circumstances of the latter were not very good, he had nevertheless said that

---

[3] Microfilm number IOR positive 11614, D654/B1/5D, No. 17 "Gombroon, Spahan, Carnemenia and Bussorah letters and papers", documents 3,4,7,8 and 9.

he had large stocks of unsold goods at Mocha and would eventually be able to clear his obligations. He added that he had indeed left 1,000 Spanish Dollars with Benidas Nihalchand on whom the respondentia bill had been issued to help clear any balance. Hope suspected that it was this 1,000 Spanish Dollars that Nihalchand had given Cowan in part payment. Hope requested Cowan to seek the assistance of Ali Razzak, governor of Mocha, in the matter when Munji Tesung would be in Mocha to appear in the case. But if nothing further could be gained, the proceeds from the sale of the goods left with Cowan as a security were to be transmitted to Hope in Dollars with any of the Company's ships bound for Bombay.[4]

III

The full potential of Robert Cowan as a private trader, however, was realized only after he returned to Bombay as governor in January 1729. His principal collaborator in this endeavour was one Henry Lowther. Lowther had first made his mark at Bombay and Surat as an agent of Commander Thomas Mathews in the early 1720s. He had joined the Bombay Council in 1725 as its youngest member. In 1728, Lowther was sent to Surat as chief of the English factory there. In a letter to Lowther dated 16 February 1729, Cowan proposed collaboration in their private trading activities with the active involvement of Laldas Vithaldas Parak, the Company's chief broker there. Cowan wrote, "A short time will give you an insight into the extensive trade of Surat in all its branches and as your post will give you unlimited credit you will have great opportunities of improving your private fortune in which I wish you all the success you desire. And as heretofore I have upon all occasions shown my **[p. 222]** readiness and inclination to do you any service in my power, you may depend on my future good offices. I have intimated to Loldas the Broker how much I interest myself in every thing that regards you. I, therefore, think you may rest assured of his faithful services. And as long as he continues to deserve it, I desire you give him your countenance and protection to gratify him". Cowan's letter went on to add "Any considerable contract or purchase you engage in I am willing to be concerned with you any part not exceeding a quarter of the whole as you shall be welcome to what part you please on any voyage I set on foot from hence of which you shall have timely notice.

---

[4] John Hope at Bombay to Robert Cowan at Mocha, 28 October 1724, Document 13; John Hope at Bombay to Robert Cowan at Mocha, 28 December 1725, Document 19, Microfilm number IOR Positive 11614, D654/Bl/5C.

Your chief care must be to get acquainted with the principal traders amongst them the *Banians* and other casts of people to which your natural affability will greatly contribute. And by them you will be informed of everything that passes in the place".[5]

The combined resources and skills of Robert Cowan, Henry Lowther and Laldas Parak soon created a situation where the Cowan-Lowther partnership emerged as the undisputed master of the Surat-Mocha trade. But the manner in which the enterprise was run had its costs and perils. Lowther was an extraordinarily aggressive and ruthless man and thought nothing of grossly misusing the Company's resources and apparatus at Surat, including the services of Laldas Parak, for the benefit of the enterprise. In February 1736, John Braddyll of the Bombay Council proffered a series of charges against Lowther at a meeting of the Council. According to Ashin Das Gupta, "That Lowther had been misappropriating the Company's money was not difficult to prove. But Braddyll gathered lurid details of what amounted to a virtual reign of terror established by Lowther at the factory. He had monopolized all trade which had any connection with the factory and any English private trader who ignored the chief of the factory had been at once ousted from Surat. Indian merchants who had attempted to stand up against the system had had 'the government set upon them'" (Das Gupta 1979: 275). Two months later Lowther disappeared ignominiously from Surat.

Laldas Parak and his sons also had their share of tribulations. In 1722, his offer to provide the Company's investment at Surat at 7 percent cheaper than the terms given by the Company's broker Rustumji in the previous year had been accepted (Das Gupta 1979: 180). The following several years witnessed an enormous increase in Laldas' role in the Company's affairs as well as in the private trading affairs of Cowan and Lowther. When Laldas died on 8 July 1732, his eldest son, Jagannathdas Laldas Parak, was taken into the service of the Company as broker. The interlocking of assets between Lowther and **[p. 223]** Jagannathdas was, if anything, even more intense and complicated than had been the case in the time of his father. The debts of the Parak family to the Company were larger than the entire annual Surat investment of the Company. Recognizing Jagannathdas's growing financial problems, a part of the Company's investment was taken away from him in the season of 1734–35 and made over to Khoja Malik and Nagar Kotta, two merchants who had been working closely with Lowther (Das Gupta 1979: 272–3). The Paraks were dismissed from the brokerage in March 1737. Jagannathdas was arrested

---

5 Microfilm number IOR Positive 11614, Document number 20.

on a visit to Bombay and the second brother, Govindas, was seized at Surat and confined in the English factory (Das Gupta 1979: 276).

What about Robert Cowan himself? As we shall see presently, he did quite well in his private trading and related ventures. But from about 1732 onward, he had reason to be increasingly concerned at the growing entanglement of his fortunes with those of Henry Lowther and the Paraks. Since he did not have much choice in the matter, however, he held on and used his influential position as governor of Bombay to make optimal use of the enormous network of private English traders in the region to promote his private trading and other interests. The way the network functioned was that the Company servants stationed at a specific factory and engaged in trade and related activities in their private capacity undertook to function as agents and facilitators for their counterparts stationed in another region. Thus they acted on each other's behalf in matters of buying and selling goods, arranging for freight cargo, remitting funds and generally looking after their interests in a mutually beneficial manner. The financial reward usually consisted of a commission charged to the beneficiary for the service provided. The rate of this commission, however, seems to have varied considerably both across services as well as clients.

IV

The principal geographical region, in which Cowan and Lowther were active, was the Middle East with the port of Mocha being the focal point with occasional forays into Jiddah and Basra. The principal Indian merchant competing with the duo on this sector was Muhammad Ali, grandson and heir of Mulla Abdul Ghafur. His dependence on the Company for passes and the availability of the Bombay marine to the latter, however, provided an edge to Cowan and Lowther over Muhammad Ali. The trade with Mocha, Jiddah and Basra was conducted in ships owned individually but mostly jointly by Cowan and Lowther, as freight cargo in ships operated by other private English traders as well as in ships freighted from Indian merchants. Indeed, buying and selling of ships as well as carrying freight cargo belonging to other merchants, both **[p. 224]** private English as well as Indian, constituted a major source of revenue for Cowan and Lowther. There were even instances when the duo undertook the construction of new ships. A case in point was the *Cowan Frigate* ("I must beg the favour of your honour's liberty to call her the *Cowan Frigate* in honour of Your Honour whose kind assistance on all occasions has enabled me to undertake this work", Lowther wrote on 25

January 1730). Its construction was undertaken in 1730 on the initiative of Lowther following assurances from the Jiddah merchants that a ship of 500 to 600 tons could easily be filled with freight cargo each year. The ship to be built on contract on the Malabar coast – traditionally the most important shipbuilding centre in the subcontinent, particularly in view of the abundant supplies of teakwood there – was designed to have a keel of 102 feet and 34 beams. It was estimated to cost around 90,000 rupees and was expected to earn a sum of Rs.50,000 as freight charges to Jiddah each year. Cowan was invited to buy whatever share he wished in the vessel because Lowther was of the "opinion whenever Your Honour returns [to England] you will find it necessary to keep some part of your fortune in India". A profit of 30 percent per annum was envisaged on Cowan's investment. Lowther requested Cowan to allow the services of one Roche to be used to supervise the construction of the ship. This man would apply for temporary discharge from the Company's service and would be provided with an advance of Rs.50,000. John Braddyll, stationed at Tellicherry, was requested in the name of Cowan to provide whatever assistance might be needed in the purchase of materials. Lowther further wrote to Cowan, "What timber and other stores I shall be obliged to provide for this ship I believe will not be subject to any Duty, as they are not for sale but to be employed in carrying a work that will yearly help to increase our customs". The Director of the Dutch establishment in Surat, Pieter Phoonsen, was requested to obtain supplies of cardage and masts etc. from Batavia. The sailors (*laskars*) were to be recruited in Bombay "most of whom come from the Sidi's country. Those from the southward do not create problems like the ones recruited here [Surat] do".[6]

Given the generally high return earned on freight traffic on the Surat-Middle East sector, the expectations entertained by Henry Lowther from the *Cowan Frigate* would indeed seem to have been quite realistic. A careful entrepreneur ready with the services of his vessel early in the season could always expect to do well. The *Edward*, of around 300 tons and bought together with its provisions and stores by Lowther from Captain Hunter in 1730 for Rs.75,000, was a case in point. Since the ship was ready to depart by 10 February, a good three **[p. 225]** weeks ahead of any other vessel, it had no problem whatever getting its full cargo for Jiddah quickly. Indeed, Lowther was in a position to pick and choose the cargo ensuring the highest possible return which was estimated at around Rs.25,000 on the outward and return trips put together. Lowther's principal competitors, Muhammad Ali and the

---

[6] Lowther to Cowan, 25 January 1730, 2 February 1730, 17 February 1730, 22 May 1731, 29 September 1731, Microfilm number IOR Positive 11613, D654/Bl/5A/6,9,11,13,38,77.

Challebys, were by no means doing nearly as well. In the case of the ship of Muhammad Ali, there were widespread fears that in view of the substantial sums owed to the governor of Jiddah, the ship might be detained there. This instilled an element of uncertainty in the minds of potential freighters.[7]

The differential advantage, often enjoyed by vessels flying the colours of one or the other of the European entities in terms of immunity from hostile action or lower rates of customs duty payable, occasionally led to attempts at camouflaging the ownership of vessels. In 1729, for example, it was reported from Surat that an understanding had been reached between Muhammad Ali and the French that the *Fateh Jang* owned by the former would be provided with French colours together with a French captain and fourteen European sailors for a trip to Mocha in return for the free transportation of 125 bales of French goods.[8]

The cargo sent to the Middle East on account of Lowther and Cowan consisted overwhelmingly of Gujarat textiles. The work of procurement was organized at major manufacturing centres such as Brodera and Broach through Laldas Parak who engaged a large number of weavers exclusively to produce for these two private English traders. An idea of the scale of the operation could perhaps be formed by the following extract from a letter from Lowther to Cowan dated 30 August 1731, "Since my last we have increased our workmen considerably and what small part of the investment is already brought in turns out exceedingly well. Loldass has just received a letter from Ahmedabad which gives him hopes that nigh one thousand weavers will come down and if so, I don't apprehend we shall fall short of the quantity of goods indented for".[9] In his letter of 2 September 1731, Lowther reported that 1,075 weavers were working for them.[10] The total number of artisans engaged on their behalf was reported to be 1,813.[11]

[p. 226] At Mocha, private English traders' goods paid only a 3 percent customs duty as against 9 percent paid by the Asian merchants. At Jiddah, the

---

[7] Lowther to Cowan, 15 January 1730, 25 January 1730, 2 February 1730, 18 February 1730, Microfilm number IOR Positive 11613, D654/Bl/5A/6,7,9,13.

[8] Dickinson at Surat to Cowan at Bombay, 4 November 1729, Microfilm number IOR Positive 11616, D654/Bl/5H/14.

[9] Lowther to Cowan, 30 August 1731, Microfilm number IOR Positive 11613, D654/Bl/5A/64.

[10] Lowther to Cowan, 2 September 1731, Microfilm number IOR Positive 11613, D654/B1/5A/65.

[11] Lowthor to Cowan, 11 September 1731, Microfilm number IOR Positive 11613, D654/Bl/5A/76.

corresponding rates were 8 and 10 percent except that the Asian merchants' goods were generally over-valued in such a way that the real burden of the customs duties on these merchants amounted to as much as 12 to 17 percent (Prakash 1998: 250). Lowther and Cowan, as indeed other private English traders, often used Mocha not as the final destination for their ships but as only the first port of call. After transacting the necessary business there, the ship would continue to ports such as Basra or Jiddah etc. Thus in 1730, the *Success* was sent to Mocha with plans to go on to Basra. In his letter of 17 February 1730, Lowther sought Cowan's consent to send rice with the ship to Mocha to be disposed of there, and coffee loaded there for Basra. According to information provided by French, a private English trader, coffee was then selling at Mocha at 70 *mahmudis* per Basra *maund* but could go up to 100 *mahmudis* in the likely event of the sultan getting embroiled in a war. In the event of Cowan not agreeing to this arrangement because of the problems he had recently had with the authorities at Mocha, the vessel would be directed to "go down to the Bay and try that market". The same letter had reported the arrival at Surat from Basra of a ship owned by Ahmad Chellaby carrying some copper on Cowan's account. Lowther hoped that Captain Hunter would offer to buy it at rupees 17 per *maund*, the same price he had paid for Lowther's lot and which was somewhat higher than the ruling price at both Surat and Bombay.[12]

V

While the Middle East was without question the principal area of operation for Cowan and Lowther, they also received goods on their own account or on that of other private English traders from places such as the Malabar coast and Bengal. A shipment of 200 *khandis* of pepper received from John Braddyll at Tellicherry in 1729 aboard the *Balls* provides the breakdown of the invoice value of the shipment. The total cost of Rs.13,458 consisted in part of (a) the base price of Rs.11,400 (b) the loss in weight amounting to Rs.427 and (c) the cost of the packing material and of the boat hire at Rs.200, amounting to a total of Rs.12,027. The remaining sum of Rs.1,431 was accounted for by (a) the prince's customs of Rs.240 (b) the Company duty of Rs.600 calculated at Rs.3 **[p. 227]** per *khandi* and finally (c) Rs.591 on account

---

[12] Lowther to Cowan, 17 February 1730, Microfilm number IOR Positive 11613, D654/B1/5A/13.

of Braddyll's commission at the rate of 5 percent of the base price plus the cost due to loss in weight.[13]

Another major branch of the Surat trade, namely that with Bengal, also attracted considerable attention from Lowther and Cowan. The goods imported into Surat included, in addition to textiles and sugar, a large volume of raw silk, while the principal item exported was raw cotton. The Dutch shipping lists strongly suggest that the rise in the private English trade was largely at the expense of that of the Surat merchants. In the early eighteenth century, these lists recorded a total of about fifty Surat ships being put to sea each year with Bengal as an important destination. By the 1730s, however, the number of Asian ships trading between Surat and Bengal had been reduced to a trickle (Prakash 1998: 249-50).

In the case of the Surat-Bengal trade, the private English traders based at Calcutta disposed of the raw cotton carried aboard the ships sent there by Cowan and Lowther; in addition to providing the return cargo consisting mainly of raw silk, both against commission. Corresponding services were provided by Cowan and Lowther at the Surat end. Captains of ships carrying the cargo were allowed a certain amount of trade on their personal account. Thus in 1731, Lowther reported that on a shipment to Bengal he had offered these captains "thirty five percent clear of all charges for their private adventures which Captain Houghton and Pelley took but the others would not".[14] It is likely that these individuals were not obliged to do any actual trading but were entitled to a certain amount of profit on a notional limited volume of trade. At times, the Calcutta merchants requested that the cotton be provided not at Surat but at Bombay. Thus in 1729, Governor Deane asked that the *Shah Alam*, on its way back from Mocha, be provided with 500 bales of cotton at Bombay. Cowan was requested to send a message to Mocha confirming whether that would be possible because the ship would call at Bombay only if the cotton were likely to be ready there. If the bales were packed tight, the ship could take in even 650 bales.[15]

The remittance of funds from Surat to Calcutta was usually organized through bills of exchange though cash was also carried aboard the ships. The most trusted Bengal *sarraf* firm on which the bills were drawn was

---

[13] Letter from John Braddyll at Tellicherry to Robert Cowan at Bombay, 31 January 1729, Microfilm number IOR Positive 11615, D654/Bl/5F/9.

[14] Lowther to Cowan, 7 May 1731, Microfilm number IOR Positive 11615, D654/B1/5A/37.

[15] Thomas Harnett at Calcutta, 16 October 1729, Microfilm number IOR Positive 11615, D654/B1/5E/21.

understandably the enormously wealthy house of the Jagatseths with its headquarters **[p. 228]** at Murshidabad. In 1734, for example, Hugh Barker, stationed at Kasimbazar – the principal raw silk emporium of Bengal – wrote to Cowan at Bombay that while a maximum of Rs.30,000 could be sent to him in cash per vessel, the remaining funds were to be sent in bills of exchange but only on the house of the Jagatseth "not knowing very well what shroff else to trust".[16] At times, a more circuitous route was necessary. The 7,000 Bombay and Surat rupees, that Jonathan Winder at Bombay wanted to send to Governor Deane in Calcutta, were first sent in a chest to Lowther at Surat in a Dutch East India Company vessel, the *Fort St. George*, "on the account and risk of Governor Deane and c. freighters of ship Drake". Lowther was then requested to obtain a bill for the amount on Fatehchand Shah of the Jagatseth house payable to John Stackhouse, the chief of the English factory of Kasimbazar. Only in the event that a bill on Fatehchand Shah could not be obtained, Lowther was to "take such secure bills as he may think proper", payable either to Governor Deane and Richard Bourchier in Calcutta or to John Stackhouse at Kasimbazar. On occasions, rather tricky situations had to be faced. In 1729, for example, Charles Grey at Calcutta reported to Cowan that when a bill for 30,000 sicca rupees on the Nawab of Dhaka was presented to the Nawab's *vakil* (attorney) for payment at Kasimbazar where it was payable, he forwarded a copy to the Nawab at Dhaka. The Nawab responded that he would pay only at Dhaka. In frustration, Grey wrote that "the nawab bears the character of a very great villain and I believe only wants to pay the bills at Dacca that he may have some advantage in paying it in old rupees or find some method to stop 2 or 3 percent when the bill is paid".[17]

The brokers of the English and the Dutch East India companies at Surat were at times also called upon to play a part in the settlement of the bills of exchange drawn on Surat. In January 1732, Lowther reported to Cowan that the two brokers were called upon to cash a bill of Rs. 210,000 drawn by the Imperial Court on the governor of Surat. "But in this they run no risk as a certain part of the revenues is made over to them for their security about which I have consulted the [Dutch] Director who is of opinion that they must assist on this occasion, and unless the governor dies suddenly they will be no sufferers nor is this anything new. . . . I beg Your Honour will not be under any concern about this affair, as Lolldas will act as cautiously as possible. But

---

[16] Hugh Barker to Robert Cowan, 5 January 1734 and 30 October 1734, Microfilm number IOR Positive 11615 D654/B1/5E/108, 154.

[17] Charles Grey at Calcutta to Robert Cowan at Bombay, 19 October 1729, Microfilm number IOR Positive 11615, D654/B1/5E/38.

unless he **[p. 229]** contributes something to secure this governor in his post, we shall have many difficulties thrown in our way noways to be avoided".[18]

In the domain of financial transactions, we must also note the considerable amount of business that Lowther and Cowan, as well as other private English traders, carried on in the field of raising respondentia loans and insurance cover to provide cargoes for their vessels. In 1730, a sum of Rs.105,000 was raised in respondentia on the *Nassau*, the respective shares of Lowther and Cowan in the total amount being 11/16:5/16. The Rs.30,000 raised on Cowan's account from the Rustumjis of Surat bore an interest of 16 percent with an allowance of 2%. The rate paid for the sum raised on the *Shah Alam* for China on account of the Bengal merchants including Governor Deane was 21.32 percent with the basic rate again being 16 percent. The underwriters for the supercargoes of this vessel were M/S Francia and Hope.[19]

VI

In this closing section of the paper, I will analyze in some detail a dispute between John Hinde, an English private trader based in Calcutta, and Khoja Zacharias Stephanus, an Armenian merchant operating out of Portuguese Goa. The dispute is of interest because of the great level of detail available on the nitty-gritty of the manner in which the network of private trade actually functioned during this period, highlighting the special risks arising out of operating in a port under the control of a different political authority. The circumstance that led to the recording of such a great level of detail on the dispute in the Cowan papers was the request that Cowan had received from one of the parties to nominate an arbitrator on its behalf.

In a letter to Robert Cowan at Bombay dated 26 June 1733, John Hinde recalled that he had received a letter from Zacharias dated 15 February 1732 intimating that he had remitted a sum of approximately Current Rupees 30,000 to Governor Deane of Bengal two years ago, as part of an arrangement whereby the governor, or alternatively M/s Hampton and Bankett, would contribute a similar sum and invest the total amount in a cargo of goods to be dispatched to Zacharias on a joint account. Since the deal had evidently not gone through, Zacharias had written to Hinde appointing him

---

[18] Henry Lowther at Surat to Robert Cowan at Bombay, 25 January 1732, Microfilm number IOR Positive 11627, D654/Bl/5Y/8.

[19] Lowther to Cowan, 18 March 1730, Microfilm number IOR Positive 11613, D654/Bl/5A/22.

his attorney for the recovery of the funds from Deane together with interest at 12 percent. However, if M/s Hampton and Bankett were independently willing to proceed with the partnership with **[p. 230]** Zacharias, they were to be allowed to do so. If not, Hinde was to try and recover the money from whosoever was in possession of it, and if he so wished to invest it in goods to be sent to Zacharias on a partnership basis. If Hinde was not interested in a partnership, then he was to simply invest the money in goods specified in a list sent along with the letter. The goods were to be freighted on the *Captain Hunter* or any other appropriate private English ship first sailing out of Calcutta.[20]

Hinde discovered that it was not possible to adhere to the twin requirements of Zacharias that the goods be procured at the prices indicated in the list and be dispatched with the first available appropriate vessel. He, therefore, decided to send them with the *Gombroon Merchant*, a ship which was under his own management and which he could afford to have delayed pending the procurement of the goods being completed. He decided to offer the owner a flat freight rate of 10 percent. The idea was to dispatch the *Gombroon Merchant* under the charge of Captain Thomas Dixon in time so as to reach Goa before the departure of the ships from there for Portugal. Dixon agreed that given the nature of the cargo which consisted mostly of gruff goods, a freight of 10 percent was eminently reasonable. The ship was dispatched on 20 November 1732 with a cargo of an invoice value of Current Rupees 25,267.[21]

However, Captain Dixon failed to reach Goa in time for the scheduled departure of the Portugal ships and Zacharias therefore refused to accept the cargo. The sequence of events that followed was recorded in great detail by one Burgess, the purser aboard the *Gombroon Merchant* who was constantly with Dixon in the latter's negotiations with Zacharias. According to this account, Dixon wrote to Zacharias on 15 February 1733, reminding him that the ship had been in Goa for 24 days and requesting him to have the freight cargo unloaded so that he could take in fresh cargo. Zacharias' response was to lodge a complaint with a Portuguese official described in the documents as the Vice-king (not the Viceroy) to the effect that Hinde ought to be made to repay to him the amount of money received by him together with interest because the goods he had supplied were not in conformity with the list sent to him. The judge appointed by the official to look into the matter duly

[20] John Hinde in Calcutta to Robert Cowan at Bombay, 26 June 1733, Microfilm number IOR Positive 11616, D654/B1/5H/14.

[21] John Hinde in Calcutta to Robert Cowan at Bombay, 26 June 1733, Microfilm number IOR Positive 11616, D654/B1/5H/14.

summoned Dixon to his office who was made to affirm on oath that the *Gombroon Merchant* indeed belonged to John Hinde. Dixon told the judge that a balance of about 8,000 **[p. 231]** rupees was left with Hinde from Zacharias' funds after procuring the goods which he offered to pay Zacharias if the latter would agree to have the ship unloaded. The judge, however, deputed two officers to visit the ship and arrange for an embargo to be put on it. The officials took an inventory of the goods and arranged for the ship's hatches to be locked and the keys taken ashore.

At this point, Zacharias offered to settle the matter if Dixon would give him the total value indicated in the invoice of the goods intended for him together with a mark-up of 20 percent. Dixon declined the offer saying the best he could do was to take the goods back and have Hinde assume responsibility for the repayment of the original sum received by him together with interest. There were rumours to the effect that orders for Dixon's arrest were in the process of being issued, prompting him to leave the ship and take refuge in the home of one D. Christopher. The orders for Dixon's arrest were indeed issued but could obviously not be carried out. Zacharias now offered to settle the matter at a mark-up of 17 ½ percent. Dixon again declined the offer telling Zacharias that he knew that his (Zacharias') normal commission for selling goods, either on his own or his principal's account, was no more than 5 percent. This made Zacharias climb further down to 15 percent. The counter-proposal made by Dixon was to take the entire cargo back on Hinde's account, dispose of it and pay Zacharias the balance of Rs.8,000 with 10 percent interest. He further proposed that the proceeds from the sale of the cargo would be deposited in a church until a final meeting ground between Zacharias and Hinde had been found.

On 14 March 1733, Burgess noted that there was no likelihood of the matter being sorted out until after the meeting of the Grand Council scheduled for the 17th of March. But no decision was taken at this meeting either and the matter lingered on. When Burgess tried to arrange a meeting between Dixon and Zacharias and asked for a written assurance that Dixon would not be arrested by the officers of the judge, Zacharias first promised that he would obtain such an assurance but later backed out saying that if Dixon "would not rely on his word he did not care nor think it proper to give any such note".

When Dixon wanted permission from the Vice-king for the *Gombroon Merchant* to leave Goa, Zacharias intimated that he would not oppose such a request. Indeed, Zacharias helped obtain the permission and the ship was brought into the river. On Dixon's advice, the officers and sailors aboard the ship left it and went to Zacharias asking for their wages for the period the ship had been under detention. When the Vice-king was approached in the matter, he termed their demand legitimate and referred them to the judge looking into the case. The judge ordered everybody to get back on the ship on pain of imprisonment, while at the same time ordering Zacharias to settle the wage claims. He now offered to settle the matter at a 10% mark-up on the invoice. **[p. 232]** In the meantime, Dixon arranged for the invoice to be translated into Portuguese for a meeting of the Grand Council scheduled for the 6th April.

On the 18th April, a communication was received from Zacharias that his total claim amounted to Rs.60,000. But he was eventually persuaded to accept a sum of 24,000 *pardaws* from Dixon together with the goods. It was agreed that the dispute would be settled through arbitration at Calcutta.[22] Before leaving Goa with the *Gombroon Merchant*, Dixon filed a claim of Rs.26,764 against Zacharias for damages incurred due to the detention of the ship. The largest single item of Rs.14,000 was in respect of compensation for the loss of business for the ship for a period of two months.[23]

John Hinde's letter to Cowan dated 26 June 1733, referred to at the beginning of this section, was a follow-up to the above proceedings. Hinde wrote to Cowan, "And I call God to witness I got nothing but my commission by them [the goods bought on Zacharias' account]. Therefore, it could not be my interest to buy them dear and therefore I am willing to make him any restitution in case I am condemned on that score. And by the same rule I hope if it appears that Zacharias has by his unprecedented method of proceeding put me to any unnecessary expenses or damages which doubtless he has, I shall have restitution made me. For which reasons I most willingly submit this affair to arbitration of such person or persons as shall be agreed upon by the Hon'ble Robert Cowan Esq. on my behalf with those that Zacharias shall appoint on his".[24]

The following day (27 June 1733), the President and Council of the English East India Company at Calcutta took cognizance of the matter and

---

[22] Mr. Burgess' minutes of Zacharias' proceedings against Dixon at Goa, Microfilm number IOR Positive 11616, D654/Bl/5H/13.

[23] Sundry damages laid by Dixon to the charge of Zacharias Stephanus Armenian at Goa for detaining the ship *Gombroon Merchant*, Microfilm number IOR Positive 11616, D654/Bl/5H/13.

[24] John Hinde in Calcutta to Robert Cowan at Bombay, 26 June 1733, Microfilm number IOR Positive 11616, D654/Bl/5H/14.

wrote a letter of protest to the Portuguese Viceroy at Goa. The following is the full text of the letter of protest.[25]

> To His Excellency the Count of Domil, Viceroy of all His Majesty the King of Portugal's settlements in India at Goa
>
> May it please Your Excellency,
> The well-known goodness and equity of your Excellency and the good harmony which has long subsisted between the King of Great Britain and His Majesty of Portugal hath encouraged us to represent to Your Excellency that several gentlemen here who entrusted Captain Thomas Dixon with a considerable sum of money on the bottom of **[p. 233]** ship Gombroon Merchant have received advice that their effects and the person of said Thomas Dixon are seized and detained at Goa at the suit of one Coja Zachary as applied for the demand which said Coja Zachary has on Mr. John Hinde, a merchant here. We cannot therefore but observe to Your Excellency that this proceeding is contrary to all the Rules of Law and Equity, it being nowhere allowable to seize one man's effects to make good the debt of another.
>
> We therefore find ourselves obliged to represent to Your Excellency the wrong which Coja Zachary has done to Captain Thomas Dixon in procuring the detention of his person, and to him and his creditors in the seizure of his effects, not doubting but Your Excellency will on consideration of this affair, cause the effects seized to be restored to the said Thomas Dixon that he may make sale thereof for the satisfaction of his creditors and permit Captain Thomas Dixton to return hither at his pleasure. If Coja Zachary has any demand on Mr. Hinde, he may empower any person to sue him in our Courts of justice here, where he will certainly recover of him whatever appears to be his due.
>
> We are to acquaint Your Excellency that as Captain Thomas Dixon is a subject of His Britannic Majesty, so we are obliged to protest and do accordingly hereby protest against you for the detention of his person and effects and do declare that you are answerable for all the damages that may be sustained thereby.
>
> We enclose Your Excellency a list of the creditors of Captain Thomas Dixon attested by the Governor of this place and the Portuguese Padri.
>
> We are Your Excellent Most Humble Servants
>
> Fort William
> 27 June 1733

---

[25] The President and Council of Calcutta – their letter and protest to the Viceroy of Goa, 27 June 1733 at Fort William, Microfilm number IOR Positive 11616, D654/Bl/5H/21.

The enclosed list of creditors had six names totalling a sum of Rs.18,766:13:9 as "Rent at respondentia at 14 percent". In addition, there are two names, one Pearson concerned in Private adventure Rs.2,180, and one Coja Soliman concerned in private adventure Rs.817:8, coming to a grand total of Rs.21,764:5:9.

On 12 January 1734, Thomas Moore at Calcutta informed Cowan that "the rest of his [Dixon's] respondentia creditors and myself have sent a brigantine to Goa this year to bring back him and his effects".[26] On 4 July, Moore got back to Cowan confirming Dixon's arrival at Calcutta. He further informed him that "the balance that Mr. Hinde has of Zacharias in his hands has been given to Dixon's respondentia creditors by which I have got near half my principal but I must confess it is more than I expected".[27] The outcome of the arbitration process, in case it was carried out, is not recorded.

In conclusion, one might briefly note that what the Robert Cowan papers establish quite conclusively is the large scale as well as the high level of **[p. 234]** efficiency and profitability that characterized the English private trading network in the Western Indian Ocean in the first half of the eighteenth century. The fact that the principal participants in the network were usually high-ranking officials in the English East India Company was a major circumstance accounting for its remarkable success.

BIBLIOGRAPHY

Das Gupta, Ashin. 1979. *Indian Merchants and the Decline of Surat c. 1700–1750.* Wiesbaden.

Prakash, Om. 1998. *New Cambridge History of India, vol 5.2: European Commercial Enterprise in Pre-colonial India.* Cambridge.

——. 2004. The Indian Maritime Merchant, 1500–1800. *Journal of the Economic and Social History of the Orient* 47.3: 435-52.

[26] Thomas Moore at Calcutta to Robert Cowan at Bombay, 12 January 1734, Microfilm number IOR Positive 11615, D654/Bl/5E/110.

[27] Thomas Moore at Calcutta to Robert Cowan at Bombay, 4 July 1734, Microfilm number IOR Positive 11615, D654/B1/5E/146.

XII

BENGAL TEXTILES IN SEVENTEENTH CENTURY INTERNATIONAL TRADE[1]

Indian textiles figured, though with a varying degree of prominence both in time and space, in several important branches of seventeenth century international trade. Among the more important of these were the intra-Asian trade, the Euro-Asian trade, the intra-European trade and the trade between Europe on the one hand and West Africa and the New World on the other.[2] Textile manufacturing was without any doubt *the* premier industry of seventeenth century India.[3] The supplies for export originated primarily in Gujarat, the Coromandel Coast and Bengal. While practically all varieties of textiles were manufactured in Gujarat, Coromandel specialized in the production of comparatively coarse varieties of cotton textiles. The specialization of Bengal consisted in the manufacture of fine cotton -, cotton and silk mixed - and silk piece-goods.

Among the cotton textiles manufactured in Bengal were both muslins and calicoes. Of the two, muslins were more loosely woven and, grade for grade, were of finer yarn. The best quality muslins were produced in and around Dacca,[4] where humidity was an advantage in the handling of delicate skeins. Of course, the finest Dacca varieties[5] were consumed almost entirely within the country for the simple reason that they were far too expensive for foreign markets including Europe.[6] The other major muslin manufacturing centers in the province were the Malda district and Shantipur in Nadia district. Some comparatively inferior varieties were also produced in Patna in Bihar and Balasore in Orissa. The principal varieties of muslins exported from Bengal (in a descending order of fineness, workmanship and cost) were: *tanzeb, terrindam, khasa, malmal, resta* and *rehing*. The staple varieties were *khasa* and *malmal,* both muslins of good quality often brocaded in gold, silver or silk threads usually in floral patterns.[7] Less often, they were instead embroidered in coloured silks in chain-stitch, in gold and silver threads or in cotton itself, which is what probably later came to be known as "chikan" embroidery.[8] Most of the pieces also had their borders woven in gold threads. That *tanzeb* was a superior version of *khasa* involving the use of better quality yarn, comparatively larger amount of embroidery work and better workmanship in general, is clear from the fact that the Board of Directors of the Dutch East India Company often reminded the Bengal factors that unless the quality of the *tanzebs* sent by them was up to the mark and the patterns sufficiently "curious," there was the risk of the Dutch merchants treating them at par with *khasas*.[9] Exactly analogous was the case with *terrindams* and *malmals*.[10] *Resta* was a muslin with stripes produced on the

This article originally appeared in Warren M. Gunderson, ed., South Asia Series, Occasional paper no. 26, *Studies on Bengal*. East Lansing, MI: Asian Studies Center, Michigan State University, Spring 1975.

loom, while *rehing* was of netlike texture made by passing a single thread of the warp through each division of the reed.[11] In 1701-02, the average price of a piece of *tanzeb*, *terrindam*, *khasa* and *malmal* was reported to be Rs. 14.25, Rs. 15.00, Rs. 8.50 and Rs. 10.50 respectively. The corresponding sale prices in the Dutch Company's autumn sale in Holland in 1703 were Rs. 25.25, Rs. 25.40, Rs. 18.00 and Rs. 15.60 respectively.[12]

The quality differential as among different varieties of calicoes was considerably more pronounced than was the case with muslins. The principal centers of production of the finer varieties were the Malda district and the area around Kasimbazar in Murshidabad district, while the coarser qualities were manufactured in Birbhum district, in Patna and in Pipli and Balasore in Orissa. The principal varieties exported from Bengal (in a descending order of fineness and cost) were *dorea*, *humhum*, *sologazi*, *chela*, *sanu*, *rumal*, *fota*, *chintz*, Guinea-cloth, *garra*, sailcloth and *dassie*. Some of these such as *fota*, *garra* and sailcloth were plain coarse calicoes with no patterns and were exported unbleached, bleached or dyed in bright shades. Others such as *humhum* and *sanu* were also plain calicoes but of finer quality. Some of the *humhum* pieces were provided with borders woven in gold threads; others were brocaded in floral patterns. *Dorea* and *chela* were fine calicoes with longitudinal stripes of varying width created on the loom, usually in blue and white yarn in the case of the latter. Occasionally *doreas* were also brocaded in floral patterns. *Dassie* was a coarse calico usually with red stripes while Guinea-cloth was a generic term for a wide range of cheap, brightly coloured and mostly striped or chequered calicoes. It was a typical Coromandel product but around the close of the seventeenth century the Dutch tried and succeeded in initiating its production in Kasimbazar in limited quantities.[13] The only calico manufactured in Bengal where patterns were created outside of the loom was *chintz* -- a coarse variety woven mainly in Patna and to a limited extent in Kasimbazar. In this case, patterns -- again, usually floral -- were created by woodblock printing, the mordants (iron for black, aluminum for red) and pigment colours (e.g., ochre) being thickened with a tree-gum.[14] Cotton-painting, i.e., the application of the dyes and mordants to the cloth freehand with a brush -- a flourishing industry in both Coromandel and Gujarat -- was unknown in Bengal.[15] In 1701-02, the average price of a piece of *dorea*, *humhum*, *sanu* and *garra* was reported to be Rs. 9.50, Rs. 5.70, Rs. 3.10 and Rs. 2.35 respectively. The corresponding prices at the Dutch autumn sale of 1703 were Rs. 17.40, Rs. 11.50, Rs. 5.10 and Rs. 4.80 respectively.[16]

Mention might also be made here of quilted bedspreads worked in chain-stitch on a coarse cotton (or jute) ground. These quilts were embroidered in pictorial designs in yellow *tussur* silk. They were manufactured in the Hugli area under Portuguese influence and exported to Europe until about the middle of the seventeenth century.[17]

Bengal was by far and most important exporter of mixed- and silk-piece-goods on the sub-continent. Mixed piece-goods were woven by the simultaneous use of cotton and silk yarns, the latter having been derived either from the regular mulberry silk-worm or from the silk-worm *anthereap aphia* that produced the wild *tussur* silk. The principal variety in the former group was *jamadani*

- described in the Dutch records as flowered *dorea* - a striped fabric brocaded in floral patterns and manufactured mainly in the Malda-Kasimbazar area. The cotton - *tussur* varieties were manufactured at several centres in Midnapore district, the most important among which was Radhanagar. Limited amounts were also produced in Malda, Hugli and in Pipli in Orissa. The principal constituents of this group were *alibanee* - multi-coloured and striped, *charkhana* - striped or chequered, *gingam* - bright coloured plain or striped and *nila* - a striped and occasionally brocaded fabric.

The silk textiles exported from Bengal were exclusively of mulberry silk except in the case of *allegia* where *tussur* yarn was also used. The principal area of production was again Malda-Kasimbazar though limited amounts of particular varieties were also produced in Radhanagar in Midnapore district. The important varieties exported (in a descending order of fineness) were: *soosy, jamawar, armosin, atlas* and *allegia*. The staple variety was *armosin* - plain, striped or chequered fine silk fabric often brocaded or embroidered in coloured silks, silver or gold threads. Thirty-two and eight tenths ounces (80 *tolas*) of silk yarn went into an *armosin* 18 yards long and 1-1/2 yards wide and containing a total of 2400 threads.[18] The shades most in demand in Europe were white, red, blue, yellow and green, and various combinations thereof.[19] *Soosy* was a silk fabric with stripes in coloured silks or gold threads; *jamawar* was a silk brocade and *atlas* was both striped and brocaded. Some *atlas* pieces were also woven in satin-weave,[20] and the shades most in demand in Europe were green, blue and coffee. Finally, *allegia* was bright coloured striped silk fabric.

The size of the pieces of textiles exported from Bengal was by no means uniform. The usual dimensions of a piece of muslin were 40 x 2 *covids*,[21] the lower and the upper bounds being 36 x 1 and 48 x 3 *covids* respectively. Muslins with a width of 3 *covids* - which could be put to an enormously larger number of uses - was a specially European-promoted innovation and appears to have been limited to *khasas, malmals* and *adathys* manufactured in Malda district. The dimensions of particular varieties of calicoes such as *dorea* were the same as of muslins though the usual size in the case of this group was 20 - 24 x 1-1/2 - 2-1/4 *covids*. The ordinary size of both mixed- and silk-piece-goods was 20 x 1 - 2-1/4 *covids* though there were important exceptions such as *charkhana* with a usual length of 35 *covids* and *soosy* with a possible length of as much as 48 *covids*.

Intra-Asian Trade

Recent research has demonstrated that in the century under discussion, several Asian countries, including most of those in the Malay-Indonesian Archipelago, besides Ceylon and Persia, depended for the bulk of their textile requirements on India.[22] While the mass-consumed inferior grade calicoes exported to these countries originated mainly in Coromandel and Gujarat, Bengal accounted for a considerable proportion of the muslins and mixed- and silk-piece-goods exported.[23] Probably the most important Asian market for Bengal textiles was Persia. The varieties exported most frequently to this market were *khasas* and *malmals* among muslins and *allegias* among silk piece-goods. Over a long period of time, the Bengal-Persia trade had grown at a steady rate and the quality and size of the piece-goods entering this trade had become so standardized that by the mid-century, a situation had arisen where merchants in Malda - the principal manufacturing centre in Bengal supplying textiles for Persia - no longer waited for formal contracts with the buyers before giving advances to weavers under the putting-out system.[24] In 1670, a Dutch factor sent to Malda to explore the possibilities of trade there reported that textiles worth about Rs. 1 million were exported annually from Malda alone to Persia.[25] Part of these textiles finally found their way to Turkey while another lot reached Italy via the overland route.[26] The Bengal-Persia trade was almost entirely in the hands of Muslim merchants from Surat and to a limited extent in that of the Armenians domiciled in India. These merchants regularly sent ships to Bengal with cotton, Persian tobacco and rosewater, and, of course, specie and purchased in return Bengal textiles and sugar, the greater part of which was sent on to Persia. Surat thus assumed the character of an important entrepot port between Bengal and Persia.[27] Bengal textiles were also exported in substantial quantities to both the Malabar and the Coromandel coasts in South India. But as in the case of Bengal-Persia and Bengal-Gujarat trade, these two branches were dominated overwhelmingly by non-Bengal merchants, mainly those from the two respective coasts.[28]

The other Asian markets for Bengal textiles were Ceylon, the Maldive islands and the Indonesian archipelago. While exports to Ceylon and the Maldive islands were confined practically to calicoes of a comparatively inferior quality, the textiles exported to the archipelago were more varied. Trade with all these places was controlled largely by the Bengal merchants.[29] But most of these merchants were Mughal state officials (from the *subahdar* down) in the province on temporary assignment or domiciled Hindu and Muslim merchants from Gujarat.[30] The share of native Bengali merchants in Bengal's foreign trade appears to have been negligible.

The total volume of Intra-Asian trade in Bengal textiles, among other goods, increased considerably as a result of the participation in this trade by the Dutch East India Company, notwithstanding the fact that the Dutch restrictions on Bengal merchants' trade with Ceylon and the Indonesian archipelago - extensive parts of which were under Dutch suzerainty or vassalage - did lead to a shrinkage of the operation of these merchants along these branches and that the volume of Dutch trade in Bengal textiles with a number of Asian markets - e.g. Ceylon, Coromandel and Malabar - was insignificant.[31] The Company exported considerable quantities of Indian textiles to the Indonesian archipelago where they were exchanged against spices and other goods. The special privileges the Company enjoyed in the greater part of the archipelago ensured for it a level of profit substantially higher than what the Asian merchants earned, which by itself was attractive enough. It should, of course, be realized that given the fact that the demand in this region was primarily for specific varieties of comparatively inferior calicoes, the share of Bengal piece-goods in the total Dutch textile trade with the region was relatively limited.

The Company's trade in Bengal textiles with Persia where it enjoyed no special privileges fell into an altogether different category. The Company found it very hard to compete with Indian and Armenian merchants who were far more intimately acquainted with the mechanics of both the Bengal and the Persian markets and had to shoulder considerably lower overhead costs. As a result, the net profit the Company earned on most of the varieties of Bengal textiles sold in Persia was rather poor. In fact, instances of Dutch factors running into net loss on particular varieties once in a while, though rare, were not unknown.[32] And yet the Company exported fairly large quantities of these textiles to Persia, particularly in the last quarter of the seventeenth and the early part of the eighteenth century.[33] The explanation, of course, was that net profit, while obviously very welcome, was not a pre-condition to trade along lines that served primarily to provide the necessary purchasing power for the procurement of items - in this case Persian raw silk and even more so the silver *abbasis* that were smuggled out - that it was profitable to procure for Europe or for other parts of Asia.

By far the most significant contribution of the Dutch East India Company to the growth of intra-Asian trade in Bengal textiles was the opening up of Japan to these piece-goods. The Portuguese had no doubt been trading with Japan from the middle of the 16th century, but there is no evidence to show that Bengal textiles were included in the cargo they sent there.[34] Again, while it is not altogether impossible that the Chinese or Japanese merchants bought Bengal textiles in Siam or other parts of south-east Asia and carried them to Japan, the quantities involved obviously could not have been significant because the Bengal-archipelago trade in silk- and mixed piece-goods - the varieties the Dutch later found marketable in Japan - had always been rather limited. While Chinese and Bengal raw silk constituted the bulk of the Dutch exports to Japan, Bengal textiles always formed part of the Dutch cargo in the post-1640 period. In 1654, Bengal *charkhanas* were sold in Nagasaki at a gross profit of 122%.[35] The following year, Bengal *taffechelas gingams* afforded gross profit of 257%.[36] The volume of Dutch textile trade between Bengal and Japan increased considerably after 1685 when the Japanese authorities restricted the proportion of raw silk in the total annual Dutch turnover in Japan - which had hitherto been around 80% - to one-third.

Euro-Asian Trade

The Euro-Asian trade in Indian textiles was comparatively limited until about 1680 whence there was a sudden and sharp increase in its volume. Essentially, this was the result of an almost revolutionary change in European fashions in wearing apparel during the last quarter of the seventeenth-century. Indian muslins and calicoes now became extremely popular all over Europe for both male and female dress.[37] In 1681, an Englist politician, Pollexfen, declared, "As ill weeds grow apace, so these manufactured goods from India met with such a kind reception that from the greatest gallants to the meanest Cook Maids, nothing was thought so fit to adorn their persons as the Fabrick from India."[38] Traditional homemade woolen stuffs were abandoned on a large scale in favour of silks and finery. Eastern silk textiles were not as fine in quality as the ones manufactured from the finest Italian and French raw silk, but they had the merit of being substantially cheaper and, therefore, within the reach of a much larger section of the community.

Given the regional pattern of specialization in the manufacture of textiles in seventeenth century India, the fastest rate of growth in the European demand for Indian textiles was registered by the varieties manufactured in Bengal. The annual orders for Bengal piece-goods from the Court of Directors of the English East India Company increased from 76,500 pieces in 1675 to 227,900 pieces in 1681 and to 457,000 pieces in 1695.[39] The English textiles manufacturers' opposition to the import of these huge quantities of Indian textiles was sufficiently vocal to lead to the passage of a Parliamentary Act in 1700 prohibiting the import for domestic use of "all wrought silks, Bengals and stuffs mixed with silk or herba, of the manufacture of Persia, China or the East Indies and all calicoes painted, dyed or printed or stained there."[40]

The rate of growth of the Dutch East India Company's import of Indian textiles into Holland was no less impressive. The last half of the seventeenth century witnessed an increase of 140% in the average annual value of the Company's imports into Holland. Over the same period, the share of textiles and raw silk in the total imports went up from 14% to 55%.[41] At the end of the century, the Company procured more textiles in Bengal than in the rest of Asia put together. In 1697, for example, out of a total of Rs. 1.57 million worth of textiles the Company imported into Holland, those originating in Bengal accounted for as much as 55%, the remainder having been procured on the Coromandel Coast, the Malabar Coast, Gujarat, Tonquin, China and Japan.[42] By the end of the century, Bengal textiles had become one of the most important - if not *the* most important - commodities in the complex of seaborne Euro-Asian trade.

Intra-European Trade

The phenomenal growth of the Euro-Asian trade in Indian - mainly Bengal - textiles was accompanied by a corresponding increase in the intra-European trade in these textiles. According to Professor Davis, two-thirds of the Indian calicoes imported into England at the turn of the century were re-exported,[43] though evidently not exclusively to other parts of Europe. By making it mandatory on the Company to re-export all patterned textiles imported from the East, the Parliamentary Act of 1700 led to a further increase in the re-export trade in Indian textiles. In an official report written in 1712, for example, Davenant estimated that over the four-year period 1702-05, England annually exported to Holland Ŀ 95,000 (approximately Rs. 760,000) worth of Indian wrought silk, Bengal mixed stuffs and calicoes painted, dyed, printed or stained in India.[44] Presumably even larger quantities would have been exported to countries which, unlike Holland, did not import Indian textiles direct.

Unfortunately, the literature on the pattern of seventeenth-eighteenth century Dutch re-export trade in commodities originating in the East Indies is so very limited and lacking in detail that it is impossible to form anything more than a very broad idea of its nature. The general picture that emerges is that Bengal piece-goods were dominant among Indian textiles re-exported to the various parts of Europe. Muslins and silk piece-goods from Bengal, particularly those brocaded or embroidered or with gold borders, seem to have been exported in fair quantities to Eastern Europe, the Baltic ports, Russia and Norway.[45] France was another major market for Indian textiles in general and Bengal silk piece-goods in particular.[46] While she, no doubt, had established an East India Company of her own in 1664, the extent of French trade in India was extremely limited during our period and Indian textiles continued to reach France mainly through the Dutch and the English. Indian textiles also figured prominently in the Dutch trade with Southern Europe and the Levant. In 1675, for example, cotton *rumals* procured in Pipli in Orissa were reported to be very "useful" in the trade with Spain and Turkey.

Europe-West Africa - New World Trade

Indian gruff calicoes - known as negro-cloth or Guinea-cloth - played an important role in the seventeenth century African slave trade. They were used first in the purchase of the slaves on the Guinea coast in West Africa and then as their staple wear in the plantations in the West Indies and the Americas. But these low-quality calicoes were procured primarily on the Coromandel Coast and as we pointed out earlier, it was only towards the end of the century that the Dutch began promoting the production of Guinea-cloth in Bengal. Even then the quantities were negligible. The number of Guinea-cloth pieces supplied by Bengal in 1706-07, for example, was only 640 pieces against an order for 20,000 pieces "or as many more as Bengal can supply." The overall role of Bengal textiles in the re-export trade to the Guinea Coast and the American colonies, therefore, appears to have been negligible nothwithstanding the fact that some of the regular Bengal gruff calicoes such as *dassie*, *garra* and *patka* might have been among the varieties re-exported to these places.

FOOTNOTES

1. The term "Bengal" is used in this paper to denote not only the territories today known as East and West Bengal but also the adjacent states of Bihar and Orissa, which together constituted a distinct political and economic region in Mughal India.

2. I do not propose to discuss in this paper the overland intra-Asian and Euro-Asian trade.

3. According to Robert Orme, "On the Coast of Coromandel, and in the province of Bengal, when at some distance from the high road, or a principal town, it is difficult to find a village in which every man, woman, and child, is not employed in making a piece of cloth." At another place, he writes, ". . . much the greatest part of whole provinces are employed in this single manufacture." Again, ". . . the progress of the linen [cotton] manufacture includes no less than a description of the lives of half the inhabitants of Indostan." (Robert Orme, *Historical Fragments of the Mogul Empire . . . from the Year 1659*, (London, 1805), pp. 409, 410-11, 413).

4. The principal centre of production was Sonargaon, about fifteen miles from Dacca.

5. The names of some of the most exquisite varieties were *shab-nam* (evening dew), *ab-i-rawan* (running water) and *bakt-hawa* (webs of woven wind). According to Tavernier, these muslins ". . . are made so fine, *you can hardly feel then in your hand,* and the thread, when spun, is *scarce discernible* (Tavernier's Travels contained in Dr. Harris' Collection of Voyages and Travels, Vol. 1, p. 811. Quoted in E. Baines, *History of the Cotton Manufacture in Great Britain* (London, 1835), p. 57).

6. James Taylor has recorded a verbal tradition according to which the very finest muslins made in Dacca in the early seventeenth century cost as much as Rs. 400 per piece, while even the most expensive varieties procured by the Dutch East India Company, for example, hardly ever cost more than Rs. 20 per piece. (James Taylor, *Sketch of the Topography and Statistics of Dacca* (1851) p. 172).

7. In the records of the Dutch East India Company, brocading is usually referred to as "woven flowers." [Orders-lists sent by the Board of Directors to Batavia (herafter orders-lists), March 1714, Koloniaal Archief No. 264, Algemeen Rijksarchief, The Hague (hereafter K.A.); March 1715 and March 1716, K.A. 265].

8. John Irwin and P. R. Schwartz, *Studies in Indo-European Textile History* (Ahmedabad, 1966) p. 49. In the Dutch records, embroidery is usually described as "flowers or patterns created by needle-sewing." (Orders - lists, March 1714, K.A. 1714, K.A. 264; March 1715 and March 1716, K.A. 265).

9. For example, the Orders - list, February 1707, K.A. 263.

10. Orders - lists, March 1703 (K.A. 262), March 1705, February 1708 and April 1709 (all K.A. 263) and March 1716 (K.A. 265); letter from the Dutch factors at Hugli to the Governor General and Council at Batavia (hereafter H.B.) 15.10.1711, K.A. 1702, ff. 92-94, I Section.

11. Irwin and Schwartz, p. 70.

12. The cost price has been calculated from the export invoices of 1701-02, H.B. 28.9.1701, K.A. 1540; Hugli factors to the Board of Directors in Amsterdam (hereafter H.XVII) 1.11.1701, K.A. 1537, H.B. 18.12.1701, K.A. 1556, and H.B. 10.4.1702, K.A. 1556. The sale price figures are based on information contained in K.A. 10228.

13. A similar attempt - motivated by a similar desire to reduce the cost of production given "the abundance of provisions" and consequently a lower cost of living in Bengal - was made in the case of two other typical Coromandel products - *salempouris* and *parcals*, but with comparatively less success.

14. Irwin and Schwartz, p. ii. Mr. Irwin has suggested (p. 45) that Patna *chintz* were cotton-paintings rather than cotton-prints and has quoted from a letter written in 1700 by the English Board of Directors in London to their factors in Bengal to substantiate this. It appears, however, that either the English directors did not quite understand the manner in which the *chintz* were patterned or that they were described in this letter as paintings rather than as prints by mistake. The Dutch procured this particular variety throughout the period of their trading operations in Bengal and the word consistently used to describe the way the pattern was made was "drukken" (to print) rather than "schilderen" - the word used to describe the process of painting. The unit established for printing *chintz* within the precincts of the Company's factory at Patna was called the "chitsen-drukkerij" and the artists "drukkers."

15. Early in the eighteenth century, the Board of Directors of the Dutch East India Company instructed the Bengal factors to persuade artisans in Patna to manufacture painted *rumals*, used mainly as handkerchiefs. Samples, apparently from Coromandel, were despatched from Amsterdam but despite strenuous efforts by both the Hugli and the Patna factors, the project proved to be more or less abortive. A small lot of 592 pieces was all that the factors succeeded in sending to Holland once in 1714. The directors found that the cloth used was not of sufficiently good quality and the standard of painting left much to be desired. Attempts to remedy these defects do not appear to have been successful. (Orders lists February 1701 to March 1716, K.A. 262-265); Explanation by Bengal factors why they were not able to meet all the orders from Holland in full (hereafter Bengal's "explanation") in years 1704 (K.A. 1584), 1706 (K.A. 1636), 1707 (K.A. 1653), 1708 (K.A. 1669), 1710 (K.A. 1688) and 1714 (K.A. 1746).

16. The cost price has been calculated from the export invoices of 1701-02, H.B. 28.91701, K.A. 1540; H.XVII. 1.11.1701, K.A. 1537; H.B. 28.91701, K.A. 1556 and H.B. 10.4.1702, K.A. 1556. The sale price figures are based on information contained in K.A. 10228.

17. Irwin and Schwartz, pp. 47-48.

18. Letter from Commissioner Van Rheede to Batavia, 6.12.1686, K.A. 1310, ff. 108vo-109vo.

19. In 1705, the directors of the Dutch East India Company asked that the *armosins* might be supplied in the following proportions: white (40%) red and blue, red and yellow and red and green (30%), red (10%), ash-grey (10%), brown (5%) and yellow (5%). (Orders-list March 1705, K.A. 263).

20. V. Slomann, *Bizarre Designs in Silks* (Copenhagen, 1953), p. 120.

21. *Covid* was an indigenous measure whose value varied considerably as between different regions. It could be as large as the equivalent of a yard or only half that much. Moreland ("Indian Exports of Cotton Goods in the Seventeenth Century", *Indian Journal of Economics*, V:3 (January 1925) apparently assumed a *covid* to be the equivalent of half a yard but the more realistic figure in the case of Bengal appears to be 3/4 of a yard (F. W. Stapel, (ed.), *Pieter van Dam's Beschryvinge Van de Oost-Indische Compagnie* (The Hague, 1932), p. 451) Vol. II, Part II.

22. For example, T. Raychaudhuri, "A Reinterpretation of Nineteenth Century Indian Economic History?", *The Indian Economic and Social History Review*, V:1, (March 1968).

23. Francois Bernier wrote in the 1660's, ". . . there is in *Bengale* such a quantity of cotton and silks that the kingdom may be called the common storehouse for those two kinds of merchandise, not of Hindoustan or the Empire of the *Great Mogol* only, but of all the neighboring kingdoms, and even of *Europe*" (Francois Bernier, *Travels in the Mogul Empire 1656-1668*, Tr. by Archibald Constable, (Oxford University Press, 1934), pp. 438-39.

24. Report on Malda by Dutch book-keeper Hendrik Cansius dated September 7, 1670, K.A. 1168, ff. 2173-74 and dated November 30, 1675, K.A. 1209, ff. 517-18; Instructions to Koopman Nicolas Coekebacker and Underkoopman de Carpentier on the eve of their departure for Malda for the purchase of textiles, dated January 8, 1676, K.A. 1209, ff. 517vo-521.

25. Report on Malda by Dutch book-keeper Hendrik Cansius dated September 7, 1670, K.A. 1168, ff. 2173-74.

26. *Ibid.*, Letter from the Board of Directors of the Dutch East India Company to the Governor-General and Council at Batavia dated 4.11.1673, K.A. 458.

27. Thus all the three ships that went from Balasore to Surat in 1683-84 as well as all the eight ships that went from Hugli to Surat in 1707-08 were on the account of non-Bengal merchants almost all of whom were from Surat. My information on Asian merchants' trade from the Bengal ports in the seventeenth and the early eighteenth century is based largely on the lists of Asian ships that arrived at and departed from Hugli and Balasore during this period. These lists were compiled by Dutch factors from the toll registers of these ports and contain details of the cargo carried, the name and occasionally the place of domicile of the merchant

on whose account the ship operated besides the name of the Captain of the ship. Some of the aspects dealt with over the following few pages are discussed in greater detail in my "The Dutch East India Company and the Economy of Bengal, 1650-1717" (unpublished Ph.D. dissertation, University of Delhi, 1967).

28. For example, all the three ships that went from Hugli to Malabar in 1713-14 were on the account of Malabar merchants. In the preceding year, out of the thirty-one ships that left Hugli for the Coromandel Coast, not one was on the account of a Bengal merchant. (Asian traders' shipping lists in the Dutch records).

29. For example, all the five ships that went from Balasore to Ceylon in 1680-81 were owned by Bengal merchants: in 1683-84, this figure was four out of five ships. Of the twelve ships that went to the Maldive islands from Balasore in 1697-98, ten were owned by Bengal merchants. All the four ships that went to the Maldive islands from Hugli that year were of Bengali ownership. Next, all the three ships that went from Hugli to Tenasserim in Siam in 1681-82 were owned by Bengal merchants. Three out of the four ships that left Hugli for the same port that year were also of Bengali ownership, though the following year, all the four ships that went from Hugli to Tenasserim were on the account of non-Bengal merchants (Asian traders' shipping lists in the Dutch records).

30. Among the most famous members of the Mughal royalty and nobility engaged in foreign trade from Bengal were Price Shah Shuja and nawabs Mir Jumla, Shaista Khan, Nawazish Khan, Khan Dauran and Naurulla Khan. Two domiciled Gujarati Hindu merchants, Khem Chand Snah and Chintamani Shah, accounted for the bulk of the trade from the Balasore port.

31. The involvement of the English East India Company -- the only other major European trading company in India in the seventeenth century-in intra-Asian trade was at best marginal.

32. For example, Bengal *garras* were sold in Combroon in 1663 at a net loss of 23% (H.B. 31.10.1663, K.A. 1135, ff. 2234vo-35).

33. On an average, the number of pieces of Bengal textile exported to Persia during this period ranged between 20,000 and 30,000. (Export invoices in the Dutch records).

34. For example, the list of goods that the "great ship" of the Portuguese carried from China to Japan in 1600 does not include a single variety of Bengal textiles. Though in the list of goods brought to Japan by the Portuguese galliots in 1637, one does find *taffechelas* and *armosins* mentioned, it is by no means certain that they had been procured in Bengal. (C. R. Boxer, *The Great Ship from Amacon, Annals of Macao and the Old Japan Trade, 1555-1640* (Lisbon, 1959), pp. 179-181, 191-196).

35. Calculated from the statement of goods sold in Japan, 1654, K.A. 1098, f. 774.

36. Calculated from the statement of goods sold in Japan, 1655, K.A. 1103, ff. 831-32.

37. According to Professor Davis, the annual import of Indian calicoes into England increased from an average of 240,000 pieces during 1663-69 to an average of 861,000 pieces during 1699-1701 (Ralph Davis, "English Foreign Trade 1660-1700," *Economic History Review*, Second Series, VII: 2, (December 1954), p. 153).

38. From a speech before the Board of Trade, Commonwealth Relations Office Library Tracts, Vol. 83, p. 50 (Quoted in Irwin and Schwartz, p. 13). Basically a similar story was told by an English merchant, John Cary, in 1695, "It was scarce thought about twenty Years since that we should ever see *Calicoes*, the Ornaments of our greatest Gallants (for such they are, whether we call them *Muslins*, *Shades*, or anything else) when they were then rarely used . . . ; but not few think themselves well drest till they are made up in *Calicoes* both Men and Women, *Calicoe Shirts*, *Neckcloths*, *Cuffs*, *Pocket-Handkerchiefs*, for the former, *Head-Dresses*, *Night-royls*, *Hoods*, *Sleeves*, *Aprons*, *Gowns*, *Petticoats* and what not; for the latter, besides *India Stockings* for both *Sexes*;" (John Cary, *A Discourse Concerning the East India Trade*, London, 1696, pp. 4-5).

39. Letter Books containing the Court of Directors' letter to the factors in Bengal, India Office Library.

40. Directors of the "New" English Company to Edward Littleton and Council in Bengal dated March 15, 1700, L.B. 11, f.173 and April 12, 1700, L.B. 11, f. 180; Directors of the "Old" Company to factors in Bengal dated January 10, 1701, L.B. 10, f. 406 and March 5, 1702, L.B. 10, f.538; S. Bhattacharya *The East India Company and the Economy of Bengal From 1704 to 1740* (London, 1954), p. 158.

41. K. Glamann, *Dutch-Asiatic Trade 1620-1740* (The Hague, 1958), Table 1, p. 13.

42. Calculated from Glamann, p. 144.

43. Ralph Davis, *loc. cit.*, p. 153.

44. S. Bhattacharya, p. 159.

45. H. Brugmans, "Handel en Nijverheid" in H. Brugmans and others, *Amsterdam in de zeventiende eeuw* (The Hague, 1901-04), part II, pp. 69-74. The French traveller, Tavernier, wrote, "But for the cloths which are ordered for *Poland* and *Muscovie*, it is necessary to have this gold and silver in the Indian style, because the Poles and Russians will have nothing to do with the cloths if they have not got the threads of gold and silver. (V. Ball (ed.) *Travels in India by Jean Baptiste Tavernier*, (London, 1889), II, pp. 28-29).

46. In 1697, for example, Bengal silk *jamawars* were reported to be doing very well in France (Orders list, March 1697, K.A. 261; Bengal's "explanation," 1699, K.A. 1516, f. 77).

XIII

From Negotiation to Coercion: Textile Manufacturing in India in the Eighteenth Century

Abstract

The paper first provides a broad overview of the structure of textile manufacturing and procurement in India in the seventeenth and the first half of the eighteenth century. It then takes up for a detailed analysis the changes in this structure in the second half of the eighteenth century as a result of the assumption of political authority by the English East India Company in the subcontinent with special reference to the case of Bengal where such authority was exercised most intensively. A market-based system was replaced by one embedded in coercion of the intermediary merchants and the manufacturing artisans. In the concluding section, the paper makes a plea for a distinction being made between the distributive justice dimension and the implications for output dimension of the changed scenario and argues that the picture of a ruined textile industry in Bengal might be in need of substantive revision.

I

India has traditionally been a major textile manufacturing nation. In the early modern period, textiles were manufactured in large quantities all over the subcontinent to provide for consumption in the domestic, the Indian Ocean as well as the world market. While an overwhelming proportion of the total domestic demand for this basic consumption good was obviously met through local village level production involving very little, if at all any, trade, the proportion of total output entering regional or subcontinental trade was by no means entirely insignificant. This was particularly true of luxury textiles where the element of regional specialization was of particular importance. Beyond the subcontinent, in the west, Indian textiles were traditionally a familiar item in the markets of the Middle East, and via these markets, to a limited extent in the markets of the Mediterranean. The fifth century A.D. cotton fragments discovered at Berenike, a harbour site on the Egyptian side of the Red Sea, are the earliest patterned textiles of Indian origin so far recovered from an archaeological context.[1] In the east, Indian textiles were traded on a much more substantial scale in mainland and island southeast Asia. A number of Indian textiles acquired from Sulawesi in Indonesia, for example, have been carbon-dated to the 14th–15th century. Textiles have reigned as a dominant aesthetic in Indonesia for centuries and have played an important role in various ceremonies in the islands. Indian textiles were quickly assimilated to fit local sensibilities and subsequently were encoded with indigenous meaning.[2]

Indeed, until the early part of the nineteenth century when the Industrial Revolution conferred a distinct cost advantage on the West, India had dominated world trade in textiles. The unquestioned domination of Indian textiles in the Indian Ocean trade has to be understood essentially in terms of the subcontinent's capacity to put on the market a wide range of textiles at highly cost-competitive terms making it in some sense the 'industrial' hub of the region sorrounded by west Asia on one side and southeast Asia on the other. As far as the European market was concerned, the quantum jump in the volume and value of the Indian textiles imported by the European corporate enterprises, mainly the Dutch and the English East India Companies, took place from the last quarter of the seventeenth century onward. This was an outcome essentially of a revolutionary change in European fashions putting Indian fine cotton and silk textiles right at the top of the fashion ladder.

Regional specialization in the subcontinent in the manufacturing of textiles was an important element in the history of the textile sector over the centuries. Coromandel on the south-east coast of India had traditionally been the leading manufacturer of relatively inexpensive cotton textiles which were either plain or patterned on the loom. They were often dyed in bright colours with plant

[1] John Peter Wild and Felicity Wild, "Rome and India: early Indian cotton textiles from Berenike, Red Sea Coast of Egypt" in Ruth Barnes (ed.), *Textiles in Indian Ocean Societies*, London and New York, 2005.

[2] Himanshu Prabha Ray, "Far-flung fabrics—Indian textiles in ancient maritime trade", in Barnes (ed.), *Textiles in Indian Ocean Societies*.

dyes. While both inferior and superior grade cotton textiles were manufactured in large quantities in Gujarat, the region also provided high-grade silk and cotton and silk mixed textiles. Bengal was the other major textile producing region in the subcontinent specializing in the production of luxury cotton, silk and mixed textiles. Given this pattern of specialization, it is not surprising that the relative share of Bengal textiles in the Indian Ocean trade—which was largely a low-cost market—was only of limited significance. But since the European market was essentially a luxury textile market, it was dominated from the very beginning by the textiles woven in Bengal except for the inexpensive cotton varieties intended for re-export to Africa and the New World. Some idea of this domination would be conveyed by the fact that, valuewise, at the turn of the eighteenth century, as much as 40 per cent of the total cargo exported to Europe from Asia by the Dutch as well as the English East India Company originated in Bengal and consisted in a large measure of textiles and raw silk.[3]

Textile production was without any doubt the premier manufacturing industry in the subcontinent. What is it that we know about the way it was organized, the methods of procurement for purposes of trade, the volume and value of trade by the Indian, other Asian and the European merchants, the scale of the industry's output, its cost structure and the profitability level and so on? Briefly, what we do know in great detail is the volume and value of the Indian textiles procured by the European corporate enterprises for export to Europe and other parts of Asia. As far as Indian and other Asian merchants involved in trade in these textiles were concerned, such information is available only on an extremely casual and sporadic basis. What we also know in great detail is the way the manufacturing production and procurement was organized. However, we know very little about the volume and value of textile output in the region, the cost structure of the industry or the level of its profitability. It is only occasionally that one gets a brief glimpse of these things and only in relation to a specific production area in the subcontinent. This paper recapitulates in Section II very briefly whatever we know in respect of these variables (except for the volume and value of trade) for the seventeenth and the first half of the eighteenth century. In Sections III and IV, we will discuss in some detail the situation in the second half of the eighteenth century which, among other things,

[3] Om Prakash, *European Commercial Enterprise in Pre-colonial India*, volume II.5 in the *New Cambridge History of India* series, Cambridge, 1998, Chapter 4.

witnessed a fundamental alteration in the conditions under which manufacturing production and procurement of textiles was carried out. A market-based system was replaced by one embedded in coercion of the intermediary merchants and the manufacturing artisans. This was a direct outcome of the availability of substantive political leverage to the English East India Company in many parts of the subcontinent and most importantly in Bengal following the grant of *diwani* rights to the Company in the province in 1765. It so happens that for this half of the century, we are somewhat better informed about variables such as the cost structure of the industry, the level of profitability and so on. For Bengal, this information is contained in an extensive documentation available in the archives of the Dutch East India Company for this period. This documentation pertains essentially to the correspondence between the Dutch and the English East India Companies regarding the alleged hindrances being placed in the textile procurement of the former by the latter. The really valuable information is often contained in the many annexures to the correspondence. While many of these documents are used, the report of the Dutch factor on a joint English-Dutch-French mission of 1767 to ascertain the relevant facts will be used in some detail to bring out the nitty gritty of the altered situation. In the concluding section, we will argue that it is important to distinguish between the impact of the change in the system of production and procurement on output as distinct from the question of the share of different groups in the value of that output. The often perceived picture of a ruined textile industry in the region might indeed be in need of substantive revision.

II

Working on the basis of the cotton yarn procured from the spinner, the basic unit of production in the manufacturing of textiles was the weaver operating as an independent artisan. To a certain extent, the production of standardized varieties of textiles for traditional markets was carried on on the basis of the weavers' own resources and at their own risk. There is evidence, for example, that several varieties of comparatively coarse cotton cloth were produced on this basis in the district of Malda in north Bengal for eventual sale to merchants engaged in trade with Pegu, north India (Hindustan) and Persia, which had traditionally been important markets for these varieties. The bulk of the marketed output, however, was produced on the basis of an agreement between merchants—many of whom were intermediary merchants known in Bengal as paikars—and weavers specifying details such as the quantity to be produced, the price and the date of delivery. A part—often a substantial part—of the final value of the contract was given in advance to enable the weaver to buy the necessary raw materials as well as to sustain himself and his family during the period of production. Clearly, the three key elements in this system were the weavers' need of finance, their relatively limited access to the market, and a desire on their part to avoid risks arising out of their inability to forecast correctly the behaviour of the demand for a given variety of textiles. This structure, which could be described as the contract system, was essentially a variant of the standard European putting-out system. Unlike in the European case, the Indian weaver bought his own raw material and exercised formal control over his output until it changed hands. Of course, the merchant who had given the advance had first claim on the output, and debt obligations often rendered the artisans subject to coercive control by the merchants.[4]

Though grossly inadequate and perhaps not entirely representative, the available evidence on the weavers' costs and the merchants' mark-up enables us to form some idea of the magnitudes involved. A 1670 report on Malda in north Bengal suggested that standardized textiles worth Rs.0.8 to Rs.1 million were sold in the district annually for export to places such as Pegu, Agra, Surat and Persia. If these were bought against cash directly from the producers who brought them into Malda rather than from the intermediary merchants, the saving in cost would be between 12 and 15 per cent. The mark-up by the merchant would, of course, be substantially greater under the contract system to compensate him for the additional risks borne. These risks were not inconsiderable. For example, a sudden rise in the cost of living in the wake of a famine, or the appointment of a particularly tyrannical official in a given area, might lead to a mass migration of the poor weavers to a more convenient location, to the great discomfiture and loss of the merchants who had entered into contracts with them and given them advances. Some data relating to 1686–7 in respect of *khasas*, a staple variety of muslin procured by the Dutch East India Company in fairly large quantities in Bengal, suggests that about two thirds of the price obtained by the weaver covered the costs of the raw

[4] Om Prakash, *The Dutch East India Company and the Economy of Bengal 1630–1720*, Princeton, 1985, pp. 98–99.

material, the remainder being the reward for his labour. The mark-up by the intermediary merchant (calculated on the basis of the price agreed upon at the time of the contract between the Company and the merchant) was 35 per cent in the case of grade I, 55 per cent in that ot grade II, and as much as 142 per cent in that of grade III.[5]

The European corporate enterprises operated in the Indian market basically as yet another group of merchants availing no special privileges in their dealings with the Indian merchants or artisans. By the same token, they were at liberty to function in the system like any other merchant group, without restriction on the use of the available infrastructure. Their factors and representatives were allowed to travel throughout the subcontinent, buy and sell where they found it most profitable to do so, and deal with their Indian counterparts on terms strictly determined by the market. The European enterprises made use of the existing procurement organization, though in course of time they did indeed introduce modifications and innovations with varying degrees of success in a variety of directions aimed at solving specific problems that they encountered. An important functionary made use of by the Europeans was the dalal (broker), an Indian employee with an intimate knowledge of both the local market and the intermediary merchants. He was ordinarily a salaried employee, and his duties included collecting information about the market price of various goods as well as identifying merchants with a good reputation for honouring contractual obligations. These merchants were brought by the dalal to the relevant company and agreements concluded between the company and each of the merchants willing to supply at mutually agreed terms. In the case of textiles, the agreement specified the quantity to be supplied, the period of delivery, and the price per piece of each of the different varieties contracted for. The merchants had the goods manufactured mainly on the basis of the contract system which, as we have seen, obliged them to give a part of the value of the contract to the producers in advance. The merchants, therefore, insisted that the company similarly give them an advance, which in the case of Bengal was ordinarily between 50 and 65 per cent. The intermediary merchants who did business with the Europeans were an extremely heterogenous group. In the case of the Dutch East India Company (VOC) in Bengal, at one end it included merchants such as Khem Chand Shah, who engaged in large-scale domestic and overseas

[5] Om Prakash, *The Dutch East India Company*, pp. 99–100.

trade and who owned several ships. At the other end, there were marginal merchants who genuinely could not have operated except on the basis of the advances received from the Company. Once the goods were delivered into the Company's warehouses, the deviation from the samples was worked out and the price finally paid to the merchants was adjusted accordingly.[6]

Peculiarities characteristic of certain regions should be noted. Probably the most important of these was the distinctly superior position of the weaver vis-à-vis the intermediary merchant in South India. Unlike in Bengal, a weaver in South India was evidently free to cancel a contract negotiated with an intermediary merchant at any time by simply returning the advance received. The merchant, on the other hand, did not possess the right to break a contract or demand the return of an advance.[7] In a situation where the average annual rate of growth of the supply of textiles failed to keep pace with the average annual rate of growth of demand for them, this would constitute an enormously important differential advantage. Around the turn of the eighteenth century when this was by and large the situation in all parts of the subcontinent, the weavers in South India took full advantage of this provision. The freedom to terminate a contract simply implied that the weaver was free to sell the finished product to the buyer willing to pay the most and use the proceeds of the sale to return the advance to the intermediary merchant. Such situations were by no means altogether rare in Bengal but in that case the diversion of output to a buyer other than the one who had provided the advance was done clandestinely and under great secrecy on both sides.

The other major difference between Bengal on the one hand and South India on the other relates to the nature of the contract between the European companies and the intermediary merchants. It was pointed out above that in Bengal the norm was for the intermediary merchant to be provided with a substantial part of the value of the contract in advance. But in South India the merchants providing cloth to the English East India Company in the early eighteenth century rarely received capital from the Company and raised much of their finance from the local bankers.[8] The closest the Dutch East India Company came to this arrangement on the Coromandel coast was the

[6] Om Prakash, *The Dutch East India Company*, pp. 102–107.

[7] Prasannan Parthasarathi, *The Transition to a Colonial Economy: Weavers, Merchants and Kings in South India, 1720–1800*, Cambridge, 2001, pp. 26–27.

[8] Parthasarathi, *Transition to a Colonial Economy*, p. 35.

essentially abortive experiment with the idea of a joint stock company. The innovation in this arrangement consisted essentially in the fact that the funds needed for investment in textiles were raised jointly by the intermediary merchants themselves rather than being provided by the Company in the form of advances to the customary extent of 50 to 70 per cent of the value of the contract. Each merchant was supposed to subscribe to the pool of funds in accordance with his share in the total value of the contract given out by the Company. These merchants were also encouraged to operate in different segments of the production areas so as to minimize competition amongst themselves leading to a rise in the cost price of the textiles procured. This was a highly welcome development from the point of view of the Company. But, over time, the distinct characteristic feature of the institution—namely, the investment by the participating merchants of their own funds in procuring the textiles obviating the need for the Company to give them advances and run the risk of bad debts arising—tended to disintegrate and the joint stock system increasingly followed the norms of the ordinary cash-advance contracts.[9]

III

The assumption of political authority by the English East India Company around the middle of the eighteenth century in each of the three major textile producing regions in the subcontinent altered the basic relationship between the Company on the one hand and the Indian intermediary merchant and the artisan on the other. The earlier relationship based on the working of the market forces of demand and supply and the absence of coercion was now replaced by one of the availability to the Company of wide powers of coercion over the Indian trading and artisanal groups. Not only were these groups no longer entitled to a market-determined return to their endeavours, they were often no longer free even to decide whether to enter into a business relationship with the Company at all. The position of these groups was further worsened by the use of its political authority by the English East India Company to increasingly marginalize the rival European trading companies engaged in the textile trade such as

[9] *Nationaal Archief* (NA), The Hague, Memoir of the outgoing Governor of Coromandel, Pieter Haksteen, for his successor, Reynier van Vlissingen, dated 20 September 1771, *Hooge Regering Batavia* (HRB) 344, ff. 53–55.

the Dutch East India Company and the French East India Company. These companies were no longer allowed to operate in the market as an equal, substantially cutting into their role as major alternative buyers of the textiles manufactured by the weavers. As one would expect, the degree of coercion in a given region of the subcontinent was directly proportional to the degree of political authority available to the English Company in that region.

Of the three major textile producing regions in the subcontinent viz. Gujarat, the Coromandel coast and Bengal, political authority capable of being misused to generate coercive control was available to the Company in its mildest form in Gujarat. Despite the assumption of political office as the *qiladar* of Surat in 1759, the Company was not really in a position to institute restrictive and coercive mechanisms for the procurement of textiles. And indeed the investment requirements of the Company at this time did not warrant any major rehauling of the existing system. It was only in the 1780s that the growing procurement of textiles by rival Europeans—the Dutch, the French and the private Portuguese traders—put the system under a certain amount of strain making the weavers increasingly unwilling to conform to the English specifications. When pressed to do so by the Bania/Parsi intermediary merchants of the English Company, what followed was a riot in 1788 by the Muslim weavers against the Parsi intermediaries. But as far as the Company was concerned, it was clear that uncertain and partial political control precluded the enforcement of coercive mechanisms for textile procurement. Conciliation rather than coercion appeared to be the Company's official watchword.[10]

It was only in 1795 that a Commercial Board was established in Surat under a Commercial Resident, the first appointee to the office being one John Cherry. Attempts were now under way to coerce the weavers to sell their goods exclusively to the Company at prices below those in the market. Cherry described the system as being moderately restrictive rather than coercive. In 1797, a set of regulations was prescribed constituting the first definitive means of control over textile producers in Western India. Among other things, these regulations prescribed that in the case of weavers who failed to deliver the textiles by the stipulated date, the Commercial

[10] Lakshmi Subramanian, "Power and the Weave: Weavers, Merchants and Rulers in Eighteenth Century Surat", in Rudrangshu Mukherjee and Lakshmi Subramanian (ed.), *Politics and Trade in the Indian Ocean World: Essays in Honour of Ashin Das Gupta*, Delhi, 1998, pp. 52–82.

Resident would be at liberty to place peons upon them to expedite the delivery. The Commercial Resident was to henceforth maintain a register of weavers and merchants employed in the provision of the Company's investment. It is, however, important to realize that even these relatively mild regulations could be framed only in the context of the expansion of English power in the region.[11]

In the matter of dominating both the rival European trading companies and, more importantly, the Indian intermediary merchants and weavers in the second half of the eighteenth century, the English East India Company was able to do substantially better on the Coromandel coast. This was the direct outcome of the much more substantive political power base that the Company had been able to build for itself in the region than had been the case in Gujarat. In the 1760s and the subsequent decades of the eighteenth century, the principal centres where the Company procured its textiles on the Coromandel coast were (a) the area around Madras where muslins and other fine textiles were manufactured (b) Cuddalore to the south which specialized in the production of calicoes and (c) the manufacturing villages in the northern sarkars where calicoes were bought through the factories at Ingeram and Madapollam. In the first of these areas, extensive *jagir* (revenue collection) rights were obtained by the Company in 1763 in the equivalent of the present day Chingleput district. Further additions to these territories were made in the subsequent decades of the century. Between the southern factories of Cuddalore (where two weaving villages of Chinnamanaikpollam and Naduvirapattu were obtained as *jagir* villages in 1762) and Madras on the one hand and those at Ingeram and Madapollam in the north, the political power that the Company was able to wrest was much greater in the former than in the latter. Both at Ingeram and Madapollam, the Company's authority was really indirect and was significantly intermediated by the zamindars of the area.[12]

The strategy followed by the Company was a simple but effective one. In the areas where significant political authority was available, including the *jagir* territories, the first step was to try and exclude rivals from operating in the area. The multiplicity of buyers which had hitherto constituted the principal bargaining strength of the weavers would thus be significantly compromised. This is precisely what the

[11] Subramanian, "Power and the Weave", pp. 68–70.
[12] Parthasarathi, *Transition to a Colonial Economy*, pp. 96–98.

Company tried to do at Cuddalore in 1766 obliging the weavers to accept advances exclusively from the Company's intermediary merchants. Following the protests from the French at Pondicherry who also operated in the area, it was agreed that the weavers could indeed work for the French but only after the contracts given out by the English Company's merchants had been duly supplied. Two years later, the intermediary merchants were dispensed with and the Company arranged to provide advances to the weavers directly. This was done by the Commercial Resident operating through gumashtas who, in turn, were assisted by brokers, an office held by head weavers in some of the villages. As an incentive, the Company agreed to provide advances on a regular basis so as to guarantee continued employment besides reducing the loom tax in the weaving villages around Cuddalore.[13]

It is, however, important to realize that while the case of Coromandel did indeed represent a much greater use of coercive authority by the English East India Company in its dealings with the weavers in the last quarter of the eighteenth century than had been the case in Gujarat, the experience of the ultimate in coercion was left to the fate of the poor weavers of Bengal. It was again in Bengal that following the battle of Plassey in 1757 the rival European corporate enterprises were most discriminated against and prevented from procuring an adequate quantity of textiles. Indeed, within a few months of Plassey, the English factors were reported to be forcibly taking away pieces woven for the Dutch. In October 1758, when the Dutch protested, the English officials promised redress but nothing was actually done. In the early 1760s, the Commercial Residents at Malda and Midnapur were instructed to ensure that the best weavers of Jagannathpur, Olmara and the neighbouring aurungs worked exclusively for the English. The public posture adopted by the English was, however, quite different. A Fort William public notification dated 28 April 1775 asserted unambiguously "that the weavers of the province of Bengal and Bihar should enjoy a perfect and entire liberty to deal with any persons whom they pleased and that no person should use force of any kind to oblige the weavers or other manufacturers to receive advances of money or to engage in contracts for the provision of clothes against their will, and that all persons

[13] Parthasarathi, *Transition to a Colonial Economy*, pp. 85–89; S. Arasaratnam, "Trade and Political Dominion in South India, 1750–1790", *Modern Asian Studies*, vol. XIII.1, 1979, p. 29.

offending against this order should suffer severe punishment".[14] It was against this background that the Dutch proposed to the English in 1767 that they should be assigned weavers in the various aurungs who would then be allowed to work for them without hindrance. The result was the setting up of a joint investigative mission of the English, the Dutch and the French East India Companies. It is the report of the Dutch representative on this mission that together with some other documents for this period constitutes the core of the material analysed in the rest of this paper.[15]

The mission was formally set up on 4 March 1767 with Johannes Mathias Ross as the Dutch representative on it along with his deputy Martinus Koning. The English representatives were John Bitter and Claude de la Porte while the French East India Company was represented by Roeland and Des Granges. Ross's instructions (formally signed by Director George Louis Vernet only on 22 April 1767) stipulated that he along with Koning would report to English governor Harry Verelst at Calcutta wherefrom they would proceed together with the English and the French representatives to the textile aurungs (a localized centre of textile manufacturing) to "investigate the best procedures to be followed to put out the contracts so that each of the three nations was served satisfactorily. Towards that end, you would make an accurate estimate of the amount of land in each aurung which was used for planting cotton as well as of the average annual output of cotton in each aurung. You would also find out the number of weavers and classify them as being of excellent, middling or poor quality". The mission was also directed to find out the number of pieces of a specified fineness that a weaver could be expected to weave in the course of a month. Ross was also asked to find out if there were persons available locally for appointment as head-dalals of the Company to whom funds could be entrusted safely.

Further, since within each aurung, textiles of different quality were produced and bleached in different hamlets of the aurung, a precise investigation was to be carried out behind the reasons accounting

[14] NA, The notification was signed by J.P. Auriol, Assistant Secretary, Appendices to the memoir of Director Johannes Bacheracht for his successor, Johannes Mathias Ross, dated 31 July 1776, HRB 246 (the volume is not foliated).

[15] The Report is entitled, "Bericht van den koopman Johannes Mathias Ross wegens de Commissie in de Arrengs [met bylagen] 1767". It was submitted to Director George Louis Vernet at Hughli on 26 December 1767. It is available at the *Nationaal Archief* (NA), The Hague, under No. 66 in the series *Nederlandse Bezittingen in Voor-Indie* (NBVI). The report is not foliated. The access code is 1.04.19.

for this phenomenon. Was it due to inherent differences in the workmanship of the weavers belonging to different hamlets or was this a function of the differing quality of water used for bleaching purposes? It was known that textiles woven in one aurung were often bleached in another for good results.

Finally, Ross was told that with a view to deriving the maximum benefit from a mission such as this, he was to collect precise information regarding the varieties of textiles produced in each aurung, the prices at which these were available there, and the varieties that could be bought or sold there at a profit. Any differences with regard to weights and measures used in these aurungs as compared to Hughli were also to be recorded.[16]

Ross and Koning travelled to Calcutta on 11 April but were told by Bitter and La Porte that they would not be ready for the trip for another two weeks. A message was subsequently received at Hughli from La Porte that the mission would start on 4 May and that they would expect the Dutch representatives to join them at Duarhatta, an aurung under the Haripal factory of the English. The team would start with the aurungs of Haripal and Dhaniakhali and then go on to Chandrakona. The English would then return to Calcutta while the Dutch and the French could continue with the mission to Santipur etc. This violated the agreement between the English governor and the Dutch director finalized in February 1767 that all aurungs where textiles were manufactured would be visited by the full team.

The Dutch team left on 23 April for Calcutta where the French had already arrived two days earlier. When the question of the number of aurungs to be visited was raised with governor Verelst, he replied that it was John Bitter who had questioned the advisability of doing all the aurungs in one trip. Verelst reiterated that the basic purpose of the mission was to have an accurate estimate of the weavers facilitating a satisfactory procurement of textiles by each of the three nations.

When the representatives of the three companies met at Bitter's house at Calcutta, Ross suggested that in order to save on time and expenses, it would be optimal to begin at Chandrakona, go on to Santipur, Kasimbazar and Bhagwangola, then cross the river and visit the aurungs at Malda, Buddaul, Jagannathpur, Handiaal, Dhaka, Bhusna and Bureng before returning home. But the English insisted that they could not be away from Calcutta for so long and would,

[16] Instructions by Vernet for Ross at Hughli dated 22 April 1767, Appendix A, Report by Ross, NBVI, 66.

therefore, insist on visiting Haripal and Dhaniakhali first. The Dutch and the French had no option but to agree. That is what explains the fact that the detailed quantitative information presented later in the paper pertains to these two aurungs. The only other aurung for which detailed information is available is that of Chandrakona. Having agreed to meet at Duarhatta on 4 May, the group dispersed.

Ross and Koning reached Haripal on 28 April. The Dutch gumashtas, however, called on them only on 1 May. By way of an explanation, it was pointed out that the fear of the English was such that all dalals and head-weavers had been busy greeting Bitter at Duarhatta with fruit and other gifts. The Dutch intermediary merchant Samram who had been sent from Calcutta to Khattorah (under the Haripal factory of the English) with instructions to join Ross at Duarhatta also joined him on 1 May. He reported that there were about 400 weavers at Khattorah each capable of producing on an average two pieces of yarn rumals each month making a total of 9,600 pieces per annum. All the weavers were obliged to work exclusively for the English. The French had put out some contracts during the preceding year but all the pieces being manufactured for them were cut off the looms and the weavers concerned meted out both bodily and monetary punishment.[17]

Samram was asked to send a circular letter to all the Dutch gumashtas and merchants to visit Ross together with their dalals. When asked at the meeting why there were serious shortfalls in the supplies against the contracts of the preceding year, the unanimous explanation offered was the high-handed behaviour of the gumashtas of the English Company and the private English traders. The English Company had reportedly forced fresh contracts on the 28th of April on the best weavers in this aurung worth 155,000 sicca rupees. This amounted to each weaver being made to accept advances in respect of the maximum amount of production that he could expect to achieve in a year's time. The private English traders were equally aggressive. Amounting to 37 in number, these individuals were completely indifferent to what they contracted for and what price they had to pay as long as they could earn a return of 9 per cent per annum on their investment. They had brought in as much as 350,000 sicca rupees for investment in the aurung. The deadly combination of the violence resorted to by the English Company and of the substantially

[17] Report by Ross, NBVI, 66.

higher prices offered by the private English traders worked towards the utter ruin of the Dutch Company.

A visitor to Ross told him under a guarantee of anonymity that the English had expressly prohibited all dalals and weavers from declaring that they (the English) ever impeded the work of procurement by the Dutch. When they were asked to present themselves at Duarhatta, they were to take the position that they served the Dutch as faithfully as they did the English. Ross was surprised that the head-gumashta of the English had even considered it necessary to recommend such a course of action to them. The fear of the English among the gumashtas and the weavers was so all-pervasive that "an English peon or an employee of equal rank was held in greater esteem by them than he (Ross) himself". There was thus no real risk of their ever declaring that they were made to discriminate against the Dutch.

On receiving information that the English had reached Duarhatta, Ross and his deputy joined them and the French there. The purpose of the English alerting their gumashtas and the dalals on the lines above became clear to Ross when he found that Bitter and La Porte were interpreting the purpose of the mission as being an investigation into the complaints of the Dutch regarding textile procurement. The Dutch were thus the complainants, the gumashtas and the weavers the persons against whom the complaints had been made, and the English the judges. This was completely contrary to the assurances given to Ross by governor Verelst at Calcutta on 24 April when he had reiterated that the purpose of the mission was to make an accurate estimate of the number of weavers and so on. The French supported Ross's stand but Bitter stuck to his position. He suggested that in order to prevent future disputes, all the pieces of textiles produced in the aurungs should be appropriated and then divided among the three companies according to their requirements. Any pieces left over were to be made available to the English private traders. When Ross pointed out that this plan was completely impractical, he was told that he was not genuinely interested in the redressal of the Dutch grievances. At this point the Dutch and the French left the meeting in protest. That is how the mission started its work.

On 6 May, Bitter ordered the arrest and despatch to Calcutta of the six weavers who had been complaining and agitating over the preceding two months about the excesses of the English gumashtas and of the low prices paid by them. The effect of this was the spread of terror among the artisans so much so that the dalals and weavers of Haripal who had earlier promised to Ross that they would jointly and publicly protest against the excesses of the English gumashtas lost their nerve and backed out of their commitment.[18]

At a dinner hosted by Ross for his English and French colleagues on 12 May, the deputy English representative La Porte, who had arrived before Bitter, was told that in view of the English order of 9 May to the weavers that over the following three months, on pain of the severest punishment, they would work for nobody other than the English, the Dutch had been unable to put out any contracts at all. The weavers still owing nearly half of the advances given by the Company in the preceding year were even offering to return them. This was because they were complaining that the English gumashtas had forced upon them contracts and advances worth more than what they could expect to produce in the course of a whole year. The weavers to whom the English had put out their contracts were precisely the ones who had always worked for the Dutch and still owed them supplies against the advances of the preceding year. All that La Porte did by way of a response was simply to shrug his shoulders saying that this could not be helped.

The next day Ross told Bitter that his belief that the aurung of Haripal was capable of producing annually only 48,000 to 50,000 pieces of textiles was misplaced and that the actual production capacity was between 90,000 and 100,000 pieces. He added that even the latter number could be enhanced considerably "only if the English desisted from using violence and force on the weavers and restored their freedom completely". In the meantime, an order had arrived from governor Verelst for Bitter saying that "the procurement of textiles for the English Company was to be regulated in such a manner as to cause the least hindrance to the procurement by the Dutch". Bitter also admitted that the aurung could probably produce 60,000 pieces annually and that the English had put out contracts for 36,000 pieces. That left 24,000 pieces for the Dutch whose duty it was to ensure that their gumashtas got hold of the necessary number of weavers. Ross asked the simple question that if the entire lot of 24,000 pieces was to be treated as available to the Dutch, what would happen to the procurement by the French, the English private traders who had already sent in as many as 350,000 sicca rupees for investment in the aurung, besides other traders.[19]

[18] Report by Ross, NBVI, 66.
[19] Report by Ross, NBVI, 66.

The English involvement in the mission came to an end on 11 June, when Bitter was instructed to proceed to Chandrakona. Ross and his deputy decided to continue on the mission and left for Dhaniakhali in the same aurung on 19 June with the intention of continuing southwards in the direction of Khirpai and Chandrakona. As for the French, Roeland excused himself from the mission thus paving the way for Des Granges to become the leader of the French assisted by one Nicolai de Faranse. The curtailed mission decided to begin with Haripal and Dhaniakhali.

Addressing the issue of the cultivation of cotton first, Ross pointed out that the local term used for the product was *kapas* and that it was grown in shrubs two to four feet high in three or four cornered balls with three kernels each. The variety grown locally was called *kali* which yielded a thinner yarn than the *baga* and the *muri* varieties, the former of which was grown in Birbhum and used in the manufacturing of *garras*. The *muri* kapas, yielding the finest yarn, was grown in the areas surrounding Dhaka which were either stony and sandy or had dense forests. This yarn was used for the manufacturing of the fine Dhaka varieties.

The *kapas* grown in and around the aurungs of Haripal, Dhaniakhali and Chandrakona was of an identical variety and the number of fields planted was regulated strictly in accordance with the amount likely to be consumed locally. There was thus no trade whatever carried on in the locally grown cotton. A bad crop then involved a rise in the price. In 1767, which was marked by an average crop, the price ranged between 7½ to 8½ ceers per sicca rupee. The equivalent of 8 ceers was 11½ lbs. Once the cotton had been cleaned of the kernels and other impurities, the yarn obtained was around 1½ ceers. It was indeed not so much a rise or fall in the price of cotton that led to fluctuations in the price of the textiles as did the wages of the spinners. *Kapas* costing ⅔ to ¾ paisas cost as much as 4 paisas to have it spun.[20]

Ross's report contains a fair amount of information on the process of the weaving of many varieties of cotton, cotton and silk mixed, as well as silk textiles, manufactured in the aurungs of Haripal, Dhaniakhali and Chandrakona in the year 1767. The survey was carried out in these aurungs because being under direct English control, the collection of information was that much easier. In the first place, the information pertains to variables such as the number of weavers, the number

[20] Report by Ross, NBVI, 66.

of looms and the number of houses (grouped in three categories of first, second and third qualities) from which the weaver households operated. This information is available in respect of each of the hamlets and villages covered by each of the sub-aurungs of the aurung to which the information pertains. This information in respect of the aurungs of Haripal and Dhaniakhali is summarized in Table 1.

According to Table 1, the two aurungs of Haripal and Dhaniakhali had between themselves as many as 164 weaving villages containing 2,745 weaver houses of which around a quarter (26.66%) were first quality, about a third (32.09%) second quality and the remaining 41.23% of third quality. Of the total of 164 villages covered by the two aurungs, while 87 fell in the 8 sub-aurungs of the Haripal aurung, the Dhaniakhali aurung contained the remaining 77 villages spread over three sub-aurungs. While 72 of the 87 villages of Haripal aurung specialized in the production of white (cotton) textiles, the remaining 15 produced silk and coloured textiles. All 77 villages of the Dhaniakhali aurung specialized in the production of silk and coloured textiles, the only exception being *sanus*, a cotton calico piece-good.

According to the table, the total number of looms in the two aurungs was found to have been 3,223 not taking into account the broken and otherwise unuseable ones. On the assumption of four weavers (one master-weaver assisted by three assistants) per loom, the number of weavers ought to have been 12,892. The survey, however, listed only 5,582 weavers suggesting a short-fall of as many as 7,310 weavers (perhaps mainly assistants). Ross attributed this immense discrepancy essentially to three factors. The first was the frequent disturbances the area had suffered from over the preceding few years. The second factor mentioned by Ross was the exceedingly "violent" and "self-centered" procurement procedures followed by the English Company obliging a large number of weavers to turn to farming and other occupations. A contributing circumstance was the large scale "recruitment by the English Company of soldiers and coolies for their army as also of labour to carry out large scale construction activity in Calcutta". Thirdly "unlike in an aurung such as Chandrakona where practically all farmers and artisans including smiths were also weavers", weaving in the Haripal and Dhaniakhali aurungs was a full-time activity.[21]

Table 2 provides a breakdown of the cost of manufacturing different varieties of cotton and cotton and silk mixed textiles between the cost

[21] Report by Ross, NBVI, 66.

TABLE I

Textiles Manufactured in the Aurungs of Haripal and Dhaniakhali, 1767

		Varieties manufactured	Number of houses (I, II, III quality)	Number of weavers	Number of looms
1.	Name of the aurung—Haripal				
	Name of sub-aurung				
	a. Teinagar				
	Number of producing villages				
	20	White textiles	366(148,107,111)	681	412
	10	Silk and coloured textiles	72(35,23,14)	153	91
Total	30		438(183,130,115)	834	503
	b. Koikalla				
	7	White textiles	126(32,41,53)	279	154
	3	Silk and coloured textiles	11(9,2,0)	25	14
Total	10		137(41,43,53)	304	168
	c. Haripal				
	8	White textiles	286(79,113,94)	609	334
	d. Mora				
	3	White textiles	61(29,20,12)	154	72
	e. Koliema				
	6	White textiles	58(31,16,11)	160	79
	f. Duarhatta				
	11	White textiles	328(154,87,87)	784	395
	2	Silk and coloured textiles	17(7,0,10)	32	24
Total	13		345(161,87,97)	816	419
	g. Aadhpur				
	7	White textiles	107(39,35,33)	241	125
	h. Raasbolhaad				
	10	White textiles	374(73,144,157)	810	423
	Total for the aurung of Haripal (sub-aurungs = 8)				
	Number of producing villages				
	72	White textiles	1,706(585,563,558)	3,718	1,994
	15	Silk and coloured textiles	100(51,25,24)	210	129
Total	87		1,806(636,588,582)	3,928	2,123

TABLE 1
Continued

2.	Name of the aurung: Dhaniakhali				
	Name of sub-aurung				
	a. Dhaniakhali				
	Number of producing villages	Varieties manufactured	Number of houses (I, II, III quality)	Number of weavers	Number of looms
	24	Silk and coloured textiles	355(63,68,224)	587	429
	b. Goerap				
	2	Silk, coloured and *sanus*	78(0,34,44)	157	96
	c. Khanpur				
	51	Silk, coloured and *sanus*	506(33,191,282)	910	575
	Total for the aurung of Dhaniakhali (sub-aurungs = 3)				
	Number of producing villages				
	77	Silk, coloured and *sanus*	939(96,293,550)	1,654	1,100
	Grand total for the aurungs of Haripal and Dhaniakhali (sub-aurungs = 11)	Varieties manufactured	Number of houses (I, II, III quality)	Number of weavers	Number of looms
	Number of producing villages				
	72	White textiles	1,706(585,563,558)	3,718	1,994
	15	Silk and coloured textiles	100(51,25,24)	210	129
	77	Silk, coloured and *sanus*	939(96,293,550)	1,654	1,100
Total	164		2,745(732,881,1,132)	5,582	3,223

Source: Adapted from Appendix L, Report by Ross, NBVI, 66.

of the yarn used and the wages bill of the weavers. This information is available for three varieties of cotton textiles and two varieties of cotton and silk mixed textiles. The cotton textiles include four kinds of *dorias* (a fine quality calico) of the standard size of 40 covid length and 2¼ covid width (the covid was an indigenous measure equalling half a yard) containing 1,100 to 1,700 threads, two kinds of *terrindams* (a fine quality muslin), again of the standard size of 40 covid length and 2¼ covid width and containing 1,100 threads, and *rumals* (a fine quality calico) of 35 covid length and 1¾ covid width containing 1,300 threads. The cotton and silk mixed varieties are *sirsick* of 30 covid length and 2 covid width containing 1,800 threads and *karraderry* of the same size and containing 1,600 threads.

What the table establishes quite explicitly is that cotton yarn of different qualities went into different varieties of the same textile. Thus while the yarn that went into the warp of the Dhaka *doria* cost 5 paisa per unit for the ground and 2 paisa per unit for the stripe, the corresponding figures for the yarn used for the Kammagora *doria* were 6½ paisa per unit and 4 paisa per unit respectively. The difference was even greater in the quality and price of the yarn used for the weft in these two varieties of *dorias*. While the yarn used for the Dhaka variety cost 6¼ paisa, the one used for the Kammagora variety cost as much as 9⅓ paisa per unit. The same was true of the *terrindams* even though both the varieties had the same number of threads.

The relative share of the cost of the yarn and of the weaver's wages bill in the total cost, however, did not differ very much across the different varieties of textiles. The share of the wages bill thus fluctuated roughly between a quarter and one-third of the total cost, being generally higher in the case of mixed cotton and silk textiles than in that of cotton textiles.

As for the factors contributing to fluctuations in the price of cotton yarn, in addition to the obvious one of fluctuations in the size of the crop, Ross drew attention to two other circumstances. One was fluctuations in the numbers of women spinners available at a point in time depending on what other employment opportunities happened to be currently available. By far the most important circumstance governing the price of yarn, however, was the volume and value of the contracts being put out at that point in time by buyers other than the English Company. In respect of each variety of yarn, the English Company fixed the price at which the weavers working for it had to be provided with the yarn, obliging the yarn producers to make up for

TABLE 2

Breakdown of the Cost of Specific Varieties of Bengal Textiles Manufactured in the Aurungs of Haripal and Dhaniakhali, 1767

S. No.	Variety	Size	Cost of yarn for the warp per piece (in sicca rupees:annas)	Cost of yarn for the weft per piece (in sicca rupees: annas)	Total cost of yarn (in sicca rupees: annas)	Per centage of total cost accounted for by yarn	Weaver's wages per piece (in sicca rupees: annas)	Per centage of total cost accounted for by the weaver's wages	Total cost per piece (in sicca rupees:annas)
1.	Dhaka *doria* containing 1,700 threads	length 40 covids, width $2^1/_4$ covids	6:6 of which 3:12 for 48 units for the ground costing 5 paisa per unit and 2:10 for 84 units for the stripes costing 2 paisa per unit	4:11 for 48 units costing $6^1/_4$ paisa per unit	11:1	73·75	3:15	26.25	15:00
2.	Kammagora *doria* containing 1,300 threads	length 40 covids, width $2^1/_4$ covids	$5{:}4^3/_4$ of which $3{:}0^3/_4$ for 30 units for the ground costing $6^1/_2$ paisas per unit and 2:4 for 36 units for the stripes costing 4 paisa per unit	5:4 for 36 units costing $9^1/_3$ paisa per unit	$10{:}8^3/_4$	75·33	$3{:}7^1/_4$	24.66	14.00
3.	Kammagora *doria* containing (unspecified) threads	length 40 covids, width $2^1/_4$ covids	4:13 of which 2:13 for 30 units for the ground costing 6 paisa per unit and 2:0 for 32 units for the stripes costing 4 paisa per unit	4:8 for 32 units costing 9 paisa per unit	9:5	74·5	3:3	25·5	12:8
4.	Sangora *doria* containing 1,100 threads	length 40 covids, width $2^1/_4$ covids	4:4 of which 2:4 for 42 units for the ground costing $3^1/_7$ paisa per unit and 2:0 for 48 units for the stripes costing $2^2/_3$ paisa per unit	3:12 for 48 units costing 5 paisa per unit	8:0	72.72	3:0	27.27	11:0

5.	*Terrindam* containing 1,100 threads	length 40 covids, width 2 1/4 covids	4:8 for 48 units costing 6 paisa per unit	6:4 for 30 units costing 8 paisa per unit	10:12	76.78	3:4	23.21	14:0
6.	*Terrindam* containing 1,100 threads	length 40 covids, width 2 1/4 covids	3:12 3/4 for 54 units costing 4 paisa per unit	4:4 1/4 for 42 units costing 6 1/2 paisa per unit	8:1	73.29	2:15	26.70	11:0
7.	*Neusdoek* (*rumal*) containing 1,300 threads	length 35 covids, width 1 3/4 covids	3:10 of which 2:10 for 42 units for the ground costing 4 paisa per unit and 1:0 for 16 units for the stripes costing 4 paisa per unit	3:4 1/2 for 42 units costing 5 paisa per unit	6:14 1/2	76.73	2:1 1/2	23.26	9:0
8.	Fine *sirsick* containing 1,800 threads (mixed silk and cotton)	length 30 covids, width 2 covids	4:1 1/4 of which 1:6 1/2 for 30 units for the ground costing 3 paisa per unit and 2:10 3/4 for 24 units of silk for the stripes costing 7 1/9 paisa per unit	4:3 1/2 for 54 units costing 5 paisa per unit	8:4 3/4 +0:8 1/4 for the colour for the silk = 8:13	67.78	4:3	32.21	13:0
9.	Fine *karraderry* containing 1,600 threads (mixed silk and cotton)	length 30 covids width 2 covids	3:12 of which 1:15 1/2 for 42 units for the ground costing 3 paisa per unit and 1:12 1/2 for 16 units of silk for the stripes costing 7 1/9 paisa per unit	4:11 for 60 units costing 5 paisa per unit	8:7	70.31	3:9	29.68	12:0

Source: Adapted from Appendix N, Report by Ross, NBVI, 66.

Notes:

1. The sicca rupee was subdivided into 16 annas = 64 paisa = 64 loads of cauris.
2. The total cost per piece as shown in the last column equals the price on the basis of which the paikars of the Dutch East India Company put out the contracts to the weavers. These prices were net prices and did not include the charges payable to the washermen, the rafugars employed to repair the muslins that might get damaged during bleaching, the brokerage of the dalals, the tolls payable at the aurungs, the cost of dressing and the cost of transport etc.

their losses by increasing the price charged to the weavers of the other buyers to the maximum extent possible.[22]

A broadly similar situation prevailed in respect of the wage rate of the weavers. The current high rate was attributable in the first place to the large quantity of the contracts being put out. But the more important factor at work was that the weavers working for the English essentially got practically nothing by way of wages with the result that in order to earn their minimum subsistence, they were obliged to ask the Dutch and others competing for their services but not in a position to dictate terms to them to pay a correspondingly higher wage rate. In the words of Johannes Mathias Ross, "We are thus obliged to pay for the English not only in respect of the weavers' wages but also the cost of the yarn, in addition to the aurung tolls etc. that the English charge us".[23]

Table 3 conveys a broad idea of the average monthly output per loom for different varieties of textiles in both the cotton textiles as well as the cotton and silk mixed textiles categories. The table assumes steady employment of the loom employing one master weaver together with three assistants further assisted by an unspecified amount of female and child labour in the family. As for the size of the pieces produced, unfortunately only the length is indicated which by and large conformed to the standard length of the pieces manufactured. As one would expect, the output was inversely related to quality (thus 5½ pieces of ordinary quality *dorias* being manufactured in a month as against 4 pieces of fine quality). An unweighted average across cotton as well as cotton and silk mixed varieties of all qualities of the standard size suggests a figure of 5⅔ pieces per loom per month giving an annual average of 68 pieces. But considering that, on an average, across each variety, a substantially larger number of ordinary quality textiles than fine or superfine quality textiles were manufactured, Ross put the average figure at 6 per month or 72 per annum. A further adjustment of this figure was necessitated, Ross pointed out, by the fact that sickness and a multiplicity of festivals often kept the weavers away from the looms. An average figure of 60 pieces per annum was, therefore, more realistic. On that basis, the figure of 3,223 looms specified in Table 1 would have yielded an annual output of 193,380 pieces across all varieties of textiles put together. But considering that the number of weavers and their assistants was no higher than

[22] Appendix N, Report by Ross, NBVI, 66.
[23] Appendix N, Report by Ross, NBVI, 66.

TABLE 3
Time Taken to Weave One Piece of Textile per Loom at the Haripal and Dhaniakhali Aurungs, 1767

Variety	Size (only length is indicated)	Superfine quality	Fine quality	Ordinary quality
Doria (cotton calico)	40 covids		7–8 days (4 pieces per month)	5–6 days (5½ pieces per month)
Malmal (cotton muslin)	"		"	"
Terrindam (cotton muslin)	"		"	"
Neusdoek (*rumal*) (cotton calico)	40 covids for fine and 32½ covids for ordinary		"	"
Sirsick (mixed silk and cotton)	24 covids	7–8 days (4 pieces per month)	5–6 days (5½ pieces per month)	4 days (7½ pieces per month)
Karraderrie (mixed silk and cotton)	20 covids	"	"	"
Rumal Sichtermans (cotton calico)	35 covids		"	
Ordinary varieties				"

Source: Adapted from Appendix O, Report by Ross, NBVI, 66.
Note: This assumes steady employment of a loom employing a master weaver and three assistants together with female and child helpers whose number is not specified.

a total of 5,582, the number of looms that could be put to use on the assumption of 4 persons to a loom would have been no higher than 1395½ yielding a total of 83,730 pieces. Finally, Ross pointed out, that if one went by the considered opinion of the knowledgeable persons in the area, the number of weavers and assistants could safely be put at 7,200 providing employment to 1,800 looms. On this basis, the average annual output in the two aurungs could be assumed to be around 108,000 pieces across all varieties of textiles.[24]

Another group of aurungs in the area for which quantitative information regarding the number of looms at work is available was that of Chandrakona and other aurungs in the vicinity. This information is summarized in Table 4.

[24] Report by Ross, NBVI, 66.

TABLE 4
Number of Looms at Work in the Aurungs of Chandrakona etc., 1767

Name of aurung	Number of looms reserved for the English	Effective number of looms available	Number of looms reportedly hidden
Chandrakona	903	896	200
Narrasjoul	231	300	50
Khirpai	350	350	50
Radhanagar	253	250	50
Ghatal	60	100	25
Udinaspur	50	50	10
Hajipur	50	60	10
Kolmisoor	0	15	0
Total	1,897	2,021	395

Source: Adapted from Appendix T, Report by Ross, NBVI, 66.

This group of aurungs lay to the south of those at Haripal and Dhaniakhali. While the Dutch carried out their procurement mainly at Chandrakona, the English trading station in the area was located at Khirpai. Similarly, the English counterpart of the Dutch procurement station at Narrasjoul was the village of Sammraat. All these centres including Haripal and Dhaniakhali were under the jurisdiction of Bardwan. Khirpai was part of the *jagir* of the Jagatseth family. Under the rubric of textile producing centres in this region, one could add Kasisjora which was under a minor raja. Legend has it that this centre was a major producer of textiles before bad management had drawn the producers to areas such as Chandrakona under the jurisdiction of Bardwan. At one point as many as 500 weavers used to operate there producing mainly for domestic consumption. Some of these weavers continued to operate there and transported their output clandestinely to the markets of Narrasjoul, Chandrakona and Khirpai. No gumashta or dalal operated from that centre any more.[25]

The aurung of Narrasjoul where the Dutch bought their textiles was adjacent to Kasisjora while the English procurement centre of Sammraat was next to the border of Bardwan. There were seven weaver villages in the neighbourhood accounting for around 300 looms. In addition to the local output, these two centres received a substantial amount of textiles from neighbouring areas. The Jagatseth family got its textiles manufactured in the area through special

[25] Report by Ross, NBVI, 66.

gumashtas. The bulk of the remaining output was acquired by the English leaving very little for the Dutch and the others.

In addition to manufacturing textiles for the Companies, this region also had about 500 looms catering exclusively to the markets of Mocha, Basra and Jidda in respect of textiles of varying length, width and prices. Each loom produced, on an average, 4 pieces per month. So in principle, the number of pieces supplied to these markets could be 24,000 per annum but the actual number was smaller because many of the weavers did not work full-time.[26]

Coming next to the aurung of Chandrakona, Ross reported that the villages and hamlets under this aurung amounted to 47 accounting for about 1,100 looms producing cotton textiles and 200 looms producing silk textiles. About 3 miles northward was Khirpai with 350 to 400 weavers. The nine paikars operating at Khirpai had many weavers also working for them at Radhanagar, Udairajpur, Duanghons, Kajipur etc. with 27 weavers even in Chandrakona. Radhanagar was about an hour's distance in the south-southeast of Khirpai. It had about a 1,000 looms and had traditionally been a major procurement centre for silk and mixed textiles produced in this entire region. It also had about 100 looms producing cotton textiles. It was well-known that the only major item procured by the Europeans in Radhanagar was *soosies*, a high quality silk textile. Other varieties produced there were mainly for sale in Surat, Mocha and Jidda etc. According to Ross's calculations, there were about 5,000 looms in Radhanagar producing silk and mixed textiles. At an average of 4 pieces per month, this would involve an annual output of 240,000 pieces worth around 15 lakhs of rupees at an average price of 6¼ rupees per piece.[27]

The English East India Company had declared raw silk produced in Bardwan, Medinipur and Kasisjora as a monopsony item. It bought raw silk from the farmers at 16 tolas per rupee and sold it to the weavers at 7 to 9 tolas per rupee. The large scale production of silk textiles had cut into the number of cotton textiles available to buyers who could not practice violence on the producers the way the English Company could.[28]

[26] Report by Ross, NBVI, 66.
[27] Report by Ross, NBVI, 66.
[28] Report by Ross, NBVI, 66.

IV

While all the European corporate enterprises—the Dutch, the English and the French—operated in the textile aurungs discussed above, by virtue of the political power enjoyed by it, the English East India Company (and by extension, the private English traders enjoying its protection) was in a category by itself. Before we go into the details of the manner in which the English grossly misused their position of authority and coerced the intermediary merchants and the weavers into working for them at terms substantially below the market, let us look at some quantitative data regarding English Company procurement available for the aurungs of Chandrakona, Khirpai and Radhanagar etc. Table 5 sets out the details of the contracts put out by the English Company at the aurungs of Chandrakona and Radhanagar etc. in the year 1767.

According to Table 5, the total number of pieces contracted for by the Company at the aurungs of Chandrakona, Khirpai and Radhanagar etc. in 1767 amounted to 28,700 pieces consisting of 15,450 pieces of *malmals*, 9,300 pieces of *dorias*, 250 pieces of *dassies* and 3,700 pieces of *soosies*. The *malmals* contracted for included 300 pieces of the usual length of 40 covids but a highly unusual large width of 3 covids. The prices for 1767 were, on an average, higher by 16 per cent than the ones for 1766. These prices were the net prices payable to the weavers and did not include the payment for the services of the washermen etc. It was stipulated in the contract that the prices indicated were in each case in respect of the first quality. Once the goods had been supplied they would be subject to be sorted into five qualities, each lower quality being evaluated at 6¼ per cent lower than the price of the quality immediately above it. Thus in the case of the wide muslins, against the price of Rs.24 for the first quality, the price paid would be 22:8 annas for the second, Rs.21 for the third, Rs.19:8 annas for the fourth, and Rs.18 per piece for the fifth quality respectively. Pieces not found good enough to qualify even for the fifth quality would be designated as 'firty' (ferretted) and would be priced at the discretion of the Company.[29] The contracts were distributed over a total of 41 paikars, the details regarding whom are summarized in Table 6.

[29] Appendix S, Report by Ross, NBVI, 66.

TABLE 5

Textiles Contracted for by the English East India Company together with their Prices at the Aurungs of Chandrakona, Khirpai and Radhanagar etc., in 1767

	Quantity (number of pieces)	Quality	Size (length & width in covids)	Last year's price per piece (in sicca rupees)	Current year's price per piece (in sicca rupees)	Value of current year's contracts (in sicca rupees)
a.	*Malmals* (fine cotton muslin)					
	300	fine	40,3	21	24	7,250
	1,000	"	40,2 1/4	16	18	18,000
	4,000	"	40,2	12	14	56,000
	750	"	40,2	13	15	11,250
	7,000	ordinary	40,2	8 1/2	11	77,000
	1,600	superfine	40,2	16 1/4	18	28,800
	800	Rasballabhpuria	40,2	13	15	12,000
Total	15,450					210,300
b.	*Dorias* (fine cotton calico)					
	3,000	fine broad stripes	40,2	12	14	42,000
	300	fine embroidered broad stripes	40,2	13	15	4,500
	1,000	small chequered	40,2	16	17	17,000
	2,000	big chequered	40,2	12	14	28,000
	3,000	ordinary	40,2	8 1/2	11	33,000
Total	9,300					124,500
c.	*Dassies* (coarse cotton calico)					
	250	small	40, 1/4	11	13	3,250
Total	250					3,250
d.	*Soosies* (fine quality silk textile)					
	1,850	diverse	40,2	8	10	18,500
	1,850	"	50,15/8	8	10	18,500
Total	3,700					37,000
Grand Total	28,700 pieces					375,050

Source: Adapted from Appendix S, Report by Ross, NBVI, 66.

TABLE 6

Distribution of English East India Company Contracts at Chandrakona etc. among Different Paikars, 1767

Name of Paikar	Number of pieces per month contracted for in 1766	Number of looms assigned to each paikar in 1766	Number of looms assigned to each paikar in 1767
a. At the aurung of Chandrakona (26 paikars)			
Kamdev Thakur	66	49	48
Raghudev Thakur	15	19	16
Janki Thakur	27	22	21
Gangaram Thakur	27	27	24
Hari Ghosal	21	18	18
Udit Thakur	18	19	19
Sadhu Kar	90	77	70
Jugal Poddar	75	57	60
Kaliram Hai	51	38	38
Gaurang Dutt	45	41	41
Govardhan Sarkar	45	40	40
Raghu Sarkar	24	25	27
Bhagirath Das	24	19	29
Motiram Poddar	24	21	21
Uknitjan Teli	30	20	22
Trilok Chaudhuri	45	28	30
Titu Sarkar	54	49	50
Trilok Sarkar	27	18	23
Lokicharan Chaudhuri	27	22	20
Jagannath Das	40	35	35
Sani Sarkar	30	29	29
Hit Kar	18	15	15
Ganesh Poddar	18	10	12
Jagannath Bairagi	15	70	12
Jugal Bari	17	8	9
Bairagidas Korni	27	26	26
Total	900	739	755
b. At the aurung of Khirpai (9 paikars)			
Sarveshwar Pahari	225	180	205
Kirparam Teli	90	72	70
Panju Datt	30	24	40
Sitaram Pal	30	24	25
Sunder Mahi	90	72	70
Manik Mondal	60	48	46
Baburam Poddar	60	48	50
Kashi Pal	30	24	25
Gokul Das	52½	42	40
Total	667½	534	571
c. At the aurung of Radhanagar (2 paikars)			
Jugal Chaudhuri	60	48	46
Motiram Dutt	30	22	25
Total	90	70	71

TABLE 6
Continued

Name of Paikar	Number of pieces per month contracted for in 1766	Number of looms assigned to each paikar in 1766	Number of looms assigned to each paikar in 1767
d. At the aurung of Ghatal (1 paikar)			
Dukhiram Doba	100	80	60
e. At the aurung of Udairajpur (1 paikar)			
Sarbjot Thakur	28	23	23
f. At the aurung of Ramjibanpur and Hajipur (1 paikar)			
Hiranand Chaudhuri	60	48	50
g. At the aurung of Sammraat (1 sarkar or gumashta being an employee of the English Company)			
(Name not given)	150	150	231
Grand Total	1,995½	1,644	1,761
For the current year (1767), the figure is 2,619 3/32 pieces per month (or 31,429⅛ pieces per annum) representing an increase, on an average, of little over 31 percent.			

Source: Adapted from Appendix U, Report by Ross, NBVI, 66.

According to Table 6, the number of pieces contracted for in the aurungs (or sub-aurungs) of Chandrakona, Khirpai, Radhanagar, Ghatal, Udairajpur, Ramjibanpur and Sammraat for the year 1766 was 23,946 (or 1,995½ per month) and for 1767, 31,429 pieces (or 2,619 3/32 pieces per month). The number of looms assigned for the purpose in 1766 was 1,644 as against 1,761 in 1767. What is very striking is the fact that these numbers suggest an obligation of providing, on an average, only 1.21 pieces per month per loom in 1766 and 1.48 pieces per month per loom in 1767. This is way below the average output of 5 pieces per month per loom suggested by Tables 1 and 3 above. Did this imply a tacit understanding between the Company and its paikars that in return for their overall cooperation in the matter of the supply of the Company's textile requirements, they would be allotted a loom capacity substantially in excess of that needed for meeting the Company's requirements. This excess capacity could then be diverted to meet the textile requirements of other buyers and markets substantially enhancing the overall business and the profit margin of these paikars. In the absence of firm information, however, this must remain only a speculative hypothesis.

What the table also suggests is a considerable variation in the number of pieces/looms allotted to individual paikars both across aurungs as well as within an aurung. Thus while in the aurung of Chandrakona, a total of 900 pieces per month was allotted to 26 paikars giving an average of 34.61 pieces per paikar, the corresponding numbers in the aurung of Khirpai were 667 pieces to only 9 paikars giving an average of as many as 74.11 pieces or more than twice the average of Chandrakona. There were also considerable variations across individuals. The person to whom the biggest contract (225 pieces per month and 205 looms) was awarded was one Sarveshwar Pahari at Khirpai. The smallest contract was for 17 pieces with 9 looms at Chandrakona. The number of looms assigned to individuals registered very little change between 1766 and 1767 except in a case such as that of Panju Datt in Khirpai where against 24 looms assigned in 1766, the number was increased to 40 in 1767. It is not entirely clear why the contract at the aurung of Sammraat was given to a sarkar (or gumashta) of the Company rather than to a paikar with a substantially enhanced number of looms being assigned to him. Finally, an analysis of the names of the paikars to whom the contracts were given shows that all of them were Hindus, mostly ethnic Bengalis, but also including the names of some Marwaris who had migrated from Rajasthan at some point. These persons, carrying the last name of Poddar, figured in the list of paikars for both Chandrakona and Khirpai. As we noted earlier, Khirpai was part of the *jagir* of the Jagatseth family, also a Marwari immigrant to Bengal.

The English East India Company's procurement of textiles in the aforementioned aurungs was coordinated by John Bitter, the Company's Commercial Resident at Khirpai. The first thing that he ordered after arriving at the Residency was a survey of the weavers and the looms available in the area and the number of pieces of textiles manufactured, on an average, in a year. He also ordered an estimate of the number of pieces contracted for and received during the preceding year by the Dutch and the French East India Companies, the English, Dutch and French private traders as well as the Indian traders. Finally, he wanted an estimate of the contracts already put out by each of these entities during the current year and the funds already invested.[30] He next ordered all the paikars supplying the English Company to appear before him to explain why the quality of the pieces delivered the

[30] Letter from Ross at Khirpai to Vernet at Hughli dated 18 July 1767, Appendix P, Report by Ross, NBVI, 66. This letter is also available in the "Memorandum concerning the principal reasons why the Dutch East India Company's trade in Bengal, particularly in textiles, has not been proceeding satisfactorily" prepared by George Louis Vernet and presented to the English governor Harry Verelst dated 10 May 1768, NA, *Hooge Regering Batavia* (HRB), 247, Appendix D. The volume is not foliated.

previous year had been not as good as of those supplied to the Dutch Company. The suppliers simply pointed out that the Dutch paid a 25% higher price. They also pointed out that it would be impossible to supply the same number of pieces (namely 21,590) as last year. The total output in the area was no higher than 42,500 pieces per annum and Bitter could expect to procure a large part of it only if he ordered the rival companies, their private traders as well as the Indian traders to leave the area. The 41 paikars listed in Table 6 were then held in detention and asked to provide the quantity listed against each in the table. Against the total requirement of 25,000 pieces (Table 5 not counting the 3,700 pieces of *soosies*), the paikars were obliged to provide a total of 31,429 pieces, the excess of 6,429 pieces being reserved for the poor-quality 'firty' pieces. Each paikar was ordered to sign a paper agreeing to supply the number of pieces recorded against his name. On refusal, each was administered ten canes on his naked skin and put in jail. They were told that if they did not sign the paper, Bitter knew of other ways to deal with them. Ross was shocked at this kind of treatment being meted out to paikars of stature, many of whom possessed assets worth Rs. 100,000 or more. After the lapse of a few days, these people came round and signed the papers. Before leaving for Sonamukhi, Bitter appointed Motiram Mohan Basak, the brother of head gumashta Radha Mohan Basak, as the first gumashta of the aurung and instructed him to ensure that each of the paikars scrupolously kept to the supply schedule agreed to by him. Ross described this man as "a rogue and a scroundrel". He treated the paikars with extreme harshness and had even whipped a paikar to death. Ross provided an instance of Basak's behaviour towards the paikars. When a paikar brought his three pieces of textiles which he was obliged to deliver daily to Basak, while two of the pieces were found to be of passable quality, the third was found to be short of its supposed width of 2¼ covids. The punishment inflicted on him was to make him rub his nose on the ground several times for a distance of 2¼ covids. He was told that he was being let off with this minor punishment because this was his first offence. The piece was returned to him with the instruction that a replacement be provided the same day before sunset. The man was obliged to buy the replacement piece from another paikar at a price four rupees higher than what he was due to receive from the English Company.[31]

[31] Ross to Vernet, 18 July 1767, Appendix P, Report by Ross, NBVI, 66; HRB 247, Appendix D.

The behaviour of the paikars towards the weavers was no better. In one instance, three weavers had reportedly brought to a paikar one piece each of a quality that the latter dared not deliver to the English head gumashta. The pieces were then tied around the necks of the weavers who were told to provide immediate replacements by buying them from others. They were escorted to their respective homes with the pieces tied around their necks by peons whose costs also they were made to reimburse.[32]

The terms and conditions the English East India Company imposed on its paikars were substantially below market. An idea of the extent of such exploitation would perhaps be conveyed by the fact that for a piece of cotton textile for which the Dutch East India Company would have offered Rs.16, the average price paid by the English East India Company was no higher than Rs.12 or 75 per cent of the Dutch price. According to Ross, this proportion would have been valid across the board. The terms of supply and evaluation were equally harsh. The pieces received from the paikars were subjected to an initial sorting from quality one to five and sent to the washermen, engaged by the Company's gumashta, for bleaching. They were then subjected to a second sorting before being sent on to the *rafugars* (the artisans engaged to repair any damage caused in the process of bleaching). The pieces were then subjected to yet another bleach before being sorted a third time. At this point, the pieces were sent on to Khirpai, chief factory of the region where the fourth round of sorting was carried out. The fifth and final round of sorting was reserved for Calcutta. As mentioned earlier, ordinarily the price paid for each descending quality on a scale of 1 to 5 was 6¼ per cent lower than that for the immediately preceding one. Pieces not found good enough to make even quality five were rejected as 'firty' (ferretted).[33]

A rough idea of what the Company subjected the paikars and the weavers to can be formed by the fact that pieces classified as third quality would gladly have been accepted by the Dutch Company as first quality at a considerably higher price. It is remarkable that even the pieces rejected by the Company as 'firty' had a profitable market. This margin was shared clandestinely between the Commercial Resident, the chief gumashta, and the paikars. To take an example from 1767,

[32] Ross to Vernet, 18 July 1767, Appendix P, Report by Ross, NBVI, 66; HRB 247, Appendix D.

[33] Ross to Vernet, 18 July 1767, Appendix P, Report by Ross NBVI, 66; HRB 247, Appendix D.

Resident John Bitter rejected 896 pieces of textiles as 'firty' that year. Many of these pieces were eventually sold by the paikars in the open market at between Rs.6½ and Rs.7 per piece higher than the price at which they had been evaluated by Company's factors before being rejected. Bitter had returned the pieces to the paikars after keeping a margin of Rs.3 per piece for himself and Rs.½ per piece for the chief gumashta Radha Mohan Basak. But even after paying Rs.3½ extra, the paikars managed to earn a net profit of Rs.3 to Rs.3½ per piece in the market for themselves.[34]

The suppliers of textiles at Khirpai estimated that the maximum that the group of aurungs under this English trading station could supply in the course of a year was around 50,000 pieces. The contracts put out by the English Company in 1767 amounted to 31,429 pieces (Table 6). The Dutch East India Company's contracts for the year were estimated at 8,100 pieces and of the French Company at 2,000 pieces, making a total of 41,529 pieces. That left a total of 8,471 pieces for all the private European traders, the Armenians as well as the Indian merchants put together. The English Company was likely to get the number of pieces that it had given out contracts for. The next group with political muscle was that of the private English traders enjoying the protection of the Company. As pointed out earlier, the cause of this group was further helped by the fact that they were quite indifferent to the quality of the pieces received as well as the cost of those pieces as long as they were able to earn a return of 9 per cent per annum on their investment. These traders, whose number was estimated at 37, were reported to have brought in as much as Rs.350,000 for investment in textiles in the area. This represented only half of the total of Rs.700,000 worth of textiles that they aimed to procure during the year. At an average cost of Rs.12 per piece, this would amount to a whopping 59,000 pieces. According to Ross's calculations, for a piece for which the English Company would pay Rs.10 and the Dutch East India Company Rs.12:7 annas, the private English traders would be willing to pay as much as Rs.14. it was, therefore, not surprising that these traders were the most preferred buyers for any clandestine supplies available with the paikars.[35]

[34] Ross to Vernet, 18 July 1767, Appendix P, Report by Ross, NBVI, 66; HRB 247, Appendix D.
[35] Ross to Vernet, 18 July 1767, Appendix P, Report by Ross, NBVI, 66; HRB 247, Appendix D.

The supplies left for the Dutch and the French East India Companies and others including the Indian traders were, therefore, quite meagre. Indeed, Ross suspected that the best that they were likely to be able to do was to get between one-eigthth and one-fourth of the total that they had intended to buy and in fact had given out contracts for during the year. In view of this situation, the paikars dealing with the intermediary merchants who had accepted the Dutch contracts indeed offered to return the money taken in advance because they believed that the weavers could still be persuaded to return the advances given to them. Given the way the English were dealing with the paikars and the weavers, the latter were likely to be affected most adversely. They claimed that on the pieces prepared for the English, not only did they get no recompense for their efforts, but in fact lost one to two rupees on the cost of the yarn that went into each piece. A delegation of weavers proceeded to Calcutta with a petition (*arzi*) requesting that the prices offered to them be increased by at least so much as to meet their costs and afford them a subsistence wage. They did manage to obtain an order directing John Bitter to do the needful. But this evidently was no more than an eyewash because Bitter not only openly disregarded the order but indeed threatened to have the weavers arrested in the event that they continued with their efforts. The phenomenon of the weavers running away from their looms and villages was, therefore, increasingly becoming a grim reality. According to a letter from Ross at Khirpai to his superiors at Hughli written on 18 July 1767, 26 weavers had fled from their looms over the preceding eight days while the flight of another 23 was imminent. When the administrator of the Jagatseth's *jagir* in the area sought the banker's intervention in the matter, the latter pleaded total inability to do anything about the English oppression.[36]

V

The extension of English power in the second half of the eighteenth century in various parts of the subcontinent was clearly a circumstance of great import from the point of view of the Indian textile manufacturing industry. In a region such as Bengal, there was a marked deterioration in the relative share in the total value of the

[36] NA, Ross at Khirpai to Vernet at Hughli, 18 July 1767, HRB 247, Appendix C_2.

textile output as far as the Bengali artisanal and the mercantile groups engaged in business with the English East India Company were concerned. This was a necessary corollary of the replacement of a market-determined relationship between the Company and these groups until about 1760 by a relationship marked by a clear-cut domination by the Company in the decades that followed. It is, however, critically important to keep the matter in perspective and clearly distinguish between the distributive justice dimension and the implications for the total output dimension of this development. It is perfectly likely that the robbing of the producers and the merchants of a part of what was legitimately due to them would have introduced some distortions in the incentive structure in the domain of manufacturing production in the textile sector. That would almost certainly have had a certain amount of negative impact on the output produced by the groups associated with the Company. But the scale of this decline as a proportion of total textile output in the province does not seem to have been anywhere near disastrous.

For one thing, the volume and value of the textile trade carried on by the Europeans from Bengal in the second half of the eighteenth century was certainly no smaller than it was in the first half; in fact it would seem to have been substantially larger. This was because the decline in the rival companies' trade—particularly that by the Dutch East India Company—was much more than made up for by the massive increase in the textile trade carried on by the English East India Company and the private English traders. Thus the annual value of the Bengal goods, of which textiles constituted a very important part, exported by the English Company rose from an average of £400,000 in the 1760s to as much as £1,000,000 and above in the 1770s and the 1780.[37] At the same time, Indian merchants continued to control the bulk of the textile trade between Bengal and other parts of the subcontinent as well as that between Bengal and other parts of Asia. Large quantities of cotton were being simultaneously carried from the Deccan to Bengal partly for use as raw material in the textile sector in the province. The picture of a ruined textile industry in Bengal which is sometimes portrayed in the literature does not, therefore, quite conform to the evidence available. This is not to suggest that the textile sector in the province would not have experienced a certain amount

[37] Om Prakash, *European Commercial Enterprise in Pre-colonial India*, p. 348; P. J. Marshall, *Bengal: The British Bridgehead, Eastern India 1740–1828*, vol. II.2 in the *New Cambridge History of India* series, Cambridge, 1987, pp. 104–05.

of dislocation in response to the pressures the English Company put on the intermediary merchant and the artisanal groups in the sector but only that the sector was resilient enough to adjust to the pressures and manage to survive intact. It was only in the nineteenth century, particularly in the second half, that the impact of the British cotton textile industry was felt with its full force by the Indian handloom sector. But even for that period, the desirability of keeping an open mind on the precise turn of events is strongly suggested by research done over the last few decades.

XIV

Long Distance Trade, Coinage and Wages in India, 1600-1960

A growing degree of monetization and an increasing use of wage labour have historically been among the more important ingredients of the process of transformation that the present day developed economies experienced in the course of their economic development. Growing monetization signified an ever-larger proportion of the total transactions being conducted in the monetized sector involving, in turn, a continuously rising supply of money in the economy. Since money consisted overwhelmingly, if not exclusively, of metals - both precious and non-precious-, the supply of money, in turn, came to be linked in a critical manner with the supply of the relevant metals. In the case of many countries, the supply of metals, particularly precious metals, was significantly dependent on imports.

Growing monetization was usually accompanied by a rising proportion of the total work force in the economy being employed on a money wage basis. While the wage rate itself would be a function of the demand and supply of the particular category of labour in question at any given point in time, the logistics of wage payments could be an important factor in determining the mix of coins of different denominations manufactured in the economy. If the norm of payment to wage labour was weekly rather than monthly, for example, a much larger component of the total coin output would probably be in smaller denomination coins. The norm of wage payment would, of course, itself be a function of both economic and non-economic factors. Consumption patterns in any society would also be subject to influence by the norm for wage payment.

Against the background of these very general observations, what was the situation like in India over the last half a millennium or so? At the very outset, it would be useful to distinguish between the pre-colonial and the early-colonial period (1600-1800) on the one hand and the colonial period

(1800-1947) on the other. This is partly because there are major differences as between these two periods in the matter of the availability of data on various economic indices, both quantitative as well as qualitative. Also, the considerations governing the output of coins and the supply of money in the economy in general were very different in the two periods. For the period between 1500 and 1800, I will argue that there was indeed a very strong causal link between long distance trade and the supply of money in the economy. This link worked through the overwhelming, indeed almost total, dependence of India during this period on imports for the supply of precious metals and to a smaller extent for that of non-precious metals including copper. As a consequence of the growing involvement of India in the early modern world economy during these centuries, there was a very large inflow of precious metals into the country with important consequences for the supply of money and the degree of monetization. One of the consequences of the accelerated pace of monetization would have been the use of wage labour on an increased scale. While the available qualitative evidence would strongly support these hypotheses, there is a great paucity of data for the period until 1800 relating to both the supply of money as well as the scale of wage employment, the usual wage rate and the frequency with which money wage payments were actually made.

The situation was completely different in the nineteenth and the first half of the twentieth century when India was under British colonial rule. As the export of Indian textiles to the West collapsed under the impact of the Industrial Revolution, India ceased to be a net recipient of precious metals from abroad. Indeed in the 1930s, large amounts of gold were exported from India to Britain on commodity account. Also, from 1893 onwards, Indian coinage ceased to be 'free' coinage and the rupee became a token coin. But while the link between long distance trade and coinage got increasingly snapped, the information base regarding the supply of money and its breakdown into currency and coins denomination improves considerably during this period. On the question of wage employment and wage rate also, the data availability during the nineteenth and the twentieth centuries is much better. But there is very little information on the logistics of the wage payments, particularly on the link between frequency of wage payment and the denomination mix of the coin/currency output. An important reason for this would seem to be that the principal unit of account in the Indian coinage, namely the rupee, was a relatively small value coin in the context of the nineteenth century levels of prices and wages. The need for smaller denomination coins was correspondingly much smaller than in the earlier period when a large part of

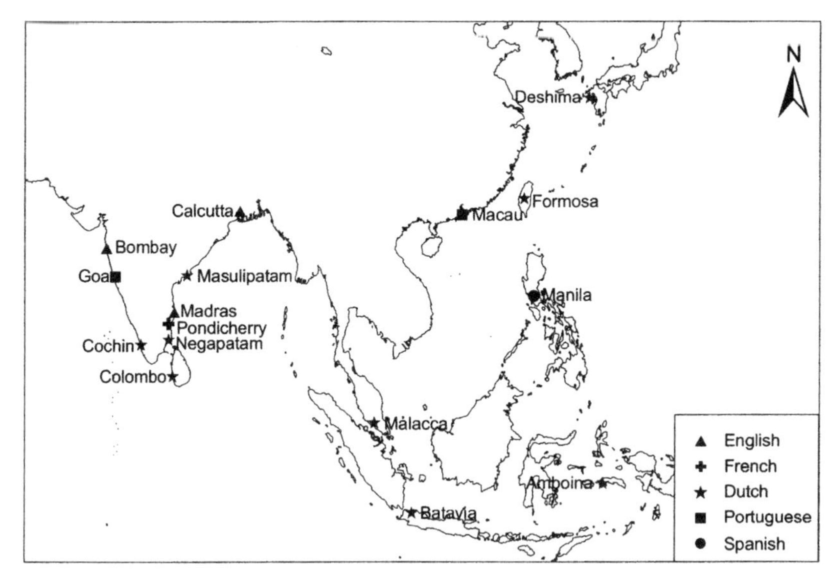

Map 13.1. Important European settlements in Asia 1650-1780

the total coin output would seem to have consisted of copper *dams* or *paisas*. Indeed, in addition to standardized money consisting of gold, silver and copper coins, Mughal India witnessed an extensive use of the so-called 'humble' money such as *cauris* (sea-shells), bitter almonds and so on to settle small value transactions including wage payments.

Long Distance Trade, Precious Metals and Coinage

In a well-known passage in his magnum opus, *An Enquiry into the Nature and Causes of the Wealth of Nations*, Adam Smith, the father of modern economic science, argued that "the discovery of America and that of a passage to the East Indies by the Cape of Good Hope are the two greatest and most important events recorded in the history of mankind"[1]. While there clearly is an element of exaggeration in this statement, it nevertheless underscores the critical role of the two events in the emergence of an early modern world economy. The three principal segments of this economy, namely Europe, the New World, and Asia came together for the first time directly as a result of the

1 Smith, *Wealth of Nations*, II, p. 139.

great discoveries of the last decade of the fifteenth century. Unlike in the case of the New World, there had been a certain amount of interaction between Europe and Asia since antiquity and there is evidence to suggest that regular trade relations between the two continents went back at least to the early years of the Christian era.

What the discovery of the all-water route via the Cape of Good Hope achieved was the overcoming of the transport-technology barrier to the growth of the Euro-Asian trade. The volume of this trade was no longer subject to the capacity constraint imposed by the availability of pack animals and river boats in the Middle East. It was indeed a critically important coincidence that the discovery of the Cape route and of the New World took place almost simultaneously. For without the enormous quantities of American silver reaching Europe through the sixteenth century, the enhanced trading opportunities between Europe and Asia opened up by the Cape route would essentially have been frustrated. Euro-Asian trade had traditionally been one involving the exchange of Asian luxury and other goods basically against European silver and, to a smaller extent, gold. This 'bullion for goods' pattern of trade was an outcome of the inability of Europe to supply goods that could be sold in Asia in reasonably large quantities at competitive terms. Europe at this time had an undoubted overall superiority over Asia in the field of scientific and technological knowledge, but not as yet the distinct cost advantage that came with the Industrial Revolution in the late eighteenth and nineteenth centuries. This put the Asian, and particularly the Indian producers, with their considerably lower labour costs and a much longer history of sophisticated skills in handicrafts of various kinds, in a position of advantage over their European counterparts in the production of a variety of manufactured goods. As a result, Europe really had no option but to pay for the Asian goods overwhelmingly in terms of precious metals. Ever since the fourteenth century or so, the output of precious metals in Europe had by and large been stagnant, raising fears of deflationary tendencies cropping up. This, coupled with the bullionist inhibitions regarding the export of precious metals, would almost certainly have created a situation where the non-availability of significant additional quantities of precious metals for export to the East would by and large have rendered the opportunities opened up by the availability of the Cape route quite redundant. It is in this context that one must appreciate the critical significance of the two great discoveries - that of the New World and of the Cape route to the East Indies - having taken place almost simultaneously. It is from this time onward that one can legitimately speak of the emergence of an early modern world economy embracing in an organic and interactive manner all three of its principal components, namely the New World, Europe, and Asia.

In so far as the trade along the all-water route in the course of the sixteenth century was by and large not at the expense of the trade along the older water-cum-land route except perhaps in the early years of the century, the Cape route did lead to a fairly substantial expansion in the overall volume and value of the Euro-Asian trade. However, it was only after the English and the Dutch were able to remove the Portuguese stranglehold over the Cape route at the beginning of the seventeenth century that the really substantive expansion in the value of Euro-Asian trade began. The English East India Company, established in the year 1600, and even more so the Dutch East India Company chartered two years later, acted as the principal agents of this expansion, assisted later in the century by the French East India Company founded in 1664. Other European enterprises such as the Danish East India Company, the Ostend Company and so forth remained essentially on the fringes.

I would like to emphasize that my formulation of the early modern world economy is very different from Immanuel Wallerstein's construct of 'world economies' based on a 'world-systems' perspective. The space available to me does not permit a proper evaluation of Wallerstein's theory but it might nevertheless be useful to recall some of the key features of his analysis. The world-systems perspective embraces the notion of both 'world-empires' as well as of 'world-economies'. A world-system, whether it is a world-economy or a world-empire, however, does not have to include the whole world so that there can simultaneously exist several world-empires as well as world-economies. A given world-economy can thus have areas external to it. There have existed in the past many world-economies, most of which became world-empires and then failed: sooner or later an imperium expanded to fill the geographical space of this economy[2].

The capitalist European world-economy, the focus of Wallerstein's analysis, arose during the period between 1450 and 1600. By the latter date, the core of this world-economy was located in north-western Europe. Spanish America and Eastern Europe (Poland and Hungary) were peripheries, but Persia, the Ottoman and Russian world-empires, the Indian Ocean area and the Far East were external to it. This world-economy had trade relations with its external areas to be sure, but since these relations were based only on preciosities, these areas were not yet incorporated into it. Some of these external areas were themselves world-economies or proto-world-economies. South

2 Wallerstein, *The Modern World-System*, I, ch. 7.

Asia (also referred to as the Indian Ocean area) was one such world-economy which got incorporated into the capitalist European world-economy only after the middle of the eighteenth century.

According to Wallerstein then, in the early modern period while South America was peripheral to the capitalist European world-economy, the Indian Ocean area was external to it. This was notwithstanding the fact that precious metals (mainly silver extracted from the mines of Potosí and Mexico) were at the heart of the commercial relations between both Europe and the New World as well as those between Europe and Asia. The rationale of this evidently consisted in the fact that while in one case Europe received the critically indispensable precious metals, in the other it lost them to its trading partner. Without bullion

> Europe would have lacked the collective confidence to develop a capitalist system, wherein profit is based on various deferrals of realized value. This is *a fortiori* true given the system of a nonimperial world-economy which, for other reasons, was essential. Given this phenomenon of collective psychology, an integral element of the social structure of the time, bullion must be seen as an essential crop for a prospering world-economy[3].

This is what made South America so valuable. In Wallerstein's words,

> The production of gold and silver as a commodity made the Americas a peripheral area of the European world-economy insofar as this commodity was essential to the operation of this world-economy, and it was essential to the extent that it was used as money. Had the bullion of the Americas all flowed out to Asia, the Americas would have been just another external arena and Europe would have been merely an axis of three arenas – America, Europe, and Asia – obtaining its Asian luxuries at the price of the goods sent to the Americas. But the Americas were not interested in exchanging their bullion, and surely not in mining it. Therefore, the Europeans first seized Inca gold, then mined Potosi and Mexican silver, seeking ever-new mining areas (of which Brazilian gold would soon be the most important). They sent settlers to control the area of the Americas politically and to supervise the economic operations, and they imported labour as well. In short, they incorporated the Americas into their world-economy, primarily because they needed a solid currency base for an

3 *Ibid.*, I, p. 46.

> expanding capitalist system and secondarily to use the surplus in trade with Asia.[4]

Asia, on the other hand, remained external to the European world-economy because all that was received from that continent were non-essential luxury goods - first spices and then the 'calicoes of the East Indies'. To quote Wallerstein yet once again,

> At this epoch, the relationship of Europe and Asia might be summed up as the exchange of preciosities. The bullion flowed east to decorate the temples, palaces, and clothing of Asian aristocratic classes and the jewels and spices flowed west. The accidents of cultural history (perhaps nothing more than physical scarcity) determined these complementary preferences[5].

The reason I have quoted Wallerstein at such great length is not really because I am particularly concerned one way or the other about his classification of the New World as a periphery and of Asia as external to his capitalist European world-economy in the early modern period. What I indeed am concerned with is the widely presumed otherness of Asia as clearly brought out in the quotations from Wallerstein above. When imported into northwestern Europe, gold and silver was a commodity "essential to the operation of this world-economy". But when imported into Asia, the same commodity becomes an item of luxury consumption used "to decorate the temples, palaces, and clothing of Asian aristocratic classes". In the case of Europe, the essential character of the import derived from its use as money: in Asia, this valuable asset was frittered away by being used "for hoarding or jewelry"[6]. Wallerstein is in very respectable company here. This is what the American scholar, Rudolph Blitz, has to say, "In the Orient much of the specie went promptly into hoards or was demonetized and became a commodity satisfying the oriental penchant for ornaments".[7] I believe that such a clear-cut dichotomy is indeed quite untenable and does not conform to a wide body of evidence available to us. Asia certainly was different from Europe but not necessarily in the matter of the role of imported precious metals in the long-term functioning of her constituent economies. And indeed whatever differences might have existed in this regard might not all have simply been a

4 *Ibid.*, II, p. 109.

5 *Ibid.*, I, p. 41.

6 Sperling, "The International Payments Mechanism", p. 450. Quoted in Wallerstein, *The Modern World System*, II, p. 109.

7 Blitz, "Mercantilist Policies and the Pattern of World Trade", p. 40.

reflection of some mystic and implicitly irrational "Oriental penchant for ornaments".

Before I come to the case of India, let me briefly quote William Atwell on late Ming China. According to Atwell,

> Japanese and Spanish-American silver may well have been the most significant factor in the vigorous economic expansion which occurred in China during the period in question. This is true not only because of its direct impact on the silk and porcelain industries, although this clearly was of great importance, but also because an increase in the country's stock of precious metals upon which economic growth and business confidence seem to have depended would have been determined almost entirely by how much silver entered the country through foreign trade.[8]

There can be very little doubt that imported precious metals had traditionally played a similarly central role in the functioning of the Indian economy. The domestic production of these metals had always been marginal in India and the internal needs of the economy for coinage, consumption, and other purposes had overwhelmingly been met through imports. Until the sixteenth century, the Middle East, which itself obtained the bulk of its supplies from Europe via the Levant, was the principal source of these imports. It was indeed not without reason that the port of Mocha on the Red Sea was often described as the 'treasure-chest' of the Mughal empire. Following the discovery of the all-water route via the Cape of Good Hope and the arrival of the Portuguese in India, the Spanish-American silver also began arriving into India directly. Another important development characterizing the sixteenth and the first half of the seventeenth century was the emergence of Japan as by far the largest Asian source of both gold and silver. Through the agency of the Portuguese private traders operating under the so-called concession system, India was among the first major recipients of the Japanese precious metals. With the large scale participation of the Dutch East India Company in the seventeenth century in intra-Asian trade as an integral part of its overall trading strategy, the volume of Japanese silver and gold reaching India through the agency of the Company became extremely large, sometimes even exceeding the quantities imported from Holland. A good amount of the Japanese silver also reached China through the agency of the Chinese merchants, who apart from the Dutch, constituted the only group of foreign merchants allowed to come to Japan during the latter's 'closed-country' era. The growing integra-

8 Atwell, "Notes on Silver, Foreign Trade, and the Late Ming Economy", p. 5.

tion of Asia into the world economy was clearly being accompanied by a growing integration of constituent economies within Asia[9].

What impact did the growing import of precious metals into India as a result of her increasing involvement in the early modern world economy have on her economy and society? We have seen above that scholars such as Wallerstein and Blitz would have us believe that unlike in the case of early modern Europe, the growing availability of these metals in an Asian society would simply have involved either an increased conspicuous consumption of these metals on the part of the aristocracy and other rich sections of the society besides their growing use in the temples, or their simply being hoarded in response to an 'Oriental penchant'. The kind of effect associated with the import of these metals into Europe would therefore not have materialized in an Asian society. By far the most concrete of these effects in the case of Europe was the so-called 'price revolution' of the sixteenth century. A similar response is ruled out in the case of Asia for the simple reason that the first link in the chain, namely an increase in the supply of money, would not have come about in the Asian economies.

In my opinion such a view is quite unjustified and needs to be revised drastically. It would seem to me that in its essentials, the situation in Asia was not very different from that in Europe. There is first of all the question of the supply of money responding to a rise in the stock of precious metals in the system. I would like to suggest that the money supply in an Asian economy such as Mughal India was fully reflective of changes in her stock of gold and silver. The treasure imported by Indian merchants into the country was against goods they had sent out the previous season, and which they ostensibly would need to invest in the procurement of goods to be sent out in the next round. Similarly, the treasure brought in by foreign merchants, including the European trading companies, was intended for investment in Indian silks, textiles and other goods. In so far as foreign coins were not allowed to circulate in India, the very first step that would need to be taken by these merchants in the matter of raising the necessary purchasing power would be the conversion of the imported bullion and coins into Mughal Indian rupees. This could be done either through professional dealers in money known as *sarrafs* or by recourse to one of the imperial mints in the empire. In either event, there would be an automatic and corresponding increase in the supply of money in the economy. It is, of course, perfectly possible that a part of the increased money supply might eventually have been hoarded or withdrawn from active circulation. But in the present state of our knowledge, it would

9 Glahn, *Fountain of Fortune*; Richards, *Precious Metals*.

probably be futile to surmise on how significant or marginal this phenomenon might have been. Some observations could nevertheless be made in this behalf. In any society, hoarding of precious metals in the form of bullion or coins would be a function of the structure of asset preferences. Given the virtual absence of deposit banking facilities in Mughal India, hoarding on a reasonable scale can very well be interpreted as a perfectly legitimate and rational form of holding liquidity. The point is that the implied irrationality in the 'Oriental penchant' kind of story might in fact never have been there except perhaps at the margin.

A growing supply of money in response to a continuing import of precious metals would presumably have had implications for the functioning of an Asian economy along lines not necessarily very different from those in Europe. I have already referred to William Atwell describing Japanese and Spanish-American silver pouring into late Ming China as possibly "the most significant factor in the vigorous economic expansion" which occurred in that country. The economic growth and business confidence associated with a rising stock of precious metals that Atwell talks of in relation to China would certainly not seem to have been confined to that country. In the case of Mughal India, for example, it would seem that the rising supply of money was leading to a significant acceleration in the process of monetization in the economy so characteristic of the period. The well-known growing monetization of the land-revenue demand during the period was clearly a part of this larger process. Another significant feature of the Mughal Indian economy was the rise of banking firms all over the empire dealing in extremely sophisticated instruments of credit. Many of these firms had enormous resources at their command. Probably the best known of these was the house of the Jagat Seths, operating from its headquarters at Murshidabad in Bengal.[10] Along with its other activities, the firm organized the transfer of Delhi's share in the land revenues collected in the province. I need hardly stress that there was an important organic link between the rise in the money supply and the growth of the banking firms in the Mughal Indian economy.

In the domain of employment, growing monetization facilitated the payment of wages in money to a growing proportion of the total work force. Logistics of wage payments would seem to be an important consideration in determining the mix of the coin output. Since paying the wages of an average workman on a daily, weekly or even monthly basis in terms of the principal coin of the Mughals, namely the silver rupee, would have been an impractical proposition, copper coins constituted a substantial proportion of the total

10 Little, *The House of Jagatseth*.

Mughal Indian coin output. This output consisted of coins of three metals - the gold *muhr*, the silver rupee and the copper *dam* or *paisa*. The basic coin constituting the principal unit of account was the silver rupee. The gold *muhr* was used mainly either for ceremonial purposes or for hoarding. The copper *dam* or *paisa* constituted a major medium of handling small-value transactions and was used extensively. A distinguishing feature of Mughal coinage was the extraordinarily high content of the relevant metal of a very high degree of purity in the coin. Thus the gold *muhr*, which weighted 169 grains troy, was practically of unalloyed metal of high purity. The alloy content in the silver rupee, which weighted 178 grains until Aurangzeb raised the weight to 180 grains, was also never more than about 4 percent. The copper *dam* weighted 323 grains till 1663-4 when its weight was reduced to about two thirds of this figure. The coins were manufactured in imperial mints spread all over the empire. The procedure followed was that of 'free' mintage under which any-one could bring bullion, old coins or foreign coins to a mint and obtain after a lapse of time new coins in exchange. The number of coins delivered against a given quantity of metal depended upon the purity level of the metal sur-rendered. This was determined at the mint. A charge was made at the mint to cover the seigniorage, the loss of metal in the process of coining, and the cost of coining, which consisted partly of the cost of the necessary ingredients and partly that of the labour involved. As far as the question of the relative valu-ation of the coin of one metal in terms of each of the other two was con-cerned, this was left entirely to the market, and depended upon the relative market supply and demand of each of the three metals.[11]

In the case of the silver rupee, the new coin delivered by the mint was known as the *sicca* rupee. The value of this coin corresponded broadly to the value of the metal contained in it, plus the minting charges including sei-gniorage. The problem of wear and tear of a coin through use was tackled ingeniously by a complex system of equivalence based on a varying degree of premium being enjoyed by a new coin over older issues. The *sicca* rupee, defined as a coin minted during the current or the previous year, enjoyed such a premium over all older issues which routinely carried the year of issue on them. The rate of this premium was controlled for all practical purposes by a class of highly experienced and influential money dealers known as *sarrafs*. Once the premium enjoyed by a new over an earlier issue exceeded a thresh-old level, the old coin would simply be brought to the mint for recoinage. This would be encouraged by the government in so far as its income from seigniorage would go up. Since the coins were intrinsic and not token coins,

11 Prakash, "On coinage in Mughal India", pp. 475-491.

the problem of debasement of coins did not plague Mughal coinage. It also seems that forgery of coins was generally not a major problem.

The Mughal coinage system involved monetary management by the state only in a limited way. The accretions to the supply of money were determined by the public itself subject to the availability of metals in the system and the capacity of the imperial mints. In this regard, the government was formally no different from any other member of the public except that its resource base was naturally larger than that of any private individual and the minting of its bullion would get priority. Further, the government could, and did, occasionally exercise its authority in directing the use of a particular metal for coinage. Thus in 1657 when an increase in the demand for copper coins in Surat took the rupee:*paisa* ratio to 1:40, while in 1642 it had stood at only 1:56, the *mutasaddi* (local governor) of Surat ruled that all copper imported into the city should be taken directly to the mint. In order to facilitate this, he banned the movement of the metal bought by the indigenous merchants from the Dutch East India Company (which was by far the single largest importer of this metal into the Mughal empire, mainly from Japan) to places outside the city. This ban remained in force over the two succeeding years.[12] Mughal imperial mints were scattered all over the empire, though clearly some were more important than others, in terms of both the number of coins manufactured as well as the geographical area within the empire over which the issues of a mint ordinarily circulated. It is also important to realize that while the business of all the imperial mints was the crafting of refined metal into coins, this could be done under different entrepreneurial and technical arrangements. The available information suggests the existence of at least two distinct models along which the structure of a Mughal imperial mint was organized. The dominant model would seem to have been the one where Mughal state officials organized the work of production themselves. The alternative organizational arrangement involved the entrepreneurial function being delegated to the *sarrafs*. What was common to the two patterns was the strict control exercised by the government on the quality of the coins manufactured.[13]

The coinage system in south India was quite different.[14] Until the Mughal conquest of Golconda in 1687, the monetary system of the region remained firmly based on gold. The standard coin was the pagoda or *hun* (53 grains) stamped with the image of Vishnu. The pagoda's subsidiary coins, the half-

12 Van Santen, De *Verenigde Oost-Indische Compagnie*, pp. 109-110.

13 Prakash, "On coinage in Mughal India".

14 Prakash, "Foreign Merchants and Indian Mints".

pagoda and the *fanam* (5 grains) were also gold. The latter, heavily alloyed, was one of the smallest gold coins known and was extensively used for ordinary commercial transactions including wage payments. A copper coin weighing between 25 and 30 grains was called 'cash'. Since 1636, the Qutb Shahs had also been minting a limited number of Mughal silver rupees to symbolize their status as tributary chiefs. After 1687, of course, the Mughals issued gold *muhrs*, silver rupees and copper coins of the usual Mughal types from the Hyderabad mint. But the production of the older indigenous gold and copper coins as well as their extensive use in the region continued for quite some time. This flexibility was possible because a centrally controlled minting structure of the north Indian variety was conspicuous by its absence in the south. In the latter region, including Golconda and the Hindu territories further south, minting was decentralized subject to licence and a fairly large number of mints operated in the area, bringing out coins which were not always comparable in weight and fineness across mints. This applied with particular force to *fanams*, where the alloy content of the coins brought out by different mints could be very different.

Coinage and Wage Payment

Coming next to the relationship between coin output on the one hand and wages and the logistics of wage payments on the other, it should be obvious that the mix of coin output in any society would be determined by the proportion of small sized transactions to total transactions including wage payments. Thus if wages are paid overwhelmingly on a weekly rather than a monthly basis, the proportion of coins of relatively smaller value in total coin output would be considerably greater than if this were not the case. This proportion would be still higher if the norm of wage payments involved daily payment. In societies with a single-metal coinage, the smaller coins would obviously be fractions of the principal coin and would bear a fixed relationship to it. This would be the case under multi-metal coinage as well provided there was a fixed relationship across coins of different metals. In such societies the production of coins of different metals and denominations would largely be a matter of metal availability and convenience. Of course, if the relative market value of different metals in terms of each other were to undergo a significant deviation from the fixed norm, coins of the metal whose relative value was on the increase would tend to be melted down.

The situation in Mughal India was more complicated than this. Not only was coinage multi-metal-gold *muhrs*, silver rupees and copper *dams* – but also 'free' with the public having the right to take bullion, old coins or foreign coins to an imperial mint for conversion after a time lag into newly minted coins. Most importantly, there was no fixed relationship across coins of different metals. As pointed out earlier, the gold *muhr* was largely a ceremonial coin also used extensively as a store of value. But it did not figure with any prominence in the settlement of ordinary transactions which were taken care of either by the silver rupee or the copper *dam*. Unless otherwise specified, a claim or an obligation stated in terms of rupees implied settlement in terms of the *sicca* rupee, namely a rupee coin manufactured during the current or the previous year. Payments made in rupee coins manufactured prior to the previous year, namely the *chalani* or the *khazana* rupees, would need to be enhanced by a market-determined premium that the *sicca* rupee carried over these coins. In practice, however, this premium was fairly defined and subject only to marginal fluctuations. The situation, however, was quite different with respect to the relationship between the *sicca* rupee and copper *dam*. According to Abul Fazl, the author of the *Ain-i-Akbari*,[15] an administered *dam*:rupee rate of 48:1 was devised around 1575 for purposes of government transactions. But the actual market rate of exchange deviated quite considerably from this ratio. The *dam* was reported to have gone up as high as 35:1 sometime before 1583 when another administered rate of 40:1 was prescribed. This is also the rate quoted for 1595-6, the year in which the *Ain-i-Akbari* was written. This often created situations of great anomaly and hardship for particular sections of the society. To take a specific case, in 1575 while the rates of salary payment that Akbar's *mansabdars*[16] were obliged to make to the troopers engaged by

15 The *Ain-i-Akbari* is part of a larger work that Abul Fazl Allami undertook on the orders of Emperor Akbar (reigned 1556-1605). The two volumes of his *Akbarnama* record the events of Akbar's reign, preceded by an account of the reigns of Babur and Humayun, Akbar's grandfather and father respectively. The third volume was devoted to recording the *Ainha-i-Muqaddas-i-Shahi* (the Sacred Imperial Regulations). It is this volume which is ordinarily referred to as the *Ain-i-Akbari*. I have used the edition translated from Persian by Blochmann, *Ain-i-Akbari*(3rd rev. and enl. edition, Delhi, 1977).

16 Under this system, all the senior military and civil administrative positions throughout the Mughal empire were held by officials known as *mansabdars*. From the time of Akbar onwards, each official held a dual numerical rank - *zat* (personal) and *sawar* (cavalry). The *zat* rank determined the official's status in the hierarchy besides his personal salary per annum, while the other rank specified the extent of the military obligations of the holder in terms of maintaining a certain number of horses, troopers and military equipment to be made available for imperial service, whenever required. The *sawar* rank also determined the annual sum of money to be reimbursed to the official against this obligation. The pay-claim of each official was met either in cash or through the grant of revenue

them were specified in *dams*, fifty percent of the actual payment was to be made in rupees, twenty-five percent in gold coins and only the remaining twenty five percent in copper *dams*. To help the cause of the troopers to the extent possible, the emperor laid down a rule that in the event the market rate of exchange between the *dam* and the rupee turned more than 40 *dams* to a rupee (the administered rate at the time being 48:1), the conversion rate actually enforced would be 40:1.[17]

The ideal way to avoid these kinds of situations would have been to enforce a fairly strict parity between the coin in which the claim/obligation was specified and the coin in which the settlement was actually made. In other words, the only way to insure a worker against the risk of fluctuations in the *dam*:rupee ratio would have been to both specify the wage in terms of *dams* as well as to make the actual payment exclusively in that coin. This was usually but perhaps not always the case. By the same token, a large payment eventually to be collected in silver rupees must also be denominated in the same coin. It is indeed the case that whatever information on wage rates is available in sources such as the *Ain-i-Akbari* is almost exclusively in terms of *dams*, irrespective of whether the basis of payment was daily or monthly (there does not seem to have been a tradition of weekly payment at all) or whether it was a time rate payment or a piece rate payment. The situation changed somewhat in the seventeenth century from about 1620 onward when one-*anna*, two-*anna*, four-*anna*, and eight-*anna* coins (all fractions of the silver rupee coin – one-*anna* coin being one-sixteenth of a rupee) were also coined, though the scale on which these small silver coins were manufactured does not seem to have been very large. The result nevertheless was that while during the sixteenth century, copper coinage was probably the dominant coinage in Mughal India, this was no longer the case in the seventeenth century. John Deyell, for example, has demonstrated an immense contraction of copper minting after the close of Akbar's reign.[18] Wage data for this period are, therefore, also found stated in rupee terms, though the overwhelming medium in which they continued to be specified was the copper *dam*.

collection rights over a specified area of land whose annual assessed revenue equalled the amount of the claim. Such areas were then known as *jagirs*. In the initial years of his reign, Akbar insisted upon meeting the pay-claims of the *mansabdars* exclusively in terms of cash but the exigencies of administrative convenience later necessitated the increasing use of the *jagir* method. By the time we reach the period of Aurangzeb (1659-1707), revenue collection rights over nearly four-fifths of the total land in the empire had been alienated to the *mansabdars*.

17 Abul Fazl, *Ain-i-Akbari*, I (1977), p.275; Habib, "A System of Trimetallism", pp. 137-170.

18 Deyell, "Long-Term Production Trends".

The only important exception to this pattern would seem to be the specification and the payment of wages as indeed other small-value transactions in terms of units of different kinds of uncoined non-standardized money alternatively referred to as 'humble' money. In Gujarat, the preferred uncoined medium of exchange was the *badam* (inedible bitter almond imported from Persia), 36 of which reportedly went for a copper *paisa* in 1646.[19] Other such mediums were pieces of lead and tin etc. But by far the most extensively used such medium at least in Bengal and other parts of Eastern India was the *cauri* or a sea-shell. In 1646, a copper *paisa* (which carried the same value as the *dam*) was reported to be commanding approximately 80 *cauris*.[20] More than a century later, a *paisa* was stated to be equal to a *ponny* of *cauris* which might well have consisted of 80 pieces.[21] The Maldive islands, south-west of Sri Lanka in the Indian Ocean, were the largest world producers of these shells at this time. In the fifteenth century, Venetian merchants conducted a re-export trade of Maldives *cauris* in the Mediterranean, from which they were transshipped across the Sahara to the gold and textile centres of West Africa. Later, in the sixteenth century, the Portuguese transferred apparently huge quantities of *cauris* from the Maldives to Portugal for re-export to Guinea, Benin and the Congo. In the Indian Ocean, the *cauris* were the principal medium through which the Maldives obtained goods such as coarse textiles and provisions like rice, oil, and sugar from major trading partners such as Bengal. Indeed, the trade with Maldives was one of the principal branches of trade carried on by the Bengal merchants from the port of Balasore in the seventeenth and the early eighteenth century. It is remarkable that at a time when trade carried on from Bengal ports such as Hugli and Balasore was undergoing an overall decline in the early years of the eighteenth century, the trade between Balasore and the Maldives was on the rise.[22] Enormous quantities of these shells thus found their way into Eastern India. While there obviously were alternative uses for these *cauris* such as for ornamentation, probably the largest single use to which they were put were as a medium of exchange. Wages are, therefore, often found recorded as both specified and paid in *cauris*.

19 Twist, *Generale Beschryvinge van Indien*, p. 58. The chapter containing this reference is reprinted, without its source being indicated, as Appendix Vc in Vol. II, Part III of Van Dam, *Beschryvinge van de Oost-Indische*, R.G.P. No. 83.

20 Twist, *Generale Beschryvinge van Indien*, p. 58.

21 *Nationaal Archief* [hereafter NA], *Voormalige Nederlandse Bezittingen in Voor-Indie* [hereafter NBV-I], No. 66, "Bericht van den Koopman Johannes Mattheus Ross wegens de commissie in de arrengs (met bylagen)", 1767. Submitted to Director George Lodewijk Vernet on 26 December 1767. Appendix N, Note 1. The volume is not foliated.

22 Prakash, "Asian Trade and European Impact" in Kling and Pearson, *The Age of Partnership*, pp. 43-70.

Even land revenue was often collected in this medium. C.R. Wilson refers to the English East India Company receiving its land revenue from *zamindars* in Calcutta in *cauris* and then converting it into rupees.[23]

The amount of information available on wage rates in different occupations in early modern India is distressingly small. It is also incapable of generating any meaningful long-term trends. But before we come to a discussion of this information, it might be useful to draw attention to some data that are available on the share of labour cost in the total cost of production of certain varieties of textiles manufactured in Bengal. The first set of data pertain to the 1680s and relate to three grades of *khasas*, a staple variety of muslins. About two-thirds of the price obtained by the weaver under the Indian variant of the putting-out system covered the costs of the raw material while the remainder was the reward for his labour. The mark-up by the intermediary merchant (calculated on the basis of the price agreed upon at the time of the contract between the Dutch East India Company and the intermediary merchant) was 35 percent in the case of grade I, 55 percent in grade II, and as much as 142 percent in grade III.[24] It is remarkable that a century later, in the case of textile after textile, the relative share of the weaver's reward in the value obtained from the European buyer had come down to a quarter.[25] The explanation almost certainly was the changed status of the labour market. The 1680's were characterized by a growing gap in the rate of growth of the demand for Bengal textiles by the Dutch and the English East India Companies and that of their supply leading to a marked increase in the bargaining strength of the weavers vis-à-vis the intermediary merchants and that of the latter vis-à-vis the Companies. The 1770s, on the other hand, were characterized by a ruthless domination of the market by the English East India Company in consequence of its newly found political leverage in the province. The poor weaver was at the complete mercy of the Company and could expect hardly anything over and above the barest minimum subsistence.

As noted earlier, the data on wage rates themselves are rather scanty and do not admit of the construction of a proper time-series. During the sixteenth century, the wage data are almost exclusively expressed in terms of copper *dams* on a daily basis. Table 13.1 lists the information available on daily wage rates in respect of two time periods. The first of these is the mid-1590s and

23 Wilson, *The Early Annals of the English in Bengal*, I, pp. 219-222; II, p. 254.

24 The precise figures were 65 per cent for grade I, 66 per cent for grade II and 68 per cent for grade III (Instructions by Commissioner Van Reede tot Drakenstein to Bengal factors of the Dutch East India Company, 21 February 1687, NA, *Verenigde Oost-Indische Compagnie (VOC)*, 1435. The volume is not foliated).

25 NA, NBV-I, 66, Note 3. The volume is not foliated.

the source of the information is the *Ain-i-Akbari* which has a brief chapter titled "On the wages of labourers" sanctioned for the imperial establishment. The second time period relates to the years 1637 and 1638, though some observations pertain to the years 1627 and 1630. The source of this set of observations is the documentation of the Dutch East India Company and these relate mainly to employees hired by the Company. The "soldiers" in this list were hired to accompany the Company's caravans carrying goods and at times specie from Agra to Surat etc. The workmen were hired in 1638 for the construction of the Company's factory at Agra. While the two sets of observations are obviously not fully comparable with each other, they nevertheless can be used to indicate the broad orders of magnitude. What such a comparison in respect of categories where information is available in both the sets reveals quite unambiguously is the distinct and substantial rise in the daily wage rate over the period. The only exception to this pattern were the lime workers.

Table 13.1. Daily wage rate in Mughal India

Category of workers	Ain-i-Akbari (1595) (in *dams*)	Dutch East India Company sources (1637-1638) (in *paisas*)
Carpenter	2-7 (for grades 5 to 1)	10-13
Bricklayer	3-3½ (for grades 2 and 1)	15
Lime worker	5-7 (for grades 3 to 1)	7
Wood-sawyer	2	12½
Bamboo-cutter	2	
Thatcher	2	
Water-carrier	2-3 (for grades 2 and 1)	
Labourer (*majur*)		4-7
Labourer in warehouse		9
Attendant		5-7
Soldier		7
Weaver		8-9
Artisan		10-12

Source: Abul Fazl, Ain-i-Akbari, *I (1977), pp. 235-236; Van Santen,* De Verenigde Oost-Indische Compagnie, *p. 102.*

How does one explain this? At least two variables need to be taken into account in this connection. One is the average price level of food items which would perhaps be the most important single constituent of the wage goods basket. The year 1638 witnessed an unusual rise in wheat prices in Agra

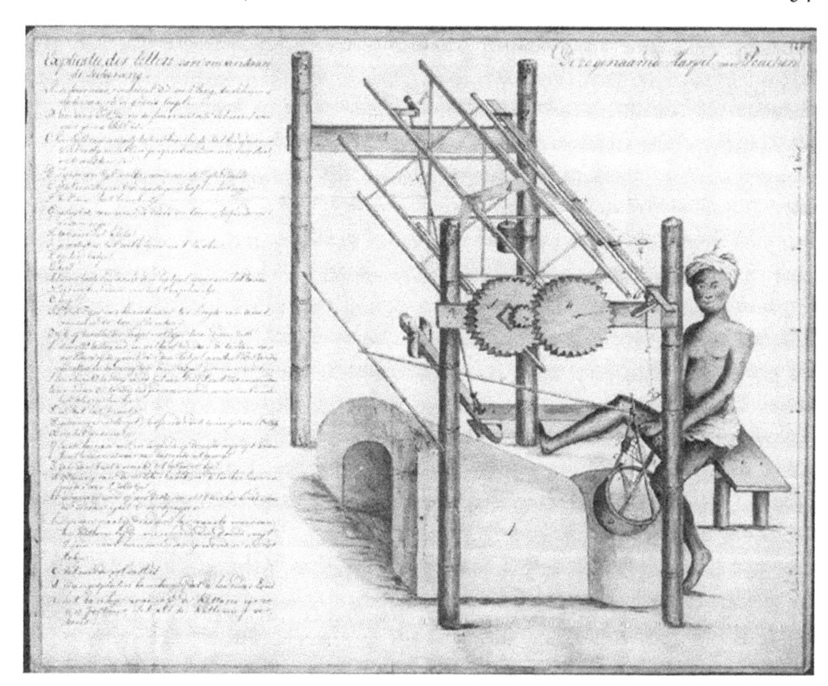

Figure 13.1. Depiction of the so-called Haspel van Pouchon: a machine that integrates the unwinding and reeling of silk in one process. Source: ARA, Verzameling Buitenlandse Kaarten, Leupe (VEL) 1107, originally attached to a letter of J.M. Ross, opperkoopman at Cossimbazar, dated 27 December 1774 (VOC 3395, ff. 142-50). Used by permission.

from 91 *paise* per *maund* of 69 Dutch ponds at the beginning of the year to Rs.1.74 on 24 April, to Rs.2.67 on 3 May to return to Rs.2.11 per *maund* on 12 July 1638.[26] It is not clear how representative or long lasting this kind of rise was but it seems to have had a hand in the rise in the wage rate. Thus Wollebrant Geleynssen de Jongh, the head of the Dutch East India Company's factory in Agra wrote that "one has now to pay the labourers and the attendants much more than before".[27]

The other variable that one needs to take into account is the changing value of the copper *dam* or *paisa* which was the medium in which the wage rate was usually expressed in relation to the silver rupee which in the course of the seventeenth century increasingly became the standard Mughal Indian coin. A quick look at Table 13.2 which gives this ratio for the years

26 Van Santen, *De Verenigde Oost-Indische Compagnie*, p. 102.

27 Van Santen, *De Verenigde Oost-Indische Compagnie*, p. 93.

between 1583 and 1702 mainly for the cities of Surat and Agra points to distinct phases in this ratio. We have already noticed earlier the difference between the administered rate of 48 *dams* and then 40 *dams* to a rupee on the one hand and the market rate of exchange on the other. In 1583 a rupee commanded only 35 *dams* in the market against the administered rate of 40 *dams* thus favouring the wage earner who was paid in *dams*. The situation, however, changed drastically in the second quarter of the seventeenth century with the rupee generally commanding fifty and more *paisas*. The high wages expressed in *paisas* that we noted earlier in respect of the 1630s perhaps need to be interpreted in this context. The picture changed drastically yet once again in the 1660s and the 1670s with the rupee commanding no more than 30 to 34 *paisas*. Unfortunately, we do not have wage rate figures for this period but the growing burden on the employers was becoming quite evident. In 1661, for example, the Director of the Dutch East India Company establishment in Surat wrote, "Considering that all wages have to be calculated and paid in *paisas*, those who are obliged to make daily wage and other small payments have to carry a distinctly larger burden".[28] Emperor Aurangzeb, who was having repairs done to his pilgrim vessel, the *Ganj-i-Sawai* the same year at Surat and was obliged to have payments made to the carpenters and other workmen reckoned in *paisas*, was similarly reported to be suffering a loss because of the "dearness of the *paisas* at Surat".[29]

From the point of view of the logistics of wage payments, it is interesting to note that according to Pelsaert, the month on occasions was regarded as consisting of forty days.[30] It is impossible to say how marginal or widespread this practice was. Also, itemized detailed information available in the papers of the Dutch East India Company on the costs incurred at the Rajmahal mint in Bengal in 1692 in coining gold bullion into *muhrs* includes items such as "sweets for the beaters" and the "cost of provisions for washermen and water carriers" employed at the mint in addition to the usual money wages paid to these categories of employees. Interestingly also, of the nine washermen employed at the mint, the seven employed on a permanent basis were paid Rs.2.75 per month while the two temporary ones received Rs.3 each.[31]

28 N.A., L. Winnincx at Surat to Directors dated 17 December 1661, VOC 1234, f.115: Van Santen, *Verenigde Oost-Indische Compagnie*, p. 115.

29 N.A., L. Winnincx at Surat to Directors dated 17 December 1661, VOC 1234, ff.115v -116: Van Santen, *De Verenigde Oost-Indische Compagnie*, p. 115.

30 Kolff and van Santen, *De Geschriften van Francisco Pelsaert.*

31 NA, VOC 1502, ff. 1387-90.

Table 13.2. Rupee: dam (paisa) ratio in Mughal India

Year	City/Region	*Dam* (*Paisas*) per rupee
1583	Agra	35
1623	Surat	57
1627	Agra	58
1630	Broach	41-43
1633	Gujarat	53-54
1636	Surat	56
1637	Agra	50-55 *
1638	Agra	55-58 *
1639	Agra	58
1642	Surat	56
1650	Surat	50
1657	Surat	40
1661	Surat	32
1662	Surat	30-31
1666	Surat	32-34
1681	Surat	30-34
1702	Surat	60-64

* *Monthly observations are available for Agra for 1637 and 1638. This figure represents the range for the entire year.*
Source: Van Santen, De Verenigde Oost-Indische Compagnie, *Tables 11 and 12, p.114.*

A Long Term Perspective

With respect to the questions of coinage and wages, there were both continuities as well as discontinuities between the pre-colonial and the colonial periods. While the degree of monetization in the economy would generally seem to have gone up in the nineteenth century, it was by no means the case that all or even the bulk of the wage payments were made in terms of money. Dharma Kumar's work on agricultural wages in the Madras Presidency, for example, establishes that in the early nineteenth century, the wages of both attached and casual workers were generally paid in grain, apart from perquisites of cloth and money.[32] A plausible explanation of the survival of a sub-

32 Kumar, *Land and Caste in South India.*

stantial non-monetized sector in India in the nineteenth and the twentieth centuries is that given the extremely high level of risk and uncertainty of Indian agriculture in conditions of erratic weather and price fluctuations, the typical farming household has always sought to protect itself by preserving an adequate minimum level of subsistence activity.

As for the system of coinage, the Mughal Indian norm of 'free' minting was discontinued as of 1893 with the closure of the Indian mints for the free coinage of gold and silver, with the government retaining the power to coin silver rupees on its own account. This was essentially an outcome of the rise in the international output of silver in the 1870s resulting in its substantive depreciation in relation to gold. As a result of this depreciation, the gold value of the rupee had fallen from about 2 shillings in 1871 to 1s.2d in 1892. This had aggravated the budgetary problem for the Government of India in so far as it had increased the burden of the home charges, namely its sterling obligations such as interest on public debt, pensions, payments to the War Office and the cost of government stores bought in England.

Between 1898-1899 and 1915-1916, a gold exchange standard operated in India. As from September 1931, following the British government's decision to abandon the gold standard, the rupee was officially linked to sterling. As for wage payments in money terms, they were now almost universally made in rupees (both notes and coins) making the production of smaller coins representing fractions of the rupee that much less necessary for the purpose. In 1918, for example, against a total of 1354 million rupees worth of notes in circulation, the number of rupee coins was 279 million and of smaller coins only 1.62 million rupees worth.[33]

A study done in the 1970s comparing the purchasing power of the wages mentioned in the *Ain-i-Akbari* for Agra with those in the Government of India's Labour Bureau's Family Living Survey of Industrial Workers in 1958-1959 for five major cities - Delhi, Kanpur, Mumbai, Kolkata and Chennai - produced the following results. For Akbar's time, the monthly average wage rate assumed was Rs.2.75. For 1958-1959, the monthly wage assumed was Rs.90 for Delhi, Rs.77 for Kanpur, Rs.104 for Mumbai, Rs.79 for Kolkata and Rs.66 for Chennai. It was found that in terms of foodgrains, the purchasing power of wages in Akbar's time was consistently higher than that in 1958-1959 in all the five cities except for one city and one commodity - *moong* (a variety of lentils) in Kanpur. The purchasing power was also considerably higher in terms of milk, curd and clarified butter, and higher by smaller margins in terms of meat. However, both Mumbai and Chennai had a substitute in 1958-1959 in the form of fish which

33 Chandavarkar, "Money and Credit (1858-1947)", pp. 762-803.

was much cheaper relatively than goat meat in sixteenth century Agra. On the other hand, the twentieth century worker could buy more of vegetable oils, sugar and jaggery, more salt and spices and more of most vegetables.[34]

A more recent study attempts a comparison of real wages of weavers in South India with those in Britain during the latter half of the eighteenth century. The price of grain in each region is used to measure real purchasing power. For South India, grain wages have been calculated in terms of rice while for Britain the grain equivalence has been expressed in terms of bread. Since bread contains only 1000 calories per pound and rice 1500, the bread figures have been converted to their grain equivalents for comparison. In the mid-eighteenth century, the wages of rural and small-town weavers in Britain are stated to have ranged from 7s to 9s a week. This could purchase 65 to 75 pounds of bread, which is calorically equivalent to 40 to 50 pounds of grain. A London weaver is believed to have made 10s 6d per week, which translated to 60 pounds of grain. The highest earnings allegedly went to the silk weavers of Spitalfields, who in 1747 earned 18s to 21s a week, the equivalent of 120 to 140 pounds of grain. In mid-eighteenth century South India, the earnings of calico weavers in Cuddalore could purchase 65 pounds of rice per week. In 1800, a more highly skilled weaver in Tanjore made the equivalent of 85 pounds of rice a week. According to data from the 1790s, the manufacturers of finest calicoes in South India earned two and a half times more per week than a Cuddalore weaver, an amount which in the 1760s could have purchased 160 pounds of rice. It is then concluded that an average South Indian weaver's wages were higher than those of a weaver in rural and small-town Britain, and comparable to those of a London weaver.[35]

It should, however, be obvious that the conclusions of such studies are subject to strong reservations. In the latter study, the principal methodological problem would seem to consist in relying exclusively on grain consumption as an index of total consumption, both food and non-food, and deriving conclusions regarding real wages entirely on that basis. Data-wise, it is not at all clear how selective or representative the observations with regard to the money wage rate particularly with regard to South India are. Also, there is no indication at all regarding the relative weights in the total weaver population of the categories producing different varieties of textiles. A range of real wages from 65 to 160 pounds of rice without any idea of the relative weights of the different components in the weaver work force in South India indeed does not tell one very much.

34 Desai, "Population and Standards of Living in Akbar's Time", pp. 53-79.

35 Parthasarathi, "Rethinking Wages and Competitiveness", pp. 79-109.

From about the 1880s onward there is a considerable body of information on money and real wage rates prevailing in different sectors of the Indian economy. An important source is the official annual publication *Prices and Wages in India* started in 1861. But there are severe problems in the use of this information arising principally from lack of comparability across time and across industries in a given sector. In brief, however, the following picture emerges. The annual average of the agricultural real wage index calculated by K. Mukherji (1890=100) stood at 93 during 1871-1873, 99 during 1878-1882 and 96 during 1896-1900. This is the overall picture. The regional picture shows greater variation. Labourers may in fact have experienced an improvement in living standards in the major cash crop growing regions. Cash crop production meant increased demand for labour with increases in cropped area and/or labour intensity. Signs of material prosperity for the rural population can in general be seen in Punjab and Bengal. For the period 1900-20, the picture is quite positive for South India. In coastal Andhra, there is evidence suggesting that real wages in the 1920s were higher than in the 1900s. In districts (especially in Madras) where commercialization combined with large net emigration, there were signs of a rise in wages. After 1920, however, most studies find the onset of a declining tendency. Money wages fell sharply during the Great Depression. In some cases real wages also fell. Dharma Kumar's conclusion that "the agricultural labourers probably felt the effect of the pressure of population after 1921 more keenly than any other group" seems valid.[36]

In the modern industrial sector the first major industry to come up was that of producing cotton textiles. The first mill was set up in Mumbai in the 1850s by a Parsi entrepreneur, C.N. Davar. In the succeeding decades, both entrepreneurship and capital in the industry continued to be wholly Indian as did the market for its output. A total absence of tariff protection or any other form of assistance by the colonial regime notwithstanding, the industry registered a rapid rate of growth. By 1914, it had become the world's fourth – or fifth – largest cotton textile industry. Information regarding movements in the wage rate in the industry begins to be available only around 1875: until 1905 the wages were quite stable. This, however, should not be construed as evidence of unresponsiveness of wages to the pressures of labour shortage. In 1897, when plague caused thousands of workers to flee Mumbai and when mills were desperately short of hands, wages rose more than 68 percent in a few short months.[37] In the twentieth century, the wage rate level rose sharply between 1914 and 1923 mainly in consequence of a sharp rise in prices.

36 Roy, *The Economic History of India 1857-1947*, pp. 80-81.

37 Morris, *The Emergence of an Industrial Labour Force in India*, p.49.

The interwar years required a contraction of the labour force as the industry struggled to resolve its economic difficulties. The years between 1926 and 1937 witnessed a steady fall in the level of wages. After 1937 the trend reversed and wages rose swiftly during World War II to the 1947 peak. But as in World War I, it seems clear that wages lagged behind wartime price rises and were pulled upward only by the cost of living.[38]

With respect to the modern industrial sector as a whole, the picture was somewhat more positive. As far as real wage movements in large scale factory industry are concerned, the best series both in terms of care of construction and explicitness of assumptions is the one by K. Mukherji. This series suggests relative stability (or slight declines) until just before World War I. From 1907-11 until immediately after the First World War there was an obvious fall while the inter-war period saw fairly significant rises in real wages. Mukherji's data deviate from conventional wisdom in their suggestion that real wages did not decline during the Second World War.[39]

Summary and Conclusions

This chapter has examined the relationship between long distance trade, coinage, and wages in India over the past half a millennium or so. Over this period, the relationship across these variables was different in crucial respects as between the pre-colonial period stretching from the sixteenth to the eighteenth centuries on the one hand and the period of British colonial rule in the country on the other. In the pre-colonial period, the amount of money supply in the economy was critically dependent upon the amount of treasure imported from the rest of Asia as well as from Europe through the agency of both the Indian and other Asian traders on the one hand and the European corporate enterprises and private traders on the other. The Mughal Indian coinage system consisted of three metals - gold, silver and copper - but was not truly trimetallic in content because of the absence of a fixed relationship across the coins of the three metals. In order to avoid inconvenience and even more so the risk arising out of the uncertainty of the changing relative value of coins of one metal in terms of those of the other two, the practice followed was to generally specify obligations/claims in terms of the coins of a particular metal as also to collect/make payment by and large in coins of the same metal. The use of gold *muhrs* was largely confined to ceremonial occasions.

38 *Ibid.*, p. 51.
39 Morris, "The Growth of Large Scale Industry to 1947", pp. 553-676.

Large transactions were specified and effected in silver *sicca* rupees while small transactions, including wage payments, were made in terms of copper *dams*. This called for a certain mix in coin output and, if necessary, the state was willing to step in to help achieve such a mix. This picture was modified to a certain extent in the seventeenth century when silver coinage became relatively more important and coins representing fractions of the silver rupee were manufactured. Monthly wages are then found stated more and more in terms of silver rupees, though daily wages continued to be expressed in copper *dams*. Non-standardized 'humble' money, particularly *cauris* in the case of Eastern India, was also an important medium of wage payments during this period. The actual amount of wage data available for the pre-colonial period, however, is rather scanty not admitting of the construction of time series or an analysis of long-term trends. But a careful analysis of the available data reveals a number of interesting outcomes. The daily wage data are overwhelmingly found expressed in copper *dams* or *paisas*. The rupee value of the wages obviously fluctuated in accordance with changes in the ratio between the silver rupee and the copper *dam* or *paisa*. It is useful to remember that between the late sixteenth and the late seventeenth century, the available evidence points to the existence of several district phases in this ratio. Whenever the value of copper coinage rose in relation to that of the silver rupee, the employers saw this as evidence of rising wage burden. The device of providing a part of the wages in kind was evidently intended as a partial protection against falling value of the copper coin and ensuring a certain minimum real wage rather than depending entirely on a purely nominal wage. One might also note that a comparison of real wages in Mughal India with the 1950s as also a comparison of real wages in South India with those in Britain in the eighteenth century was found to be exercises fraught with many problems.

The pattern of relationship between long distance trade, coinage, and wages was qualitatively of a very different kind in the nineteenth and the first half of the twentieth century. Following the stoppage of the import of treasure, there no longer was any relationship of consequence between the first two of the three variables. Free minting of the Mughal Indian vintage was abandoned towards the end of the nineteenth century and the money supply henceforth consisted overwhelmingly of notes though rupee coins and coins representing fractions of the rupee continued to be manufactured. The information on wage rates begins to be substantial from about the 1880s onward but problems of coverage and comparability abound making it possible to make only general statements regarding long-term trends.

Bibliography

Abul Fazl, *Ain i Akbari*, Translated and edited by H. Blochmann and H.S. Jarret, revised and enlarged by Jadunath Sarkar, 3 vols (3rd rev. and enl. edition, Dehli, 1977).

Atwell, William S., "Notes on Silver, Foreign Trade, and the Late Ming Economy", *Ching-Shih Wen-t'i*, 3:8 (1977), pp. 1-33.

Blitz, Rudolph C., "Mercantilist Policies and the Pattern of World Trade, 1500-1750", *Journal of Economic History*, 27:1 (1967), pp. 39-55.

Chandavarkar, A.G., "Money and Credit, 1858-1947", in: Dharma Kumar (ed.), *The Cambridge Economic History of India, II, c. 1757 - c. 1970* (Cambridge, 1983), pp. 762-803.

Dam, Pieter van, *Beschryvinge van de Oostindische Compagnie*, edited by F.W. Stapel and C.W.Th. van Boetzelaar, 4 vols, 7 pts ('s-Gravenhage, 1927-1954).

Desai, Ashok, "Population and Standards of Living in Akbar's Time: A Second Look", *The Indian Economic and Social History Review*, 15:1 (1978), pp. 53-79.

Deyell, John S., "Long Term Production Trends for Copper Coins in the Mughal Empire", a note appended to Habib, "A System of Trimetallism", in: John F. Richards (ed.) *The Imperial Monetary System of Mughal India* (Oxford, 1987), pp. 160-170.

Glahn, Richard von, *Fountain of Fortune: Money and Monetary Policy in China, 1000-1700* (Berkeley, CA, 1996).

Habib, Irfan, "A System of Trimetallism in the Age of 'Price Revolution', Effects of the Silver Influx on the Mughal Monetary System", in: John F. Richards (ed.) *The Imperial Monetary System of Mughal India*, (Delhi, 1987), pp. 137-170.

Kolff, D.H.A. and H.W. van Santen (eds), *De Geschriften van Francisco Pelsaert over Mughal Indie, 1627: Kroniek en Remonstratie* (The Hague, 1979).

Kumar, Dharma, (ed.), *The Cambridge Economic History of India*. Vol. II (Cambridge, 1983).

Little, J.H., *The House of Jagatseth* (Calcutta, 1967).

Morris, Morris David, *The Emergence of an Industrial Labour Force in India, A Study of the Bombay Cotton Mills, 1854-1947* (Berkeley, CA, 1965).

Morris, Morris David, "The Growth of Large Scale Industry to 1947" in: Dharma Kumar, *The Cambridge Economic History of India*. Vol II (Cambridge, 1983), pp. 553-676.

Parthasarathi, Prasannan, "Rethinking Wages and Competitiveness in the Eighteenth Century: Britain and South India", *Past and Present*, 158 (1998), pp. 79-109.

Prakash, Om, "Asian Trade and European Impact: A Study of the Trade from Bengal, 1630-1720", in: Blair B. Kling and M.N. Pearson, *The Age of Partnership: Europeans in Asia before Dominion* (Honolulu, 1979), pp. 43-70.

Prakash, Om, "Foreign Merchants and Indian Mints in the 17th and Early 18th Century", in J.F. Richards (ed.), *The Imperial Monetary System of Mughal India* (New Delhi, 1987), pp. 171–192.

Prakash, Om, "On coinage in Mughal India", *The Indian Economic and Social History Review*, 25:4 (1988), pp. 475-491.

Roy, Tirthankar, *The Economic History of India 1857-1947* (Delhi, 2000).

Santen, H.W. van, *De Verenigde Oost Indische Campagnie in Gujarat en Hindustan, 1620-1660* (Leiden, 1982).

Smith, Adam, *An Inquiry into the Nature and Causes of the Wealth of Nations*, edited by H. Campbell and A.S. Skinner, 2 vols (Oxford, 1976).

Sperling, J., "The International Payments Mechanism in the Seventeenth and Eighteenth Centuries", *Economic History Review*, 2nd series, 14:3 (1962), pp. 446-468.

Twist, Johan van, *Generale Beschryvinge van Indien* (Amsterdam 1648).

Wallerstein, Immanuel, *The Modern World-System*. Vol. I: *Capitalist Agriculture and the Origins of the European World-Economy in the Sixteenth Century*, vol. I (New York, 1974).

Wilson, C.R., *The Early Annals of the English in Bengal*, 3 vols (London, 1895-1917).

XV

Trade and Politics in Eighteenth-century Bengal

In his well-known 1940 essay reviewing Volume IV of Godée Molsbergen's *History of the Dutch East Indies* covering the eighteenth century, Jacob van Leur put forth the unexceptionable proposition that it was not possible to write the history of Indonesia in that century in terms of the history of the Dutch East India Company. He then widened the canvas from Indonesia to Asia as a whole, put forth a case for the autonomy of Asian history in relation to that of Europe, and argued that the 'unbroken unity' of Asian history from the seventeenth to the nineteenth century 'makes the category Eighteenth Century useless as an instrument for ordering the facts in that historic landscape'.[1] While there probably is a certain amount of validity in this argument in relation to Indonesia, it certainly is far too sweeping when considered with reference to individual major Asian regions. Indeed, given the large size and the enormous diversity that characterized the Asian continent, it would be unrealistic to expect that over any given period of time, similar developments would characterize the history of the various major segments of the continent.

As far as South Asia is concerned, the eighteenth century does without any question constitute a distinct category in its history. This was the century between two empires. The Mughal empire had lost its cohesion with the death of Emperor Aurangzeb in 1707: the British were unable to consolidate their position in India until the early years of the nineteenth century. The collapse of the centralized Mughal empire had witnessed the emergence of a number of successor states. Some of these had evolved out of the fiefs of local Mughal governors as in Awadh, Bengal, Hyderabad or the Carnatic. Alternatively, they had emerged from the jurisdictions established by successful rebels such as the Maratha generals or the Sikhs of the Punjab. How did these successor states fare during the eighteenth century both politically and economically?

According to scholars such as Irfan Habib and M. Athar Ali, the successor states were not quite able to cope with the changing situation and there was in all probability a general decline in the standard of economic performance. Habib sums up the eighteenth century as a period of 'reckless rapine, anarchy and foreign conquest'.[2]

This view has been challenged over the last decade or so by several of the so-called 'revisionist' historians - Muzaffar Alam, Chris Bayly, Burton Stein, André Wink and others. In the words of Stein, most of these scholars

> agree that the rural economy over most of the eighteenth century India enjoyed substantial, if uneven, growth notwithstanding both the destructive wars culminating in those which won the subcontinent for the British, and the supposed political disorder in many areas. It is claimed that new, smaller states with efficient tax gathering procedures replaced the Mughal military imperial order, that market networks proliferated and became to a degree interlinked, that a more prosperous agriculture came into being with increased commodity production as a result of rural investments by the revenue farmers of the time, that all of this was buoyed up by an ever-increasing level of international trade in which Indian artisans, merchants and especially bankers played key and lucrative roles, and that this phase of political economy obtained until the first quarter of the nineteenth century.[3]

The portrayal of the eighteenth century in the historiography thus ranges from one of political chaos and great instability to exactly the opposite of that characterization. In the matter of economic performance, the range of possibilities stretches from decline to stagnation to growth. What also emerges from these writings quite unambiguously is the large variation in developments through the century in both the political and the economic sphere across different regions of the subcontinent.

What was the situation like in Bengal, which had the distinction of both being among the first successor states to emerge within the framework of the Mughal empire, and also being the first region to be taken over by the English East India Company nearly half a century later, formally inaugurating the era of colonial rule in the subcontinent? The man responsible for creating a near-autonomous successor state in Bengal was Murshid Quli Khan, an extremely able but equally ambitious Mughal official, sent to the province at the turn of the century with a specific brief to try and increase the revenues that the imperial government at Delhi received annually from the province. By scrupulously ensuring that the annual flow of the *khalisa* revenues to Delhi not only continued uninterrupted but in fact registered an increase over time, Murshid Quli succeeded in creating a mutually beneficial working partnership with the imperial government. His own price in the bargain was to obtain near-autonomy from the centre. An important milestone in the emergence of this situation was the 1716 conferment on Murshid Quli Khan by Emperor Farrukhsiyar of the office of the *subahdar* or *nazim* (governor) in addition to the office of the imperial *diwan* that he already held. This was the first time that the two key offices were combined in one person in any province. The arrangement suited both sides. The Centre got its revenue regularly while Murshid Quli, though not formally independent of the Mughal empire, enjoyed an enormous degree of freedom in which to manoeuvre within Bengal. The successor state thus created survived Murshid Quli's death in 1727 until the forces of Robert Clive defeated those of *Nawab* Sirajuddaulah at Plassey in 1757 and installed in his place a puppet administration. In 1765, the English East India Company coerced the imperial administration into formally appointing it the *diwan* of the province. The emperor was sanctioned an annual tribute of Rs 2.6 million. The *nawab* of Bengal retained the office of *nazim* with formal responsibility for defence, law and order and the administration of justice according to Islamic law. However, as a military entity, the *nawab* was reduced to insignificance. He was granted a fixed allowance for his court expenses and such activities as he tried to undertake. The rest of the revenues of Bengal were at the disposal of the East India Company.

In the case of Bengal, then, the eighteenth century consists of two distinct time-periods with the cut-off point lying somewhere around 1760. Quite apart from its political dimension, the distinction is of key importance in an evaluation of the standard of economic performance and achievement that characterized the province through the century. The introduction of alien rule introduced important modifications in the structure of economic organization at a variety of levels. Probably the most basic of these was an alteration in favour of the English East India Company and the private English traders (most of whom were also employees of the Company) of the pattern of distribution of the overall income and output generated in the economy. Van Leur's observation that 'Though Plassey, like the capture of the town of Jakarta in 1619, may be a landmark in the light of later history, at the moment of the military feat itself it held no preponderant significance, and there was no drastic change as a result of it' only underscores his inadequate grasp of the South Asian scenario.[4]

In the domain of political stability and the state of law and order, the situation in Bengal in the first half of the eighteenth century was certainly no worse than it had been during the seventeenth. If anything, Murshid Quli Khan's grip over the administrative machinery in the province was firmer than had been the case under his predecessors. It is true that a certain amount of political dislocation was caused in the early 1740s as a result of the Maratha incursions into the province. But that was essentially a temporary phase and things were by and large back to normal by the end of the decade. In brief, the picture of political confusion and unrest associated with the declining power of the Mughals in the first half of the eighteenth century is certainly not applicable to Bengal.

As in the rest of the subcontinent, an overwhelming bulk of the total output in Bengal was generated in the agricultural sector. By all accounts, Bengal was amongst the most fertile of the major Indian regions. The high level of productivity achieved embraced both food production and commercial crops. The latter, including such items as mulberry, cotton, and sugarcane, were highly market-oriented, and the acreage and output responded quickly to changes in market demand. To take an example from the early years of the eighteenth century, while urging the imperial authorities to settle their dispute with the Dutch in Bengal, Murshid Quli wrote in 1706 that following the closure of the Dutch factory at Kasimbazar two years earlier, the Hollanders' demand for raw silk had registered a considerable decline, leading to a substantial shift of land away from mulberry into rice and pulses. This had had an injurious effect on the income from land revenue inasmuch as mulberry lands were assessed at Rs 3 per *bigha*, whereas the corresponding rates for rice and pulses - being lower-value crops - were only Rs 0.75 and Rs 0.37 per *bigha* respectively. This could be reversed only if the Company were persuaded to reopen its factory at Kasimbazar.[5]

There is no evidence whatsoever to suggest that this highly positive picture underwent any deterioration in any sense through the remaining part of the eighteenth century. Indeed, the rising sums of land revenue collections in the province might well point to an increasingly more productive and efficiently organized agricultural sector. Between 1700 and 1722, the actual amount of revenue collected in the province per annum is reported to have gone up from Rs 11.72 million to Rs 14.11 million - an increase of over 20 per cent.[6] In the absence of a marked or sustained rise in the general price level in the province during the relevant period, it would be unrealistic to dismiss a revenue increase of this magnitude simply as an adjustment to rising prices.[7] Philip Calkins has suggested that Murshid Quli's revenue reforms tended to depress the weaker and less efficient *zamindars* and intermediate landholders, while allowing the stronger and more efficient ones to survive.[8] On the whole, there was a more intensive squeezing of the intermediary groups as a whole, a phenomenon unlikely to obtain for any length of time in a situation of non-growing output.

What about the non-agricultural sector? It is now established that the structure of manufacturing production in India had attained a high level of development and sophistication before the arrival of the Europeans in the Indian Ocean at the beginning of the sixteenth century. If one looks at the structure and the dynamics of the Indian Ocean trade around this time, it is clear that India played a central role in this structure. In part, this indeed was a function of the mid-way location of the subcontinent between West Asia on the one hand and Southeast and East Asia on the other. But much more important was the subcontinent's capacity to put on the market a wide range of tradeable goods at highly competitive prices. These included agricultural goods, both food items such as rice, sugar and oil as well as raw materials such as cotton and indigo. While the bulk of the trade in these goods was coastal, the high seas trade component was by no means insignificant. The real strength of the subcontinent, however, lay in the provision of large quantities of manufactured goods, the most important among which were textiles of various kinds. While these included high-value varieties such as the legendary Dhaka muslins and the Gujarat silk embroideries, the really important component for the Asian market was the coarse cotton varieties manufactured primarily on the Coromandel coast and in Gujarat. There was a large-scale demand for these varieties both in the eastern markets of Indonesia, Malaya, Thailand and Burma as well as in the markets of the Red Sea, the Persian Gulf and East Africa. While it is impossible to determine precisely what proportion of total domestic demand for mass consumption textiles in these societies was met by imports from India, the available evidence would seem to point in the direction of this not being altogether insignificant. India's capacity to manufacture these textiles in large quantities and put them on the market at highly competitive terms made it in some sense the 'industrial' hub of the region surrounded by West Asia on one side and Southeast Asia on the other. By at the same time providing an important market for the specialized agricultural, mineral and other products that her trading partners were in a position to supply in order to pay for the Indian textiles and other goods, India significantly enhanced the basis of trade in the Indian Ocean region. It is really in this sense that the critically important role of India in the structure of early modern Asian trade needs to be assessed.

Following the arrival of the Europeans in the Indian Ocean, and particularly since the coming of the Dutch and the English East India Companies at the beginning of the seventeenth century, the volume and the value of the trade from India increased substantially. Bengal figured prominently in the trade between Europe and Asia, providing at the end of the seventeenth century no less than 40 per cent of the total Asian cargo (valuewise) that the Dutch and the English Companies sent to Europe each year. The goods procured in Bengal consisted overwhelmingly of textiles and raw silk. Bengal also figured prominently in the substantial intra-Asian trade carried on by the Dutch Company, supplying raw silk for the critically important Japan trade and opium for the Indonesian market. The structure of manufacturing production in Bengal responded most positively to the spectacular expansion in the international demand for her products.

The highly market-responsive and cost-competitive structure of manufacturing production in Bengal and other parts of the subcontinent was conditioned to a significant degree by the availability of a sophisticated infrastructure of institutional arrangements and specialized services that the manufacturing sector was able to draw upon. This infrastructure enabled the Indian artisan, the Indian merchant, the European trader and the Indian *sarraf* to work in tandem to produce a certain result which was of mutual benefit to all of them. Among other things, this infrastructure consisted of elements such as an advanced state of division of labour coupled with the emergence of a labour market, price responsive marketing systems, merchant groups capable of good organization and collective defence, highly developed accountancy skills, a sophisticated imperial minting organization ensuring utmost quality control of the coins issued, and a highly developed credit organisation in which the instrument of the *hundi* was used both to raise short-term credit as well as to arrange for interregional transfer of funds efficiently and inexpensively.

Did this structure undergo any particular stress or deterioration in Bengal during the eighteenth century (or at least during its first half), generating, in turn, adverse consequences for the level of trade and, more generally, for the overall scale of economic activity in the non-agricultural sector in the region? There really is no particular evidence to suggest that this happened. It is true that the Maratha incursions into the province in the 1740s had led to a scarcity of grain, shortage of labour and generally rising cost levels. As a result, among other things, the production and procurement of textiles for export had suffered quite severely. In 1744, for example, it was believed that the fortunes of several of the merchants supplying textiles to the Dutch Company were under strain. These suspicions were confirmed in 1746 when it was learnt that four important merchants operating in the major textile centre of Shantipur near Dhaka - Hinkar Chaudhury, Jag Bhushan, Gokul Chand and Bhagwan Gopi Chand - together with their associates, Radhamohan Chaudhury and Radhakant Chand, had been financially ruined. The Company suffered considerable losses in the form of debts owed by these merchants. The principal corrective step the factors sought to take was to require the merchants to provide sureties. But the local *sarrafs* and bankers, who would have been acceptable to the Company as guarantors, flatly refused, saying it was too risky a proposition.[9] It should, however, be emphasised that this kind of situation was essentially a temporary aberration caused by specific circumstances. By the end of the decade, things were by and large back to normal.

The increasing body of privileges enjoyed by the English East India Company in the region, mainly in the context of the royal *farman* granted to it by Emperor Farrukhsiyar in 1717, is often quoted as another distortion this period witnessed involving a curtailment of the rights and privileges of the ordinary Indian merchants. One such special privilege accorded to the English related to their exclusive use of the Murshidabad mint three days a week 'if it be not against the King's interest'. In fact, however, this privilege was never actually made available to the English. This would seem to have had indirectly something to do with the power and influence enjoyed by the house of the Jagat Seth at the Murshidabad court. But as I have argued in some detail elsewhere, the suggestion that the Jagat Seths then managed to appropriate for themselves the exclusive right to use the Murshidabad mint, forcing everyone else to sell their bullion to them and obtain coins in return on terms less favourable than if they had had their own access to the mint, is equally incorrect. There is abundant evidence to show that the Dutch East India Company, for example, continued to have significant quantities of silver minted at the Murshidabad mint.[10] There was thus no departure from the Mughal norm of allowing, in principle, everyone access to the mint.

As for the actual movements in trade from Bengal by the various groups - European and Indian - involved in it, the picture for the first half of the eighteenth century is essentially one of net growth, though the share of the

Indian merchants in the total intra-Asian trade during the period almost certainly declined. As far as the Euro-Asian trade, which was carried on exclusively by the Europeans, was concerned, the period was marked by significant growth. The average annual value of the Dutch East India Company's exports from Asia to Europe increased from *f*5 million during 1698-1700 to *f*6.42 million during 1738-1740. The corresponding figures in the case of the English East India Company were *f*4.56 million and *f*7.66 million respectively. The late-starting French East India Company had also done a considerable amount of catching up with the value of its annual exports during 1738-1740 standing at *f*4.61 million. In the case of both the Dutch and the English East India Companies, by far the most important Asian trading region during the period was Bengal. This reflected the dominant role of textiles and raw silk, Bengal being for the former the most important and for the latter practically the sole source of supply, in the total exports from Asia. In the case of the Dutch Company, the exports from Bengal accounted for 40 per cent of the total Asian exports during the 1690s, 1700s and 1710s, for 35 per cent during the 1720s, and for as much as 47 per cent in 1735-1736. The figure in the case of the English East India Company was 42 per cent during 1698-1700 and as much as 66 per cent during 1738-1740.[11]

As an integral part of its overall trading strategy, the Dutch East India Company also engaged in a substantial amount of trade within Asia. India, and particularly Bengal, played an important role in the Dutch intra-Asian trading network. The key Bengal commodities entering this trade were raw silk for the Japanese market which provided precious metals in return, and opium for the large and growing market of the Indonesian archipelago. The servants of the Company also engaged in a large volume of intra-Asian trade on a clandestine basis in high value low bulk commodities such as Bengal opium. For a short period between about 1720 and 1740, the French East India Company also engaged in a limited amount of intra-Asian trade in collaboration with both its own employees and other traders - Indian and European. Some of these employees operating on their individual accounts included well-known names such as Mahé de la Bourdonnais and Joseph François Dupleix.

The largest single group of European traders engaged in private trade between one region of India and another and between India and other parts of Asia was, of course, that of the English traders, including both Company servants as well as others. The private English trade in Bengal had started out late in the seventeenth century at the Hugli and the Balasore ports. Following the founding of Calcutta in 1690, the bulk of the English trade had begun shifting to that port. The early years of the eighteenth century witnessed a remarkable growth in the volume of the English private shipping at Calcutta. The fleet consisted of about twenty ships in 1715; by the 1730s the number had doubled. The principal trading links of the Calcutta shipping at this time were westward - with Surat, the Persian Gulf and the Red Sea. A Dutch shipping list pertaining to Calcutta listed for 1734 the departure of sixteen private English ships westward - nine for Surat, two for Gombroon and Basra, one for Basra alone, two for Mocha and one each for Jiddah and Sind. A ship to Surat reportedly carried an average of Rs 70,000 worth of goods in addition to the freight cargo, a ship to the Persian Gulf Rs 150,000 to Rs 200,000 worth of goods plus freight cargo, while a ship to the Red Sea carried, in addition to the freight cargo, Rs 300,000 worth of goods.[12] The differential advantage enjoyed by the English in the form of an exemption from transit and customs duties in Bengal, subject only to the payment of a token annual sum of Rs 3000, was evidently an important factor enabling them to draw more and more trade to themselves.[13] However, adverse political conditions in the western Indian Ocean, combined with general instability in Bengal in the 1740s following the Maratha incursions into the province, provided a damper on the trade between the two regions.

The eastward trade carried on by the private English merchants from India consisted essentially of three segments - Southeast Asia, the Philippines and China. The first of these stretched from ports such as Pegu, Tenasserim-Mergui, Ujang Salang, Kedah and Aceh - all on the eastern littoral of the Bay of Bengal - to Ayutthaya in the Gulf of Siam. The port frequented in the Philippines was Manila and that in China Canton. Until about 1760, the eastward trade was dominated by English shipping based at Madras with the role of the Calcutta shipping in this trade being rather limited. Thus the number of vessels going eastward from Calcutta was reported to be four each in 1704-1705 and 1705-1706 and three in 1706-1707. Again, in 1734, against sixteen departures from Calcutta westward, only four were recorded eastward. Also, the average value of the cargo carried by a ship going eastward was estimated at no more than Rs 60,000. The 1734 figure was by and large representative of the situation in the 1730s and the early 1740s.[14]

The picture is much less clear when it comes to movements in the Indian merchants' shipping from the ports of Bengal in the course of the eighteenth century. I have shown elsewhere that a detailed analysis of the Dutch shipping lists pertaining to the Indian merchants' trade from the Bengal ports of Hugli and Balasore between 1680 and 1720 suggests a rather mixed picture. Bengal's trade with Surat, the Persian Gulf, and the Red Sea was dominated by merchants based at Surat, while that with the Malabar and the Coromandel coasts was carried on predominantly by merchants based at the two respective coasts. The broad conclusion suggested by the number of vessels that left Hugli for these areas is that the Coromandel trade was on the increase, although there was no clearly discernible trend one way or the other in the trade with Surat, the Persian Gulf, the Red Sea and the Malabar coast. The picture is much clearer with regard to the branches of trade controlled by the merchants based in Bengal: Ceylon, the Maldive islands, and the eastward branch including Burma, Siam, Sumatra, the Malay peninsula and the Philippines. The trade with Ceylon practically dried up and the eastward trade suffered a heavy decline, but the trade with the Maldives increased substantially. The overall position in relation to all the branches of trade from Bengal taken together was, therefore, mixed, with no clear trend in many branches, a clear decline in trade along others, and an increase along two branches. A distinct feature of the decline in the important eastward trade was the near-complete withdrawal by Mughal state officials who had traditionally dominated this branch of trade.[15] Unfortunately, no specific study of the movements in the Indian merchants' trade from Bengal in the period after 1720 has yet been carried out. But even if it turns out that the period between 1720 and the mid-eighteenth century witnessed a decline in the overall volume and value of the Indian merchants' trade from the ports of Bengal, such a decline would in all probability have been more than compensated for by the rise in the English merchants' trade between Bengal and other parts of Asia. And then, of course, there was the substantial rise in the Euro-Asian trade over this period carried out by the European trading companies from the region.

The period until the 1750s, then, was marked by a practically continuous rise in the volume and value of the intra-Asian and the Euro-Asian trade from Bengal, though the share of Indian merchants in the intra-Asian trade would almost certainly have registered a decline. The trade carried on by the Europeans, particulary the corporate sector, had significant positive implications for the economy of the region. Because of the inability of Europe to provide goods that could be sold in India in reasonably large quantities at competitive terms, there was a chronic and substantial excess of commodity exports from India over the commodity imports from Europe. This export surplus had to be settled regularly through the import, by the European companies, of large quantities of precious metals into India, imparting to the trade a 'bullion for goods' characterization. Interestingly, in the context of the existence of a certain amount of slack in the economy, this pattern of trade tended to become an instrument of growth for the economy of the relevant Indian region. Ordinarily, an increase in foreign trade in an economy leads to an increase in the output of export goods and a decline in the production of goods that are now being imported in a larger quantity. By definition, the net result of growing trade is an increase in the value of total output in the economy. But in the case of trade of the kind that took place between Bengal (and other Indian regions) and Europe until about the mid-eighteenth century, the gain resulting from an increase in the value of trade would be much more substantial. In view of the imports being mainly of precious metals rather than ordinary trade goods, the decline in the domestic production of import-competing goods would at best be marginal. The increase in exports (and export surplus) would then ordinarily involve a net increase in output and income. This increase could have been achieved through an increase in productivity per unit of input through technological change, a reallocation of resources so that more of the high-value export goods were produced, and/or a fuller utilization of existing productive capacity and an increase in capacity itself, creating more employment.[16]

The two major groups directly affected by the growth in the value of the European trade were the merchants dealing with the companies and the artisans who manufactured the export goods. The intense and growing competition among the various European companies, particularly the Dutch and the English, for Bengal goods such as textiles and raw silk increasingly turned the market into a sellers' market. This was reflected in the growing bargaining strength of the merchants vis-à-vis the companies. By the same token, the artisans were able to extract much better terms from the merchants. Writing in 1700, for example, the Dutch factors at Hugli made the following observation: 'The merchants inform us (and on investigation we find that they are speaking the truth) that because of the large number of buyers in the weaving centres and the large sale of textiles, the weavers can no longer be coerced. They weave what is most profitable for them. If one does not accommodate oneself to this situation, then one is not able to procure very much and the supplies go to one's competitors'.[17] It is thus clear that the 'gains from trade' were not confined to any particular group, but were indeed transmitted in some measure or another all the way down to the level of the humble artisan.

With the English East India Company takeover of Bengal after the battle of Plassey, this favourable configuration of circumstances, by which foreign trade served essentially as an instrument of growth in the economy, was rudely terminated. A new phase in the eighteenth-century history of the region had begun. But before we go into the principal elements characterizing this discontinuity, it is important to emphasize that in one important respect there was a basic continuity in the period before and after 1760. This was the continuing vitality and market responsiveness of the structure of production in the region under grossly adverse circumstances. In a situation where the average annual English company exports from the region increased from *f*4.4 million in 1760 to an incredible *f*12.5 million by the end of the 1770s, accompanied by a gross deterioration in the terms and conditions under which the suppliers and the artisans were obliged to operate, the structure of commercial agricultural, and manufacturing production in the region showed no signs of crumbling and continued to deliver.

The first major element of discontinuity in the new situation was the near-stoppage of silver imports by the European companies into Bengal. This was partly an outcome of the availability to the companies of large amounts of rupee funds owned by private European traders of various nationalities and waiting to be remitted home against bills of exchange payable at various European capitals. In the case of the Dutch East India Company, for example, this was an important factor leading to a decline in the value of the precious metals imported into the region from *f*4.72 million in 1751-1752 to *f*2.63 million in 1761-1762, and a mere *f*0.39 million in 1770-1771. In the case of the English East India Company, the Bengal revenues officially accruing to it after 1765 provided yet another major source of investment funds which were used not only in Bengal but also in Madras and Bombay and even in China. To that extent, the Company's exports from Bengal became 'unrequited' and a drain on the region's resources. In the words of the Parliamentary Select Committee of 1783,

> A new way of supplying the Market of Europe, by Means of the British Power and Influence, was invented; a Species of Trade (if Such it may be called) by which it is absolutely impossible that India should not be radically and irretrievably ruined, although our Possessions there were to be ordered and governed upon Principles diametrically opposite to those which now prevail in the System and Practice of the British company's Administration.

The Committee also noted that:

> In all other Countries, the Revenue following the natural Course and Order of Things, arises out of their Commerce. Here, by a mischievous Inversion of that Order, the whole Foreign, Maritime Trade, whether English, French, Dutch or Danish arises from the Revenues; and these are carried out of the Country, without producing any Thing to compensate so heavy a Loss.[18]

Quite apart from the drain of resources dimension of the altered pattern of the English company's trade from Bengal, the cessation of silver imports effectively meant the demise of the centuries-old 'bullion for goods' character of the Indo-European trade. In the altered state of affairs, the 'gains from trade' in terms of increases in income, output and employment along the lines discussed earlier would no longer accrue. The post-1760 period also witnessed a basic alteration in the ground rules the English Company followed in its dealings with the merchants and the artisans supplying it with the textiles and other export goods. These dealings were no longer governed by the market forces of demand and supply. Through an extensive misuse of its newly acquired political power, the Company subjected suppliers, artisans and peasants to complete domination, imposing upon them unilaterally determined terms and conditions including monopsony, which significantly cut into their margin of profit. This misuse of authority was not confined to the English Company but was also extensively resorted to by its servants engaged in intra-Asian trade on their private account. In the rest of this paper, we will examine this process in some detail with reference to two major commodities - textiles and opium, trade in the latter of which was confined to the private traders.

In the case of textiles, the English Company made use of the so-called *gumashta* system of procurement which became the principal vehicle through which the Dutch and the French East India Companies were marginalized and the weavers obliged to produce for the English Company subjected to intense coercion. For purposes of procurement, the Company divided the province of Bengal into segments, each of which consisted of a group of production centres called *aurungs*. Each group contained a string of procurement stations, one of which was designated as the principal station where the chief *gumashta* of the group, responsible to the Commercial Resident, was based. The chief *gu-mashta* received from the Company both a salary (a modest sum of around Rs

50 per month) as well as a commission. He operated with the Company's funds and was, in principle, responsible for any bad debts that might arise from the sums advanced to him. Each of the subordinate trading stations was manned by a *gumashta* and a *dalal* who dealt with the weavers. Alternatively, the chief *gumashta* might operate directly through *paikars*, a group that was a counterpart of the *dalals*.

On the strength of the Company's political authority in the region, the *gumashtas/dalals/paikars* enjoyed a position of unquestioned domination over the weavers and forced upon them terms considerably below the market. The Company's operations at Khirpai provide a good example of the manner in which the system was run. Soon after the Company had been granted *diwani* rights in 1765, the Commercial Resident of the area arranged for information to be collected regarding the number of weavers, looms, pieces of textiles of different kinds manufactured in each *aurung* in his area in a year, the number ordinarily procured by rival European trading companies as well as private merchants each year, and so on.[19] Since the Company's textile requirements took precedence over everyone else's, individual *paikars* of the Company were allotted weavers who were banned from working for anyone else till such time as they had met their contractual obligations towards the Company. The terms offered by the Company to the *paikars* and in turn by the latter to the weavers were extraordinarily poor. The perennial complaint of the weavers was that the price allowed them by the Company hardly enabled them to cover the cost of the raw materials. In 1767, the weavers went so far as to send a delegation to Calcutta with a petition (*arzi*) requesting that the prices offered to them be increased by at least enough to afford them a subsistence wage. They did manage to obtain an order directing the Commercial Resident, identified in the Dutch report as one Bathoe, to do the necessary. But this evidently was no more than an eyewash because Bathoe not only openly disregarded the order but indeed threatened to have the weavers arrested in case they continued with their efforts.[20]

The pieces of textiles received from the *paikars* were classified by the Company's evaluators from quality one to five. Pieces not found good enough to make even quality five were rejected as 'firty' (feretted). A rough idea of what the Company subjected the weavers to can be formed by the fact that pieces classified as third quality would gladly have been accepted by the Dutch Company as first quality at a considerably higher price.[21] It is remarkable that even the pieces rejected by the Company as 'firty' had a profitable market. The margin between the price that these pieces fetched in the open market and the rate at which they had been evaluated by the Company before being rejected conveys some idea of the extent of the exploitation of the weavers. This margin was shared clandestinely between the Commercial Resident, the chief *gumashta* and the *paikars*. To take an example from 1767, Resident Bathoe rejected 896 pieces of textiles as 'firty' that year. Many of these pieces were eventually sold by the *paikars* in the market at between 6.5 to 7 rupees per piece higher than the price at which they had been evaluated by the Company's factors before being rejected. Bathoe had returned the pieces to the *paikars* after keeping a margin of 3 rupees per piece for himself and 0.5 rupees per piece for the chief *gumashta* Radhamohan Basak. But even after paying 3.5 rupees extra, the *paikars* managed to earn a net profit of 3 to 3.5 rupees per piece in the market for themselves. Besides, the Company also exploited the weavers by manipulating the raw material market to its advantage. It was reported in 1767, for example, that Resident Bathoe had bought silk yarn from the producers at 16 *tolas* to a rupee and had supplied it to the weavers of silk textiles at 7 to 9 *tolas* per rupee. The profits were shown in the Bardwan accounts of the Company.

Another major item the English procured in Bengal was opium, produced mainly in adjoining Bihar. But unlike in the case of the textiles, the market for opium was confined to Asia, mainly the Indonesian archipelago and later China. The role played by the English Company in the opium trade was confined by and large to the procurement of the commodity on a monopsonistic basis from 1773 onward and making it available to individual English traders. The actual trade in the item was carried on by these traders, most of whom were also employees of the English company, operating in their private capacity. Before the Company itself monopsonized the procurement of the commodity in 1773, the individual traders also operated, as far as possible, on a monopsonistic basis and acquired opium at a price distinctly lower than would have obtained in a free market situation. Indeed, the resultant high profit margin made the opium trade an important vehicle of the generation of private English fortunes in Bengal.

The first important case available of an English Company servant trying to monopolize opium on his private account is that of William McGwire, the chief of the English factory at Patna. In 1761, he 'persuaded' *Naib-subedar* Ram Narain to issue a *parwana* stipulating that McGwire would have the exclusive right to engage with the suppliers of opium for the procurement of the drug. McGwire tried to have this arrangement legitimized by Calcutta and in the process even offered a share in the profit from the venture to Governor

Vansittart. But the latter refused to succumb to the temptation and ordered a withdrawal of the *parwana*.[22] That, however, did not deter McGwire's successor, William Ellis, from grossly misusing his official position to coerce the suppliers to provide him the drug at prices considerably below the market.[23] From 1765 on, the English Company factors at Patna agreed to carry on this business on a somewhat more organized basis. They decided to act jointly and divide the profits from the venture on the basis of each person's status in the hierarchy. These individuals generally did not engage in internal or international trade in the item on their own and sold it on a monopoly basis to the prospective drugtraders, who would include Indian merchants, other private English traders, the Dutch Company etc. The gross profit earned by the Patna factors has been estimated to have ranged between 175 per cent and as much as 300 per cent.[24] But considering that the arrangement did not have Calcutta's approval and the machinery of enforcement available to the Patna factors was of necessity limited, it would seem that the proportion of total marketed output that passed through the hands of these factors was perhaps not very large.

The situation was altered radically in 1773 when the English Company decided to assume monopoly rights in the drug for itself. The arrangement was for the Company to organise the procurement of the drug on an exclusive basis and then arrange for its sale to prospective traders through public auctions held at Calcutta. It was maintained that given the 'dispositions and the habits of the natives', a monopoly was essential.[25] Earlier, Vansittart's minute which had formed the basis of the 1773 decision had elaborated on these 'dispositions and habits' by noting that 'had every merchant free liberty to make them [the suppliers and producers] Advances, they would receive Money in Abundance, they would dissipate a part of it, they would be unable to manufacture opium sufficient to complete their Engagements'.[26] In order to further justify the measure, the Company even helped to create a myth that a state monopoly of opium had always been the norm for India. In a memorandum sent to the Dutch factors at Hugli, Governor-General John Macpherson and the Calcutta Council observed:

> The opium of this country was always managed by the native government as a monopoly and we have the evidence before us of a person who held a considerable office at the Buxbandar for above sixty years, and who is now alive that opium and saltpetre were purchased by the foreign companies as they could from the

> persons enjoying the exclusive privilege of this monopoly in like manner as by private merchants.[27]

Benoy Chowdhury has also suggested that 'before the monopoly of the East India Company was established in 1773, the Patna merchants had a monopoly right of purchasing opium from the peasants'.[28] The implied basis of this statement is a 1788 report by Ram Chand Pandit, an opium agent of the English Company. But in effect all that this report talks of is the financing and the exercise of a certain amount of control on production and processing of opium by a group of Patna merchants.[29] An examination of the extensive reports filed by the factors of the Dutch Company at the time do not suggest the existence of either state monopoly or of anything like a monopsonistic relationship between a group of Patna merchants on the one hand and the suppliers and the producers of opium on the other. Given that at the time of the British takeover of Bengal, the Dutch Company was the single largest buyer of opium in the market, the existence of a monopsony even in a diluted form is hardly likely to have been passed over by the factors in silence.[30] The 1773 English Company monopoly, therefore, must be viewed as an 'innovation' with rather important consequences.

Initially, the monopoly pertained to the Bihar opium and excluded the marginal amount produced in the province of Bengal. In principle, the monopoly implied that the entire output of the drug in Bihar would have to be handed over to the Company at a price determined unilaterally for the year. The amount so collected was then sold off to traders in the drug at public auctions held in Calcutta. The mechanics of the system of collection were as follows. Initially, a contractor was awarded the contract for a year at a time. Although applications were invited from interested persons through public notices in English, Persian and Bengali,[31] the selection was made by the Governor-General-in-Council essentially on a patronage basis rather than on the basis of any objective criteria prescribed for the purpose. From 1781 on, the contract was given for a period of four years at a time. When the first four-year contract expired in 1785, the patronage system of awarding it was replaced by one whereby it was given to the highest bidder at a public auction organized for the purpose.

The Company paid the contractor at a specific price communicated to him in advance for each chest of opium delivered.[32] Half the expected value of the entire lot was given to him in advance out of which he was expected to give cash advances to the peasants producing opium. The contractor was subject to a penalty of Rs 100,000 in the event of being found supplying opium to anyone other than the Company.[33] All opium was to be collected at Calcutta in a crude state where it was to be 'manufactured' under the superintendence of a nominee of the Company.[34] From 1775 on, the revenues from opium were treated as excise or tax funds rather than as profit from trade. The management of the opium business continued to be with the Board of Revenue till 1793 when it was transferred to the Board of Trade.[35]

In 1797, the contract system was abolished in favour of an agency system involving the Company's direct control over the cultivation of opium. The production was henceforth to be restricted to Bihar and Banaras and discontinued in Bengal. Two Company officers were appointed Opium Agents with headquarters at Patna and Banaras respectively. The formal legislation defining the basic principles of the new system was set out under Regulation VI of 1799. This edict, although supplemented by further Acts in 1816, 1857 and 1870, continued to regulate the opium production and marketing enterprise until the early twentieth century.[36] All private cultivation of poppy was banned. The peasant was forced to cultivate a specific plot of land and to deliver its entire production at a fixed government price to the Agent. If a peasant failed to cultivate the full amount of land that he was required to and on which he had been given an advance, he was obliged to pay back pro-rata three times the value of the advance for the shortfall in the total area cultivated. If it were established that the shortfall in output had been due to negligence on the part of the peasant, he was to repay the proportional amount of advance with 12 per cent interest. If an illicit sale was established, the rules provided for the confiscation of the lot besides a fine at a rate of 4 rupees per *seer*. If confiscation of the lot was not possible, the fine was to go up to 10 rupees per *seer*. By Regulation VI of 1816, the rates of the fines were increased to 8 and 16 rupees per *seer* respectively. The rate of interest to be charged on the advances returned because of shortfall in supply was at the same time doubled to 24 per cent.[37]

If a peasant decided to be in the business of producing opium, he had no option but to deal with the Company. But in principle, he had the right not to be in the business of producing opium and reject the offer of a cash advance in return for pledging his crop to the English Company agent. The 1773 document which had specified the clauses of the opium monopoly had clearly laid down that 'no cultivator will be forced to cultivate poppy against his inclination'.[38] Regulation VI of 1799 had repeated 'but it is left entirely at the option of the Ryot or Cultivator, to enter into engagements on account of

Government at a settled price, or to decline it altogether'.[39] But the possibility that the rights of the peasants were not fully protected and that an element of compulsion was introduced into the picture is strongly suggested by the need for Governor-General Cornwallis to make the following stipulation in 1789. He decreed that henceforth a contractor could not 'compel the ryots to engage for the cultivation of a greater number of *beeghas* than they cultivated the preceding year'.[40] Also, if for some reason, a particular peasant was simply not able to continue engaging in opium cultivation, then he was required to give up his land as well since it had been earmarked for opium. The land was then assigned to another peasant undertaking to produce opium.[41]

The terms of the contract given to the peasant were enforced quite rigorously. The true beginnings of the Company's monopoly system could perhaps be placed around September 1775, when the opium contract was awarded to one Griffith. This man arranged for *parwanas* to be issued to officials in the opium districts obliging them to ensure that nobody other than his agents had access to the drug.[42] In 1776, when some Bengali merchants managed to give out opium advances clandestinely, a strongly worded letter was despatched to the *pargana* officials, holding them directly responsible for such unauthorized deals. They were directed to have a public announcement made that if an opium supplier or cultivator had accepted a cash advance as part of a clandestine deal, he was not to feel obliged either to honour the contract or return the advance. Any complaint that might be preferred against him in this connection would not be entertained by the administration.[43]

The opium enterprise was clearly of great advantage to the English East India Company, the contractors and other intermediaries participating in the enterprise as well as the private English traders engaged in the opium trade. Many of the intermediaries and the traders were servants of the Company. From the point of view of the Company, an obvious advantage was the accretion of Bengal's revenues. The documentation of the Company suggests that between 1773-1774 and 1784-1785, though there were significant annual fluctuations, there was a generally upward trend in the revenue from opium. From a low of £14,256 in 1774-1775, the revenue went up to £49,572 in 1778-1779 and to £78,300 in 1783-1784, though in 1784-1785 it came down to £53,348.[44] As a proportion of total Bengal revenues, the revenue from opium is estimated to have accounted for 5.2 per cent in 1792, 7 per cent in 1812, 10 per cent in 1822, and as much as 20 per cent in 1842.[45] Another important consideration was that the Company's direct involvement in the opium business put it in a position to encourage and facilitate the export of increasing quantities of Bihar opium to China. For one thing, this stopped the drain on specie from Bengal to China to pay for the tea procured there for the European market. Indeed, in the course of time Indian opium and cotton became the principal medium of payment for Chinese tea.

The opium contractors were also known to have made handsome profits from the enterprise. It has been suggested that in the early years of the monopoly system, a contractor could stipulate for £10,000 from a subcontractor, who could himself stipulate for £17,000 from yet another subcontractor, who was still able to make a handsome profit.[46] While it is not at all certain how representative these figures over time are, they nevertheless suggest the existence of a very positive situation from the point of view of these people. Finally, as far as the private English traders engaged in it were concerned, the advantages of the opium enterprise consisted not only in high rates of profit, but also in making the opium trade with China the principal vehicle for the transmission home of the profits earned in India. This was done by placing the proceeds from the China sales of opium at the disposal of the Company factors in Canton in exchange for bills on London.

The China trade was also largely instrumental in bringing about what Holden Furber has termed the 'commercial revolution' in the Indian Ocean trade. This revolution, completed by the 1780s, consisted in the first place of a complete domination of trade in the Indian Ocean and the South China Sea by English shipping based in Calcutta and Bombay, and in the second, of an increasingly central and indeed dominant position of the trade with China and Malaya in the private English merchants' trade from India. Curiously, however, the expansion in the private English merchants' trade with China had a certain amount of positive spin-off effect on the Indian merchants' trade with the Southeast Asian ports. In the context of the growing need for Southeast Asian goods saleable in China, the trade in the ports of the region had revived. This revival, in turn, had promoted to a certain extent the Indian merchants' trade with ports such as Aceh, Tenasserim, Phuket, Kedah and Johore.

To conclude, the eighteenth century, consisting of two sub-phases with the cut-off point lying somewhere around 1760, constituted a distinct category in the history of Bengal. The successor state established in the province in the early years of the century by Murshid Quli Khan turned out to be a perfectly stable political entity till it was itself overrun by the English East India Company in the 1750s, inaugurating the establishment of colonial rule in the subcontinent. In the domain of economics, there is nothing to suggest that the agricultural sector experienced any particular problems during the century. The rising revenue collections over the first quarter of the century might even point towards a growing agricultural output. The non-agricultural sector, supported by an efficient infrastructure, also continued to be extremely vigorous and highly cost-competitive. The volume and the value of trade from Bengal, both intra-Asian and well as Euro-Asian, was continuously on the increase through the century, though the Indian merchants would seem to have increasingly been edged out from intra-Asian trade by their private English counterparts. The other important group that was a victim of the English misuse of their newly acquired political power in the province in the period after 1760 was that of merchants and artisans supplying goods to the Company and the private English traders. The unilaterally determined terms and conditions forced upon these groups robbed them of their legitimate share in the benefit accruing from growing output and trade. At a macroeconomic level, the post-1760 period also witnessed a growing drain of resources from the province in the form of 'unrequited' exports to Britain financed by the diversion of Bengal revenues to the procurement of these goods.

Notes

1. J.C. van Leur, *Indonesian Trade and Society: Essays in Asian Social and Economic History* (The Hague 1955) 284.
2. Irfan Habib, *The Agrarian System of Mughal India, 1556-1707* (Bombay 1963) 351.
3. Burton Stein, 'A Decade of Historical Efflorescence', *South Asia Research* 10/2 (November 1990) 132-33.
4. J.C. van Leur, *Indonesian Trade and Society*, 273.
5. Om Prakash, *The Dutch East India Company and the Economy of Bengal, 1630-1720* (Princeton 1985) 25.
6. Appendix no.6 to John Shore's 'Minute on the Rights of Zamindars', West Bengal Government Archives (Calcutta), Board of Revenue, *Proceedings*, April 2, 1788, vol. 127, 539-540. Quoted in Philip B. Calkins, 'The Formation of a Regionally Oriented Ruling Group in Bengal, 1700-1740', *Journal of Asian Studies* (1970) 799-806. Note the proximity of the figure of Rs 14.11 million to that of Rs 14.28 million, the figure that emerged after the 1722 revision of the Bengal land revenue. The *khalisa* component of the latter figure was Rs 10.96 million. W.K. Firminger ed., *The Fifth Report from the Select Committee of the House of Commons on the Affairs of the East India Company, 1812* II, Appendix 4, 186 and 191.
7. For evidence on movements in the general price level, see Om Prakash, *The Dutch East India Company and the Economy of Bengal*, Chapter 8.
8. Philip B. Calkins, 'The Formation of a Regionally Oriented Ruling Group in Bengal', 803.
9. Memorandum by Jan Kersseboom, the outgoing director of the Bengal factories, addressed to his successor, Louis Taillefert, 16 February 1755, General State Archives, The Hague (ARA), VOC Archives (VOC) 2862. The volume is not foliated.
10. Om Prakash, 'On Coinage in Mughal India', *The Indian Economic and Social History Review* 25/4 (October-December 1988) 475-491.
11. Om Prakash, *European Commercial Enterprise in Pre-colonial India*, New Cambridge History of India Series (Cambridge, 1998).
12. P.J. Marshall, *East Indian Fortunes: The British in Bengal in the Eighteenth Century* (Oxford 1976) 85-86.
13. This privilege had been secured first in 1651 by misrepresentation of facts pertaining to the *farman* granted by Emperor Shahjahan in 1650. It had been formalized in February 1691, see the *hasb-ul-hukm* issued under the seal of *wazir* Asad Khan. The royal sanction was received in 1717, see the well-known *farman* granted by Emperor Farrukhsiyar and the *hasb-ul-hukm* issued under the seal of the grand *wazir* Sayyid 'Abd Allah Khan. The privilege was meant for the English company goods alone, but was widely abused to include the private traders' goods. The latter often abused it further by assuming, against a consideration, the ownership of the Indian merchants' goods.
14. P.J. Marshall, *East Indian Fortunes*, 85-88.
15. Om Prakash, *The Dutch East India Company and the Economy of Bengal*, 222-234.
16. For details of this argument, and an estimate of the additional employment generated

by European trade in Bengal in the late seventeenth and the early eighteenth centuries, see Om Prakash, *The Dutch East India Company and the Economy of Bengal*, Chapter 8.

17. Explanation by the Dutch factors of why the orders were not supplied in full, 1700, ARA, VOC 1638, ff.17-19, section 2.
18. 'Ninth Report from Select Committee Appointed to Take into Consideration the State of the Administration of Justice in the Provinces of Bengal, Bahar and Orissa', 25 June 1783, India Office Library (IOL), L/Parl/2/15.
19. J.M. Ross at Khirpai to Director at Hugli, 18 July 1767, ARA, Hooge Regeering Batavia (HRB), Appendix D, 247.
20. J.M. Ross at Khirpai to Director at Hugli, 16 May 1767, ARA, HRB, Appendix C2, 247.
21. J.M. Ross at Khirpai to Director at Hugli, ARA, HRB, Appendix A, 247.
22. 'Secret Memoir Concerning the Directorate of Bengal Left by Outgoing Dutch Director Louis Taillefert for his Successor George Louis Vernet', 17 November 1763, ARA, HRB, 246, f.205; Memoir of Dutch Director in Bengal at Hugli, Johannes Bacheracht for his successor, J.M. Ross, 31 July 1776, ARA, HRB 252, ff.114-115; 'Extract of the Proceedings of the President and Council at Fort William in Bengal in their Revenue Department, the 15th October, 1773', Appendix 57 to the Ninth Report from the Select Committee, IOL, L/Parl/2/15; P.J. Marshall, *East Indian Fortunes*, 118-119.
23. Memoir of Bacheracht for Ross, 31 July 1776, ARA, HRB 252, ff.115-116; Enclosures to the memoir of Bacheracht for Ross, 31 July 1776, ARA, HRB 253, f.6.
24. Memoir of outgoing Dutch Director of Bengal, George Louis Vernet for his successor Boudewyn Verselewel Faure, dated 8 March 1770, ARA, HRB 249, ff.85-86; Extract Bengal Revenue Consultations, 23 November 1773, Appendix 57, Ninth Report, IOL, L/Parl/2/15; P.J. Marshall, *East Indian Fortunes*, 146.
25. Governor-General John Macpherson and Council at Calcutta to Eilbracht and Van Citters, members of the Dutch Council at Hugli, 8 September 1785, ARA, HRB 211 (unfoliated).
26. Extract, Bengal Revenue Consultations, 23 November 1773, Appendix 57, Ninth Report, IOL, L/Parl/2/15.
27. Governor-General John Macpherson and Council at Calcutta to Eilbracht and Van Citters, members of the Dutch Council at Hugli, 8 September 1785, in 'Correspondence Exchanged between the English Authorities in Bengal and the Servants of the Dutch Company there, 1785', ARA, HRB, 211 (unfoliated).
28. Benoy Chowdhury, *Growth of Commercial Agriculture in Bengal, 1757-1900*, I (Calcutta 1964) 6.
29. S. Sanyal, 'Ram Chand Pandit's Report on Opium Cultivation in 18th Century Bihar', *Bengal Past and Present* 87 (1968) 181-189; J.F. Richards, 'The Indian Empire and the Peasant Production of Opium in the Nineteenth Century', *Modern Asian Studies* 15/1 (1981) 62.
30. Indeed, a Dutch memoir from 1776 explicitly says that while some attempts had been

made during the pre-1757 period to monopsonize opium, these had never been successful. Memoir of Director Bacheracht for his successor, Ross, 31 July 1776, ARA, HRB 252, f.117.

31. For a sample of the public notice, see Extract Bengal Revenue Consultations, 23 May 1775, Appendix 62, Ninth Report, IOL, L/Parl/2/15.
32. The price paid to the first opium contractor, Mir Manir, was Sicca Rs 320 per chest. In respect of the lots procured in Ghazipur and some other districts outside Bihar and held in *jagir* by Nawab Shuja-ud-Daula, a price of Sicca Rs 350 per chest was stipulated. Extract Bengal Revenue Consultations, 23 May 1775, Appendix 62, Ninth Report, IOL, L/Parl/2/15.
33. Extract Bengal Revenue Consultations, 23 November 1773, Appendix 57, Ninth Report, IOL, L/Parl/2/15.
34. Ibid.
35. Second Report of the Select Committee, 1805, IOL, L/Parl/2/55, collection 55, f.21.
36. J.F. Richards, 'The Indian Empire and the Peasant Production of Opium', 64.
37. Benoy Chowdhury, *Growth of Commercial Agriculture in Bengal*, 42.
38. Extract, Bengal Revenue Consultations, 23 November 1773, Appendix 57, Ninth Report, IOL, L/Parl/2/15.
39. Second Report of the Select Committee, 1805, IOL, L/Parl/2/55, collection 55.
40. Benoy Chowdhury, *Growth of Commercial Agriculture in Bengal*, 51.
41. Ibid.
42. Minutes of the Dutch Council at Hugli, 13 October 1775, in Enclosures to the memoir of outgoing Director Bacheracht, ARA, HRB 253 (unfoliated); Letter from Gregorius Herklots to the Council at Hugli, 20 October 1775, ARA, HRB 253 (unfoliated).
43. *Parwana*, 8 March 1776, available in Minutes of the Hugli Council meeting, 28 May 1776, Enclosures to the memoir of Bacheracht, ARA, HRB 253 (unfoliated).
44. 'An Account of the Annual Profits Arising to the Company from Opium in Bengal from the Acquisition of Diwani to the Date of the Latest Advices from Bengal', IOL, Parl/L/2/20, collection 20, f.1.
45. Tan Chung, 'The British-China-India Trade Triangle, 1771-1840', *The Indian Economic and Social History Review*, 11/4 (1974) 422-423.
46. P.J. Marshall, *East Indian Fortunes*, 203.

INDEX

For Product Safety Concerns and Information please contact our EU representative GPSR@taylorandfrancis.com Taylor & Francis Verlag GmbH, Kaufingerstraße 24, 80331 München, Germany

T - #0080 - 160425 - C0 - 224/150/21 - PB - 9781138375833 - Gloss Lamination